Capital Crimes

Max Décharné is a writer and musician. He is the author of seven previous books, including *King's Road*, *Hardboiled Hollywood*, *Straight from the Fridge, Dad* and *A Rocket in my Pocket*. He has been a regular contributor to *Mojo* magazine since 1998, and also writes for a variety of other publications. In his music career, he has released eleven albums and numerous singles since 1991. He lives in London.

Praise for *Capital Crimes*

'Read this book and London will never look the same again'
Loud and Quiet Magazine

'With a darkly evocative sense of place and period, this is a shocking and often poignant history of human nature's most violent impulses, and the vibrant city that forms their backdrop'   *Good Book Guide*

'A fascinating, sideways view of London's real underground'
Choice Magazine

'An insightful and multi-layered depiction of crime in London'
Raven Crime Reads Blog

Capital Crimes

Seven Centuries of
London Life and Murder

MAX DÉCHARNÉ

arrow books

Published by Arrow Books 2013

2 4 6 8 10 9 7 5 3 1

Copyright © Max Décharné 2012

Max Décharné has asserted his right under the Copyright, Designs
and Patents Act, 1988, to be identified as the author of this work

First published in Great Britain in 2012 by Random House Books
Random House, 20 Vauxhall Bridge Road,
London SW1V 2SA

www.randomhouse.co.uk

Addresses for companies within The Random House Group Limited can be found at:
www.randomhouse.co.uk/offices.htm

The Random House Group Limited Reg. No. 954009

A CIP catalogue record for this book
is available from the British Library

ISBN 9780099539025

The Random House Group Limited supports the Forest Stewardship
Council® (FSC®), the leading international forest-certification organisation.
Our books carrying the FSC label are printed on FSC®-certified paper. FSC
is the only forest-certification scheme supported by the leading environmental
organisations, including Greenpeace. Our paper procurement policy can be
found at www.randomhouse.co.uk/environment

Typeset by Palimpsest Book Production Ltd, Falkirk, Stirlingshire
Printed and bound by CPI Group (UK) Ltd, Croydon CR0 4YY

For Katja

CONTENTS

INTRODUCTION

This is a book about murder. It is also a history of London, reflecting the changing face of the capital from the fourteenth to the twentieth centuries. At the start of this story, the entire population of the city would have fitted roughly four times into the current Wembley Stadium; by the end, it had risen to more than eight million. From a time when the modest capital was slowly recovering from the Black Death, to the days when it had become a vast metropolis littered with bombsites following the Blitz, many things altered, but the grim fact of murder remained a constant.

Each chapter deals with an individual homicide – some notorious, some lesser-known – set against the background of the times in which it was committed, including major events such as the Peasants' Revolt, the Gordon Riots and the Zeppelin raids, alongside technological advances such as the development of the railways or the invention of the telephone. All these played a part in the criminal history of a city which had for hundreds of years resisted the very idea of a standing police force.

Until the 1960s, the shadow of the death penalty lay over any London murderer. Many such crimes were committed for age-old reasons like jealousy or financial gain, yet there were also significant differences from century to century in the conditions that led to murder, and society's reaction to the event. Elizabethan Londoners could expect to lose both ears for trespass and both hands for sheep stealing, to be dragged behind a boat between Lambeth and Westminster for adultery, to be burnt at the stake for heresy or boiled alive in lead for poisoning a man. Compared to these, the simple rope at Tyburn starts to look like an understated measure.

Every city has its murderers. Punishing them is one thing, arresting them quite another. In the days before regular policing, if the culprit was not discovered red-handed, they might well not be caught at all. Life was cheap, and detection a late-blooming science.

At the time of the Norman Conquest, a murderer was generally fined according to the relative importance of the dead person, with the going rate for a citizen of London set at one hundred shillings during the reign of Henry I. In the medieval city, the monarch lived in constant fear of being overthrown by contenders to the crown, and so law-makers were more concerned with suppressing treason, political unrest and heresy. Simple homicide came somewhere further down a long list of capital felonies which also included 'hunting by night with painted faces and visors', 'stealing of hawks' eggs' and, of course, 'conjuring, sorcery, witch-craft and digging up of crosses'.

By the eighteenth century, London had become one of the world's largest cities, the principal hub of international trade and the heart of the original industrial revolution. In the narrow, insanitary streets of the crowded metropolis, where doctors killed more than they cured and many children died before the age of two, murder was just another of the many hazards of everyday life. To 'dance upon nothing' – criminal slang for death by hanging – was the customary punishment for murder. Yet this was only one of two hundred capital offences, alongside crimes such as theft of a sheep, robbing a house or picking someone's pocket for goods worth more than a shilling. Counterfeiting the coin of the realm was held to be treason and therefore still carried the brutally extreme sentence for men of being drawn and quartered, and for women, burning at the stake.

With such a lengthy selection of capital offences, it might be expected that London in those days had a police force of considerable size, but the opposite is true. The Bow Street Runners, Henry Fielding's legendary mid-eighteenth-century group of constables, never numbered more than fifteen operatives in all their years of existence. Prior to the founding of the Runners in 1748, the apprehending of criminals was in the hands of a selection of self-appointed 'thief-takers'; bounty seekers who collected a fee from the government for every conviction. Many of those drawn to this profession were little better than those they hunted, and Jonathan Wild, the most famous thief-taker of them all, was himself eventually hanged at Tyburn in 1725.

There had been a long-standing abhorrence in the public mind towards the notion of an official police force: such things were held to be utterly foreign, a sinister tool favoured by despots and absolutist monarchs. When the Home Secretary Robert Peel finally introduced London's first properly constituted police force in 1829, he was at pains to dress them in clothing which aped current civilian dress, in an effort to play down any suggestion that this was some kind of para-military organisation.

As society changed, London became used to the idea of bobbies on the beat, yet for a long time investigative methods were haphazard at best. It was Charles Dickens, a friend of several early Scotland Yard officials, who introduced the wider public to the word 'detective' in his 1853 novel, *Bleak House*, when an officer of the Yard presents himself by saying, 'I am Inspector Bucket of the Detective, I am.' If this might sound modern to our ears, other factors clearly belong to a bygone age. Public executions continued outside Newgate prison until 1868, and although London's first telephone exchange opened in 1879, it wasn't until 1901 that a telephone was finally installed at New Scotland Yard, prompting a sceptical sergeant to comment, 'I don't know what we're coming to – if this sort of thing goes on, we'll have the public ringing us up direct.' By the same token, when Sir Francis Galton published a book called *Fingerprints* in 1892, outlining the groundbreaking method for identifying individuals, this heralded the development of forensic methods of crime investigation. However, well into the twentieth century Scotland Yard operatives were still arriving at murder scenes to find that local officers had already allowed the body to be moved, clothing burnt, floors scrubbed and surfaces wiped.

As time passed and science gave the police ever increasing weapons in the hunt for murderers, the movement towards the abolition of capital punishment also grew stronger. Catching such criminals was in theory becoming easier, but the question of how the justice system should then punish them had become highly controversial by the 1950s. Following the last hangings in England on 13 August 1964, the practice was halted, before being abolished in 1969 – which may perhaps have come as a relief to the Kray twins, who were convicted of murder that same year.

The murderers and victims featured here span many eras and social classes: from a pair of working-class brothers in Deptford a hundred years ago to a member of King James I's inner circle at the end of Shakespeare's time, or an everyday eighteenth-century Islington highway robber, an East End plague nurse of the Restoration, and a prime minister during the Napoleonic Wars. Some of these cases were thoroughly documented at the time, while others came and went leaving the briefest trail of paper to record a violent death and the reasons behind it. Not every one of those accused may have been guilty, and there are at least two examples here where the killers went unpunished. They all, however, reflect the years when murder in London was a capital crime.

Max Décharné
London, June 2012

ACKNOWLEDGEMENTS

I'd like to say a heartfelt thank-you to my agent, Caroline Montgomery of Rupert Crew Limited, who first recommended me to Random House, for her careful reading of all the various incarnations of the text, and her very helpful suggestions throughout. Similarly, sincere thanks are due to my editor, Nigel Wilcockson, whose idea gave rise to this book, for his help, encouragement and understanding during the past three years. I'm deeply indebted to Gemma Wain for her insight and first-class advice during the revision stages, to Sophie Lazar for bringing it all together, Rachael Ludbrook for the very fine front cover, and all at Random House who have made it a pleasure from start to finish.

Given that most of these murder cases stretch back hundreds of years, I did not expect to conduct interviews during the writing of the book, but I was fortunate to learn that my friend Martin Hart had first-hand memories of the Styllou Christofi case. I'm grateful to Martin and his wife Valerie for meeting me in the Magdala pub to share their impressions of Hampstead in the 1950s.

Thanks are due to the volunteers who run the River Police Museum in Wapping for their kindness and knowledge. I would also like to thank the staff of the Westminster Reference Library, the British Library, the Guildhall Library, the Bodleian Library and Alexandra Park Library. The magnificent website www.oldbaileyonline.org has been invaluable, as has the John Johnson Collection of Printed Ephemera. In addition, I would like to extend my gratitude to the Reverend Charles Burney, who departed this life in 1817, but left behind the finest collection of English historical newspapers in the world.

Finally, and most of all, deepest thanks and love to my wife Katja, for her many careful and insightful readings of each stage of the text, and her total support throughout, without which there would have been no book at all.

Wat Tyler slain at Smithfield by William Walworth,
Mayor of London, in the presence of Richard II

ONE

REVOLTING PEASANTS
1381

Imagine a city with no police. A city that is crowded, dirty and teeming with livestock; where fresh water is even harder to come by than food, and you can starve to death in the street as people pass on by because they have problems enough of their own. Crime is ever-present, and violence is an everyday reality. If a man should take it upon himself to break down a stranger's door with an axe and set about despatching all those inside, what is to stop him, and who will catch him afterwards if he gets away?

London in 1381 was just such a city. Worse still, there was a heavily armed, rampaging mob at its gates who had already torn up most of the laws of the land, leaving a trail of destruction and death in their wake. For those inside the city walls, news was scarce, fragmentary and unreliable. Who were these people? What did they want, and how many would they kill in order to get it?

This was a time of fear and paranoia, in which the old order of daily life no longer applied, and of riot and unrest, during which the gates of the city and even the walls of the Tower of London proved no defence against the attackers. It was a time when the reeking waters of the Thames were clogged with broken finery looted from John of Gaunt's palace on the Strand, and the spikes on top of Old London Bridge wore a brand-new grisly trophy – the severed head of the Archbishop of Canterbury.

If such a man had fallen victim to the mob, who then was safe?

A thousand years after the departure of the Romans, there was still only one bridge spanning the Thames, but London had grown from a regional centre into the largest, and richest, city in England; by 1381, it stretched from the Aldgate and the Tower in the east to the Lud Gate and the convent of the Black Friars in the west. In the previous century, it had also become the unquestioned seat of government, ending the former system whereby the monarch would spend much of their reign travelling the nation with a large entourage, effectively taking the entire administration along with them. Parliament, the law courts and the king's household were now firmly centred on London and its near neighbour, Westminster, two cities joined by a route along the river called the Strand. Fifty years earlier, the city had boasted a population of somewhere around 100,000 – huge by the standards of the middle ages – yet the combined effects of famine and the Black Death of 1348 had seen it reduced to about a quarter of that number. For many inside London's walls, life was brief, easily forfeited, and – for those in the lower orders – hardly their own in the first place. Three hundred years after the Norman Conquest, an estimated fifty per cent of all Englishmen were still villeins or serfs, in bondage to a lord or to the local clergy. The status of such people had been carefully defined by Anglo-Norman lawyers such as Henry de Bracton, who characterised them as one who 'ought not to know in the evening what work might be demanded of him tomorrow.' Not exactly slaves, but neither were they free.

The indigenous peasantry were constrained while they lived, and of little account if they were murdered. Indeed, under William the Conqueror in the eleventh century, a law had been introduced by which an entire district became liable for payment of the blood-money for the murder of a Norman, unless the residents could either produce the killer or prove that the victim was English, and therefore relatively expendable. Killers in 1381 did not always suffer the death penalty, and many murders were still punished by fines, mutilation or exile, but execution was becoming more common. In the centuries since the Conquest, there had been a gradual rise in the number of executions for murder, with guilt usually being attested to by jurors or men of local standing, and the matter frequently settled through ordeal by boiling water or by fire. In addition, since 1221, anyone convicted of treason was now subjected to the process of being hanged, drawn and quartered. This was quite a contrast to the situation which had existed in Anglo-Saxon times, when murderers were not often executed, but rather sentenced to pay a fine, two-thirds of which went to the king and only a third to the victim's family.

In fourteenth-century London, since there were no police, the local community was relied upon to keep a lookout for crime. In the event of a murder, it was the duty of anyone who found a body to raise a hue and cry. This meant letting four of your nearest neighbours know of your discovery, and then jointly contacting the local bailiff and coroner, who in turn summoned a jury. All able-bodied men in the district were obliged to respond when a hue and cry was raised and assist local officials in pursuit of those who had disturbed the king's peace.

The victim's body would be examined for any evidence of wounds, strangulation or the like. Murder trials were astonishingly swift by modern standards, lasting just a matter of minutes; there was no provision for any witnesses to speak in defence of the accused, and the verdict regarding guilt or innocence was based on public opinion and 'common knowledge'. Thus anyone considered to be of bad character who might conceivably have had a motive for a killing, or who had been seen acting suspiciously in the neighbourhood, stood little chance of acquittal. However, under this system, the determined criminal wishing to commit murder could considerably lower their chances of ever being apprehended for the crime. They had only to wait for an opportunity to do it without witnesses, and then have the good sense to relocate to the other side of the city, or another town or village altogether.

One very contentious aspect of the legal process was the part played by the figures of dubious standing known as questmongers or assizers. These two terms essentially described the same occupation, which was held in very low esteem by the public. Questmongers were in effect professional jurors, defined in Chambers & Daunt's *A Book of London English, 1384–1425* as people who 'made a profit out of inquests, whether by giving false evidence, or holding the inquest. These semi-legal busy-bodies are continually referred to with disfavour and classed with lawyers and false jurors.' Bishop Latimer, in one of his sermons written in the sixteenth century, reinforced the poor opinion of the breed, saying: 'Scripture doth shew what a thing it is, when a man is a malefactor, and the *questmongers* justify him, and pronounce him not guilty.' As for the equivalent term 'assizer', or 'sysor', it's probably enough to say that in William Langland's narrative poem *Piers Plowman*, written around 1380, the character named 'False' rides on an assizer. In short, they were popularly considered to be willing to swear any kind of untruth in return for bribes, even if it might cost the defendant their life or result in a murderer going free.

Being an assizer was not a well-loved profession at the best of times, but it was frequently a lucrative one. Among those in London who had turned the trade to their own good account over the years was a certain Roger Legett, who had a house outside the city walls, in the fields of Clerkenwell, an agricultural area known for its fresh water and farming, but also for its brothels. In times of peace, this would have been a reasonably pleasant location, away from the noise and bustle of the narrow medieval street-plan enclosed within the old fortifications of London itself. Yet, with a new and unpredictable enemy approaching the metropolis from several directions, it would have been dangerously exposed.

The threat bearing down upon the city in June 1381 was what became known as the Peasants' Revolt. Led by men such as Wat Tyler, Jack Straw and the rebel preacher John Ball, it was the culmination of decades of instability throughout the kingdom. The old social order, shaken by the effects of famine and the plague, had been further weakened by the imposition of a series of hugely unpopular poll taxes between 1377 and 1381.

Anyone associated with the hated taxes became fair game to the rebels. As the person most identified with the introduction of these taxes, John of Gaunt, duke of Lancaster and the kingdom's effective ruler, was one of the principal targets of the uprising, but there was a wave of antagonism directed at anyone connected with the legal system. The contemporary chronicler Thomas Walsingham wrote in his *Historia Anglicana* that they 'began to execute all the lawyers in the land whom they could capture – not only apprentices but also old justices and all the kingdom's jurors, without respect for piety; for the rebels declared that the land could not be fully free until the lawyers had been killed.' Roger Legett was not exactly a lawyer, but as a questmonger, the rebels would have considered him a legitimate target.

On Thursday, 13 June 1381, anyone attacking Roger Legett's Clerkenwell home would not have found him there. Leaving it shuttered and boarded as far as possible, he had fled, seeking the protection of the city. Perhaps Legett had heard reports of the Kentish rebels massing at Blackfriars, and the destruction they had wrought in Southwark on having found London Bridge closed to them. He might even have learned that quest-mongers' houses had been targeted on that occasion – a powerful argument in favour of fleeing in search of a safer haven within the metropolis. Stories of rebel actions in the Canterbury area, and in Essex, would have been current in the city; rumours of lawyers and petty officials attacked or killed, and reports of how it was dangerous to be identified with the jury system, or even to be able to read and write.

In those days it was customary to go about armed, even when no imminent danger threatened. Legett would have taken some food and wine, and what money he could carry – gold or silver – to guard against most eventualities, and he might have worn a disguise. If the common people were rising up against their superiors, then fine clothes or obvious outward signs of wealth were to be avoided. He was a refugee in his own city, looking for a bolthole in which to rest until the storm passed.

From his house near the Priory of St John, his journey took a south-ward direction to the city's ancient Roman walls, which had enclosed London since the second century and still contained the vast majority of its inhabitants. His route followed the path of the Holborne – a tributary of the Fleet River, which snaked its way down from the Northern Heights and acted as a thoroughfare for bringing valuable goods such as wool, timber, cheese and corn into the city. He might have been able to see smoke rising ominously from the various trouble spots, or to hear the distant sounds of conflict and destruction floating across the open fields. He would have been wise to keep one hand on the reins of his horse and the other on his sword. The laws of the land had been overturned and were lying in the gutter, and a man alone might well be stopped, ques-tioned, robbed or killed by one of the roving gangs of rebels.

Roger Legett's chosen place of refuge, once he had managed to enter the city proper, was St Martin's-le-Grand. This venerable monastery was regarded as the most hallowed place of sanctuary in the capital, and its bell had for centuries rung the curfew for the surrounding area at night, after which anyone still abroad was liable to arrest. Having reached here, his troubles were far from over, but his chances of survival were greatly improved.

In normal times, Roger Legett would have been perfectly safe in St Martin's. Sanctuary was not just a custom, it was enshrined in law, based on the principle that Church ground came under separate jurisdiction. Fugitives seeking shelter within church walls had a certain number of days in which their safety was guaranteed, and their food and drink provided, after which time the clemency – and the food – ended. They then had the option of remaining where they were and facing starvation, or heading straight for the nearest port and going into exile. If they left the building and went out into the community without leaving the country, the local population had permission to kill them on sight.

Legett probably sought sanctuary with the intention of remaining only a day or so until the unrest had passed, then resuming his normal life. It was prudent for all those with some connection to the legal system to keep a low profile during the chaos of the uprising. However, he might have had an additional reason. Roger Legett had acquired a reputation for cruel behaviour some years earlier, due to his malicious habit of setting traps, 'hidden engines of iron', close to his home in the long grass of Fikettesfield, just south of Lincoln's Inn Fields. They were devices not unlike those which poachers might use to snare a rabbit, but he was not hunting for food. The intention, for his own twisted amusement, was to injure unsuspecting students and apprentices from the nearby Inns of Court, who used this stretch of open ground for recreation. Legett obtained a pardon for this callous offence, but his actions had probably not been forgotten or forgiven by the local residents, and at a time when the mob were taking to the streets, it was surely wise to seek sanctuary until order was restored.

During the first few days of the revolt, as the flames and smoke rose from numerous public and private buildings, records of the legal system were cast onto the fires and practitioners of the law were hunted down as enemies of the people, it must have seemed as if the world would never be quite the same.

Inside his place of refuge, Roger Legett would have stayed as near to the altar as possible, in the hope that if any intruders broke through, they might be awed by the proximity of this religious symbol and refrain from any violence in such a place. There would have been others there who had also been drawn by the supposed protection offered by St Martin's-le-Grand – a motley selection of the fearful, the guilty, the aged and perhaps even some convinced that the final judgement was at hand. Rumour penetrated even these walls, and the attackers had now breached the city's defences. Kentish rebels had gained access to the city when the gatekeepers of London Bridge – the sole southern approach – let down the drawbridge, while those from Essex passed easily through the Aldgate. The latter, one of the six original gates of the old city, stood just to the west of the modern tube station that bears its name, where the roads Duke's Place and Aldgate now meet.

While Roger Legett was marked out for possible ill-treatment because of his trade and his past behaviour, others were targeted merely because they were different, making this a dangerous time to be a foreigner in London. The *Anonimalle Chronicle*, probably the most reliable contemporary account of the Peasants' Revolt – written by someone thought to have been a member of the king's entourage in the Tower and a witness to many of the events he describes – records the rebels' brutal pursuit of a group of Flemish merchants. These people had sought sanctuary in the church of St Martin Vintry, which until the Great Fire stood on College Hill, midway between the modern tube stations of Mansion House and Cannon Street:

> ... they went to the church of St Martin's in the Vintry, and found therein thirty-five Flemings, whom they dragged outside and beheaded in the street. On that day there were beheaded 140 or 160 persons. Then they took their way to places of Lombards and other aliens, and broke into their houses, and robbed them of all their goods that they could discover. So it went on for all that day and the night following, with hideous cries and horrible tumult.

Lombards and Flemings would have stood out – they were easy targets in an era when to be foreign was to invite immediate suspicion and distrust. Indeed, shortly before entering the city by way of London Bridge, the rebels had taken the time to destroy a Flemish-staffed brothel in Southwark, owned by the mayor of London, William Walworth: 'And on this same day of Corpus Christi, in the morning, the commons of Kent broke down a brothel [*une measone destwes*] near London Bridge, occupied by Flemish women who had farmed it from the mayor of London.'

In the midst of this chaos, in which all manner of old scores were settled – notwithstanding the genuine grievances which were being aired on behalf of the poorer sections of society – Roger Legett, cooped up in the monastery of St Martin's-le-Grand, had good cause to worry about his own fate, yet only a sketchy idea of what was happening out in the streets.

Today, the former site of St Martin's-le-Grand is marked by the street of the same name, which runs north from St Paul's Cathedral. It lay directly on the traditional route taken by condemned prisoners being brought from Newgate prison, just outside the western walls of the city, to the execution place at Tower Hill. Over the years, a significant number of these prisoners escaped to the monastery and were granted sanctuary, although the doors were generally barred to Jews and to traitors. Roger Legett might justifiably have felt that he had reached a place of safety, but the normal rules did not apply at this time. As Thomas Walsingham put it: 'Nor did they show any reverence to holy places but killed those whom they hated even if they were within churches and in sanctuary.' Indeed, the *Anonimalle* also records that the man in charge of the Marshalsea prison in Southwark fell victim to the mob despite having sought sanctuary in Westminster Abbey:

> . . . he was near the shrine of St Edward, embracing a marble pillar, hoping for aid and succour from the saint to preserve him from his enemies. But the commons wrenched his arms away from the pillar of the shrine, and dragged him into Cheap, and there beheaded him

Cheapside, or Cheap, was a traditional rallying point for the city. The street at that time was London's principal marketplace, a central hub from which radiated various roads and alleys containing a wide selection of guilds and trades. Present-day street names record some of their former specialisations: there were dairymen in Milk Street, shoemakers in Cordwainer Street, goldsmiths in Goldsmith Street, and bakers in Bread Street. On Cheapside itself lay a public water fountain, or conduit, called the standard, next to which stood a cross. It was located in the very centre of the medieval city, opposite the southern end of Honey Lane, a short distance east of the top end of Bow Lane (both of which survive), and not far from the thirteenth-century church of All Hallows. The fountain supplied the local populace with drinking water, brought in lead pipes all the way from the leafy outlying village of Paddington, and was a natural gathering point in a reeking, overcrowded city where most water was tainted and undrinkable.

Traditionally, the standard was also a place of execution. In 1196, William fitz Osbert, also known as William Longbeard, had been cornered in the nearby church of St Mary-le-Bow and dragged by force of arms to the standard and beheaded. Then, in 1326, Edward II's Treasurer, Walter Stapleton, bishop of Exeter, met a similar end, taken at sword-point from within St Paul's Cathedral and beheaded at the standard.

St Martin's-le-Grand, Roger Legett's place of refuge, was but a few paces west from the Cheapside standard, and at this time sanctuary was clearly not infallible. In fact, even the city's most formidable bastion, the Tower of London, proved useless in protecting some who sought shelter inside. Hundreds were to die across the city during the rising, which at one stage threatened to overthrow some of the most powerful figures in the land. The following day, Friday, 14 June, both the king's treasurer, Robert Hales, and his chancellor, Simon Sudbury, Archbishop of Canterbury, were dragged from the Tower despite a guard of some six hundred soldiers, executed, and their heads exhibited above the gateway on Old London Bridge. The rebels nailed a mitre to the top of Sudbury's head so the crowds could identify him. He was a natural target, because in an era when many of the highest administrative posts in the country were held by churchmen, he was also a lawyer, a diplomat and, since 1375, chancellor of England, which made him the man ultimately responsible for the imposition of the poll tax.

Sudbury and Hales met their end on the Friday. By this stage, whatever news may have been filtering through to those inside the precincts of the monastery of St Martin's-le-Grand, Roger Legett, at least, was no longer there to hear it.

The rebels were deliberately targeting anything and anyone connected with the apparatus of the law. They went to the Temple to destroy not only the buildings but also 'all the books, rolls and remembrances' they found there. Such was their mistrust of the legal system, that they 'had it cried around the city that all lawyers, all the men of the Chancery and the Exchequer and everyone who could write a writ or a letter should be beheaded, wherever they could be found'. They also broke open Westminster and Newgate prisons, freeing everyone confined there, presumably because if the law was false, and the law had put them there, then they deserved to be set free.

As a well-known – or even notorious – questmonger, Roger Legett was an obvious target for the rebels. Although the deaths of anyone not part of the aristocracy rarely merited a personal identification in the works of contemporary historians and scribes, Legett's particular end was deemed worthy of note by the eyewitness scholar who wrote the *Anonimalle Chronicle*, even on a day of much bloodshed, when the king himself was besieged by the mob in the Tower:

> This same Thursday [13 June 1381] the said commons came to St-Martin-le-Grand and dragged out of the church from the high altar a certain Roger Legett, an important assizer; they took him into the Cheap where his head was cut off. On that same day eighteen persons were beheaded in various places of the town. At this time a great body of the commons went to the Tower of London to speak with the king. As they could not get a hearing from him, they laid siege to the Tower from the side of St Katherine's, towards the south. Another group of the commons, who were within the city, went to the Hospital of St John, Clerkenwell, and on their way they burnt the place and houses of Roger Legett, questmonger, who had been beheaded in Cheapside, as well as all the rented property and tenements of the Hospital of St John they could find.

When the rebels reached St Martin's-le-Grand, the monastery's ancient walls gave Legett no protection. Whether he fought or attempted to reason with them, appealing to the sanctity of the place, it was all to no avail. Taken prisoner, possibly already wounded at this stage, Legett was carried forcibly the few hundred yards south into Cheapside. Turning the corner into the main street, having almost certainly attracted a larger crowd of onlookers, street ruffians or the merely curious, they would have then dragged him due east, and halted by the waters of the standard. He must have known where they were taking him, and a growing sense of horror and fear would have overtaken him as he realised what was about to happen – if, indeed, the mob were not already gleefully shouting in his face the details of his imminent end. Cheapside would have been crowded with people, most of them armed; a scene of noise, smoke, brandished weapons, stray cattle and dogs, and filth littering the ground. It would have taken a brave passer-by indeed to intervene at this stage and prevent Legett's murder.

This was a crime committed in broad daylight by an unknown number of people, presumably convinced that they had right on their side. His severed head was raised above the jeering crowds, yet another death in a tumultuous week of bloodshed. Those who killed Roger Legett were clearly making a public spectacle of the event, taking him to a symbolic location as if this was a judicial execution. His death, and that of many others during the revolt, would have been seen as retribution for his past conduct and his method of earning a living.

As for the legality of the proceedings, Wat Tyler and his followers were in the process of attempting to revoke virtually all of the existing laws of England, seeking to return to a previous era which they held to have been more just. Tyler is said to have predicted that soon all laws in the country would issue from his mouth, although given that all accounts of the uprising were written after the event by chroniclers who were very much hostile to the rebels, it is not always possible to trust the reports of what was said, and by whom. There was certainly a lynch-mob mentality at work during those days; the chronicler known as the monk of Westminster spoke of the crowd 'running wild like the most rabid dogs', Walsingham called them 'rustics, and most inferior ones at that', while another contemporary scribe, Henry Knighton, labelled them a 'criminal mob'.

Of course, by the time these reports were written, the young king and the mayor of London had faced down the rebels at a very tense armed gathering at Smithfield, the city had returned to something like normality, and Tyler's head had gone to decorate the row of spikes on Old London Bridge.

At this time, centuries before the advent of an organised London police force, a crime such as the death of Roger Legett, which took place amid the chaos of an uprising against Church and State, would have only a small chance of being solved. London lay under a pall of smoke from the numerous burning and looted buildings, and the scores of heads that had been struck off decorated not only London Bridge but also the city's gatehouses. Legett's own head very likely wound up in such a place, and may well have been paraded through the streets by the mob; its particular fate is not recorded. Part of the citizenry was out in the streets engaged in the violence, while the rest were inside their own homes with all the doors and shutters bolted, waiting for the turmoil to pass. Neither faction was likely to assist with a hue and cry, should any bailiff or constable have been brave enough to attempt to call for one. At a time of popular revolt when six hundred fully armed men in the Tower seemingly stood helplessly by as the rebels took out the king's treasurer and his lord chancellor for summary execution, those who killed Legett in the middle of one of London's busiest streets would have felt little fear of retribution.

Pinning the blame on anyone for the various murders that took place in London during the days of the revolt was a complex undertaking; punishing the leaders, though, was another matter. Some, such as Wat Tyler, had died during the uprising, but others were hunted down afterwards. John Ball, the itinerant preacher – who gave a sermon to the commons as they massed on Blackheath before entering the city, uttering his famous egalitarian rallying cry, 'When Adam delved and Eve span / Who was then the gentleman?' – was arrested in Coventry, where he had fled after Tyler's death at Smithfield. As one of the acknowledged leaders of the uprising, Ball was tried at St Albans on 12 July, and hanged, drawn and quartered there days later, in the presence of the king.

Yet a surprisingly high number of those who were found to have taken part in the killings, looting and destruction were subsequently pardoned in the aftermath of the revolt. These even included the five London aldermen who were indicted on the very serious charge of treacherously opening up the southern drawbridge of London Bridge and inviting in the rebels. Given the severity of the disturbances, it is remarkable that only around a hundred people are thought to have been executed on charges of having participated in the rising (although the various contemporary chroniclers painted a far more bloodthirsty picture of the revolt's suppression).

As for the murderers of Roger Legett, their fate is unknown. It may well be that no one in particular out of the mob that dragged him away from the high altar of St Martin's-le-Grand to his death in Cheapside was ever identified and tried for the crime. Alternatively, even if they were, it's possible that they may then have been pardoned. Over in Somerset, far from the main centres of unrest, one Thomas Engilby seems to have taken advantage of chaotic times to pay off an old score in Bridgwater. He was charged that on 19 June, just a few days after the crisis in London, he had burnt down several houses, beheaded one Walter Baron, and had forced his own housemate, John Bursy, to behead another man named Hugh Lavenham. It was said that 'Thomas placed Hugh's head together with that of Walter Baron on lances over the bridge at Bridgwater.' The natural assumption might be that Engilby would suffer the death penalty for such behaviour, but instead, he received the king's pardon, which in Richard's own words, justified the decision thus: 'Nevertheless, we by our special grace and because of this present feast of Easter, and on the condition that he behaves well to us and our people henceforward, have pardoned Thomas.'

If this was not a hanging offence, then those responsible for Legett's death might also have been afforded similar leniency. An amnesty was granted to nearly all of those who had participated in the rising, the monarchy evidently finding it more practical to offer pardons in return for money. A list was drawn up of people excepted from the general pardon, but even some of those were eventually set free, such as the Essex peasant leader John Awedyn, despite being described in his indictment as 'one of the rebels against the lord king in the city of London'.

On balance, it's more likely than not that the killers of Roger Legett went unpunished. He seems to have been singled out by the mob as a representative of the hated legal system – indeed, as one who profited from it even at the expense of other men's lives – and also because those Londoners with long memories might have recalled his sadistic habit of setting iron man-traps. It may be that it was only his local notoriety that caused his name to appear in the *Anonimalle*, when hundreds of other victims of the revolt went unrecorded, and so his fate was remarked and noted down, at a time when usually only the deaths of the wealthy and important were included in the chronicles. Nevertheless, to the unknown scribe who gave us the account of his death, Legett may have seemed a largely innocent victim, an upright citizen. Those writing directly after the revolt's conclusion had precious little sympathy for the rebels' motives, finding their actions utterly criminal. In killing Legett, or a Lombard, or an officer of the crown, the rebels were striking at the established system, and were roundly condemned by the chroniclers for this.

We know virtually nothing of Legett's life, and just a few spare details of his death. He was one of many who perished in the very heart of London, on one of the capital's bloodiest days. Order was swiftly restored, the hated poll tax was repealed, and yet the state of villeinage lived on for over a century. The revolt had been crushed, but attempts to rid the capital of everyday murder would prove less successful.

Old St Paul's Cathedral towering over London in 1540,
with the ancient city walls and gates clearly visible

MURDER IN THE CATHEDRAL
1514

In the early years of the reign of Henry VIII, over a century after the Peasants' Revolt, the population of London was just starting to rise, having remained static around the figure of 60,000 since the days of the latter upheaval. This was the beginning of a sharp expansion which saw the number of inhabitants triple within a hundred years. Under Henry's father, Henry VII – who ruled until 1509 – the nation had gradually returned to stability after the bitter divisions of the Wars of the Roses, but in terms of everyday crime, things were much as before, according to a despatch written around 1500 by a Venetian envoy to his superiors back home:

> There is no country in the world where there are so many thieves and robbers as in England; insomuch that few venture to go alone in the country excepting in the middle of the day, and fewer still in the towns at night, and least of all in London.

This was still, in 1514, a Catholic nation. The Reformation had not yet begun in earnest, here or in mainland Europe (Martin Luther's written complaints about the state of the Church would begin in 1517).

Henry VIII, according to a contemporary account by Sebastian Guistiniani, was 'very religious. Hears three masses daily when he hunts, and sometimes five on other days'. A twenty-three-year-old monarch who had been on the throne for five years, Henry had spent much of that time not in religious disputes, but making his name in the traditional manner of English kings, waging war on France. The king's home nearest the city, Westminster Palace, which had served England's monarchs for centuries, had been badly damaged by fire two years earlier, leaving him with no proper London residence except for the Tower. Work would begin in 1515 on building Henry an alternative palace to Westminster, in a more central location at Bridewell, where the Fleet River meets the Thames, close to the highest peak of the city skyline, Old St Paul's Cathedral.

It is difficult to overstate the extent to which St Paul's dominated the surrounding area. There had been a cathedral on this site dedicated to the saint since the year 610. The first, dating from the reign of King Ethelbert, was destroyed by fire in 961. Rebuilt, it then survived through the early days of the Norman Conquest until it too was swept away by flames in 1087. The colossal structure that replaced it – known today as Old St Paul's – was eventually consecrated in 1148, having survived another serious fire during its construction. A central stone tower was added a century later – topped by a wooden spire encased in lead, rising to a height of four hundred and forty-nine feet – and by 1327 a further enlargement and reconstruction of the entire building had been completed. Sir Christopher Wren's seventeenth-century St Paul's which survives today is a magnificent structure, and at three hundred and sixty-four feet was until 1962 the tallest building in London – Old St Paul's, however, was longer, wider and considerably taller. The former was constructed at a time when the city held upwards of half a million people – how much more dominant and awe-inspiring must Old St Paul's have seemed in the far smaller London of 1514, with a population roughly one tenth the size? A symbol of the colossal power of the Church, looming far above the surrounding rooftops, it cast a literal and psychological shadow over those who walked the streets below. Raised to the glory of God, its sheer scale carried a measure of intimidation.

By the time Henry VIII came to the throne, the spire of St Paul's was topped by a fifteen-foot-high gilded cross containing the relics of several saints, to ward off lightning bolts and other less temporal dangers. Bones and other assorted bits and pieces supposedly taken from the bodies of illustrious Christians were widely venerated at the time, and each significant place of worship would be expected to have its own collection. In St Paul's, the lengthy list of relics included a piece of the True Cross, some blood of St Paul, the hand of St John, some hair of Mary Magdalene, a knife of Our Lord and even some milk of the Virgin. (Exactly how all these things were supposed to have survived for a millennium and a half and also to have found their way to England was perhaps a mystery equal to any of those occupying the theologians of the nation.) Presiding over this impressive collection, and the building itself, was the Dean of St Paul's, Dr John Colet (although he himself disapproved of the cult of relics and also of pilgrimages). Colet knew Henry well, and frequently had his support at a time when the preaching of a sermon could land its author in gaol or worse.

Religion was a serious business. In the years immediately after the Peasants' Revolt, the first full translation of the Bible into English had been produced, inspired by the teachings of the theologian John Wyclif, which so threatened the established order that even the possession of a copy became a capital offence. The Bible in Latin required churchmen to explain it. In English it was dangerous, since anyone who could read might quote selectively and interpret its meaning for their own ends. The Church wished to retain control, and heretical followers of Wyclif, known as Lollards, were often burnt at the stake for their beliefs. In 1499, twelve recanting Lollards had been forced to do penance outside the cathedral at Paul's Cross, near the eastern nave, surrounded by unlit wooden faggots as a warning of where their heresies might lead. At the opposite end of the building, forming the south-west corner of St Paul's, was the Lollards' Tower, which served as a prison for those suspected of such crimes.

Yet for all the splendour of the building itself, and the pomp and wealth of the churchmen within, the average Londoner often showed a lack of respect, indifference or even outright hostility to religion. A cathedral on the scale of St Paul's might have been designed to inspire awe in the surrounding population, but in many cases it clearly did no such thing, as Keith Thomas states in his landmark work, *Religion and the Decline of Magic*:

> . . . virtually every kind of irreverent (and irrelevant) activity took place during divine worship. Members of the congregation jostled for pews, nudged their neighbours, hawked and spat, knitted, made coarse remarks, told jokes, fell asleep, and even let off guns.

St Paul's itself was used for all sorts of purposes by the citizens; as a meeting place, business house, or a place of entertainment. In 1411, the religious authorities had found it necessary to issue a decree forbidding wrestling inside the building, but this was mild compared to the problems in the thirteenth century, when 'by the lurking of thieves and other lewd people, in the night time, within the precinct of this churchyard, divers robberies, homicides and fornications, had been oft times committed therein'.

However, to fall foul of the Church and its systems of authority could be very dangerous. Bishops and archbishops sat in the House of Lords, playing an active part in the governance of the nation, and were directly involved in the censorship of printed materials and the organisation of universities. There also existed an entirely separate legal system run by the Church, distinct from the common law of the land. Ecclesiastical courts dispensed justice on a wide variety of moral issues relating to marriage, divorce, adultery, money lending, the probate of wills and many other aspects of private life. In those last decades before Henry VIII quarrelled with Rome, tore up the rulebook and drastically curtailed the role and influence of the Church, it played a key role in the fabric of the nation, and when its authority was challenged by any individual, was capable of responding with an iron fist.

Richard Hunne was a prosperous Londoner. A member of the Merchant Taylor's Company, one of the most important City Livery Guilds, he lived in the parish of St Margaret's, New Fish Street Hill, which would later be at the epicentre of the Great Fire of London in 1666. (Wren's Monument, commemorating the fire, stands on the former site of this parish church.) Despite his wealth and social standing, Hunne seems to have had a low opinion of the established Church, and his father-in-law, Thomas Vincent, was a prominent Lollard.

Richard's infant son Stephen died in March 1511, aged five weeks. As was relatively common in wealthy families, Stephen had been put out to nurse. He had been sent to Whitechapel – a supposedly healthy outlying district of farms and fields – and his funeral service took place in the 'white chapel' which originally gave its name to the whole district, the church of St Mary Matfelon. It had long been the custom for the families of the deceased to pay a form of death duty to the clergy who officiated at the funeral, which was known as the 'mortuary'. In this case, the priest, Thomas Dryffeld, claimed Stephen's burial cloth as a mortuary, but Richard Hunne refused. To the mind of the recently bereaved father – no lover of the Church at the best of times – this probably seemed an insulting demand; the priest, of course, saw things differently. From this seemingly trivial dispute arose something far more serious.

Dryffeld eventually responded by taking the matter to the ecclesiastical courts and obtained a judgement in his favour at the Archbishop of Canterbury's court of audience at Lambeth on 13 May 1512. All would probably still have been well if the matter had been allowed to rest there, but neither side showed that inclination.

Later that year, Hunne attempted to attend mass at St Mary Matfelon but was refused entrance on the grounds that he had been excommunicated. His action may well have been a calculated provocation, to see if there would be a reaction. Hunne now fought back, accusing the priest of attempting to subvert the king's authority by having used an ecclesiastical court, and obtained a writ of *praemunire facias*, which is defined by the *Oxford English Dictionary* as 'prosecuting abroad a suit cognizable by English law' – in other words, the Church was unjustly imposing foreign laws upon the people of England. This action of Hunne's struck at the basis upon which the ecclesiastical courts were founded, and even though his writ was rejected in 1514, the threat had been made, and the Church authorities moved swiftly against the man who had issued it.

There was already grave unease among the clergy at an act of parliament passed two years earlier which had removed legal immunity for minor Church officials – clerks, sub-deacons and the like – so that they could now be tried by the lay courts. Priests, bishops and archbishops were still exempt, even if the crime involved was murder, but this was a worrying development. For centuries, members of the Church had been protected under 'benefit of clergy', and were dealt with by ecclesiastical courts; often very leniently. This change in the law under Henry VIII, restricting their privileged status, posed a serious threat, and was condemned in 1514 by the pope. Richard Hunne could scarcely have picked a worse time to mount any kind of challenge to the authority of the ecclesiastical courts.

As a wealthy man and recently bereaved father, with a longstanding distrust of the Church and its power, Richard Hunne may well have pursued his actions out of emotion rather than calm reflection. In initially refusing to hand over the mortuary as requested, and so picking a fight with a minor priest, he had registered his protest. If he had stopped there, and paid the tribute once the court had found against him, that would very likely have been the end of the matter. Instead, he raised the stakes considerably by taking the matter to the court of king's bench – not just a secular court, but the highest in the land. He sued Dryffeld the priest for slander, and then rounded up several other more senior clerics in his action, including the summoner Charles Joseph, who reported directly to the Bishop of London, Richard Fitzjames.

In threatening the bishop and questioning the right of the ecclesi-astical courts to pass judgement on the actions of citizens, Hunne was treading on extremely dangerous ground. Indeed, his case now attracted the attention of one of the most important political figures in Henry's kingdom, William Warham, who was not only Archbishop of Canterbury but also Lord Chancellor; the man who had crowned the king in 1509. Warham's response was to begin proceedings to try Hunne for heresy. Eventually, after the dispute had rumbled on at a low level for a couple of years, on 14 October 1514 a forbidden Wyclif Bible was conveniently discovered hidden away in Richard Hunne's house, triggering his arrest.

Until this point, Hunne had been a rich merchant pursuing his grievance through the courts; now he was an accused man, taking on the considerable might of one arm of the State. As a suspected heretic, he was imprisoned not in the Tower of London, but in a building at the heart of the Church's power in the capital, Old St Paul's, in the so-called Lollards' Tower. By calling attention to himself through his court action, some might say he had invited retribution – in the words of a Japanese proverb, 'the nail that is sticking up will be hammered back down'.

Since Wren's cathedral is slightly smaller than the one it replaced, the site of the Lollards' Tower, which formed the south-western end of old St Paul's, is today covered by the steps and paving stones directly outside the Great West Door of the present building. The wealthy Hunne was confined here in a cell just like any common prisoner, directly on the orders of the Bishop of London, Richard Fitzjames. The earliest account of the case, *Hall's Chronicle*, published some thirty years after these events in 1548, put it like this:

> This yer in December ther was one Richard Hun a marchat tayllor of London in Lollers tower by the commaundment of the Bishop of London, called Rychard Fitziames & doctor Horsey his chaunceler . . .

This somewhat dry summary scarcely hints at the implications of the situation. The reality for Richard Hunne, after the initial satisfaction of having stood up to his powerful adversary had faded, would very likely have been a mixture of fear and depression. Once confined inside St Paul's, he had access to no one and was completely at the mercy of the Church authorities, who could now dictate the course of events. This was a psychological contest in which one side held all the trump cards, and they soon made their first move. Dr Horsey, the bishop's chancellor, had primary responsibility for the prisoner, and it was on his order that Hunne was taken on 2 December to Fulham Palace to be interrogated by Bishop Fitzjames.

This was a journey west, through the Lud Gate (with its crop of severed heads on spikes), along Ludgate Hill, crossing the Fleet River; along Fleet Street and Temple Bar, then over the Strand Bridge, past the rebuilt Savoy Palace and the Thames to the south and the greenery of the Convent Garden to the north; following the river through the separate settlement of Westminster, the tiny village of Chelsea and finally the tranquil countryside of Fulham, traditional retreat of the bishops of London since the eleventh century. The journey took Richard Hunne from the noise and stench of the very heart of the capital city to a place of rural seclusion – of farmyard smells, birdsong and the fresh breeze from the river – then all the way back to the Lollards' Tower. It was the last he would ever make.

The prisoner was probably not in a fit state to appreciate any of the sights that passed on the long road to Fulham, weighed down as he was by an exceedingly heavy chain and collar around his neck, placed there on the orders of Dr Horsey, as *Hall's Chronicle* recounts:

> Also before Hun was caried to Fulham, the Chaunceller commanded too
> be put uppon Huns necke a greate coller of Iron with a greate chayne
> whiche is to hevy for any man or beast to were and longe to endure.

For Richard Hunne, a man of wealth and position, accustomed to the finer
things in life, the indignity may even have been worse than the considerable
discomfort. Criminals and malefactors were supposed to be treated thus,
not respectable members of city livery companies. If this was a measure of
the confidence with which Church officials felt able to act, the implications
were disturbing.

Hunne's place of interrogation at Fulham, like his prison in the city, was
a church. He was questioned in the chapel of Fulham Palace by
Dr Horsey in the presence of the bishop, Richard Fitzjames. According to
the official record, he stood accused of a list of offences, all of which would
have identified him as a religious troublemaker. The first charge made him
out to be one who would strike at the very economic roots of the Church:

> That he had read, taught, preached, published, and obstinately defended,
> against the laws of Almighty God; that tithes, or paying of tithes, was
> never ordained to be due, saving only by the covetousness of priests.

The next two charges went even further, suggesting that he had blackened the name of every member of the clergy by saying 'that bishops and
priests be the scribes and Pharisees that did crucify Christ, and damned
him to death', and that 'bishops and priests be teachers and preachers,
but no doers, neither fulfillers of the law of God; but catching, ravening,
and all things taking, and nothing ministering, neither giving'. These
kinds of sentiments were probably voiced in pubs and taverns across the
city by men in trusted company when the drink began to take hold.
However, if Richard Hunne had said anything remotely like this within
earshot of anyone with Church connections, then the man clearly had a
death wish. Of course, just because he was charged with such offences,
it does not follow that they were true.

Still, this was not all. Further charges related to Hunne's alleged defence
of the opinions of a convicted heretic called Joan Baker, and his supposed
statements that 'the bishop and his officers are more worthy to be punished
for heresy than she is'. Finally, there was the question of the Wyclif Bible
supposedly found at his house, along with other banned books:

That the said Richard Hun hath in his keeping divers English books, prohibited and damned by the law; as the Apocalypse in English, Epistles and Gospels in English, Wickliff's damnable works, and other books, containing infinite errors, in the which he hath been long time accustomed to read, teach, and study daily.

With such a programme of determined anti-clericalism every day, it is a wonder he found time for his business affairs. In fact, the sheer number of suicidally dangerous offences against the Church which Richard Hunne was alleged to have committed begins to make this roll-call look about as trustworthy as the litany of 'evidence' commonly presented at twentieth-century Stalinist show trials. However, this was not a public hearing, but a closed interrogation in a private location, at which all manner of pressure could be brought to bear upon the prisoner. Whatever actually transpired that day, the result was that a document was written, purported to be in Hunne's own hand, in which he admitted these heresies and submitted himself humbly to the judgement of the Church. Perhaps not surprisingly, the veracity of this document would later be called into question.

The case presented that day by Dr Horsey drew a picture of Richard Hunne as an intemperate anti-clerical zealot, reading and spreading heretical opinions throughout the city, and openly challenging the Bishop of London and his officers. As the saying goes: give a dog a bad name . . . . . . and hang him.

Back at the Lollards' Tower, Hunne was placed under even closer arrest than before. It was decreed that he was now only allowed one meal a day, and the man formerly responsible for his day-to-day care, Charles Joseph the summoner, handed over his duties to John Spalding, a bellringer, reputed to be 'simple'. Perhaps Joseph was considered to be sympathetic to the plight of the prisoner; more likely, though, he was replaced with someone more pliant, in order to facilitate the next move, which was not long in coming.

It was 4 December 1514, two days after his secret interrogation at Fulham. The boy responsible for bringing Richard Hunne his meagre daily meal was let into the cell as usual by two of the Bishop's men. This may well have been one of the few times the prisoner had any company at all during the day, and therefore the child might have expected this chained-up, older man to engage him in brief conversation. Today, however, there was no chance of that. On entering the room, the three of them found the merchant hanging lifeless from an iron staple by a silk noose; he had died in the night.

In a later era, this would have been the moment to summon an ambulance, the police, and perhaps a forensics team. Instead, Dr Horsey was sent for, who proceeded to act almost as a combination of all three. He examined the scene and then declared unequivocally that Richard Hunne had hanged himself.

Horsey, as the Bishop of London's right-hand man, was certainly someone whose opinion would have carried weight, but even so, the death in custody of a man of Hunne's wealth and social standing required an inquest. The body was left exactly where it was, and the following day, 5 December, the cell was visited by the coroner William Barnwell and twenty-four citizens to inquire into the death. It may have been four centuries before the development of forensic crime scene examinations, yet for the time, this was a surprisingly thorough inquest, which was set out in detail in the account given thirty years later in *Hall's Chronicle*.

What they found was immediately suspicious: the noose of silk was not securely fixed to the iron staple, yet Hunne's neck had been decisively broken. It was also obvious that Hunne's hands had been bound, and they concluded that there was nothing solid anywhere in the cell upon which the prisoner might have stood in order to hang himself – the one stool available being so rickety that 'any man or beast myght not touche it so little but it was redy to fall'. There was a candle set up some distance away from the body which had been neatly snuffed out, and it appeared that whoever had done this, it could not possibly have been Hunne. There seemed to be no possibility that the 'soft sylken gyrdell' would have been able to break his neck in that position, and when they opened up his coat, a large quantity of blood was found underneath:

> Whereby it appereth plainly to us all, that the necke of Hun was broken, and the great plenty of blude was shed before he was hanged. Wherefore all wee fynde by God and all our consciences that Rychard Hun was murthered: also we acquyte the sayde Richard Hun of his aune deathe.

Everything that they saw in that cell convinced them that Hunne had not killed himself, and that he had been violently murdered, which given that he had been confined in supposed high security by the Church – with access denied to friends and family members alike – raised the formidable question: how had his captors let this happen? Some, of course, went further, and assumed that Richard Hunne had in fact been assassinated on the direct orders of the clergy.

The news spread quickly through the city, giving the Church authorities much concern, for, as Bishop Fitzjames wrote to the very powerful Bishop Thomas Wolsey when the death first became public, the average Londoner hated the Church so much that they would 'cast and condemn my clerk though he was as innocent as Abel'. This seemingly disrespectful attitude on the part of the general populace is not that hard to understand. Recent popes had included Alexander VI (died 1503) – who fathered two of the most notorious Borgias, Lucretia and Cesare, and would make anyone a cardinal if they could pay the correct fee – and Julius II (died 1513), who had several daughters, was riddled with syphilis, and had almost certainly bribed his way to the top. The new pope, Leo X, was at least not a womaniser like his predecessors, but only, as a contemporary wrote, because he was a devotee of 'those pleasures which cannot, with decency, be named'. Clearly, the last thing that the Church needed at this point was another blow to their moral authority, and the inquest's conclusion that Richard Hunne had been murdered while in clerical custody, at the very heart of St Paul's itself, was hardly the kind of publicity they were after.

Endeavouring to fight back, Bishop Fitzjames and his supporters then elected to take what to modern ears sounds like an incredible step: they would try the corpse for heresy, presumably reasoning that if they blackened Hunne's name then no one would continue to defend him. Bizarre as this idea may seem, there were precedents for it in the history of the Church. In the year 897, the new pope, Stephen VII, had the corpse of the previous pope but one, Formosus, exhumed, dressed up in pontifical robes and then put on trial. Found guilty, the body was mutilated, briefly buried, exhumed again and then thrown in the Tiber, from where it was later rescued and reburied secretly by supporters of the deceased. Stephen VII was himself strangled shortly after, but a decade later, Pope Sergius III had what remained of the much-battered corpse of Pope Formosus exhumed and put on trial yet again. Declared posthumously guilty for the second time, the body of Formosus was beheaded and thrown once more into the Tiber. If the rotting corpse of a dead pope could be repeatedly dragged in front of the religious courts, then surely a recently deceased London merchant was fair game, or so it might have seemed to Bishop Fitzjames.

So it came about that on 16 December 1514, the mortal remains of the late Richard Hunne were brought before the Church authorities and formally tried for heresy. It is a measure of how seriously the Church authorities took the matter that the dead man had ranged against him in the court not just Richard Fitzjames, Bishop of London, but also – according to John Foxe in his *Book of Martyrs* (1563) – the bishops of Durham and Lincoln, together with 'six public notaries, his own register, and about twenty-five doctors, abbots, priors, and priests of name, with a great rabble of their common annointed catholics'. Quite what Hunne would have pleaded in front of such an august assembly under other circumstances is impossible to say, but in this instance, it can be assumed that he maintained a suitably impassive countenance while the learned gentlemen read out the case against him. Unsurprisingly, not least because of the inability of the accused to answer the charges, they found him guilty, and sentenced him to the common fate of heretics in England, to be burnt at the stake. Four days later, what was left of Richard Hunne was publicly incinerated at Smithfield – an action which prompted considerable public revulsion. Normally, the crowds would play along with such an event, perhaps jeering at the condemned and taunting them in their agony; in this case, the public scorn was reserved for the executioner and those who had ordered this farcical procedure.

Smithfield – where Wat Tyler met his end during the Peasants' Revolt, and scene of the riotous yearly bacchanal known as Bartholomew Fair – had long been one of London's places of execution. Ever since the passing of the Act *De Haeretico Comburendo* in 1401, many Lollards had been burnt at the stake at Smithfield. In 1494, these included eighty-year-old Joan Broughton, together with her daughter. Most recently, in 1511, John Bannister and William Succling had gone to the stake after being tried by Bishop Fitzjames. Huge crowds generally turned out for such events, but the sight of the remains of a man who had been dead for several weeks being tied up and publicly burnt on the orders of the Church was hardly likely to be greeted with cheers or approval from the London mob. As an improvised strategy for covering up an inconvenient death, the trial and 'execution' backfired, to the extent that Henry VIII himself was moved to ask questions about the case.

In the event, the matter was deemed worthy of 'tryall of the lawe', as *Hall's Chronicle* puts it, whereby Dr Horsey, the bellringer John Spalding who had been in charge of the keys to Hunne's cell, and the summoner Charles Joseph, responsible for the day-to-day care of the prisoner, were indicted for murder. At their trial, Charles Joseph began by making a confession which implicated several others. He first stated categorically that the supposed handwritten confession signed by Hunne on the day of his interrogation at Fulham had been wholly forged by Dr Horsey, and went on to describe how he and Horsey and Spalding together had killed Richard Hunne in his cell, then faked the appearance of suicide:

> . . . we founde Hun lyenge on hys bedde, and than Mayster chaunceller sayde, lay handes on the thefe and so al we murthered Hun, and than I Charles put the gyrdell aboute Huns necke, and than Ihon Belrynger and I Charles dyd heve up Hun and Master Chaunceller pulled the gyrdell ouer the staple and so Hun was hanged.

This damning confession was backed up by the evidence of Charles Joseph's maidservant, who testified that he had later admitted to her 'I have distroyed Richard Hun'. It was further stated at the trial that on the day before the death of the prisoner, Dr Horsey himself had visited Hunne in his cell in order to ask forgiveness for what was about to happen, as one John Fixe related: '. . . the said chancellor came up into the said Lollard's Tower, and kneeled downe before Hun, holding up his hands to him, praying him of forgivenes of all that he had done to him, and must doe to him.'

As one witness followed another – John Spalding, bellringer; Thomas Chitcheley, tailor; Thomas Symondes, stationer; Robert Johnson, publican; John Enderby, barber – the evidence against the accused seemed overwhelming. The men on trial all worked directly for the Bishop of London, and the death in question had taken place in one of the most important Church properties in the country. Small wonder that Bishop Fitzjames was moved to write personally to Wolsey, one of the king's inner circle, asking him to stand up for Horsey, his 'poore chaunceller', on trial for murder in the 'vntrewe [untrue] quest' to find out about the death of Richard Hunne. In the letter, he claimed that the damning statements of Charles Joseph were made under the influence of torture ('payne and duraunce'), and that Horsey was innocent of all charges.

Fitzjames might have considered Horsey falsely accused, but the jury did not, and the bishop's chancellor was duly found guilty of murder.

Two acts were then brought before parliament in February 1515. One restored to Richard Hunne's heirs his considerable fortune of £1,500, which had been forfeited by his conviction for heresy. The second endorsed the verdict of the jury, and called for action against Dr Horsey. During the parliamentary debate for the latter Act, Bishop Fitzjames stood up in front of the assembled lords and swore that the trial jury were false, perjured *caitiffs* [worthless wretches] and that the only person responsible for Hunne's death was the prisoner alone, who had hanged himself. He begged the lords to intercede in this matter, otherwise 'I dare not kepe myne awne house for heretiques'. In short, back me up, or the heretics will take over, and even my palace at Fulham will be unsafe.

The lords were not convinced, and ratified the verdict of the jury. This meant, at the very least, that the Bishop of London was thought to have employed several murderers among his entourage, and at worst, might well be implicated in both the death and the cover-up. Yet the power of the Church remained very substantial, and Henry VIII was still some decades away from picking a decisive battle with the men of the cloth.

In the event, despite one of the Bishop of London's trusted officers being found guilty in open court of premeditated murder, Dr Horsey's fate was not sealed. Fitzjames appealed directly to the king, and it seems a deal was struck. Horsey, who had been hiding in Lambeth Palace, appeared again in the law courts, presumably as a humble gesture, offering to submit to whatever judgement might be required, whereupon the Attorney-General announced that he would not be taking the matter any further. The case was therefore closed, Horsey stood acquitted, and went immediately to start a new life in Exeter, several days' carriage ride away from London. He remained there until he himself died, yet continued to be the Bishop of London's chancellor for another sixteen years.

Hunne's case was just one of over sixty heresy hearings dealt with in the Bishop of London's diocese between 1511 and the death of Fitzjames in 1522, but it remains the one for which the latter is most remembered. John Foxe devoted a great deal of space to this affair in his *Book of Martyrs*, published in 1563 – within living memory, yet separated in time from those events by the tumultuous upheaval of the Reformation and Henry's dissolution of the monasteries. Within a few decades of the death of Hunne – a man who had unwisely threatened the long-established power and jurisdiction of the Church – the religious map of London would be changed beyond all recognition. Churches, monasteries, convents and palaces were sold off on Henry's orders to the highest bidder or given away to favoured courtiers. Some of these buildings were destroyed, others became hospitals or found other uses, such as St Mary Graces, near the Tower, which was turned into a naval supply yard.

Old St Paul's itself still stood, neglected, in the heart of the city – its monuments and shrines broken up or defaced, the churchyard becoming a centre for the new book trade. The lofty wooden spire of the old cathedral, with its towering cross containing martyrs' bones, caught fire and collapsed in 1561, but the building still cast a giant shadow over London, until another fire a century later laid waste to the entire structure, along with most of the city.

In a metropolis built largely of wood, fire was an ever-present enemy. It regularly broke out in the teeming, crowded streets, bringing down buildings and sometimes whole districts. At the last, fire also disposed of what was left of Richard Hunne; a dead man tried for heresy, who outlived his infant son by just two years.

Ducount in bonis dies suos, & in puncto ad
inferna descendunt. JOB. XXI.

H Holbein in.

A wealthy woman falls into the clutches of a skeleton in an illustration from the
sixteenth-century *Dance of Death* series by Hans Holbein the Younger

THREE

FILTHIE LUSTES
OF WICKED WHOREDOME
1573

In Elizabethan London, time-honoured entertainments such as drinking, gambling, cock-fighting, bear-baiting and bull-baiting occupied the free hours of the general public, much to the annoyance of puritan preachers such as John Northbrooke, who expressed his disapproval in *A Treatise against Dicing, Dancing, Plays, and Interludes, with Other Idle Pastimes* (1577). He also deplored the inadequacy of legislation governing football matches, calling those involved 'loitering idle persons, ruffians, blasphemous swinge-bucklers and tossepots'. Dancing – a favourite pursuit of Queen Elizabeth herself – was of course the Devil's work, and an incitement to lust, but Northbrooke reserved perhaps his greatest contempt for the 'mummers' who put on plays:

> Satan hath not a more speedie way and fitter schoole to work and teach his desire, to bring men and women into his snare of concupiscence and filthie lustes of wicked whoredome, than those places and playes, and theatres are.

As a drama critic, John was very much ahead of the pack, since London's first purpose-built theatre had only opened in 1576, the year before he wrote his *Treatise*. It is hardly surprising that the capital's first home of drama was sited outside the city walls, beyond the reach of the more stringent regulations prevailing in the metropolis. Opened by James Burbage, it stood in sparsely populated ground, on the road which ran north out of Bishopsgate, between Shoreditch and the Finsbury Ditch. Since there was no other competition, the building was called simply The Theatre.

As more playhouses were built and plays written, so too came further moralistic publications denouncing them, but drama also had its supporters in court circles. Burbage's troupe of players was under the patronage of Elizabeth's favourite, Lord Robert Dudley, earl of Leicester – a cultured man who supported not only the theatre but also painters and musicians (although he, too, drew the line at football). Plays were given on temporary stages at court in front of the nobility, and also in impromptu spaces such as inn yards, as had long been the custom. James Burbage's purpose-built theatre, designed to mimic the galleried layout found in London inns, proved to be merely the start: over the following four decades there appeared the Fortune, the Curtain, the Cockpit, the Blackfriars Playhouse, the Globe, the Rose, the Hope and the Swan.

With all this theatrical activity, the question naturally arose among the relevant authorities as to what subject matter might be fit for presentation on the stage. To hear the puritans tell it, theatres were centres of lust, debauchery and wickedness. They also depicted a variety of crimes; up to, and including, murder.

Murder was of course hardly unknown in Elizabethan London, and it is understandable that playwrights might wish to depict it on the stage. However, in most instances, the examples shown would probably have been historical scenes, such as Brutus stabbing Julius Caesar. Cases taken from recent daily life would have been quite another matter, especially if some of those involved were still alive.

In modern times, murder has generally been regarded as the most serious offence on the statute books. Yet from a criminal's point of view, killing a man in sixteenth-century England was not necessarily any more risky a business than merely stealing his money, since in law, highway robbery was punishable by death. Some crimes were held to be worse than simple murder. As far as the State was concerned, offences which threatened either the power of the monarch or that of the Church were considered the most serious, and thus deserving of extreme punishments. Debasing or counterfeiting the coin of the realm, which in principle threatened the entire validity of the money supply, was therefore classified as treason; in 1570, for example, a man named Philip Mestrell was hanged, drawn and quartered at Tyburn for counterfeiting. If the latter offence was held to undermine the fabric of the State, so too was the case of a man who was 'hanged, headed and quartered' in 1581 for begging while using a licence upon which he had forged the queen's signature. No one, except the beggar himself, died as a result of this crime, but it was felt by the authorities to be serious enough that his body should be divided up into pieces and those parts displayed in several cities to serve as a warning to others not to follow his example.

A comprehensive round-up of the various punishments on offer in the 1570s was set down by William Harrison in his *Historicall Description of the Iland of Britaine*. He was also a cleric of somewhat apocalyptic hue, convinced that Satan was attempting to destroy Elizabethan England by means of Popish plots. A native Londoner – born in Cordwainer Street, Cheapside, in 1535 – Harrison would, like most city residents, presumably have witnessed a variety of criminals being subjected to the noose, the stake, the pillory and the branding iron. This was not an era for the squeamish: poisoners were boiled to death in lead, heretics burnt alive, sheep rustlers had both hands chopped off and, as for those who had the temerity to commit suicide – 'such as kill themselves, are buried in the field, with a stake driven through their bodies'.

After noting that hanging was the customary punishment 'in cases of felonie, manslaghter, roberie, murther, rape, piracie, & such capitall crimes as are not reputed for treason or hurt of the estate', Harrison then claims that – contrary to whatever might be the situation in other, less civilised lands – 'our condemned persons do go so cheerefullie to their deaths, for our nation is free, stout, hautie, prodigall of life and bloud'.

The three volumes of Harrison's *Historicall Description* were substantial enough in their own right, but were actually written and published as the preface of a much larger, indeed monumental, work of history which had a great effect upon the way in which the nation viewed its own past: Raphael Holinshed's *Chronicles of England, Scotland and Ireland* (1577), which weighed in at a magisterial 2,835 small folio pages. Included in this vast work were the basic stories that underlie Shakespeare's *Macbeth* and most of his history plays, but in addition to recording tales of the violent death of a king in the eleventh century, the *Chronicles* also gave details of a notorious murder which had taken place just four years earlier, in 1573: 'The five and twentith of March being wednesdaie in Easter weeke, and the feast of the Annuntiation of our ladie, George Browne cruellie murthered two honest men neere to Shooters hill . . .'

Now part of south-east London, Shooters Hill in those days was a lonely countryside location at Woolwich, between the Royal Palaces of Greenwich and Eltham. Through it ran the main road into London from Kentish towns such as Rochester and Dover. The hill had long been a favourite spot for highwaymen and robbers to lie in wait for rich travellers (far easier to hide in the woods before making an attack, and melt away into the greenery, than risk the same action in town or village, where the locals might give chase or draw their own weapons). In order to discourage such behaviour, the rotting bodies of executed robbers were displayed on gibbets along the roads where they had plied their trade, which made the ride into London from south or north a gruesome business at the best of times.

There is no record of exactly how Shooters Hill gained its name, but the common theory is that it was much used for archery practice. Certainly, this is where Henry VIII came with Catherine of Aragon on May Day, 1515, and was treated to a display of skill by two hundred bowmen, led by a man dressed as Robin Hood.

Robberies and murders on sparsely populated roads such as this were hardly unusual, but the particular case noted by Holinshed attracted far more than the customary attention. John Stow, another great chronicler of Elizabethan times, also devoted a fair amount of space to an account of the murder. Of the 'two honest men' that Holinshed mentioned above, Stow says: '. . . the one of them was a wealthy merchant of London, named George Sanders, the other John Beane of Woolwich.'

Here, of course, was a possible reason for the attention; although one victim was a servant, the other, George Sanders (or Saunders), was a rich Londoner, who lived near the church of St Dunstan's in the East, between the Tower and London Bridge. Since well-off road travellers were a prime target – whether in town or in outlying districts – robbery might have been initially suspected as the motive for the murders, but then there would have been little to distinguish this particular case from many others. In fact, this was not a theft with violence; it was a deliberate, pre-arranged homicide.

By rights it should have been a simple expedition; a relaxing stroll in the country. George Sanders and his young servant, John Beane, had broken their journey from London the previous day with an overnight stay at the Woolwich home of a Mr Barnes. Now, early on the morning of 24 March 1573, the two men set off on foot in a southerly direction through open countryside, heading for the village of St Mary Cray, not far from Orpington. For someone used to the bustle and dirt of Elizabethan London, this would very likely have been a pleasant start to a quiet day.

As they walked along the woodland paths of Shooters Hill, the early morning mood of calm was shattered by the sudden appearance of George Browne, who had been lying in wait for them. It is possible that Browne had been stalking them for some distance, or perhaps he simply chose a spot along the way that he knew would effectively conceal him from view. Whatever the explanation, he certainly seems to have had the advantage of complete surprise; all three men would have carried weapons as a matter of course, but George Browne had his already in hand. Within seconds, the brutal assault was over, and Browne was riding away, attempting to put some distance between himself and the gory scene he had left behind.

The merchant George Sanders was killed outright. Before making his escape, Browne must have assumed the servant to be equally lifeless, but, according to John Stow's account:

> . . . John Beane having ten or eleven wounds, and being left for dead, by God's providence revived again, and creeping away upon all four, was found by an old man and his maiden, and conveyed to Woolwich, where he gave evident marks of the murderer.

In other words, Beane was able to describe his attacker, and though fearfully wounded, he somehow lived until the following Monday. Medicine in the sixteenth century was primitive by modern standards and the servant's wounds were extensive, and so there was probably nothing much that could be done for the young man except to make his last hours as comfortable as possible – although his end may of course have been hastened by accepted medical 'cures' of the day such as bloodletting. Crucially, though, because John Beane hung onto life for a few days, giving an account of the last moments of George Sanders and the appearance of the assailant, the manhunt which followed was based upon solid information.

Even given this advantage, the results were spectacularly successful. In the normal way, anyone robbing or killing travellers on a lonely stretch of country highway might justifiably feel that the real danger lay in being observed and apprehended at the scene of the crime. Having made their escape into the surrounding countryside – especially by means of a horse, which in an hour might easily cover ten miles on an unobstructed track or road – the immediate danger of capture would have passed. The object then would be to go to ground somewhere safe, attracting as little notice as possible. However, problems arose if the fugitive was in some way well known to those in pursuit, and distance alone might prove of little help. This must certainly have been the case for George Browne, since three days after the crime was committed, he was apprehended almost forty miles away at Rochester in Kent, brought back and identified by the dying servant. Even today, this would be a swift result, but in an age with no police force, in which communications between towns could take days or even weeks, this was fast work indeed. It is not recorded how the authorities were able to lay their hands on the fugitive in a distant location so soon after the manhunt began – the assumption must be that his identity was known to them, and the homes of his friends and family considered as possible places of refuge. The fact that Shooters Hill lay on the main road from London out to the coast raised the distinct possibility with the pursuers that Browne might choose to flee not to the cover of the metropolis but in the opposite direction, to the sea and maybe beyond. He might have been observed at one or other of the inns or taverns along the way, resting his horse or stopping for a hurried meal. What the reports state is that he was eventually arrested at Rochester in the house of a relative. It was said that he had been attempting to escape to Holland.

───────⟡───────

Having left two men for dead in an isolated location, Browne had very likely thought that he could vanish into the early morning and that would be an end of it. Now, he found himself trussed up and subdued, with time enough on the long, uncomfortable journey back towards the capital to brood upon the fate which awaited him.

With Browne now in custody, the true story gradually began to unfold. The prisoner was examined by the officers of the Queen's Majesty's council, and made a wide-ranging confession. Exactly what kind of pressure might have been brought to bear upon Browne during the examination is not recorded, but the methods employed were probably severe. Of course, if William Harrison is to be believed – according to his *Historicall Description of the Iland of Britaine* – torture was something employed by the rulers of barbarous foreign lands, and not approved of in England: 'To use torment also, or question by paine and torture, in these common cases, with us is greatly abhorred.'

Yet surviving official records of the day say otherwise: in 1570, the Lieutenant of the Tower was given written instructions by the Privy Council in the case of one John Felton to have him 'brought to the place of torture, and put in fear thereof; and if they shall perceive him still to be obstinate, then to spare not to lay him upon it, to the end he may feel such smart and pains thereof as to their discretions shall be thought convenient'. The rack was not the only option at that time; another was to be confined in a completely dark, subterranean chamber in the Tower there to be attacked by numerous rats which infested the place at high tide. Faced with such ordeals, it is not surprising that some prisoners chose to make full and frank confessions.

Whether by force, or just possibly out of repentance, Browne admitted his own guilt, and told a tale which condemned him but also implicated several others. What had initially seemed like an isolated highway robbery was now shown to be a conspiracy.

George Browne revealed that after stabbing George Sanders and John Beane, he then sent word of his actions by messenger to a wealthy widow named Ann Drewry, who lived in London. He explained that Drewry was the person who had told him, by means of a secret letter, of the route that Sanders would take and when to waylay him. For Browne to send his own message, directly after the murder, was an extremely risky undertaking, since the information could of course hang him if it fell into the wrong hands. The man who carried the news between Browne and Drewry was her servant Roger Clement, whom the other conspirators nicknamed 'Trusty Roger'.

As soon as Roger had set off to inform Ann Drewry of events, Browne made haste to nearby Greenwich Palace, where Queen Elizabeth's court was in residence. Although not of high status himself, he probably knew several members of the retinue, and his intention would have been to show his face and thus establish some kind of alibi there. However, shortly after he arrived, news of the murderous assault reached the court. It would have shocked Browne to learn that he had left an eyewitness behind, severely injured but still alive; as a result of this, he seems to have changed his plans and left almost immediately for London.

George Browne covered a lot of ground in the next few days. Having travelled from Shooters Hill to Greenwich and then into the city directly after killing George Sanders, he arrived at Ann Drewry's house, yet she would not meet with him in person, probably out of caution. Instead, the servant Trusty Roger received him, and handed over the very considerable sum of £20, which Drewry had raised by pawning a quantity of gold or silver items – an amount presumably agreed beforehand as George Browne's reward for the assassination of Sanders.

Mistress Drewry had been careful to conduct matters by means of her servant, but by the day after the murder it was clear that the affair was beginning to unravel. Word was out that the second victim had given a description of his attacker. Despite having received a payment the previous day equal to that of the yearly income of a small farmer, George Browne was sent a further £6 by Ann Drewry, with a message that he should now 'shift for himself'. Understandably, he decided to flee the capital, where his face was known and there were few if any places for him to hide: a city of 75,000 people was huge by the standards of the day, but still not really big enough to provide total anonymity for a wanted man. Like many who fell foul of the authorities in that era, he judged that flight across the Channel was a far safer bet. However, as John Stow relates in his additions to Harrison's *Historicall Description*, the authorities were never very far behind:

> Nevertheless the lords of the Queen's Majesty's council, caused speedy and narrow search to be made for him, and upon the eight and twentieth day of the same month, he was apprehended in a man's house of the same name at Rochester.

In confessing his part in the murder, Browne had swiftly implicated Ann Drewry and her servant, Trusty Roger. When this pair were also brought in for interrogation, they in turn revealed the name of the fourth and final conspirator – George Sanders' own wife, Anne Sanders.

The large amount of money paid to George Browne would have been temptation enough for some, but in fact, he was no mere hired killer, and his overwhelming motive was something else entirely.

This was a crime of passion, fuelled by Browne's feelings for the wife of George Sanders. Having once encountered Anne Sanders by chance at the house of Ann Drewry, he was so infatuated that he immediately asked her name and where she lived, announcing that he had determined then and there to marry her. Browne clearly knew her friend Drewry, but this did not prevent him from giving her up to the authorities in his confession. However, nothing in his version of events even hinted at the involvement of his great love, Anne Sanders.

Now that Mistress Drewry and Trusty Roger were also under interrogation, Browne's shielding strategy proved useless, as Roger offered a version of events in which Anne Sanders was the chief instigator of the plot to kill her husband, and had directly contributed to the money paid out after the killing. Browne himself seems to have spent most of the time following his arrest attempting to protect the reputation of Anne Sanders; he admitted that he was in love with her, and said that he had on several previous occasions made unsuccessful attempts to kill George Sanders, without her knowledge. As for Ann Drewry's role in all this, Browne maintained that she had promised to help him marry Mistress Sanders. Holinshed gave this account of his testimony:

> . . . he confessed the deed (as you have heard) and that he had oftentimes before pretended and sought to doo the same, by the instigation of the said mistresse Drurie, who had promised to make a marriage betweene him and mistresse Sanders, (whom he seemed to love excessivelie) neverthelesse he protested (though untrulie) that mistresse Sanders was not privie nor consenting thereunto.

Thus the conspirators in the plot fell one after another under interrogation like a series of dominoes, as Browne implicated both Drewry and Roger, then Roger implicated Anne Sanders.

Having admitted his own guilt in the murder, George Browne was sent to be tried at the court of King's Bench, in Westminster Hall, on 18 April. The verdict being a foregone conclusion, he was swiftly convicted and sentenced to be hanged at Smithfield two days later. At the trial and even on the scaffold, he denied vehemently that he had ever slept with Anne Sanders, or that she was in any way a party to his crime. Standing before the considerable crowd with the rope around his neck, he took advantage of the tradition that allowed the condemned to address the onlookers, 'at which time also untrulie (as she hir selfe confessed afterward) he laboured by all meanes to cleere mistresse Sanders of committing evill of hir bodie with him, and then floong himselfe besides the ladder'.

George Browne's corpse was briefly hung up in chains at Smithfield, and then, as was the custom, it became one of the regular gruesome sights confronting travellers on the old Roman road across Shooters Hill; chained up and twisting in the breeze until there was little left to see.

The murderer himself might have been hunted down, tried and executed, but the case itself was far from over, and it continued to generate a great deal of interest both among the general public and also the higher echelons of Queen Elizabeth's court. The interrogation of Mistress Drewry and Trusty Roger carried on, with the latter having belied his nickname and implicated Mistress Sanders. However, there was a further complication, since Anne Sanders was pregnant, either with George Browne's child or her husband's. The authorities waited a short while until the baby was born – what became of it afterwards is not recorded – and then promptly sent her to the Tower:

> And after mistresse Sanders being delivered of child and churched (for
> at the time of hir husbands death she looked presentlie to lie downe)
> was upon mistresse Druries mans confession, and other great likelihoods,

likewise committed to the tower, and on wednesdaie the sixt of Maie she was arreigned with mistresse Drurie at the Guildhall.

The Guildhall, like its counterpart Westminster Hall, was used for important trials (it was here that Lady Jane Grey had been sentenced to death for treason alongside her husband twenty years earlier). Drewry and Sanders were jointly charged with having procured the murder by letter, having knowledge of the crime, and with financially assisting the murderer after the event. Both of them entered a plea of not guilty.

Trial proceedings in those days were very brief, and to mount any kind of a defence was difficult; indeed, by the time things had come this far, the result was often a foregone conclusion. The two women were found guilty, as was 'Trusty' Roger Clement when tried for his part in the same offences two days later, and all three were then sentenced to be hanged together at Smithfield.

Although condemned, Anne Sanders still protested her innocence, and the authorities spent several days attempting to secure her confession. Various clerical men were given the task of persuading her by means of argument to admit to the crime, and a stay of execution was announced in order to facilitate this. However, when the original execution date came round, Sanders was allowed to overhear from her cell – whether deliberately or not – two gentlemen discussing 'the gallowes that was set up', and the fear of impending death apparently prompted her admission of guilt.

Yet this was not quite the end of the matter. In a further twist to the tale, a minister named Mell – who seems to have fallen in love with Anne Sanders quite as swiftly as George Browne had done sometime earlier – hatched a plan to secure her freedom. Mell went to Mistress Drewry, asking her to change her testimony and say that Sanders had known nothing of the plot. This she eventually agreed to do, but Mell let slip word of his intentions to a third party, who promptly betrayed him to the Privy Council. As a result, no pardon was forthcoming, and Anne Sanders, Ann Drewry and Trusty Roger were all taken to Smithfield for execution on 13 May, with Mell sentenced to be pilloried there at the same time, so that he was forced to watch the whole proceedings.

When the day dawned, huge crowds lined the route all the way from Newgate to Smithfield. The intense public interest generated by this killing is attested to by an anonymous pamphlet published shortly afterwards, entitled *A briefe discourse of the late murther of Master George Saunders*. It states that the event drew 'so great a number of people as the lyke hath not bene seene there togither in any mans remembrance'. They climbed roofs, knocked out windows, and even clung to steeples in order to view the prisoners.

If it seemed that half of London had turned out to watch the executions – including the earls of Derby and Bedford – the condemned did not disappoint their audience. Mistress Drewry, a widow, announced to the bemused crowd that she had not, in fact, poisoned her own late husband, and Anne Sanders, the primary focus of attention, repented out loud of her sins in her relationship with George Browne and for having planned the murder. They stood together on a cart with Roger Clement, the ropes around their necks as they prayed for forgiveness, then the vehicle was driven away underneath them.

For the conspirators, this was the end, yet their tale had an afterlife which few could have foreseen at the time.

The first response to the public interest in this murder case was the pamphlet previously mentioned, whose full title was almost as long as its contents: *A briefe discourse of the late murther of Master George Saunders, a worshipfull Citizen of London: and of the apprehension, arreignment, and execution of the principall and accessories of the same.* Issued shortly after the executions, it was printed in the shadow of St Paul's at Knightrider Street by Henry Bynneman – not some cheap sensationalist, but one of the most important English printers of the sixteenth century. In fact it was he, four years later, who would issue the first edition of *Holinshed's Chronicle*. Similarly, the author of *A briefe discourse* was no hack; this anonymous publication cloaked the identity of Arthur Golding, a man from a wealthy family, whose usual writings consisted of respectable translations from the classics. Golding's rendering of Ovid's *Metamorphoses* – the first to appear in English – influenced dramatists such as Shakespeare and Marlowe. His murder pamphlet, although it sought to strike a high moral tone, also had a direct effect upon the newly flourishing English stage.

A briefe discourse proved so popular that it was reprinted in 1577. It was the basis for the account of the George Sanders murder that appeared in *Holinshed's Chronicle*, which in turn was used by John Stow for his retelling of the case. Golding's work also influenced other writers, such as Stow's friend Anthony Munday, whose *A view of Examples, meete to be perused of all faythfull Christians* (1580) gave a colourfully moralistic account of the Sanders affair:

> This George Browne (before named) addicted to the voluptuousnesse of this vaine world, to unlawfull lyking, to runne at his libertie in all kinde of lewde behavior, murdred cruelly maister George Saunders, an honest, vertuous, and godly Cittizen.

In the language of a hellfire preacher – 'O, minde most monstrous! O, heart most hard! O, intent so yrksome! . . . Through the lewde life of one man six lost theyre lyves' – Munday held these events up as a dreadful example of the consequences of unclean living. He was not just a religious writer, however. By the 1590s, he was also a very respected playwright and sometime actor, whose works were presented regularly at the Rose theatre – indeed, he was ranked among some very exalted company by the Elizabethan writer Francis Meres in 1598:

> . . . the best for Comedy among us bee, Edward, Earle of Oxforde, Doctor Gager of Oxforde, Maister Rowley once a rare Scholler of learned Pembrooke Hall in Cambridge, Maister Edwardes one of her Majesties Chappell, eloquent and witty John Lilly, Lodge, Gascoyne, Greene, Shakespeare, Thomas Nash, Thomas Heywood, Anthony Mundye our best plotter, Chapman, Porter, Wilson, Hathway, and Henry Chettle.

Despite the growing number of theatres and playwrights, there was still a strand of thought that held them to be an abomination. Officially, the question of the fitness or otherwise of dramatic productions was strictly controlled by a censor called the Master of Revels. Yet this did not deter an anonymous author of the late 1580s or early 1590s from writing a play directly inspired by the then-famous murder of George Sanders, which used the real names of all of the principal characters.

The work was eventually published in 1599, and its title made no pretence of hiding the identities of those involved. It was called *A Warning for Faire Women, Containing the most tragicall and lamentable murther of Master George Sanders of London Marchant, nigh Shooters Hill, Consented unto by his owne wife, acted by M. Browne, Mistris Drewry and Trusty Roger agents therein: with their severall ends.*

The playwright used a method that remains popular with tabloid newspapers up to the present day; describing immorality in elaborate detail while simultaneously decrying it. The action begins with the figure of History entering through one door carrying a drum and a flag, while Tragedy enters through another door 'in her one hand a whip, in the other hand a knife'. Clearly, the blame here is to be laid squarely at the feet of Anne Sanders, the 'faire' woman of the title.

The figure of Tragedy acts as a kind of chorus throughout, at one point entering with a bowl of blood, calling forth her Furies and uttering lines such as these:

> Bring forth the banquet and that lustful wine,
> Which in pale mazors made of dead men's sculls,
> They shall carouse to their destruction.

Fuelled by the drinks served by the Furies, Mistress Sanders, wearing a black veil, is led forward by a figure representing Lust to meet George Browne. Chastity, dressed in white, tries to hold her back, but Mistress Drewry pushes Chastity away. Browne and Sanders then embrace.

Most of the key elements of the real-life story are played out in this allegorical form – depicting events that had taken place only a few years earlier, well within the living memory of the audience. Indeed, there were very likely some who came to the play who witnessed the last moments of Browne, Sanders, Drewry and Clement at Smithfield. Today it would probably be the subject of numerous lawsuits, but these were the very early days of English drama and the censorship of the stage. Quite what the deceased originals of these characters would have made of such a representation is hard to imagine, but then, John Reginald Christie, hanged for murder in 1953, would probably also have been astonished if anyone had told him that he would one day be portrayed on the big screen less than two decades later by Richard Attenborough.

The strange literary afterlife of this notorious Elizabethan murder case prefigured the rise of a whole industry devoted to pamphlets and books such as the *Newgate Calendar*, giving accounts of famous crimes and their perpetrators. Within another half-century, all the theatres were torn down by the parliamentarians, and Shakespeare himself went unperformed for several decades until the Restoration in 1660. The public taste for murder tales, however, showed no sign of diminishing.

These Swanlike notes, sung so inspirdly
to thy untimely fall, proves most exact
Lines drawne from Life; & by swift Prosodie
Showes but thine owne Soules Prophecie in Act
Thy Name, and Vertues live, So kill thy Mould
was all Imprisonment; and Poyson could.

But thy more heavenly-Selfe from double chaines
sett free (alone), Thy Body, and the Tower
In that Supreme unpartiall Court remains
wher nor Ambition, Envy, Lust, Save power,
Redeem'd from poysonous plotts from Witches dire
from Westons & St. Apothecaries. Sarme & D.

Sir Thomas Overbury

FOUR

MURDER UNDER THE GUISE
OF FRIENDSHIP
1613

The early seventeenth century in England was a time of great learning and advances in the sciences, yet belief in witchcraft was still widespread, and the line between scientific knowledge and the occult was sometimes hard to discern. Respectable citizens seeking to learn the whereabouts of missing persons or property turned regularly to astrologers, who were also consulted about the advisability of impending sea voyages, likely marriage prospects, the causes of illness, the legitimacy of children and a hundred other questions.

The king himself, James I, had a great interest in learning of all kinds. In many ways one of the most intellectual monarchs the country has known, he wrote and published books and articles, and highlighted the risks inherent in the new habit of smoking in his *Counterblaste to Tobacco* (1604); 'a custom loathsome to the eye, hateful to the nose, harmful to the brain, dangerous to the lungs, and in the black stinking fume thereof nearest resembling the horrible Stygian smoke of the pit that is bottomless'. Four centuries later, medical opinion concurs, yet this was also a man who as king of Scotland published a book about the dangers of witchcraft (*Daemonologie*, 1597), and established commissions to deal with the supposed supernatural threat posed to his life by the North Berwick coven. Shakespeare himself created literature's most famous witches in one of his new plays, *Macbeth*, the first recorded performance of which, 20 April 1610, at the Globe Theatre, was noted in a manuscript called the *Bock of Plaies*, written by one of the premier occultists of the age, the astrologer Simon Forman.

A play featuring witchcraft and a Scottish king would have had a particular resonance in the London of those days, only seven years after James I had come down from ruling north of the border. As a

Stuart, James was well aware that the reigns of several of his ancestors had been ended by the assassin's knife and that high position was no safeguard against murder – indeed, he customarily wore thick padded clothing not unlike a modern flak jacket to ward off possible attacks. James also wrote about the divine right of kings, and in the year under discussion he was sole ruler, having temporarily dispensed with parliament altogether. He was distinctly uncomfortable in the presence of strangers, but favourites of the king were fortunate indeed. To be close to the monarch was no small achievement; there were many titles and honours at his discretion, and for those who enjoyed the king's favour, all things might be pardoned, including murder.

The mysterious death of Sir Thomas Overbury in the Tower of London in 1613 involved several of the king's inner circle. Put simply, Overbury seems to have been murdered because his friends in high places were significantly outnumbered by his enemies. Being incarcerated in one of the capital's most secure buildings ought to have served as some form of protection for Sir Thomas, but it was a place where titles or influence could prove no defence, and death might come in various guises, not simply the headsman's axe on Tower Hill.

Thomas Overbury – like many through the centuries who found themselves imprisoned in the Tower – was accused of displeasing the monarch. Generally held by contemporary witnesses to be an arrogant, self-important man with few of the social graces useful for making and keeping friends and allies, Overbury had risen not as a protégé of James I, but rather as the close associate and advisor of Robert Carr, the king's favourite. Carr was a Scot like James himself, and had travelled south with him in 1603 as a page in the king's retinue. Winning the king's good graces, he had risen steadily to become variously Viscount Rochester, keeper of Westminster Palace, Privy Councillor, Knight of the Garter and Lord Treasurer of Scotland. In the year of Overbury's murder, 1613, Carr ascended even higher, and was created earl of Somerset and Baron Brancepeth.

Carr's ever-increasing social and political advancement had for a long time also benefitted his close friend Overbury. However, as the regularly replenished crop of formerly illustrious heads on Old London Bridge reminded passers-by, a fall from grace could be swift.

Sir Thomas began life in relatively comfortable circumstances. As the son of a Warwickshire landowner, he was not an aristocrat, but very far from being a peasant – in short, a gentleman. His father, the MP Sir Nicholas Overbury, owned a manor house in Warwickshire called Compton Scorpion, eight miles south of Stratford-upon-Avon. Thomas, the third of Sir Nicholas's children, was born at the manor in 1581. Educated at Oxford University, Thomas Overbury then studied law at the Middle Temple in London. One of his friends at this time was the playwright and poet Ben Jonson – a decade older and already very well known – who mentions Overbury in his writings. Jonson's greatest success had been *Every Man in his Humour* (1598, staged by Shakespeare's own theatre company, the Lord Chamberlain's Men, with William himself in the leading role). Once James I ascended the throne in 1603, Jonson soon became a favourite of the royal family, devising elaborate masques for their entertainment in collaboration with Inigo Jones. One of these, entitled *Hymenaei*, was performed at court on 6 January 1605, to celebrate the marriage of Frances Howard to the earl of Essex. As it turned out, this was not a happy union, and Lady Frances would also later play a pivotal role in the death of Sir Thomas Overbury.

From around the year 1604, Overbury developed what would prove to be the defining friendship of his life, with Robert Carr. He eventually became, in Sir Roger Wilbraham's words, Carr's 'bedfellow, mynion, and inward councellor, for which he was much envyed in Courte'. This close relationship aided him greatly when Carr – now Viscount Rochester – rose to a position where he functioned essentially as a kind of private secretary to King James. As a result, Overbury in turn achieved a position of great influence, handling state papers and helping to shape the advice which the less-intellectual Rochester gave to the monarch. In effect, he became the power behind the power behind the throne, and was understandably regarded with suspicion, wariness and envy in some court circles.

Overbury's upward rise may be measured by the fact that he was given the gift of a salt works by James I in 1607, and knighted the following year. Like the king, he too was a man of letters. He coined epigrams, and shortly after his death, a series of satirical descriptions of various London characters was published under his name: *a Canting Rogue; a Devillish Userer; a Reverend Judge; an Arrant Horse-courser; an Ignorant Glory-hunter; a very Whore*. One of them – *a Courtier* – might have been taken by some of his friends to be a self-portrait:

> . . . his surest marke is that he is to be found only about princes . . . He puts more confidence in his words than meaning, and more in his pronunciation than words . . . Neither his motion, or aspect are regular, but he mooves by the upper *spheares*, and is the reflection of higher substances.

His enemies, however, jealous of his ascendency, might have pointed instead to the character called *an Intruder into favour*:

> He is a *mountaines monkie*, that climbing a tree, and skipping from bough to bough, gives you backe his face; but come once to the top, he holds his nose up into the wind, and shewes you his tayle.

It is now generally held that these works are probably not in fact by Overbury himself, but they sold well at the time when his murderers were up for trial, and ran through many editions during the reign of James I. Several generations later, John Aubrey summed up the received opinion of the man in his late seventeenth-century work, *Brief Lives*: 'Sir Thomas Overbury was prouder than Sir Walter Raleigh, who was damnable proud.' Viscount Rochester, the king's favourite, was also none too popular in certain quarters, but when he too joined the ranks of Overbury's enemies, the latter's downfall was assured. Some at court felt that it had been particularly unwise of Overbury to ridicule his friend Rochester's new love, Frances Howard, in a poem entitled *A Wife*, although it's not entirely clear that she was the inspiration for this work. As for Overbury himself, he seems never to have married, and his relationship with Rochester was certainly the closest he ever enjoyed. When this connection was broken, his position in the court hierarchy became dangerously insecure.

The Tower of London had been standing guard over the eastern edge of the walled city since the reign of William the Conqueror, five and a half centuries earlier. A collection of interlinked buildings surrounded by a wall which in places was fifteen feet thick, it was ringed by a moat a hundred feet wide at its fullest extent. Serving as a combination of fortress, armoury, royal palace, menagerie, mint, administrative centre, torture chamber and place of execution, it had also housed selected prisoners ever since 1101, when Ralf Flambard, Bishop of Durham, became its first inmate. The walls of the Tower were ninety feet high, yet Ralf managed to escape down a rope; many later prisoners were not so fortunate. Some lived in relative comfort, their quarters fitted out in a reasonable approximation of conditions outside. At the other extreme, there were those who were made to endure the confines of the Little Ease, a claustrophobic cell only four feet square, too small for either standing or lying down. In early years the fortress merely served to confine prisoners, but from 1446 the rack had been employed – known as the Duke of Exeter's daughter, after the man who, as Constable of the Tower, had introduced it – and the brutality really set in once Henry VIII became king in 1509. The list of illustrious names who had been imprisoned, tortured and then executed there was long indeed by the time Overbury was incarcerated. Even Elizabeth I, half a century earlier, had been locked up in the Tower some years prior to becoming queen, and might easily have become one of its many victims, as she acknowledged at the very start of her reign: 'Some have fallen from being princes of this land to being prisoners in this place. I am raised from being a prisoner in this place to be prince of the land.'

Many of the precise facts surrounding the imprisonment and murder of Sir Thomas Overbury will never be known. Even the cause of his incarceration is a matter of dispute. On the face of it, his confinement was due to having refused to serve when the king offered him the post of ambassador at a European court (the precise location is not clear, although some of Overbury's jail statements make reference to France). It also seems likely that the king himself had a grudge against Sir Thomas, probably on account of the latter's influence on Rochester. Since James's feelings for his favourite were in many ways like those of a fond and jealous husband, to appear in the guise of a rival for Viscount Rochester's attention had its risks. As for the queen, by all accounts she found it hard to tolerate Overbury, and would likely have been pleased to see him removed from court in this way. Most importantly, though, Overbury had offended his closest ally, Rochester himself. Because of his place in the king's affections, Rochester was now one of the most powerful men in the land, and had also begun an affair with a member of one of the nation's great dynasties, Frances Howard, daughter of the first earl of Suffolk. This romance was fraught with complications, given that Frances was still married to Robert Devereux, third earl of Essex. It was Overbury's recklessness in criticising Rochester's new liaison – and questioning the virtue of the lady herself – that alienated the couple and provoked his eventual downfall.

It's not hard to see why Overbury would have opposed Rochester's attachment to Frances Howard or the machinations aimed at securing the annulment of her marriage to Essex that would leave her free to marry her lover. Sir Thomas rightly concluded that if this came to pass (as it eventually did, shortly after his death), the chief influence in Rochester's life would be Frances.

The plot to ensure Overbury's imprisonment was hatched by members of the Howard family, probably with the help or acquiescence of their new ally, Rochester. Once there, Overbury would be in no real position to object to the planned divorce between Frances and Essex, and her proposed marriage to Rochester. With the powerful Howard faction now manoeuvring against him, and the king and queen regarding him with displeasure, Overbury suddenly found himself taken to the Tower on 21 April 1613, his refusal to serve as ambassador the outward excuse for his arrest.

When Overbury arrived in the Tower, its most famous inmate was Sir Walter Raleigh, who had been confined there in relative comfort with his wife and children at the top of the Bloody Tower since 1603, writing his *History of the World*. This three-storey building had originally been known by the less emotive name of the Garden Tower, but some time after Edward IV's sons were murdered there in 1483, it acquired the name 'bloody', and it was here that Sir Thomas Overbury was brought and held. (Other parts of the fortress were nicknamed with equal candour – the Flint Tower was known as Little Hell, and in the reign of Elizabeth I the Devereaux Tower was called Robyn the Devyll's Tower).

Among the Tower's other inhabitants were two leopards, eleven lions, three eagles, two owls, a jackal and two mountain cats, although bears often had a rougher time of it, being baited to death in a special pit within the Tower walls – a favourite pastime of the king.

Overbury may have expected to be pardoned after a short interval, or at least have taken heart from the fact that some, like Raleigh, had survived there for years. For the time being, however, his evenings were regulated by the chimes emanating from the octagonal Bell Tower, which sounded in accordance with regulations laid down six years before: 'When the Tower bell doth ring at nights for the shutting in of the gates, all the prisoners, with their servants, are to withdraw themselves into their chambers, and not goe forth that night'. With time on their hands, many Tower prisoners carved their names and family crests upon the walls of their chambers, sometimes reflecting upon their circumstances, such as one member of the Pole family, who left this inscription in 1564: 'To serve God. To endure penance. To obey fate is to reign.'

As for Sir Thomas, he never again left the confines of the building, and within five months, he was dead.

In the early days of his imprisonment, Thomas Overbury was indeed cut off from contact with the outside world. The Lieutenant of the Tower at that stage was Sir William Wade, who so successfully prevented anyone from communicating with the prisoner that Rochester was denied access. This did not fit in with the plans of those who had engineered Overbury's incarceration, and Wade was soon dismissed from his post. According to court gossip, the new Lieutenant, Sir Gervase Elwes, was not only placed there through the influence of the Howard family, but had also paid a significant sum of money for the post into the bargain. Promoted by the king, apparently at the behest of the Howards and Rochester, Elwes was likely to do as he was told, as was his newly appointed Under-keeper, Richard Weston, who had only recently spent time carrying secret messages between Rochester and Lady Frances during their affair. Hence, the two people most concerned with the supervision of Overbury, and who constituted the prisoner's only link to the outside world, were very much beholden to the Howard family.

As for Overbury's own relations, his father Sir Nicholas certainly took a great interest in his fate, as his siblings seem also to have done, but they were very much kept at arm's-length by the terms of the close confinement under which he was held. Since Overbury was suspected of blackening Frances Howard's reputation through his anonymous writings, removing him to a secure place had effectively muzzled this dissenting voice. Lady Frances, however, seems to have eventually taken this reasoning to its logical conclusion: why settle for a temporary silence, when his mouth might be stopped permanently?

With a more co-operative Lieutenant of the Tower now in place, the way was clear for Lady Frances to arrange for various gifts of foodstuffs – tarts, jellies and the like – to be sent to the prisoner over a period of several months. In his isolated state, already in uncertain health before he even entered the Tower, Overbury had only these packages and the occasional letter to connect him with anyone outside the walls. Unfortunately for him, the food was later revealed to have contained a mixture of no less than eight different poisons, including several varieties of arsenic, cantharides and even powdered diamond dust. In order to obtain such items, Lady Frances had turned to an associate of hers, one Anne Turner, the widow of a society doctor, whose own source for these dangerous substances was an apothecary of dubious reputation called Franklin. It was said in some quarters that Anne Turner was a white witch, although the line between supposed witchcraft and orthodox medicine in those days was sometimes rather blurred. What is certain is that she and Lady Frances had visited the occultist and astrologer Simon Forman shortly before his death in 1611, apparently seeking potions with which her ladyship could alienate the affections of her then husband the earl of Essex, and attract Robert Carr, Viscount Rochester. It was natural therefore that Frances should seek Turner's help and connections once more when she required potions of a different and more deadly kind.

At the same time that Frances and Anne Turner were sending poisoned food in to the prisoner – some of which Weston seems to have disposed of harmlessly before it reached its intended victim, perhaps out of sympathy – Overbury was also carrying out a secret correspondence with Rochester, ironically by means of messages also concealed in food. Since his health was delicate, Sir Thomas concocted a plan to win the king's sympathy and thus his own freedom by appearing to be wasting away, and so arranged for various emetics to be sent to him. Not knowing that he was writing to the very people responsible for his confinement, Overbury willingly dosed himself with potions which further weakened his constitution at a time when it was already under severe assault from secret poisoning. His smuggled messages to Rochester at this time, some of which survive, make piteous reading: '. . . to this Friday morning my heat slackens not, my water remains as high, my thirstiness the same, the same loathing of meat, having eaten not a bit since Thursday . . .'

Sir Gervase Elwes seems to have discovered at an early stage that his deputy Weston was attempting to bring poison to their captive. Yet Elwes, who owed his appointment to the influence of the Howards, raised no alarms at this point, while the health of the prisoner grew slowly worse. Sir Thomas was attended by various distinguished physicians during his confinement, but they might not have noticed obvious signs of poisoning. This was an age in which medical opinion still favoured the use of controlled bloodletting as a cure for many ills, and there were some who felt that the safest treatment was to avoid the attentions of doctors altogether, as the 'cure' might easily prove more deadly than the illness.

One thing is certain: cut off from his family, betrayed by his former friend, beset by doubts and weakened by the combined effects of pre-existing illness and systematic poisoning, Sir Thomas Overbury was a man whose fate was effectively sealed. Having endured months of pain and discomfort, he finally died alone in the Bloody Tower on 14 September 1613 and was swiftly buried on the instructions of Henry Howard, earl of Northampton, who wrote as follows to Elwes:

Noble Lieutenant. If the knave's body be foul, bury it presently. I'll stand between you and harm; but if it will abide the view, send for Lidcote [Sir Thomas Overbury's brother-in-law, the main family member engaged in trying to secure the prisoner's release], and let him see it, to satisfy the damned crew. When you come to me, bring me this letter again yourself with you, or else burn it.

Clearly, these are the words of someone not exactly distressed at the recent death, and evidently with something to hide. For the time being, though, Overbury was safely dead. Frances' previous marriage was soon nullified, she and Rochester were then married, and by the time questions were seriously being asked about the death of this all-but-friendless man in the Tower, Northampton himself had died, taking his secrets with him.

On 19 October 1615, Sir Edward Coke, Lord Chief Justice of England, announced to those assembled in the Guildhall, that 'of all felonies, murder is the most horrible; of all murders, poisoning the most detestable; and of all poisoning, the lingering poisoning'.

This opening statement, offered at the trial of the first of several people accused of arranging Sir Thomas Overbury's death, reflected the horror felt among London society when the circumstances of his protracted demise began to emerge, some two years after the event. The punishment on the statute books at that time for wilful poisoning, as Sir Edward reminded his listeners at the start of the proceedings, was boiling to death (although none of the accused eventually suffered this fate). A short while later, the first defendant in this case, Richard Weston, was brought before the court, and charged that he:

> . . . being about the age of sixty years, not having the fear of God before his eyes, but instigated and seduced by the devil, devised and contrived not only to bring upon the body of Sir Thomas Overbury, kt., great sickness and diseases, but also to deprive him of his life.

This talk of the devil was more than a figure of speech. Like James I, Sir Edward Coke seems to have believed sincerely that the devil was active in the land, and held witches to be a real and present menace, defining the latter elsewhere as 'a person that hath conference with the Devil to consult with him or to do some act'. Richard Weston, Under-keeper to Sir Gervase Elwes, Lieutenant of the Tower, stood accused of poisoning, not witchcraft, but his motives were attributed to something far more powerful than mere malice. As an officer whose post had given him daily access to the prisoner, Weston was the prosecution's initial target. Once convicted, he would pave the way for a selection of much more illustrious individuals to be brought in as accessories; in particular, Lady Frances Howard, whose agent Weston was thought to be, and also Rochester, her new husband, now earl of Somerset. Indeed, much of the evidence quoted at the trial of the latter couple was derived from Weston's earlier confessions. However, these would have been made under threat of torture, which leaves them somewhat open to question.

The evidence against Weston was damning. In the legal custom of the time, charges were read out as statements of fact, as if already proven; they were essentially a recitation of the guilty actions of the accused, with little chance for them to offer any considered defence. Statements obtained by various confessions – however they might have been extracted – were then presented to the court as unassailable truths. Thus it was categorically stated of Weston that he had poisoned Overbury, and then requested payment from Anne Turner for this service:

> Weston having given this poison, which wrought very vehemently with him by vomits and extreme purging, he presently demands his reward of Mrs Turner, who replies, *that the man is not yet dead: perfect your work, and you shall have your hire.*

At Weston's trial it was further asserted as fact that Robert Carr had sent Overbury a white powder, urging him to take it, with the following words: 'It will make you more sick; but fear not, I will make this a means for your delivery, and for the recovery of your health.' The record of the state trial continues:

> *Sir Thomas Overbury*, never dreaming of base treachery, but conceiving it as a friendly policy, received the said powder, which wrought upon him more vehemently; whereupon his sickness grew more vehement or violent, and his languishment increased: which white powder, upon *Weston's* confession, was poison.

Here it is obvious that the trial of Weston is a mere prelude to the indictment on murder charges of a much more important figure, Robert Carr, and those around him. Indeed, Carr's wife, Frances Howard, was expressly implicated later in the same account, when it was stated that the poisoned food was 'provided by Mrs Turner, with the knowledge of the said countess'.

The prosecution cast their net wide, and some of the highest names at court were entangled within it.

Robert Carr had risen far and fast since catching the eye of his monarch a decade earlier, and yet by the time the murky business of the Overbury poisoning was being held up to the light in a series of court cases in 1615–16, the carefully woven threads of his dazzling career were already beginning to unravel. In the immediate aftermath of Overbury's death, it had not seemed so; created earl of Somerset and Baron Brancepeth, he had finally married Frances Howard on 26 December 1613, and the following year was made Lord Chamberlain, Lord Privy Seal and Warden of the Cinque Ports. The king's long-time favourite, it seemed, was now enjoying all that the heights of power had to offer.

Yet there was trouble on the horizon. James I had lately taken a liking to another handsome gentleman of the court, George Villiers, whom he had first noticed when visiting the country home of Sir Anthony Mildmay in August 1614. Immediately appointed a cupbearer to the king, the following year Villiers was both knighted and made a gentleman of the bedchamber – a valued position which gave him intimate and regular access to the monarch. His rise to the unofficial position of king's favourite would prove even swifter: a little over two years after their first meeting, James created Villiers earl of Buckingham, saying that he loved him 'more than any other man'. By this time, however, his former rival, Carr, was comprehensively disgraced.

The trial of Robert Carr, earl of Somerset, took place on 25 May 1616 – a little over a month after the death of Shakespeare – before a jury of peers of the realm. On the day preceding, his wife Frances Howard had been similarly tried on murder charges relating to the death of Overbury. In both instances, the principal reason for proceeding against them was the confession made by Richard Weston, former Under-keeper of the Tower. Unlike her husband, Lady Frances pleaded guilty, apparently in a state of some distress, after hearing the charges read to her:

> The countess of *Somerset*, all the while the indictment was reading, stood, looking pale, trembled, and shed some few tears; and at the first naming of *Weston* in the indictment, put her fan before her face, and there held it half-covered till the indictment was read.

Her guilty plea was met with praise from the Attorney-General, Sir Francis Bacon, who noted that the others already tried for involvement in the crime – Richard Weston, Sir Gervase Elwes, Anne Turner, who had obtained the poisons and then paid Weston his fee, and James Franklin the apothecary, who supplied the poisons – had 'at their arraignment persisted in denial'. It did them little good, since they were all executed in 1615. Their trials had merely been a prelude, however, to the main event, as could be seen from the parade of more than twenty lords who were lined up to hear the case, not to mention eight judges including Sir Edward Coke, Lord Chief Justice of England, and Sir Henry Hubbart, Lord Chief Justice of the Common Pleas. That such a trial was something out of the ordinary was highlighted by Bacon in his opening remarks: 'This is the second time since the king's coming, these thirteen years, that any peers have been arraigned.'

Following the guilty plea entered by Frances at the outset, the proceedings largely consisted of a résumé of the facts as they were understood – or as the State would wish them to be – and served mostly as a lesson to any others of high rank who might feel that they could do murder with impunity. In a country where the king himself had a morbid fear of assassination, it was important that examples should be set. Bacon issued a warning on behalf of the monarch when outlining the particular transgression that Overbury's murderers had committed:

> . . . a particular offence to a private subject, against those that have been so high in the king's grace and favour, and therefore deserve to be written in a sun-beam. But his being the best master in the world, hinders him not from being the best king; for he can as well plane a hill, as raise a valley: a good lesson to put to my lords the peers; he is lieutenant to him that is no respecter of persons.

The countess of Somerset's trial laid out the bare bones of the conspiracy as it appeared at the time, and charged that she and her husband the earl were 'the procurers of Overbury's death'. In truth, so much had already been said about them during trials the previous year that their reputations were already severely damaged. Indiscreet notes from Frances to Anne Turner and to the astrologer, Simon Forman – headed 'Burn this letter' and signed 'your affectionate loving daughter' – had been read out in open court during Turner's trial, together with various items provided by Forman's widow, which brought an authentic whiff of brimstone to the proceedings:

There was also shewed in court certain pictures of a man and woman in copulation, made in lead, and also the mould of brass, wherein they were cast, a black-scarf also full of white crosses, which Mrs Turner had in her custody. At the shewing of these, and inchanted papers and other pictures in court, there was heard a crack from the scaffolds, which caused great fear, tumult and confusion among the spectators, and throughout the hall, every one fearing hurt, as if the devil had been present, and grown angry to have his workmanship shewed, and this terror continuing about a quarter of an hour . . .

Small wonder that the Lord Chief Justice, Sir Edward Coke, summed up by telling Anne Turner that 'she had the seven deadly sins; viz. a whore, a bawd, a sorcerer, a witch, a papist, a felon, and a murderer, the daughter of the devil *Forman*', and called upon her to repent.

By immediately pleading guilty at her own trial, Lady Frances kept the proceedings to the bare minimum, opting to throw herself on the king's mercy. She was probably aware that the only other time when a peer had stood trial during James's reign, execution had not followed even though a sentence of death had been pronounced. In her case, she would have known that a capital sentence was inevitable, but would have been hoping that the king would shortly afterwards show clemency. When asked if she had any statement to make before sentencing, she replied: 'I can much aggravate, but nothing extenuate my fault; I desire mercy, and that the lords will intercede for me to the king.'

She was then sentenced to be taken to the Tower, to await death by hanging.

The trial of Frances' husband, Robert Carr, earl of Somerset, took place the following day, and differed markedly in that he opted to plead not guilty. The king's former favourite had dressed carefully for the event, in black satin, lace and velvet, but his condition showed in his face, as the transcript records: 'his visage pale, his beard long, his eyes sunk in his head'. The case against him was stated plainly by Serjeant Montague, in a bleak summary of the slow destruction of the prisoner Overbury in the Tower:

> *Robert*, earl of *Somerset*, stands indicted as accessory before the fact, of the wilful murder and poisoning of Sir *Thomas Overbury*, done by *Weston*, but procured by him ... *Weston*, at four several times, gave *Overbury* four several poisons, the first May the 9th, 1613, that was *Rosalgar*, carrying this poison in one hand, and his broth in the other; the second was June following, and that was *Arsenick*; the third was July the 10th following, and that was *Mercury Sublimate* in tarts; the fourth was September the 14th following, and that was *Mercury Sublimate* in a clyster, given by *Weston* and an apothecary yet unknown, and that killed him.

Shortly afterwards, the Attorney-General, Sir Francis Bacon, rose to present the case for the prosecution, calling the crime, 'murder under the guise of friendship'. Overbury himself, in a letter addressed to Carr during his last weeks in the Tower, accused him bitterly of betraying him. He said that he had written his own account of all that had happened, and claimed that he had given it sealed in trust to a friend, although this may have been an empty boast, and just how Overbury was supposed to have contacted this unknown friend is unclear. The contents of the supposed document were obviously designed to threaten Carr, as the conclusion of Overbury's letter makes clear: '. . . So thus if you will deal thus wickedly with me, I have provided that whether I die or live, your shame shall never die, nor leave to be the most odious man alive.'

That it should be Bacon who was the prosecutor in the trials of both husband and wife was ironic, since in December 1613 he had helped create the *Masque of Flowers* that was performed to celebrate the marriage of Carr and Lady Frances, just as Ben Jonson had written one for her previous marriage. A distinguished man of letters and philosopher, as well as a politician, Bacon brought all his eloquence to the task of addressing the court and laid out the cause of the break between the former close friends, Carr and Overbury:

> For it fell out some twelmonths or more before *Overbury's* imprisonment in the *Tower*, that the earl of *Somerset* fell into an unlawful love towards that unfortunate lady the countess of *Essex*, and to proceed to a marriage

with her: this marriage and purpose did *Overbury* mainly impugn, under pretence to do the true part of a friend, for that he accounted her an unworthy woman. But the truth was *Overbury*, who (to speak plainly) had little that was solid for religion, or moral virtue, but was wholly possessed with ambition and vain-glory, was loth to have any partners in the favour of my lord of *Somerset*; and especially not any of the house of *Howards*, against whom he had always professed hatred and opposition.

Bacon accused the earl of having been the 'principal actor' in the events leading up to Overbury's murder, and claimed that 'you did continually hearken to the success of the impoisonment, and that you spurred it on, and called for despatch, when you thought it lingered'. Since Carr had chosen to plead not guilty, full and lengthy charges were laid against him, and several of Overbury's letters to him from the Tower, pleading for help, were read out in court, as well as those he had received from the earl of Northampton, implicating him in the poisoning. Calling upon Carr to answer the charges, Bacon mentioned that because of his wife's confession the previous day 'there is great hope of the king's mercy, if you now mar not that which she hath made'. Nevertheless, Carr asserted at the start 'I am confident in my own cause', and went on to distance himself clearly from his wife and her fate:

> Whereas it is pretended that I should cause poisoned tarts to be sent to him to the *Tower*; my wife in her confession saith, that there were none sent but either by me or her; and some where wholesome, and some not: then it must needs follow, that the good ones were those which I sent, and the bad hers.

Clearly, whatever love had once existed between the couple had by now evaporated under the strain of the case, and the earl was at pains to put the blame squarely upon his already convicted wife. Much argument then followed, but the end result was the same. The jury of his peers unanimously returned a verdict of guilty and Carr received the same death sentence as Frances. Before he was conveyed to the Tower, he too begged the lords to beseech the king for mercy.

The king's justice could be dispensed in any manner he saw fit, and, content with his new favourite, George Villiers, he seems to have been inclined to show his former favourite a little mercy. Lady Frances, who had pleaded guilty, was pardoned just two months after her trial, on 13 July, but she and her husband Robert Carr were held in the Tower until January 1622. The latter, who had disputed the charges against him, was freed at the same time as his wife in 1622, but had to wait until 1625, shortly before the king's death, for his own pardon. As it happened, he outlived not only the king but also the new favourite Villiers (who was assassinated in Portsmouth in 1628), and Frances (who died in 1632), hanging on in relative obscurity himself until 1645, but never regaining the heights of power he had attained before Overbury's murder. Despite Carr's attempts to place the blame for that crime squarely on his wife's shoulders during his own trial, the couple lived quietly together at Chiswick until the death of Lady Frances.

Carr and his wife had steered a very risky path in a dangerous age, but the lingering affection of the king for his former favourite very likely saved them from execution. Hardly a bloodthirsty man himself, he seems to have been content to let them be sidelined into obscurity, considering it punishment enough. Others of lower social standing had already been hanged for the crime, and the monarch's will, in this age, was able to override all other considerations: was this not, after all, a man who had written a learned treatise on the divine right of kings?

Sir Thomas Overbury's family may have been deeply angry and frustrated at this outcome, but there was nothing to be done. As for the man himself, he remains there still, interred in the Chapel Royal of St Peter ad Vincula, just inside the north-west corner of the Tower walls.

An engraving by George Cruikshank showing a
sixteenth-century execution on Tower Green

FIVE

CHEERFULLY TO THE STAKE
1675

In the second decade after the restoration of the monarchy, London was a city of around half a million people, still recovering from the twin hammer-blows of the plague year 1665 and the Great Fire of 1666. These two great public disasters affected all Londoners both rich and poor, although the wealthy at least had the option of temporarily leaving the city during such times, and carrying away their goods and valuables. One of those on a much lower income who stayed behind to take her chances was a woman called Elizabeth Lylliman (or Lillyman). She is said to have tended to people stricken with the plague, without herself succumbing to it. Her good fortune continued the following year when the fire laid waste to roughly four fifths of the houses within the city, since she lived in an outlying eastern district untouched by the flames. Elizabeth's luck, such as it was, ran out a decade later, when she found herself arraigned at the Old Bailey on 7 July 1675, charged with murder.

Elizabeth and her husband lived in a very narrow, twisting rat-run called Swan Alley, outside the city walls on the very eastern edge of London, where buildings gave way to open country. Their home lay a little to the north of the Tower and the slaughterhouses of East Smithfield, and just below the road leading out to the leafy hamlet of Whitechapel. Swan Alley itself ran between two substantial north–south thoroughfares: at the western end, a road called The Minories, and at the eastern, Mansell Street, which bordered on a large open square of land known as Goodman's Fields. The Minories, named for the order of nuns who had inhabited the area in the thirteenth century, was known for its gunsmiths and armourers. Goodman's Fields was a 'tenter ground'; an open area of land used for cloth-drying, where woven material was stretched out on wooden frames called tenters, and secured by tenter-hooks. Today, there is nothing left of Swan Alley itself, although a newer east–west thoroughfare called Portsoken Street follows its approximate route.

Naming roads after swans was quite common in London: there were at least a dozen Swan Alleys in that era, not to mention a clutch of Swan Yards, Courts and Stairs. As names go, in a city that was teeming with livestock and birds of all kinds, it was unremarkable, especially when compared to other London thoroughfares of the time such as Thieving Lane, Whores Nest, Pissing Alley, Cutthroat Lane, Melancholy Walk, Labour in Vain Street, Foul Lane, Cats Hole and Blowbladder Street.

Although some roads in the centre of the city were paved, out here on the periphery the traveller would usually encounter just a mixture of mud and stones, mixed in with dung and household waste of all kinds, and possibly some dead animals lying around to trip the unwary. During the plague year of 1665, all dogs and cats in the city had been killed by order – several hundred thousand of them – in an effort to stop the spread of disease, but they had since returned in great numbers. The air itself was frequently dim and smoky, owing to the Newcastle sea coal burnt in most London fireplaces, and available light was further diminished by the overhanging upper storeys of houses, which jutted out above the roadways, enabling opposite neighbours to reach out and shake hands from across the street from their bedroom windows, should they be so inclined. Swan Alley would have been just such a dingy, claustrophobic thoroughfare, of a type that had been common in the city since early medieval times, and which Sir Christopher Wren had hoped to sweep away with his ambitious post-fire proposal for a new London of wide, expansive boulevards. In the end, his plans came to nothing, because existing homeowners were keen to hang onto their territory, and the old medieval street plan was essentially rebuilt as before. The considerable task of clearing away the ruins of Old St Paul's Cathedral from the site where torrents of molten lead had rained down from the roof had not long been completed. On 21 June 1675 – the day before Elizabeth Lylliman was arrested – the first stone of Wren's new St Paul's was put in place.

It was not only cathedrals that were rising from the ashes. During the time of Cromwell's Commonwealth, theatrical performances had been outlawed and theatres demolished, but with the restoration of the monarchy, drama returned to the capital. Old plays were revived, and many new dramatists appeared on the scene, some writing works that would have shocked the puritan sensibilities of the previous generation. The popular image that comes down to us of the age of Charles II from Restoration comedies is of a knowing, witty society with decidedly modern views about sex. Indeed, one of the best known and most controversial of these, William Wycherley's *The Country Wife*, was given its first performance in January 1675, presented in the brand-new theatre in Drury Lane which had been designed by Wren. In this fashionable setting, cuckoldry and adultery are the stuff of comedy, yet there was a darker side to the age, and anyone falling foul of the law might see themselves facing punishments of medieval ferocity.

Elizabeth's husband, William Lylliman, was, according to the pamphlet *A Complete Narrative of the Trial of Elizabeth Lillyman,* 'a lusty comely man, and not above thirty years of age or thereabouts'. In this broadsheet, published shortly after her death as a result of great public interest in her case, the spelling of her surname differed from that in the court records – this was an era when there were still no fixed spellings for most words. It is from this publication, which is far more extensive than the short report from the Old Bailey, that most of the facts about her are known.

A cooper by trade, William Lylliman made varieties of casks, hogsheads, firkins and other wooden items for a local brewhouse, and was apparently a 'civil, honest, laborious person'. It is hard to know how much credence to give to the view of the couple in the pamphlet, which presents the recently deceased William in glowing terms throughout, and Elizabeth as a woman of many faults even prior to the murder. Although generally referred to in the neighbourhood as a nurse, she is said to have had little or no regular employment, and 'pretended sometimes to take in clothes to wash, yet she did not do any considerable matter of work, but lived a life somewhat extravagant and expensive for one of her condition'.

As a couple, William and Elizabeth seem an odd match. By 1675, they had been together for just one year, but no reason is given as to why this thirty-year-old man had married someone nearly twice his age. Measured against the shorter life expectancies of the seventeenth century, Elizabeth would have been considered an old woman. It's certainly possible that she had money, since it is stated that this man was 'the sixth that she had', so she may have been a widow with her own house, or funds. The *Complete Narrative* claims that in the early days of the marriage Elizabeth did 'extremely dote upon' her husband, but it was not long before her suspicions got the better of her, and drove her ultimately to murder:

> . . . being herself near three-score, she was not a little tainted with the poison of jealousy, which often is the disturber of the discreetest marriages, and therefore might without matter of wonder prove the bane of this lascivious heart. Baiting her controversies sometimes on that account (for which 'tis generally believed she had indeed no occasion) till Satan taking the advantage of her being in one of these jealous moods (in which she used often to threaten she would do him a mischief) prevailed on her barbarously to imbue her hands in his blood.

Elizabeth Lylliman was accused of petty treason, an offence which had been on the statute books since 1351 and carried the severest penalties, different for each sex. Men found guilty of this crime were hanged, drawn and quartered – a protracted ordeal whose reality was even more of a barbaric spectacle than one might imagine. The victim would first be hanged, but not to the point of death:

> Then to be cut down alive, and to have his Privy Parts cut off and burnt before his Face, as being unworthily begotten, and unfit to leave a Generation after him. His Bowels and inlay'd Parts taken out and burnt, who inwardly had conceived and harboured in his heart such horrible Treason. After, to have his head cut off, which had imagined the Mischief. And lastly, his body to be quartered, and the Quarters set up in some high and eminent Place, to the View and detestation of Men, and to become a Prey for the Fowls of the Air.

It is small wonder that several public hangmen were reputed to have had to drink themselves virtually insensible before performing such tasks. Samuel Pepys witnessed this grisly process on 13 October 1660, at the public execution of one of the men who had signed the death warrant of Charles I, giving rise to one of his most frequently quoted diary entries:

To my Lord's in the morning, where I met with Captain Cuttance, but my Lord not being up I went out to Charing Cross, to see Major-general Harrison hanged, drawn, and quartered; which was done there, he looking as cheerful as any man could do in that condition. He was presently cut down, and his head and heart shown to the people, at which there was great shouts of joy.

The word 'cheerful' sounds an odd choice to the modern ear, but Pepys used it again two years later when describing the demeanour of three more of the regicides as they passed him on a cart heading for the gallows at Tyburn to be hanged and quartered. This, of course, was the punishment for killing the king, the most serious kind of treason, yet men found guilty of petty treason were held in law to merit the same fate. The sentence for women convicted of petty treason was different, certainly, yet equally harsh: they were burnt at the stake.

As a punishment, burning was closely associated with religious offences. In the previous century, during the reign of the Catholic Queen Mary, it was Protestants who were burnt for heresy. Now, the tide of persecution had turned, and Catholics went in fear of the stake. The House of Commons had been debating finally abolishing Henry IV's law of 1401 for the burning of heretics, *De Haeretico Comburendo*, but a glance at the *London Gazette* for 14 June 1675 shows advertisements for two different books warning of the dangers of the old religion: *The Abominations of the Church of ROME* and another with an even more pointed title, *The Burnt Child dreads the Fire*.

Attempts by priests and Jesuits to convert the nation back to Catholicism were held to be treasonous, and those responsible were burnt. Equally threatening by the standards of the day – and therefore equally harshly punished – was the crime of petty treason. This charge was levelled in cases where people attempted to overthrow what was seen as the natural order of lay society, just as heretics were held to be trying to subvert the natural order of religion. It was a charge reserved for those who struck out at their superiors, such as servants who murdered their employers. Wives killing husbands were very much included in this category, since, in law, the woman was definitely the junior partner in any marriage. Elizabeth Lylliman, a woman thought to have murdered her husband, could have expected no other charge.

Elizabeth was brought in front of the judges at the General Quarter Sessions of the Old Bailey in 1675, one year after the authorities began publishing proper records of such trials so 'that the punishments inflicted on a few may by an Exemplary Caution create fear in all'. On that day, she was lined up alongside the usual collection of prisoners, whose offences ranged from mild to serious, and justice was dispensed very quickly, as was the custom:

> At the Sessions at the Old-Bayly, there begun the 7th of July instant, were Tryed a great number of Malafactors, for Crimes of various and sundry natures, as Murthers, Robberies, Burglaries, Cheats, Libellers, and other Enormities . . . it is strange to see what a speked mass of loathsome crimes present themselves at these times amongst the wicked Heard that are brought before this great Tribunal, to receive the due reward of their wickedness.

Standing in the dock at one of the most important law courts in the country, Elizabeth Lylliman would have had only a very small part to play in the short proceedings which determined her fate. The evidence presented that day was brief and to the point, characterising her as a vicious felon – 'a person of some fifty years of age, old both in years and wickedness' – who had struck down an innocent man for the flimsiest of reasons. It was a domestic dispute between a husband and wife from a poor district in East London, briefly analysed and then judged, before the gentlemen of the judiciary moved on to other matters; more work for the legal scribes, another date for the executioner's diary.

On the afternoon of Tuesday, 22 June 1675, William Lylliman returned home to Swan Alley from his job at the brewhouse, to find that Elizabeth was not there. She was a couple of streets away, 'at an Ale-house hard by in Glasshouse Yard at Ninepins'. Glasshouse Yard was just south of Goodman's Yard; the latter still exists today. The glasshouse itself was one of a number established towards the end of the previous century, when Venetian glass-blowers first came to London and set up in business producing mirrors, bottles and the like. Ninepins, the game of skittles which Elizabeth was playing, was, according to the seventeenth-century writer Henry Peacham the Younger, one of the most popular of the age: 'The most ordinary recreations of the Countrey are football, skales or ninepins, shooting at butts [etc.].'

His wife not being at home, William decided to visit a nearby cobbler friend who ran a stall outside their house in Swan Alley, taking some food with him – 'a piece of cold mutton, and a dried mackerel' – which he intended to eat at a nearby pub. He seems to have invited his friend to come along with him for a drink, and also had a favour to ask, since he apparently had no cutlery with him: 'Before Lillyman went into the Alehouse he asked the Cobbler for a knife to cut out his victuals, who lent him a very sharp long one, which their trade commonly use to pare heels with.'

It was just a short walk to the pub in Glasshouse Yard, where his wife was playing ninepins in the skittle alley. William probably knew that she would be there and had chosen this hostelry out of the many in the area for that reason. Upon arrival, he sent a message to Elizabeth by means of one of the staff, asking if she would like to come inside to the main bar and join him. It is hard to say how long Elizabeth had already been enjoying the facilities of the alehouse, but by all accounts she had been engaged in that time-honoured pursuit once described by Raymond Chandler as 'doing next week's drinking too soon'. In this somewhat charged state, she reacted badly to an offhand witticism made by the woman at the alehouse who brought her news of William's arrival:

> . . . a Servant maid (unluckily as it proved in the consequence, but very innocently intending it only for jest and merriment) said to her: 'Ah Mistress Lillyman, little do you think that your husband and I have been together and that he gave me a bottle of ale at your house.'

Whether this was a wise thing to say to a woman 'elevated with drink' is debatable, but Elizabeth apparently took the remark at face value and began an angry exchange with her husband. This, however, was not a slanging match in front of a drunken group of onlookers in a crowded bar; the couple were in a private room, with no other witnesses. Although many alehouses in those days were simply dwellings that happened to sell alcohol and food – with just the front room or parlour serving as the drinking area – this establishment was on a much larger scale, with various rooms available, some of which were intended for those who wanted privacy. The beginnings of their argument were observed by others, but by the time things became serious the couple were completely alone, as both the landlady and her serving woman had left the room – 'the woman of the house being gone for a pot of drink, and the maid for a loaf for him'.

Exactly what happened next is impossible to say. Those in nearby rooms may well have heard shouting or the crashing sounds of overturning furniture, but perhaps not; there would have been plenty of random noise in such an alehouse to drown out much of what happened, not to mention the ever-present crashing of ninepins from the adjoining skittle alley. Fights would have been a normal part of life in such a place, in a society where beer was strong and drinking often began at breakfast. Even if any sounds did escape from the room, a dispute between husband and wife was a commonplace enough occurrence, not usually meriting investigation. At any rate, it appears that no one raised the alarm. It seemed just another ordinary afternoon at the alehouse. Yet when the serving woman returned to the Lyllimans' room with the bread, she found William clutching his chest, saying that his wife had stabbed him. At first, he asked the maid to fetch his friend the cobbler from outside, then however made his own way to the door, saying: 'Ah Countryman! This wicked woman my wife has stabbed me with the knife I borrowed of thee!' Elizabeth immediately denied the accusation, saying 'I stab thee Love? Why wilt thou say so? I have not touched thee.' She went forward to kiss William, but he pushed her away with the words, 'Ah wicked woman thou hast killed me!'

The *Complete Narrative* states that at this point there was nothing in the outward appearance of William to suggest any injury, since the blood had yet to show through his clothing. A wound from an extremely sharp knife can often show surprisingly little evidence at first, despite the severe damage it can cause. Soon afterwards, however, it became clear that something was desperately wrong, as William suddenly collapsed in sight of everybody. Carried into a larger room in the pub by his friend the cobbler – perhaps because they sought a table of sufficient size upon which to lay him – the injured man mustered enough strength to point to the left-hand side of his chest and say, 'Here, here my wife hath killed me.'

Having uttered this last accusation, William Lylliman lost consciousness and died a few minutes later, leaving Elizabeth to the mercy of the
crowd. She then confirmed their opinion of her likely guilt by attempting
to flee via the back door of the alehouse, 'but neighbours stopped her
and sent for a constable, who carried her before a Justice of the Peace'.

In these times, it was still normal for the State to rely on bystanders
and members of the public to apprehend any suspected wrongdoers, and
while there were constables, they did not belong to any kind of larger
organised body. The role had existed since at least the fourteenth century
– a local person who was the first line of defence in the State's attempts
to uphold the law – yet there was no chain of command and no senior
officers directing affairs. In theory, a constable was supposed to keep
order in the parish and his duties were loosely defined, although if a
crime was committed, his principal task would be to hold anyone captured
by the public until such time as the justice system could deal with them.
The idea that one of these familiar figures, as well as the public, might
give chase after lawbreakers was certainly well established – for instance,
at the start of the seventeenth century William Kemp wrote that he had
danced 'like one that had escaped the stocks, and tride the use of his
legs to out-run the Constable'.

Had Elizabeth managed to flee the area and make her way to a different
town, she might never have been discovered and tried for murder, but
even then – with no means of support – she might have starved to death
thereafter. Once apprehended, with witnesses to swear that she had been
condemned in her husband's dying words, her trial and conviction were
little more than a formality. However, when initially questioned by the
Justice of the Peace, Elizabeth is said to have acted as if nothing whatever
had happened:

> At her examination there, she behaved herself very strangely, seeming
> altogether unconcerned at what she had done, and laughing at it: amongst
> many other silly answers, was this one, 'I wish my hands may never see
> my eyes, if I killed my husband.'

Elizabeth herself may have refused to take the matter seriously, if this
account is to be believed, but this particular murder case generated enormous interest among a hardened public which had seen countless fatalities
during the plague year. In the London of that time – with health care

primitive and even that only available to the few – death was ever-present, sometimes violent, and often mysterious. For the previous eighty years or so, attempts had been made to record the number of yearly deaths and christenings within the city by means of Bills of Mortality, which also endeavoured to list causes of death. The bill for the year in which Elizabeth Lylliman was tried, 1675, gives a figure of 17,224 burials spread across all the London parishes, within and without the walls (compared to 11,775 christenings). As for the causes of death, these were many. Some explanations seem clear enough: there were those said to have starved (2), drowned (57), been poisoned (4) or died in childbed (284). Yet others apparently perished that year of the King's Evil (60), St Anthony's Fire (5), Blasted and Planet (2), of the Megrims (5) or from Rifling of the Lights (172). However, there were surprisingly few executions, and a fair number of those sentenced to death by the courts were subsequently allowed to live. Only eighteen people suffered capital punishment in London that year: clearly then, alongside those hung for simple robbery, the case of a woman accused of murdering her husband was something out of the ordinary.

On the day of her trial, 7 July 1675, Elizabeth Lylliman was brought to the Sessions House from the adjoining Newgate gaol where she had been held. The court was situated on a road called Old Bailey, which eventually led to the building itself being known by that name. This was a brand-new structure, completed only two years earlier, since the previous courthouse was destroyed in the Great Fire. Newgate had also been burnt to the ground in the same conflagration, and the rebuilt prison opened a year before the new Sessions House.

After waiting together with the day's other prisoners in the yard outside, which was surrounded by a spiked wall to prevent escape attempts, Elizabeth was taken into the courtroom itself. Compared to the Old Bailey's modern incarnation, this room had one very obvious difference – there were only three walls, the fourth side being open to the air. This was a deliberate attempt to mitigate the effects of the diseases which prisoners brought along with them, specifically 'gaol fever', the virulent form of typhus endemic in the prisons of the day.

Spectators gathered in part of the yard from where they could observe the proceedings, and witnesses customarily waited in nearby pubs until they were called, there being no rooms as yet allocated in the Sessions House for that purpose. When it came time for Elizabeth to stand in the dock, she faced the judges and the witness box, with members of the jury arranged to both left and right. There was also a large mirror hanging above her, designed to reflect the light from the windows onto her face, so that members of the court could better observe her reactions.

During this particular session, which lasted four days, a wide variety of people stood in this same dock. It was a cosmopolitan group, including a couple of horse thieves, a Swiss pickpocket, a French jewel thief, a highway robber, and a woman who had 'stripped children of their cloaths'. At the end of the last day, six men and women were sentenced to be transported, ten to be branded ('burned in the hand'), and a further ten to be hanged. The published court record makes this sound almost like an everyday occurrence, an impression reinforced by Pepys, who would visit the 'Old Bayly' reasonably regularly for meetings, but occasionally also watched the proceedings, as on 2 September 1663, when he saw a servant maid convicted of stealing various items from her master: '. . . a silver tankard, a porringer of silver, and a couple of spoons'. He noted in his *Diary* that the woman 'likely will be hanged', but seems more concerned that this example should serve as a lesson to him to seek good character references when next hiring 'mayds'.

On the day of her trial among a group of prisoners accused of more everyday crimes, Elizabeth Lylliman's brief moment in the dock was certainly, despite the crowded schedule, very much the main event. The distinguishing factor of her short time in the dock was her odd behaviour, as the trial transcript notes:

> . . . her carriage was very strange both at her Arraignment and Tryal, for after her Indictment read, and the Clark demanded her Plea to the same, she fell into a kind of passion, and desired of the court that she might see her dead Husband before she pleaded, which she insisted upon with seeming earnestness for some time; but this appeared to the Court to be but a mad kind of Artifice, designed out of her feigned passionate Zeal to her Murthered Husband to take off the suspicion of her being instrumental to his death . . .

In the end, Elizabeth was persuaded to enter a plea, at which she said, 'not guilty'. Witnesses were then called: the woman who ran the alehouse, the serving girl from the same establishment, and the cobbler whose knife had been borrowed by William. According to the fuller account given in the *Complete Narrative*, when the maid appeared on the stand, Elizabeth 'fell into another passionate fit, calling her many base, scurrilous names in open court'. She vehemently denied all the charges made against her, but very unwisely also insisted that she had been tempted to attack the serving woman that afternoon in the alehouse.

Despite the *Complete Narrative* asserting that William initially showed no outer signs of having been attacked, the court testimony in the Old Bailey transcript painted a much more graphic picture of the murder scene, in which it was claimed that the weapon was clearly visible to those entering the room:

> . . . while the Fish was a broyling, the people of the house being gon out of the Room, at their return, they found poor Lylliman with the aforesaid knife in his body, and the blood streaming out after it in this condition.

In the face of such statements, there was probably not much that Elizabeth could have done, although her own reported behaviour in court seems to have further sealed her fate. However, it probably made little difference one way or the other. In those days circumstantial evidence and the testimony of bystanders and character witnesses were practically all that the courts had to consider: being found in the company of her stabbed husband and condemned out of his own mouth, there was virtually no chance of Elizabeth escaping a guilty verdict. To those sitting in judgement, it appeared an open and shut case:

> So that the matter being evident, the jury brought her in, *guilty of the indictment*. And accordingly she received the usual sentence for persons of her sex, in cases of petty treason, that is to say, to be *burned until she be dead*.

The published record offers few clues as to why, if Elizabeth Lylliman murdered her husband, she was moved to do so. The most obvious suggestion was that of insanity – temporary or otherwise – which was also their explanation for her behaviour in court:

. . . when she came to the bar, she did, as formerly, passionately request to see the body of her husband before she died, saying she could not else dye in peace. But this action of hers, was suspected rather as a fit of raving, than the result of a considerate mind, from one who so apparently proved to be his Murtheress.

Having received a sentence of burning, Elizabeth Lylliman was taken on Monday, 19 July 1675, to Tower Hill, where she was awaited by the already notorious public executioner, Jack Ketch. Memorably described in a pamphlet of 1679 as 'the redoubtable Squire Ketch, Death's Harbinger, Pluto's Van-courier, Vice-roy of Fate, and sole Monarch of the Triple Throne', he was a man whose name eventually passed into London folk-lore as an all-purpose nickname for whoever held the post of public executioner. Ketch had a reputation for brutality, drinking on the job and rank incompetence – best illustrated by his botched attempts at beheading William, Lord Russell, in 1683, and the duke of Monmouth in 1685, following which he was lucky to escape from the angry crowds with his own life.

In cases of burning such as this, it was customary for the exe-cutioner to strangle the victim first before applying a flame, as this was felt to prevent unnecessary suffering. Since there is no mention in the *Complete Narrative* of any unforeseen or unusual events at Elizabeth's execution, she was probably already dead before the fire was lit.

A decade or two later, once the deregulation of the press had led to an explosion of newspaper publishing in London, such a case would have been covered in great detail. At that time, however, the government's official paper of record, the *London Gazette*, was far more concerned with news of the current military campaigns in Germany, interspersed with bland reports of Charles II's movements between London and Windsor. Yet the issue published on 21 June, the day before the murder, carried an advert for a book with an ironically appropriate title: *The Christian's Defence against the Fears of Death. With resonable Directions how to prepare our selves to Dye well.*

Soon after being sentenced to such a horrific end, according to the *Complete Narrative*, Elizabeth 'seemed scarce at all sensible of her condition', but in the days that followed, while still denying the murder, she apparently told friends and visitors that she had 'been a grievous sinner for many years'. It is claimed that she eventually confessed her guilt to ministers in her cell, and her last reported words on the scaffold, if accurate, uphold this view:

> Good people you are come to see the sad end of a miserable woman. I have been a scandalous liver ever since I was fifteen years old, and now God almighty has taken this time to punish me for all my wickedness; I cannot but acknowledge the murder of my dear husband, although I must needs say, I never intended it, but did it in my passion, and it is well known among my neighbours how dearly I loved him, I pray God I may be an example to you all, and that though I suffer this cruel death here, I may be delivered from the pains of hell fire forever.

The anonymous writer of the *Complete Narrative* seems to have been struck by her repentant and dignified behaviour on the scaffold, and his choice of words unconsciously echoes that of Pepys, quoted earlier, after watching the execution of Major-General Harrison:

> And after some private prayer by the minister, she kneeled down herself and prayed very earnestly, which much affected the standers-by, and after went cheerfully to the stake where she suffered.

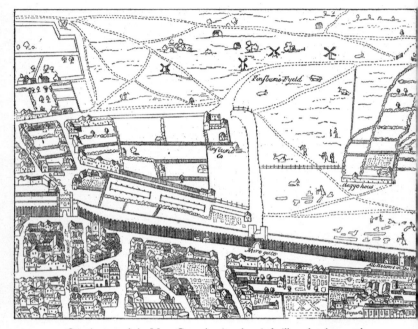

Cripplegate and the Moor Gate, showing the windmills and archery yards
of Finsbury Fields, from a map by Ralph Agas (1540–1621)

SIX

DYING FOR A DRINK
1695

There is not much left of Grub Street. Even the name itself was changed in 1830 to Milton Street, and during the mid-twentieth century many of its buildings were swept away by the Blitz. Some of what remained was then lost to the huge post-war construction project which eventually gave rise to the Barbican Centre. Opened in 1982, this twenty-acre concrete complex of arts venues and housing developments was partly built over the southern end of what used to be Grub Street. The surviving northern section which ends at Chiswell Street, near the old Truman Brewery, is still there at the time of writing, although the building work continues and a giant crane dominates the skyline.

At the end of the seventeenth century, however, Grub Street was in the process of becoming famous – a byword for the hack writers and newly emerging journalists who flourished in the wake of the Licensing Act of 1695, which ended almost a hundred years of State censorship of publications. In short order, ten London newspapers appeared as rivals to the government's own *London Gazette*, and the area around Grub Street gradually became known as the haunt of many a new journalist, satirist or jobbing writer. By 1730, the name was such a common shorthand term that it was commemorated in the title of Richard Russell and John Martyn's satirical weekly the *Grub Street Journal*, while two decades later, Dr Johnson enshrined it in his *Dictionary of the English Language* (1755) as follows:

> *Grub-street*, the name of a street in London. Much inhabited by writers of small histories, *dictionaries*, and temporary poems; whence any mean production is called *Grub-street*.

The original Grub Street ran north from just outside the old city walls, near to Cripplegate. Directly to the west lay the open spaces of Moor Fields, and to the north, the archery grounds of Finsbury Fields, where many windmills once stood. The Elizabethan historian John Stow provided a brief glimpse of the Grub Street of those days in his *Survey of London* (1598):

> In the East ende of Forestreete is More lane: then next is Grubstreete, of late yeares inhabited for the most part by Bowyers, Fletchers, Bowstring makers, and such like, now little occupied, Archerie giving place to a number of bowling Allies, and Dicing houses, which in al places are increased, and too much frequented.

Two years after this description was published, Edward Alleyn built the Fortune Theatre a few hundred yards north of Grub Street – a circular wooden structure very similar to the Globe in Southwark. Alleyn grew very rich promoting theatrical productions and bear-baiting events, giving generously throughout his life to the parish of St Giles without Cripplegate, in which lay Grub Street.

The church of St Giles still stands. Almost completely surrounded by the Barbican development, it can be seen from the terrace of the arts centre, across a short stretch of ornamental water. Oliver Cromwell was married in this church in 1620, and in its crypt are buried the remains of former Grub Street resident John Foxe, who published *The Book of Martyrs* in 1587, and those of the writer John Milton, who had lived nearby in the street called Barbican from 1645 onwards. It might be supposed that Milton lent his name to Grub Street when it was renamed in 1830, but the architect James Elmes, writing the year after the change, denied this: 'It is now called Milton-street, not after the great poet of that name, as some persons have asserted, but from a respectable builder so called, who has taken the whole street on a repairing lease.'

Even when Milton lived in the area, during the latter stages of the Civil War, Grub Street was already home to many printers of books and pamphlets: Bernard Alsop, at 'Grub Street, near the Upper Pump', Thomas Dunster 'at the Red Lion in Grub Street', or Mark Rookes, who published *Bloody Newes from Ireland* (1641) at 'Grub Street neere to the Flying Horse'. In this era before the days of street numbering, it was common to include in the address local landmarks such as public water pumps, or more often, alehouses and taverns such as the Red Lion and the Flying Horse mentioned here. Throughout the length of Grub Street, many of the narrow alleys and courtyards radiating off to the right and left of the main thoroughfare appear to have been named for the pubs which stood at their corners, such as Boar's Head Court and Red Lion Court at the northern end, or the Greyhound Inn to the south.

Inns provided food and lodging for travellers, as well as drinks, but even the humble alehouse, which might only be essentially a private dwelling offering a simple range of home-brewed refreshments, would generally abide by established notions of hospitality. A 1602 description of an alehouse, quoted by Peter Haydon in his book *Beer and Britannia*, gives some indication of how drinkers could expect to be treated, in this case by the landlady or the servants:

> If either the hostess or her daughter or the maid will kiss handsomely at parting, it is a bird line to draw the company hither again the sooner. She must be courteous to all . . . for she must entertain all good and bad, rag and tag, cut and longtail. She suspects tinkers and poor soldiers most, not that they will not drink soundly, but that they will not lustily. She must keep in touch with three sorts of men, that is the maltman, the baker and the justices' clerks! . . . Her ale, if new, looks like a misty morning, all thick: well if her ale be strong, her reckoning right, her house clean, her fire good, her face fair and the town great or rich, she shall seldom or never sit without the chirping birds to bear her company.

At a Grub Street hostelry not unlike the kind described above, a brutal murder took place in December 1695. The victim was a landlord, rather than a landlady, but he would also have been used to welcoming all kinds of people, 'good and bad, rag and tag, cut and longtail'. In this case, however, the drinkers did not depart quietly at the end of the evening with a kiss from the serving woman.

On the evening of 14 December 1695, Robert Maynard, Samuel Mercer and George Draper stopped at the house of George Stockton, seeking refreshments. It was a dark time of the year, just a week away from the shortest day. The streets were poorly lit in those times, if at all, and most people in search of a drink would not necessarily have gone more than a short walk away from where they lived. It is probable therefore that these men were already familiar with George Stockton's establishment and knew something about the owner. Maynard was certainly a local man, a resident of the parish of St Giles without Cripplegate, and might even have been a regular at the place.

Indoors, the light would have come from just a handful of candles, and from the fire – a welcome sight in the middle of winter. It would be gloomy to modern eyes, but cosy all the same, despite the clinging smoke from the sea coal burning in the grate. From the outside, some alehouses were almost indistinguishable from normal dwellings, and in earlier centuries would have been identified by just a wooden stake or a garlanded pole, but since the 1500s wooden inn signs had begun to make an appearance. These might hang on bars protruding from the wall of the establishment, or be suspended from a post which stood in front of the building. Pub names derived from a variety of sources, some of which were quite straightforward: royalty (the King's Head), heraldry (the Bear & Ragged Staff – the crest of the Warwick family), religion (the Mitre), or trades and professions (the Three Jolly Butchers). Others were of more obscure origin, as the writer Joseph Addison noted in the *Spectator* in 1711:

> Our streets are filled with blue boars, black swans, and red lions; not to mention flying pigs, and hogs in armour, with many other creatures more extraordinary than any in the deserts of Afric . . . The fox and goose may be supposed to have met, but what has the fox and the seven stars to do together? And when did the lamb and dolphin ever meet, except upon a sign-post?

If these were considered odd, a century later, when Napoleon was thinking of invading England, his failed attempt was mocked in one of the most singular alehouse signs, My Arse in a Bandbox.

In Grub Street, the pub names were more in the common run. Near the northern end was the Boar's Head, one of many animal signs around town. The Cross Keys, located about halfway down the road, denoted either a locksmith or the arms of the papacy (still a common sign even at a time when Catholics were held to be plotting to overthrow the king). As for the Flying Horse, this was inspired by a type of public game offered by the house in question, as noted in Hotten and Larwood's mid-Victorian study of inn signs:

> It was the name of a popular amusement, which often consisted in a swing, the seat of which formed a wooden horse. This the ambitious youth mounted, and as he was swinging to and fro he had to take with a sword the ring off a quintain. If he succeeded, his adroitness was rewarded either with a number of swings gratis, or an allowance of beer. Such a *Flying Horse* served for a sign to an alehouse in Moorfields in the time of Queen Anne . . .

Not everyone who drew a sword at an alehouse had such innocent intentions. John Aubrey wrote in 1692 that the Fleece in Covent Garden had been 'very unfortunate for homicides; there have been several killed – three in my time. It is now a private house. Clifton the master hanged himself, having perjured himself.'

While the name of George Stockton's hostelry has not been preserved, it is still possible to reconstruct the events leading up to his murder. It is known that his three customers, Maynard, Mercer and Draper, drank ale that night – a cheaper option than wine – which suggests that these men were from the poorer section of society. Having consumed their first drinks, probably served in leather or ceramic tankards, they then ordered food, as the court record noted: 'after a while they had a Pound of Sawcidges for their Supper'.

Late in the evening, having finished a round of drinks and eaten their food, Maynard, Mercer and Draper then prevailed upon the landlord for more hospitality, at which point things took a severe turn for the worse. In a scene which has been played out in numerous drinking establishments down through the ages, the patrons demanded service, and the proprietor wanted to close up and go to bed. In this instance, however, the former refused to leave, as the court transcript states: 'Then they called for Hot-Pots of Ale and Brandy, and the deceased pulled out his Watch, and told them that it was late, it being almost Twelve a Clock, and he did not care to draw any more.' Brandy was becoming harder to find in the 1690s because of the war with France, so this would not have been a cheap option, although if these men had come with the prior intention of robbing the place, they would scarcely have worried about settling the bill anyway.

It is a measure of Stockton's relative wealth that he was able to pull out a pocket watch. Watches had been around in primitive form since the previous century, but it was only in the last two decades that the technology had advanced to the point where they were becoming reliable, greatly aided by Thomas Thompion's invention of the cylinder escapement in 1694. The majority of the population would not have had a timepiece of any kind, so for the landlord to produce such an item was a sign of his status, and perhaps not the wisest course of action in front of strangers. It may even have been the sight of this precision instrument, its case of silver or gold reflecting the light from the fire, that prompted Maynard and his associates to thoughts of crime that evening. As the Reverend Edmund Hickeringill wrote in 1705, 'Pocket your Watch, and Watch your Pockets.'

What happened next seems to have been something more than the usual escalation of a drunken argument. At first 'they pressed him that they might have but one more, and they would be gone', but this was evidently met with another refusal. A pub landlord soon learns how to defuse such a situation and make it clear that the evening is over – this is probably something that George Stockton would have faced every few days, and in most cases the inebriated guests would have taken their leave with perhaps just a few muttered complaints. This, however, was different. Upon hearing the landlord's response, Robert Maynard alerted his companions with a pre-arranged signal, and then the three of them viciously attacked Stockton: '. . . the Prisoner cried Come, which being a Watch-word, they all rose up and laid hands upon him, and tied the Neckcloth about his Throat, so that his Tongue came out of his Mouth, and bound him.' Maynard and the others had the advantage of surprise, so that the landlord was overpowered before he even sensed danger. The scarf around Stockton's throat was pulled so tight that he could scarcely breathe, as if they were trying to choke him to death. Set upon so suddenly, outnumbered, in considerable pain, and probably in fear of his life, George Stockton's only hope would have been that these were just thieves, but it would have been a slim one. If all they had wanted was to immobilise him before robbing the place, their actions thus far would have been enough; however, Robert Maynard quickly went further, and Stockton's fate was sealed:

. . . then the Prisoner called to one of them to lend him his Pistol, which he did, and he struck the deceased three blows upon the forehead, and he fell down with his face upon the Hearth, and the Prisoner said that now he would lye quietly.

Whether he died by strangulation, or the blows to the head, this seems to have been the end of George Stockton. Having removed the landlord, the three men then proceeded to tie up what appears to have been the sole other occupant of the house, identified only as 'the deceased's Kinswoman'. She was secured to a chair and gagged, but apparently not otherwise harmed, leaving the criminals a free hand to loot the building. Whether they knew it beforehand or not, there were certainly some portable goods worth stealing. From the evidence provided later by the surviving victim of the raid, they found on the upper floors of the house 'four Silver Tankards, and some Gold, and other Goods which she could not name'. Tied to a chair by three men, and with her relative brutally murdered, she must have been terrified that a similar fate lay in store for her. Having killed once, they had nothing to lose by eliminating the only witness.

Some thieves, with a dead body lying by the hearth, another victim bound and gagged in the same room, and a selection of looted gold and silver items in their hands, would have made a swift getaway, but not in this case. They apparently 'did tarry in the house for some time', and were careless in their actions into the bargain. While there was no need in those days to take trouble about fingerprints, it has never been a good idea for murderers to leave their personal belongings at the scene of the crime, especially if they live just a short distance away and are known in the neighbourhood. Yet this is precisely what happened.

All things considered, the wisest course would have been to leave the district entirely. As far as is known, this was the strategy adopted the following day by two of the men, Samuel Mercer and George Draper, who, at the time of the trial, were named as accomplices, but listed simply as 'not yet taken'. Robert Maynard failed to flee, and did not even take the precautionary measure of lying low. News of the brutal death of a local pub landlord would have been the talk of the parish, discussed on doorsteps and in alehouses, yet Maynard ventured out into the streets near the murder location the following day to visit his usual barber – with the intention of altering his appearance by having his hair cut short.

If Maynard normally had longer hair, this implies that he was not usually in the habit of wearing a wig, since most of those who did would habitually keep their own hair underneath trimmed very short for the sake of comfort. Heads would be shaved in order to accommodate the wig, which helped with the fit and also prevented the wearer from feeling too warm. By having his hair cut short, and then adopting a wig, Maynard would thus have been able to disguise himself to a certain extent.

In his diary entries, Samuel Pepys recorded his struggles with the new fashion for wig-wearing during the summer of 1663. On 9 May, visiting his barber Mr Jervas, he tried on several 'periwiggs'. Although he remained unconvinced of the need for one, he admitted to himself that 'the pains of keeping my hair clean is so great'. Good wigs were not cheap, and there was always the risk of infection from the hair that was used. Ever since the returning Charles II had brought the fashion to England in 1660, wigs had become an important article of attire, so that a news item in the *London Gazette* for the month of Maynard's trial makes a point of stressing the lack of a wig as one of the principal means of identifying a pair of suspected criminals:

> John Mills aged about 27, and Oliver Mills his Brother, aged 31, both lusty plump persons, fresh colour'd, and wearing their own hair, have fraudulently deceiv'd a Person of a sum of Money; and are since Absconded . . . . . . Whoever shall give notice of both, or either of them, at the Angel and Crown Coffee-House in Threadneedle-street, so as they may be secured, shall have his Charges born, and be well rewarded.

Not only could barbers provide wigs, shaves, haircuts and hat-care, they were often the first port of call for minor surgery and rudimentary dentistry, hence the blood-red stripes of the poles which identified their places of business. They were therefore likely to know their customers quite well, which, in Robert Maynard's case, proved to be his undoing. Having gone to his regular barber the evening after the murder in order to buy a 'peruke' (wig) and have his hair cut off, he was identified by that self-same barber as the owner of a hat which had been left behind at the scene of the crime by the murderers. Hats, like wigs, were reasonably valuable and sometimes needed attention, and at the trial, Maynard's barber was able to testify that the item did indeed belong to the defendant, and 'swore positively that that was the Prisoner's Hat, for he had brushed it several times'. In their carelessness, the murderers had left behind them not only this hat, but also a green apron; either of which, in the days before the mass production of clothing, ran the risk of being individual enough to identify them.

On 27 February 1696, the Sessions House at the Old Bailey opened up for several days of trying assorted prisoners, among them Robert Maynard. Presiding over the trials were the Lord Mayor of London, Sir John Houblon, and Sir Salathiel Lovell, Recorder of the City of London, together 'with several others of His Majesties Justices for the City of London, and County of Middlesex'. During the following week they heard a large number of cases, many of them petty crimes which these days would merit little more than a caution or a minor custodial sentence, but which carried the death penalty then.

Sir John Houblon, a wealthy man with close links to the king, had subscribed the considerable sum of £10,000 when the Bank of England was established in 1694, and served as its first governor. The Recorder, Sir Salathiel Lovell, was perhaps a more controversial figure, accused by some of being corrupt and in league with thief-takers – those shadowy figures who made bounty money bringing in people for arrest, of whom the most notorious example was the early eighteenth-century criminal Jonathan Wild. One of Lovell's great preoccupations at this time was with 'coiners' and 'clippers'. These were people who debased, mutilated or counterfeited the coin of the realm at a time when the demands of the war had driven the nation's silver reserves to dangerously low levels. This, of course, would also have been a major concern of Houblon as governor of the new bank. Parliament had lately passed an act entitled *To prevent counterfeiting and clipping the Coin,* ascribing the problem largely to a conspiracy of Jacobites and Jesuits, and the *House of Commons Journal* for 1694–5 stated:

The current Silver Coin had for many Years began to be clipped and adulterated; and the Mischief of late had been so secretly carried on, by a Combination of all People concerned in the Receipt of Money, and so industriously promoted by the Enemies of the Government, that all Pieces were so far diminished and debased, as that five Pounds in Silver Specie was scarce worth forty Shillings, according to the Standard: Besides an infinite deal of Iron, Brass, or Copper, washed over, or plated.

Several of the prisoners brought before the bar during the session at which Robert Maynard was tried were accused of coinage offences, which were classed as high treason, and appeared in the court record as follows: 'T-J- of the Parish of Saint Michael's Cornhill, in the Ward of Cornhill, was indicted for High-Treason, for Clipping 100 Halfcrowns on the Four and twentieth of December last', and Robert Creed, of Frying Pan Alley in the Parish of Saint Giles without Cripplegate, accused of clipping halfcrowns, shillings and sixpences. Both, however, were acquitted.

These crimes took place at a time when printers were beginning to exploit the public appetite for news about crime and criminals, issuing pamphlets that told of the life stories or last dying words of notorious felons. The records of proceedings from the Central Criminal Court at the Old Bailey provided a ready-made subject, and in the 1670s they began being published – a very successful enterprise which continued until 1913. The earliest surviving published Old Bailey record dates from April 1674, so when Robert Maynard came to trial in 1696, his moment in court was also preserved for posterity.

As a result of that publication, a picture emerges of the day that Maynard was tried. Even though this was the most important court in London, the majority of cases concerned simple offences of theft: James Knowland, charged with stealing 'a Silver Scissar Cafe, value 10s. and an Essence Bottle 2s'; Catherine Davies, who admitted unlawfully taking 'two Watches with silver Cases' worth £10; the team of Abigail Kelly (alias Baily, alias Grig) and Mark Fenton, said to have stolen '120 pair of mens Shooes' valued at £27; George Bowyer, indicted for 'feloniously stealing from Margaret Battey, Spinster, a Brass Kettle, val. 4s.'; and Richard Lewis, accused of picking what must have been a very roomy pocket belonging to Michael Rixon, since it contained '86

Guineas, one other 20s. piece of Gold, and Eleven Pound 15 Shillings and Sixpence'.

So it went on, with each prisoner spending a minimum of time in the dock; clippers next to thieves, petty criminals alongside murderers, nearly all at risk of the gallows. Robert Maynard was not the only person standing trial for a killing at this session. John Sharp, the survivor out of two men who had fought a duel on open ground near the present site of King's Cross station, was accused of having murdered his opponent, but in the end he was found guilty of manslaughter. Duelling, though not exactly respectable, was not seen in the same light as a crime such as Maynard's, and the jury might well have been predisposed to mercy in Sharp's case.

Given the state of evidence-gathering and the continuing reliance upon simple character references and witness statements, a great deal hinged upon the appearance of the accused and how they conducted themselves in the witness box. If a prisoner made a good impression, or seemed to be a gentleman, they stood a chance of persuading the court of their innocence. Christopher Billop was charged at these same sessions with forgery – an offence generally punished with both a fine and one or more appearances in the pillory, which might prove fatal. At his trial, the question of his good character was paramount:

> The Prisoner's Counsel alledged, that the Prisoner was a Person that had been a very noble Captain, and had done great Service for the Kingdom, and called Persons of very great Quality, and divers worthy Citizens to his Reputation, who said that they could not think him guilty of such a Crime. The Jury found him not guilty.

Robert Maynard had no hope of adopting a similar course. Indeed, he seems to have admitted right away that he came from the lower levels of society, who lived on their wits and might easily find themselves on the wrong side of the law. His whole defence strategy was based on a claim of mistaken identity. The barber swore that the hat found at the scene of the crime belonged to Maynard, but the prisoner denied this and gave an alternative reason for having changed his appearance. He explained that he had his hair cut short because he was intending 'to fight a man' – perhaps reasoning that longer hair might afford a hand-hold when grappling with an opponent. Maynard even went so far as to admit to being on the run from the authorities, but not because of any fear of a murder charge: '. . . he said that he had absconded from his Lodging for a great while, he hearing that there were Warrants out against him for Clipping.'

At a trial presided over by the governor of the Bank of England and another judge with a reputation for actively pursuing offenders who debased the coin of the realm, Maynard chose to argue that he was the kind of person who was likely to be wanted for such crimes. It was certainly a risky strategy, since coiners and clippers, if found guilty of high treason, were hanged, drawn and quartered. Perhaps he felt that there was little or no evidence to convict him of such a charge, and it might help him avoid being linked to the cold-blooded murder of George Stockton, which would carry a certain sentence of death by hanging. Yet even leaving aside the barber's evidence concerning the hat, there would also have been the eyewitness testimony of Stockton's relative. She was able to make an identification of those responsible, despite the trauma of the attack and the poor light inside the alehouse.

In the end, Robert Maynard's defence strategy, such as it was, proved to be of little use. It seems that the witness statements of Stockton's kinswoman, and that of the local barber, were enough to place him squarely at the scene of the crime, and the jury therefore returned a verdict of guilty.

———

There is no record of Samuel Mercer or George Draper ever standing trial for their part in the murder of George Stockton, so they seem to have made a better job than their associate of going to ground after the events of that night in 1695. Robert Maynard alone was left to face the gallows at Tyburn. Indeed, if the testimony is to be believed, he took the leading part in instigating the murder and dealt the fatal blows with the pistol.

The scene confronting him on his final day would have been very similar to that recorded in a pencil-and-wash drawing of an execution at Tyburn by the artist Marcellus Lauron in the previous decade, now preserved in the Pepys Library in Cambridge. A crowd of Londoners in broad-brimmed hats surround the structure known as the triple tree – the fifteen-foot-high triangular gallows constructed in 1571, from which anything up to twenty victims could be hanged at the same time. In this picture, six people are standing on a cart underneath one of the cross-beams, with nooses around their necks. A hangman adjusts the rope above one of them, as a clergyman tries to obtain a last confession of guilt from a prisoner. Underneath the hangman's cart, a dog wanders through the scene between the wheels, apparently oblivious to the events taking place. Several armed men stand close, to prevent any rescue attempt, while various members of the crowd are on horseback, the better to view the proceedings. In later years, wooden grandstands were built to oblige the crowds, but the impression given in this particular illustration is of a smaller and less dramatic event – which may be misleading, since a crowd of 20,000 are known to have attended the execution of fifteen criminals in 1651.

All around among the onlookers, hawkers sell food and drink, or broadsheets purporting to contain the last dying confessions of the criminals, as pickpockets work the crowd, attempting to steal people's money while their attention is distracted by the spectacle. If caught, they too would have had their day at Tyburn.

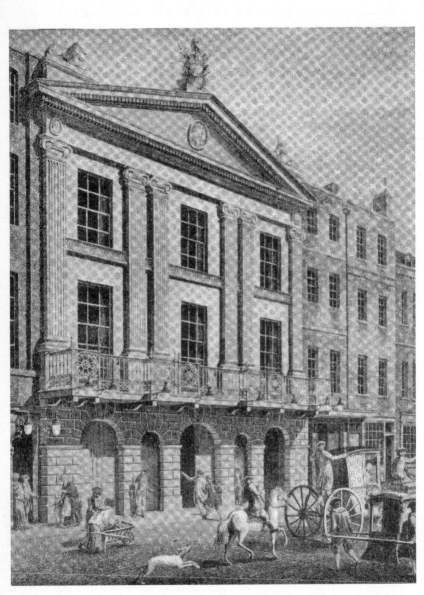

Drury Lane Theatre, Covent Garden

SEVEN

RIOTING AND DRUNKENNESS, CHAMBERING AND WANTONNESS
1716

To Londoners, hangings were a familiar sight. Since the end of the twelfth century, all manner of people had taken the one-way cart to Tyburn; it was one of the great spectacles of the city. Condemned men and women were brought from Newgate prison up through Holborn and along what later became Oxford Street to be 'turned off' by the public hangman, cheered or booed by the public according to their crimes. Some, like the self-styled 'Thief-Taker General', Jonathan Wild, were pelted with all manner of missiles throughout the length of their journey, while others met with a fair amount of sympathy, and might stop off at alehouses to drink their way to the gallows as if at their own wake.

For the most part, those who ended their days at Tyburn were drawn from the lower sections of society. Many had earned their place through simple crimes of theft, such as eleven-year-old James Lanman, sentenced to death in 1722 for stealing a silver snuff-box. Children seldom received capital sentences, however, and the majority of youngsters brought before the judges at the Old Bailey were either whipped, marked down for transportation to the colonies, or – as in the case of ten-year-old watch thief Owen Cheslyn in 1766 – acquitted purely on account of their age.

Among the general run of poverty-stricken housebreakers, petty thieves and coiners who troubled the Central Criminal Court, the sight of any prisoner who might be described by the hacks of Grub Street as a gentleman was enough to provoke a flurry of reporting in the news-sheets littering the coffee house tables of London. One such case which held their attention in January 1717, concerned an alcohol-fuelled late-night argument in Covent Garden between several men of quality, in which a man lost his life when confronted by some others who, the papers felt, were old enough, and rich enough, to have known better.

The question of young gentlemen roaming the town late at night picking violent quarrels with random strangers had excited much comment during the previous five years; an apparently new menace to society from groups of men calling themselves 'Mohocks' or 'Mohacks' (a corruption of the word 'Mohawk'). Richard Steele drew attention to them in the *Spectator* in 1712:

> . . . I could not forbear communicating to you some imperfect Informations of a Set of Men (if you will allow them a place in that Species of Being) who have lately erected themselves into a Nocturnal Fraternity, under the Title of the *Mohock Club*, a Name borrowed it seems from a sort of *Cannibals* in *India* . . . An outrageous Ambition of doing all possible hurt to their Fellow-Creatures, is the great Cement of their assembly, and the only Qualification required in the Members. In order to exert this Principle in its full Strength and Perfection, they take care to drink themselves to a pitch, that is, beyond the Possibility of attending to any Motions of Reason or Humanity; then make a general Sally, and attack all that are so unfortunate as to walk the Streets through which they patrole. Some are knock'd down, others stabb'd, others cut and carbonado'd.

A generation later, the distinguished letter-writer Lord Chesterfield claimed that the club itself had never existed, but the public at the time certainly seems to have believed in them, as this news item from the 12 March 1712 issue of the *British Mercury* shows:

> One Mr. M—— d of Greys Inn, cutting a Gentleman that justled him, over the face, was pursued by the Mob as a Mohock, and had been destroy'd by them, had not the Constable convey'd him away in a Coach before a Magistrate. Yesterday morning were taken six of the Mohocks, and bound over, having before they were taken, been well beaten by the Watch.

Late-night encounters with the constable and the roving members of his watch were the chief hazard faced by anyone drunk, incapable or up to no good. They were employed by the parish authorities, and as the writer Guy Miege stated in his book *The Present State of Great Britain and Ireland* (1707), 'the common Officers appointed to seize upon Malefactors, are those we call Constables'. Although London was still over a century away from having a properly constituted police force, these patrols served to monitor, and to some extent regulate, the life of the streets. As can be seen from the above newspaper report, they were not averse to handing out their own version of on-the-spot physical justice, and commentators of the time also allude to the watch's propensity for demanding bribes from those they waylaid. One of Grub Street's finest, the writer Ned Ward, recorded a nocturnal encounter with these roving officers in his satirical monthly journal, *The London Spy* (1698–1700). The Spy and his companion are stopped in the street by the Constable – 'another midnight King of Clubs . . . going his progress round his scanty dominions attended with his whole court of ravenous mobility' – who suspects their motives for walking the streets so late at night:

> He demanded of us, after an austere manner, who and what we were . . . [Spy replies] 'We are very sober, civil persons, who have been about our business and are going quietly to our habitations.' 'Civil and sober persons,' said he, 'how do I know that, Mr Prattlebox? You may be drunk for aught I know, and only feign yourselves sober before my presence to escape the penalty of the act.' My friend put his hand in his pocket and plucked out a shilling. 'Indeed Mr Constable,' says he, 'we tell you nothing but the naked truth. Here is something for your watch to drink. We know it is a late hour, but we hope you detain us no longer.'

Patrols such as this had responsibility for a few streets and would be based in a special building or lodge, about the size of a garden shed, usually sited in the middle of a main thoroughfare. For the Covent Garden area, one was located directly in front of the church of St Mary le Strand, just east of the entrance to Somerset House, near the southern end of Drury Lane. A similar watch house lay further north, in High Holborn, a little to the south of Bloomsbury Square, whose patrols covered the northern part of the lane. In a busy, all-night entertainment area like Covent Garden these watchmen would have had quite a job on their hands.

London in 1716, at the very start of the Georgian era, was a place where great elegance and wealth rubbed shoulders with the direst poverty. Wren's new St Paul's Cathedral now fully dominated the London skyline, although minor additional work was still being carried out. It was a spectacular monument to the spiritual life of the city, while Covent Garden catered more for the needs of the flesh, as the writer Tom Brown noted in the following description of various London locations from his satirical work *Amusements, Serious and Comical* (1707):

> Coffee and Watergruel to be had at the *Rainbow* and *Nando's* at Four. Hot Furmety [a milky wheat dish] at *Fleet-bridge* by Seven. Excellent Pease-potage and Tripe in *Baldwins-gardens* at Twelve. At night much Fornication all over *Covent-garden*, and five miles round it. A Constable and two Watchmen killed, or near being so, in *Westminster*, whether by a Lord or a Lord's Footman, the Planets don't determine.

Clashes between the watch patrols and inebriated late-night revellers were a common occurrence. Since almost everyone went about armed as a matter of course, it did not take much for these arguments to become dangerous or even fatal. On one of the very last days of 1716, three men of a somewhat Mohock persuasion encountered the watch at 11 pm in Drury Lane. They were drunk and aggressive, yet – judging from their dress and their manner – clearly not from the lower classes, and so the patrol moved away, seeking to avoid a confrontation. A short while later, the same three men quarrelled with a couple emerging from a nearby tavern. Swords were drawn, and within minutes, a man lay dead.

A restless, raucous area known for its brothels, alehouses, coffee houses, market and theatre, Covent Garden acted as a magnet for the many who sought amusement or some kind of oblivion.

Since London was by this time well on its way to becoming the busiest port in the world, it is not surprising that a great many seafaring men on shore leave found their way to Covent Garden. One such was Captain Robert Faulkner, who ventured up Drury Lane on the evening of 30 December 1716, apparently determined to sample a fair amount of what the district had to offer.

Drury Lane, in addition to its other attractions, was the site of one of London's only playhouses, the Theatre Royal. First constructed in 1663 to hold Thomas Killigrew's King's Company, it had burnt, like much else in the city, during the Great Fire three years later. Rebuilt for the then-considerable sum of £4,000 by Sir Christopher Wren, it prospered, although a few weeks prior to Captain Faulkner's ill-fated visit to the area, the theatre had witnessed drama of another kind, when a certain Mr Freeman, 'a mad gentleman' with an income of £2,000 a year, attempted to assassinate the Prince of Wales during a performance.

Exactly how Captain Faulkner had spent the earlier part of that day is unclear, except to say that heroic quantities of alcohol must have been involved. This, in itself, would hardly have been unusual in early eighteenth-century London; water was generally polluted and a menace to health, so most people would start their day with a 'morning draught' of beer or claret, as anything brewed, fermented or distilled was considered safer. Drinking continued steadily throughout the day, and so it is no surprise that a seafaring man on leave ashore at 11 pm might be three sheets to the wind.

There was no play performance listed in the newspapers for that Sunday night at the Theatre Royal. The previous evening His Majesty's Company of Comedians had staged a production of *The Maid's Tragedy* by Beaumont and Fletcher – 'at the Desire of several Ladies of Quality', as the advertisements billed it – but Captain Faulkner seems to have been looking for ladies of another kind.

Just a few doors away from the theatre in Drury Lane was one of the best-known brothels of the area, run by Mother Elizabeth Wisebourn.

Something of the combustible flavour of this district is captured in a news-sheet of 1719 called the *Original Weekly Journal*, which ends by highlighting the wealth of Sally Salisbury, one of the leading courtesans associated with Mother Wisebourn's establishment:

> Last Saturday Night a great Quarrel arose among the Gamesters at the Faro Chocolate House near Covent Garden, where Oaths and drawn Swords flew about like Thunder and Lightening [sic]: Three of the Gamesters were ran thro' the Body; and one had his Nose and Eyebrows cut off with a Sword, and now lyes ill of his Wounds at the Rose Tavern . . .
>
> We hear that Sally Salisbury, a noted Lady of Pleasure, is setting up a Chariot, and has hired a Coachman and two Footmen.

Newspaper reports of the events of that evening state that Faulkner was in the company of Mary Lewis, 'a Lewd Woman of the Town', and ran into trouble when outside a pub off Drury Lane. On their arrival at the Horseshoe Tavern, they had already been, in the language of the time, somewhat 'nazy' or 'cup-shot' from the quantity of alcohol consumed. This particular hostelry was in one of the many narrow alleys which led off the main street to right and left, by the name of Colson's Court. It ran between Drury Lane and Great Wild Street – now simply called Wild Street. Today, Colson's Court, along with almost all of the alleys flanking Drury Lane, has been lost to redevelopment, and a block of flats occupies the ground.

John Wilson, landlord of the Horseshoe, later testified to the inebriated state of Faulkner and Mary Lewis, and recalled his attempts to provide the captain with safe transport for the journey home by calling for a sedan chair and two chairmen. It would have been wise for Faulkner to have climbed unsteadily into such a conveyance and allowed himself to be ferried home at this point, but for some reason he instead attempted to proceed on foot, still in the company of Mary Lewis.

The watch would have regularly encountered groups of well-dressed, intoxicated young men, and were aware of how readily they might reach for their swords on the flimsiest of pretexts. Nine times out of ten it would have been easier to turn a blind eye to the drunken insults and move along. This seems to have been the course adopted by the patrol that first encountered Johnson Burdet (or Burdett), Thomas Winchurst and their friend Mr Moore in Drury Lane that night. Three members of the watch faced three argumentative 'gentlemen', as they later testified:

> Kelson, Shaw, and Calson, three Watchmen, depos'd, That on the 30th of December last, at about 11 a Clock at Night, they going to enquire for their Master, the Constable, met the Prisoners in Drury-Lane in Company with one Mr. Moor, not yet taken, who seem'd to be in a very quarrelsom Humour . . .

To hear them tell it, the officers tried hard not to provoke the three men, despite a series of taunts directed at them by Moore (later reported by one newspaper to be the Bishop of Ely's son). The exchange between the two parties went as follows:

Moore: 'What are you the Walking Watch?'

Watchman: 'We are the Watch.'

Moore: 'God damn you, You'll dance all Day long after a Gentleman to get a Pint of Drink of him.'

Watchman: 'We ask nothing of you, Sir.'

Moore: 'God damn you, if you did, I would sooner give you the Point of my Sword in your Guts than Three Halfpence, and I would kill a Dozen of you for that Many.'

Winchurst: 'So would I, if I had a Sword.'

As Ned Ward suggested in the *London Spy* extract quoted earlier, the nightly watch patrols had a reputation for demanding drinking money from anyone they met late at night. However, if the watchmen's account of this conversation is accurate, Moore at least seems to have been itching for a fight, and doing his best to provoke it. Oddly enough, for a gentleman in those days, Winchurst was unarmed. The patrol decided to take the prudent course and not rise to the challenge. Elsewhere in their testimony, they suggested that they had encountered these gentlemen on previous occasions, and were wary of them on that account:

[The watchmen] thinking them bent upon Mischief, (having taken Notice of some of them before for such Enterprizes) to avoid a Fray turned away from them, going down Colson's Court to seek for the Constable at the Horseshoe-Tavern.

As it happened, the patrol looked for the man in charge of their watch in the same pub where Captain Faulkner and Mary Lewis had spent the last couple of hours, but he was not there. Upon arrival, they chanced upon Faulkner just as he was leaving, 'and a Woman with him Arm in Arm'. The captain had somehow managed to pay his bill, but it is a measure of how drunk he must have been that the landlord was not content to see him going off with Lewis in this fashion, and came out of the building to ask the sedan chair porters why they had not taken Faulkner as arranged. The landlord's wife later testified that she had been worried the captain would be robbed by Lewis on his way home, and therefore urged her husband and the two chairmen to go out and see to his safety.

However, in the dimly lit passage known as Holford's or Holliford's Alley that ran past the back door of the tavern, trouble had already broken out. In their befuddled state, Faulkner and Lewis ran straight into the three drunken gentlemen whom the watch had encountered earlier, and the narrowness of the alley left little room for each group to pass. Burdet, Winchurst and Moore deliberately 'jostled the Deceas'd and the Woman against the Wall, and backwards and forwards, giving very bad Language'.

Faulkner was certainly outnumbered, but as a member of one of the armed services, he would have been no stranger to a fight, and was, of course, intoxicated just like his opponents. He protested vociferously, demanding to know what they meant by such behaviour, but if he thought that this would provoke an apology, he was mistaken. All he received by way of a reply was a torrent of abuse, and the cry, 'Damn ye ye Dog do you resent it?', after which Winchurst – having no weapon of his own – urged Burdet to use his sword. 'Damn ye, draw!', he shouted at his friend, who then complied, lunging several times at the captain with it before the latter had a chance to draw his own. In the confined, dark space of the alley, things had escalated from shoving and name-calling to the clashing of steel in a very short time. Neither side was in much condition to try anything sophisticated, but edged weapons in the hands of drunks are a dangerously unstable combination.

As the members of the watch had earlier suspected, the three young men were determined to pick a fight with anyone who might come along. The brief combat was a haphazard business, and in the confusion Mary Lewis was wounded in the thigh. Seconds later, Burdet backed away several yards and then 'advanc'd with a furious Push' upon the captain and ran him right through the heart, falling over on top of him as he did so. Faulkner collapsed immediately with a twelve-inch deep wound in his chest, having caught his assailant a minor blow on the chin with his own sword.

The tavern keeper, and the chairmen who accompanied him, had arrived on the scene just in time to see the murder. They rushed to pick up both Faulkner and Burdet from the floor of the alley and stood them up against its walls, probably not realising quite how serious the captain's injuries were. The situation became only too clear when the sailor slid down from this position to the ground and had to be carried back into the tavern, at which point his gaping wound was discovered. A surgeon was immediately sent for, but by the time he arrived, Faulkner had died.

As for the suspected Mohocks, the mysterious Mr Moore had somehow already made his escape, despite the bystanders, but Johnson Burdet and Thomas Winchurst were held at the scene by a combination of Wilson the landlord, the chairmen, and members of the watch who had been in the tavern.

It was a senseless murder, carried out in the heat of the moment when all parties were roaring drunk, the victim being completely unknown to his killers. They stood to gain absolutely nothing from such a crime, and were stupid enough to commit it in full view of a group of watchmen. The attack was even witnessed by residents whose windows overlooked the alley, who also later gave evidence. If there was indeed at that time something called the Mohock Club of wealthy, bored young men, stalking the city inflicting random violence on strangers for the sheer pleasure of it, these three were ideal candidates for membership.

By the reign of George I, London had a variety of daily and weekly newspapers reporting on local, national and international events. Although late-night skirmishes in town were hardly uncommon, the fact that the victim in this case was a distinguished captain of the Royal Navy, and his attackers gentlemen, made this particular crime especially newsworthy. Faulkner died in the very last hour of 30 December 1716, and all through January the case was reported from a variety of angles by the principal news-sheets – a form of detailed coverage that would not have been possible a century earlier. However, these published accounts owed much to rumour and speculation, with even basic facts such as the names of those involved often becoming scrambled and mistaken.

The *Evening Post*, reporting the arrests on 1 January 1717, for instance, managed to print the wrong names for two of the three people involved: 'Last Monday Mr. Burdet and Mr. Webster were committed to Newgate for killing Captain Godfrey, having quarrell'd about a Woman.'

A rival publication, the *Weekly Packet*, noted that a coroner's inquest had found the two suspects guilty, and at least managed to spell the victim's name correctly, but still changed the name Winchurst to Webster. When the trial date at the Old Bailey was set for 14 January, the press coverage already left no room for the idea that the prisoners could be innocent, as if the verdict of the coroner was sufficient in itself. The report in the *Evening Post* of 5 January was unambiguous about who might be responsible for the crime:

> Last Night Capt. Robert Faulkner (by Mistake said to be Capt. Godfrey) who was killed by Mr. Burdet and Mr. Winchurch, was bury'd at St. Bride's Church. The Coroner's Inquest have found 'em guilty of Murder.

In the issue of the *Daily Courant* published on the same day, these spare details are fleshed out with more of a concern for the life and career of the victim, who is portrayed as a hero of the Royal Navy, a long-time commander of a man-o'-war who had served his country faithfully. In addition, the social status of one of the prisoners is highlighted. This case was obviously more notable than the average bar-room squabble among the lower classes, whose perpetrators were regularly carted off to Tyburn with little fuss.

On the day of the Old Bailey trial, there were many witnesses lined up against Burdet and Winchurst. In addition to the watchmen (Kelson,

Shaw and Calson), were Captain Faulkner's evening companion Mary Lewis, the tavern landlord John Wilson and his wife, and the chairmen and sundry residents of Holford's Alley. Short of standing up on the stage of the Theatre Royal and committing murder there, the accused could hardly have arranged a more comprehensive set of witnesses to their crime. From the official account of the moment when Faulkner and his companion were jostled by the three men in the alley, it is evident that not only were the latter very much the worse for drink, but also that various sexual taunts were made in order to provoke the captain:

> They met the Prisoners in Holford's Alley leaning their Heads against the Wall as if they had been Vomiting, and that presently Mr. Winchurst turned to the Deceas'd and the Woman, as did also Mr. Bardet, and both of them jostled the Deceas'd and Woman very rudely, Winchurst making use of very bawdy obscene Language.

If this report is to be believed, the captain's initial response to such treatment was commendably mild. He apparently said 'Fie! Gentlemen, what do you mean? Why are you so uncivil? Why do you affront me and my Wife?' Faulkner may well have used the word 'wife' at this time in an effort to shame the three men into desisting, or else this was merely an invention of the prosecuting counsel, intending to make all of the captain's actions and words seem reasonable and polite in the face of hostility. Faulkner's protests had no effect, and seeing a sword raised against him, he drew his own weapon and 'endeavour'd to put himself in a Posture of Defence as well as his present unhappy Condition would permit', yet soon fell in the face of Burdet's vigorous attack.

The accused's explanations, such as they were, had little chance of success in the wake of the testimony offered by the various witnesses. Johnson Burdet stated simply that 'he thought the Deceased's Sword was drawn when he drew his; and that he had no Malice against the Deceased, having never seen him in his Life'. In other words, a drunken misunderstanding, with no harm intended. As for Thomas Winchurst – who had not dealt the fatal blow but was charged with urging Burdet to draw his sword in the first place – his plea was equally weak. He said that he had been unarmed, held no grudge against Faulkner, and that it was a minor misunderstanding which had unfortunately turned sour. He even tried to paint himself as a moderating influence and potential peacemaker. Mostly, though, he blamed the alcohol:

> Winchurst pleaded that they had been drinking, and very much in Drink as well as the Deceased; and that the Alley was narrow, and that so they might jostle one another by chance, and that they did not do so designedly: He likewise insisted upon it that he had neither Sword nor Stick, nor had any Malice against the Deceas'd, he being a Stranger to him. He pleaded likewise, that he would have prevented the Mischief, crying out, Sieze their Swords, Sieze their Swords, which the watch acknowledged; but at the same time depos'd, that he did not do so till he saw the Deceas'd kill'd. And was the principal Cause of his being kill'd, in being the first Beginner in the Fray, and the most violent Promoter of this Disaster.

Perhaps understandably, the judges Sir Thomas Bury, Chief Baron of the exchequer, and Sir John Pratt, Justice of the King's Bench, had little time for such arguments. In particular, they rejected the claim that the prisoners had no animosity towards the deceased, commenting that 'those Persons who went upon such Adventures, first to pick Quarrels with peaceable Persons they met, and unknown to them too, and afterwards kill them, had Malice against all Mankind'. To put it another way, these were the actions of Mohocks.

As was common in such cases, the main defence consisted of the summoning of various persons to speak on behalf of the accused and their good reputations, but apparently these witnesses offered little in the way of positive testimony, and the jury 'considering the Barbarity and Inhumanity of the Crime', found Burdet and Winchurst guilty on all counts.

The case and verdict were reported at length in the following day's papers. The *Evening Post* made it their lead item of crime news, and then gave a round-up of other cases, noting the mild sentence passed upon John Humfreys ('indicted for speaking Seditious Words against his Majesty, That King George is an Userper to the Throne, and for drinking the Pretender's Health, by the Name of James the Third'), and that Jonathan Wild – 'Head Theif [sic] Catcher in England, as he stiles himself' – had been taken into custody. Wild eventually became one of the most notorious criminals of the century, but for the moment, Burdet and Winchurst were the men in the spotlight. Less than a week after they were sentenced to death, the following advert appeared in the *Daily Courant*:

> This Day is Published, The whole Proceedings at the Sessions-House in the Old-Baily, with the Particular Account of the Tryal's of Mr. Burdett and Mr. Winchurch, who were found guilty of the *Wilful Murder* of Capt. Robert Faulkner. Printed for J. Philips, and sold by J. Roberts near the Oxford-Arms in Warwick-lane. Price 3.d.

In fact, this contained little that the average gentleman would not have been able to find through following the news-sheets. The real enthusiast would have had to wait for the slim publication issued just after the execution, that claimed to be a letter 'From Mr J Burdett . . . to some Attorneys Clerks of his Acquaintance', in which the penitent murderer sets out a series of reflections upon his life. The aim of the text was to demonstrate his newly awakened religious sensibilities, and – 'as wicked as I have all my life been, and as hardened as I now am' – implore his friends not to follow in his footsteps.

Burdet, or more likely a ghost-writer, sets the scene in his cell in Newgate, with his family weeping before him:

> My Mother and a Sister sit or Kneel continually before me, the very Pictures of Sorrow in Despair . . . The very Keeper turn'd away his head, the other day, for sadness, to see how we were together; which wounded me so deep, that had I any Instrument of Death by me, I could not surely have outlived that moment.

However, it was probably not the scenes of repentance, but the descriptions of a career of debauchery, that most helped to sell the booklet, providing an insight into the mind of a Mohock:

When I consider in what manner I have led my Life, for the seven or eight Years last past of it; and recollect how almost every Day and every Night thereof has been fill'd up with strange Impieties and Profanations of one kind or other, with execrable Oaths, unheard-of Blasphemies and Curses, with almost a perpetual Drunkenness, with Whoredoms and Adulteries never to be numbred up, and Villanies of every kind that can be thought upon . . . such a Life·as this has found the End it righteously deserv'd: it ended in the killing of a Man; a Stranger, inoffensive, unprovoking. I ran him through the Heart, thoughtless of Death, impenitent, and unprepared. I gave him not a Moment's time to recommend himself to God's Mercies.

Publications such as this – in which the criminal almost always experiences a religion-inspired change of character in the condemned cell – were enormously popular. For every person who attended the executions, there were perhaps another five or ten who wished to read about the case.

At the end of January, as the date of their execution drew near, Burdet and Winchurst were again singled out for special attention by the press, and when the time came, each made the journey to Tyburn in his own carriage, which was decked with mourning. The other condemned made do with two of the carts generally employed for this purpose. They were Thomas Whitehead (21), a burglar from Shropshire; Will Farendine (23), a housebreaker from Coventry; Mary Pierce, alias Cook (40), a shoplifter from Lancashire; and Will Ashdon, who had been sentenced to hang for stealing a looking-glass. While the procession was making its way westward from Newgate to Tyburn, there was a moment of drama when a last-minute reprieve came through for Ashdon. The *Weekly Journal* reported that he was 'taken out of the Cart betwixt St. Sepulchre's Church, and Snow-Hill Conduit, and carried back to Newgate'.

There was no reprieve for the two men found guilty of the murder of Captain Faulkner. In accordance with the custom, the prison chaplain, known as the Ordinary of Newgate, not only preached to the condemned men in their final days, but also noted down their stories, and published them at 8 am on the day following their execution. The Ordinary at this time was Paul Lorrain, former secretary to Samuel Pepys. He made a considerable amount of money publishing these semi-official texts, whose purpose was part religious instruction and part crime reportage. According to Lorrain's account, Burdet and Winchurst died calm and remorseful, and made a point of claiming publicly that their elusive friend Mr Moore had played no part in the killing. The Ordinary recorded their last words, and also inquired into their origins:

[Johnson Burdett said] he was 23 years of age, born at Sandon in Essex, of good and virtuous Parents, who gave him a liberal Education; and designing to bring him up to the Law, did at first put him to an Attorney here in London; but growing loose and unruly, he soon left him, and would not apply himself to any thing that was commendable, but follow'd ill Company, that made him a greater Deboshee than he was before, and with them spent Days (and Nights) without number, in rambling abroad, in Rioting and Drunkenness, in Chambering and Wantonness . . . [Thomas Winchurst said] he was 20 Years of age, born in Whitecross-street, in the Parish of St. Giles Cripplegate, London: That he liv'd two Years with an Attorney; but having no Inclination to the Study of the Law, or any thing relating to that Profession, he left him, and then betook himself to the same loose and vicious Courses as his Companion Mr. Burdett did.

Because of the proliferation of newspapers, and the popularity of rush-released publications such as the proceedings of the Old Bailey, and the Ordinary of Newgate's accounts, there is far more personal information available about the crimes and criminals of the early Georgian era than for a murder in Shakespeare's time. With this abundance, however, came contradictions. Although Lorrain's account was criticised at the time for attempting to make the life stories in his texts fit in with a ready-made concept of sin and repentance, at least these snippets were based upon face-to-face interviews in the condemned cell. While the Ordinary had written that Burdet was twenty-three and came from Sandon, readers of the description of the hanging published in the following day's *Weekly Journal or British Gazetteer* were confidently informed that he was twenty-two and 'the Son of a Clergyman in Leicestershire'.

All the accounts certainly agree that the two 'unhappy Gentlemen' met their end with dignity, and the press reception accorded them was extremely sympathetic. This is perhaps surprising, given the senseless brutality of the killing, and probably owed a lot to their social station. The *Weekly Journal*, for example, said that the pair 'behav'd themselves with a very Christian and Gentlemanlike Behaviour, and died with great Penitency for the Crime they were condemn'd', and wrote of 'this unhappy Murder, which by an untimely End cut them off in the prime of their Youth'. The likely market for newspapers and crime booklets would have included many young gentlemen from similar backgrounds to the accused, which may explain such favourable reporting, but it is not hard to imagine what the relatives of Captain Faulkner might have made of this.

For a snapshot of Burdet and Winchurst's final day on earth, here is their contemporary Tom Brown again, conjuring up a typical hanging day at Tyburn at the start of the eighteenth century:

> Mr. Ordinary visits his melancholy Flock at *Newgate* by Eight. Doleful Procession up *Holborn-hill* about Eleven. Men handsome and proper, that were never thought so before, which is some Comfort however. Arrive at the fatal Place at Twelve. Burnt Brandy, Women, and Sabbath-breaking repented of. Some few Penitential Drops fall under the Gallows. Sheriff's Men, Parson, Pick-pockets, Criminals, all very busy. The last concluding peremptory Psalm struck up. Show over by One.

In the end, as Steele had warned in the *Spectator* when first informing his readers about the Mohocks, the latter would have done well to 'take warning from the Club of Duelists; and be put in mind, that the common Fate of those Men of Honour was to be hang'd'.

William Hogarth, *The Idle Prentice Executed at Tyburn*, from the
1747 series *Industry and Idleness*

EIGHT

JOHN DAVIS, HIGHWAYMAN
1731

In 1731, Britain was four years into the reign of a new king, George II. The political scene was dominated by Robert Walpole, later spoken of as the nation's first prime minister; a man who, according to his biographer, Edward Pearce, 'ran bribery and corruption on an industrial scale'. Then, as now, life in the capital was a great deal easier if one had wealth, and the luxurious lifestyles of some were funded by robbing those below. This practice was perhaps best summed up by Dennis Bond, longstanding Member of Parliament for Poole – expelled from the house that year for colossal fraud involving the public purse – who uttered the phrase, 'Damn the poor, let us go into the City where we may get money.' Neither were the clergy immune to such tendencies, as the king himself pointed out, calling Bishop Hoadly 'a canting hypocritical knave to be crying "The kingdom of Christ is not of this world" at the same time that he receives £6,000 or £7,000 a year'. If this sounds modest, consider that in 1712 John Campbell, second duke of Argyll, purchased the country house and substantial estate of Kenwood, between Hampstead and Highgate, for just £4,000.

As for the poor themselves, life was generally a scrabble to earn a few pence to keep starvation at bay, and on the thirteen hanging days each year at Tyburn, many of the prisoners there were being executed for the petty theft of items worth only a pound or two. Yet the distance between the common thief and those in power was not so great, in terms of how they behaved and the methods they employed to gain their ends. Walpole himself had been satirically compared to that famous deceased son of Tyburn, the 'Thieftaker General' Jonathan Wild, in the theatrical success of the era, *The Beggar's Opera* (1727), and the link was not as far-fetched as it might seem. Wild was a favoured agent of the law before falling foul of it himself, while the future prime minster had been expelled from the Commons in 1712 and imprisoned in the Tower on a charge of 'a High Breach of Trust and notorious corruption'.

Sometimes it must have seemed as if half of London's 600,000 inhabitants were trying their hardest to rob the other half.

Standing in the dock at the Old Bailey on 14 July 1731, John Davis was facing the death penalty. This, in itself, was nothing out of the ordinary, since the statute books of the time contained numerous offences deemed to merit hanging, and Davis was in a high-risk profession, that of highwayman. His was a way of life that provoked fear and fascination in almost equal measure among eighteenth-century English society. Numerous pamphlets were published that told the stories of highwaymen's robberies or their last words on the scaffold, and to pay a last visit to notorious men of the road in the condemned cells at Newgate was a popular pastime among the gentry. After execution, the tattered remains of these felons could be seen on any of the approach roads to London, picked clean by the birds and swinging in the wind as a warning to any who might imitate their crimes.

John Davis would eventually have his brief hour of posthumous glory in the exploitative literature of the day – meriting a mention in volume two of the anonymous best-seller *The Tyburn Chronicle or Villainy Displayed in all its Branches*, and also in James Guthrie's rush-released pamphlet *The Ordinary of Newgate – His Account of the Behaviour, Confessions and Dying Words of the Malefactors Who Were Executed at Tyburn on Monday the 26th of this Instant, July 1731*. A short life and a public death: these were the usual prospects of the average highwayman.

Justice was handed out incredibly swiftly at the Old Bailey in the eighteenth century, and the July sessions which took place from Wednesday 14 to Saturday 17 were much like any other. Whereas today a murder trial might last weeks or even months, the court records show that on these four days evidence was heard and sentence passed on a remarkable fifty-nine cases brought before the court, many of them capital offences. With no organised police, no forensics and only the

word of a few citizens to consider, the magistrates presided over a production line of justice, weighing each life in the balance in a matter of hours
or even minutes.

The prisoners who appeared in the dock during that session – brought
up singly from the filthy gaols which were so disease-ridden that any stay
of more than a week or so was apt to finish off both guilty and innocent
alike – stood for a few brief minutes while their sins were paraded and
their fate decided: William Nebury (bigamy), Jane Vaughan (shoplifting),
Antonio Key (pick-pocketing), Hugh Cambell (animal theft), Martha
Busby (infanticide) – the faces came and went. In the main, these were
not the glamorous sorts of crime that captured the popular imagination:
after all, this was a city in which a significant slice of the population relied
upon crime purely in order to survive.

While in theory all these defendants faced the threat of hanging, in
practice it was usual for most sentences, including murder, to be down-
graded to either transportation, or being 'burnt in hand' – branding on
the thumb by the official executioner with the letter 'T' for theft, 'F' for
felon or 'M' for murder. Of those sentenced that day, three were ordered
to be burnt in hand, thirty-two to be transported, and only eight to be
hanged. Antonio Key, Jane Vaughan and Hugh Cambell were shipped off
to a harsh life working alongside slaves in His Majesty's colonies; William
Nebury was burnt in hand, presumably with the letter 'F'; Martha Busby
was one of the few acquitted that day, for lack of evidence. Out of the
eight destined for Tyburn, seven were highwaymen.

Islington was John Davis's home district, and his hunting ground as a
highwayman. North from Clerkenwell, at the very edge of the city, fields,
orchards and farms stretched out on either side of one of the northern
routes out of London. This isolated thoroughfare later evolved into what
is now Upper Street, but in those days it was merely a stretch of toll road
through undeveloped country which went by the name of the Islington
Road. With the Skin Market and then the Mad House on the right (the
area today around Northampton Square, immediately south of the Angel)
and the New River Head waterworks on the left (close to where Sadler's

Wells Theatre now stands), the route led to the turnpike gate marking the southern end of the Islington Road, after which there was little but open ground – ideal territory for anyone lying in wait for late-night wayfarers on the northern approaches. Although the popular image of a highwayman might be of someone on horseback far out in the countryside, many worked on the fringes of the city itself, where trees, barns or hedges provided plentiful shelter.

When the law finally caught up with Davis, he was charged with a number of crimes, which were listed in the trial transcript as follows: 'Theft with violence: highway robbery, killing: murder, theft with violence: highway robbery, theft: simple grand larceny'. The similar nature of the indictments matches the repetitive pattern of his robberies.

The first of the charges levelled against him that day was this:

> John Davis, of St. Mary Islington, was indicted for assaulting William Walker Esq; in a Field and open Place near the King's Highway, putting him in Fear, and taking from him a Coat, Waistcoat, a Pair of Breeches, Hat, Wig, Sword, and Nine-pence Half-penny in Money, the 10th of July, in the Year 1730.

Davis and an unidentified companion had attacked Walker at 10 pm as he was making his way 'between Islington and Oldstreet Church, in Company with one Edwards, a Painter'. This was the very border of the city, where the land immediately north of St Luke's Church and Old Street Square was occupied by market gardens and orchards. The semi-rural nature of the district was echoed in the place names along the southern side of Old Street itself: Tripe Yard, Goat Alley and even Farm Yard.

Walker and Edwards were attacked on a simple road through the open fields, before they had reached the first buildings around Old Street, and in the confusion of the scuffle, Edwards managed to escape. Drawing his own sword, Walker succeeded in running through Davis's accomplice, but was then brought down by blows from some implement 'so that he lay 3 Months at Islington before he recovered of his Wounds and Bruises'. Once injured, Walker submitted, declaring that he had money hidden in his shoes, and was then relieved of most of his clothing and possessions. Given that he had fought back courageously, he was lucky not to have been murdered outright by the pair, but it may be that they believed him to be already mortally wounded.

William Walker and his companion were running a serious risk in crossing dark fields on foot late at night. This was an era when coaches would gather at inns on the outskirts of London and wait until there were enough of them to pass together in a group across Blackheath, the better to protect themselves from assault. Similarly, the dance halls and watering holes of the Northern Heights in the neighbourhood of Hampstead made a point of advertising not only their various entertainments but also the fact that they could provide an escort of several stout and heavily armed men to accompany patrons safely home down Highgate Hill. However, Walker might have been undaunted by walking abroad in such locations because he himself was perhaps more accustomed to being the hunter than the victim in these circumstances. Indeed, the confrontation between him and Davis appears to have been a case of one highwayman being held up by another, and when Walker eventually came forward to identify Davis as a robber, the latter swiftly returned the compliment. On Davis's evidence, Walker himself was brought to trial as one of the defendants in another case heard that day, accused of theft with violence and highway robbery:

> William Walker, of Pancras, was indicted, for that he with one Morgan Jones, not yet taken, did assault Thomas Lane on the Highway, putting him in fear, and taking from him a Watch, value 3 l. a Ring, value 10 s. a Coat with Plate Buttons, value 3 l. and divers other Things, the 24th of March, in the Year 1730.

In the end, he was cleared for lack of a positive identification, since Thomas Lane could not swear that this had been the man who had assaulted him in the dark that night. As can be seen from the charges, the coat that was taken was held to be of equal value to the victim's ring. In an era when servants earned three or four pounds a year, their masters might spend a pound or more just on a pair of shoe buckles, and at the lower end of the market, the windows of the shops along the Strand were full of second-hand items such as vests, stays, handkerchiefs, buttons or gloves – everything wearable could command a price. While, in our age, a street robber might steal a mobile phone or a laptop, in the 1730s they might take the clothes from your back, your wig and your shoes. Hence, the many stories of highwaymen leaving their victims not only bereft of jewellery and purses, but also stripped and shivering by the side of the road.

Although William Walker was found not guilty in the case against him, the jury that day were more than convinced that John Davis had been the man who had assaulted and robbed him in Islington in 1730, and Davis was duly sentenced to death for this crime. Immediately afterwards, however, Davis was tried in a separate case on the more serious charge of murder:

> . . . for assaulting Thomas Tickford, and giving him one mortal Wound with a Pistol in the Head, of the Length of half an Inch, and the Depth of 3 Inches, the 17th of July, in the Year 1730.

This indictment was linked to the next, for the violent robbery of the victim's brother during the same incident:

> . . . for assaulting Henry Tickford on the High-way, at the same time, and taking from him a Handkerchief, Hat, Hat-band and Gloves, and 19 d. in Money.

While Davis's previous robbery had been committed virtually on his own doorstep in Islington, he had then ventured further afield. On this particular July evening in 1730, he travelled west through the undeveloped countryside, past the conduits and the waterworks, and an isolated cluster of buildings and cultivated fields known as Black Mary's Hole (a hundred yards or so to the east of what is now King's Cross Station). Moving on through the virtually featureless, darkened landscape, passing the tiny settlement of Pancras and some odd man-made fish ponds in the district that later became Euston, he would have arrived at a lonely stretch of open road known as Fig Lane. Here, he encountered the Tickford brothers.

Fig Lane ran west to east from a country inn called the Lord Southampton's Arms across to the hamlet of Pancras, and there were no buildings whatever along its entire length. At the western end, it joined the main route into London from Highgate, roughly near the site of what is now Warren Street tube station. Travellers approaching London on this road often broke their journey or changed horses at the well-known coaching inn Old Mother Red Cap's (now the World's End pub, opposite Camden Town tube), and anyone planning to continue heading south on this route would have been preparing their money ready to pay the turn-pike tolls at Tottenham Court.

Thomas and Henry Tickford were travelling south down the Highgate

Road, returning to the city from Hendon, having attended the funeral of another of their brothers. At the junction by the Lord Southampton's Arms, they turned east off the main thoroughfare into Fig Lane, perhaps in order to avoid the tolls of the Tottenham Court Road, and at this lonely spot were waylaid by John Davis and an unnamed accomplice. The attack was made late at night, and the victims would have been well advised to have made the journey either in a larger group or at least heavily armed. Yet it may be that no other people were available to make up the numbers, and anyway, a scared traveller with a weapon was probably no match for an habitual criminal with his finger on the trigger.

The hold-up itself was brutally simple: Davis hid behind a post; his partner lay concealed in a ditch. According to the transcript, Davis showed himself and his loaded pistol, before uttering the classic phrase 'stand and deliver'. Thomas Tickford was then shot full in the face by both assailants, and although it was obvious that this would prove a mortal wound, the unfortunate man survived for an agonising thirty-three hours. It would be logical to assume that the robbers would have had no scruples in finishing off their other victim, yet, incredibly, Henry managed to convince Davis to show him mercy and later told the court that

> . . . the Prisoner took his Wig, and look'd upon it by Moon-light, that one of them was for killing him too, that he begg'd hard for his Life, and said, it was very hard that one Brother had been killed in coming from another Brother's Funeral, and that the Third must be killed too; that at length the Prisoner said, no, leave him alive to bury the old Rogue his Brother.

Perhaps fearful that there might be other members of the funeral party following close behind, the two robbers made their escape down the empty road, very likely eastwards in the direction of Islington. Henry Tickford managed to summon assistance, either from another traveller or from the nearby inn, to carry off the still-living Thomas, since one Mary Tickford later gave evidence at the trial 'that the Deceas'd was brought Home at about Two o'Clock in the Morning in a miserable Condition, wounded in the Forehead and Cheek'. The magistrates at the Old Bailey also heard the testimony of a surgeon, Mark Hawkins, who told the court 'that he was call'd to Thomas Tickford at Two o'Clock in the Morning, and found that his Wounds were Mortal; and afterwards upon opening his Head, found that one Bullet had gone quite through the Cheek, and the other was lodged in one of the Cotes of the Brain'.

Having escaped into the night, John Davis might well have avoided being tried for the crime if he had then called a halt to his illegal activities for a while, but his criminal habits were ingrained. Just as, in a later century, Al Capone was convicted for income tax evasion rather than his numerous other offences during his bloody rule in Chicago, the crime that led to the downfall of John Davis was equally pathetic and mundane, the theft of some beer. At a time when few people would trust the water in London, everyone – adults and children alike – habitually drank alcohol to quench their thirst. Much of this was very potent, but for children, or any who did not wish to become too intoxicated, there had for hundreds of years existed a weaker brew known as small beer. Davis the murderer and highwayman was finally apprehended on 1 June 1731, for the comparatively trivial crime of 'stealing a Cask of Small Beer, value 4 s. 6 d. the Property of John Brown', as the *Daily Courant* reported, 'and likewise, on his own Confession, for being concerned in several Robberies on the Highway'.

Once in prison and awaiting trial, Davis was available for inspection by any of the numerous individuals who, having been robbed or assaulted, made a habit of searching the lock-ups of London in hope of identifying the culprit. The callous violence shown by Davis during the Fig Lane robbery suggests that he had few qualms about taking a life, yet if he had been more ruthless in finishing off his victims, there would have been no one still around to identify him, and the case would probably have failed for lack of supporting testimony. However, Davis seems to have largely convicted himself out of his own mouth when he was in custody, confessing to his part in the highway robberies but denying murder. Quite what he hoped to gain by this is hard to say, since any of these charges were enough to hang him, but he might have hoped for a more lenient sentence in the case of a robbery conviction.

On the day of his brief trial, there never seemed much likelihood of John Davis avoiding the noose. Evidence was heard from a pair of witnesses who both seem to have been acquaintances of the accused, putting him squarely at the scene of the killing. Sarah Carter testified that Davis had admitted in front of her that he had been involved in the Tickford hold-up but had not been the one to pull the trigger. Jonathan Broadhurst also 'had heard the Prisoner own that he was concern'd in this Robbery, and had the Prosecutor's Hat, Gloves, Handkerchief, and Money'.

This latter testimony, combined with the prisoner's own prior admissions, effectively sealed his fate. The court duly found Davis guilty of the robbery and murder of Thomas Tickford, and pronounced a second death sentence. In the more trivial matter of the stolen cask of small beer, it was not felt necessary to proceed, owing to the previous two guilty verdicts.

Newspapers published the following day provide a snapshot of life in the capital at that time, in which the sentence passed on John Davis was just one more everyday occurrence:

> Yesterday at the Sessions at the Old Baily, the three following Persons were Capitally convicted, viz.
>
> John Davis, for two Robberies on the Highway, and a Murder.
>
> John Drinkwater and Bernard Fink, for a Robbery of the Highway.
>
> The Gentleman who had the Misfortune to kill the Boy at a Billiard Table, by a Blow on the Head, was try'd for the same, and found guilty of *Manslaughter*.

In the case of the last news item, the paper seems to have been somewhat biased in favour of the defendant – perhaps on account of his higher social status – and so did not identify him by name. This was, in fact, a certain Captain Piggott, who had beaten a young man to death at the Castle Coffee House, yet escaped with the relatively mild punishment of being burnt in the hand. To modern sensibilities, branding carries an air of more archaic forms of justice, and the newspapers that week also reported a case heard at a sessions house near the Barbican which harked back even more strongly to the days of seventeenth-century witchcraft trials:

> Last Wednesday a woman was try'd before the Bench of Justices at Hicks's-Hall, upon an Indictment of defrauding one Mrs. Newton, of 12 l. 13 s. on Pretence of being a cunning Woman, or Fortune-teller, and as such, of being capable to bring home safe her Son from the East-Indies in a Whirlwind; and also of procuring three Men to fall in Love with the said Mrs. Newton. After a long Hearing of the Evidence the Defendant was acquitted.

This was the decade that saw the birth of key figures who later drove the Industrial Revolution – such as mechanised spinning pioneer Richard Arkwright (b. 1733) and steam engine developer James Watt (b. 1736) – and yet the suggestion that an old-style 'cunning woman' could employ magic to fly someone home from abroad by means of a whirlwind was deemed credible enough to bring a case in front of London magistrates. Times were changing, but old beliefs died hard.

John Davis met the traditional fate of the highwayman – a death sentence handed down at the Old Bailey, followed by slow strangulation on the gallows in front of a jeering crowd. The date was set for Monday, 26 July, a fortnight after his conviction. In a city where the time-honoured business of public execution was still one of the great popular spectacles, his end would have certainly been an event, but it was one among many.

After all, death, in Hogarth's London, was ever-present and easy to come by: most children did not live to reach adulthood; measles or smallpox could carry off rich and poor alike at a moment's notice; and few people who entered what hospitals there were ever emerged alive, so riddled were those establishments with disease. On balance, few among the poor probably expected to survive much beyond their twenties, and thus the criminal life with its promise of short-term gain had an undoubted allure, despite the shadow of Tyburn.

Although the court case had revealed a certain amount about Davis's activities during the robberies that led to his downfall, it was left to the prison chaplain, James Guthrie, Ordinary of Newgate, to extract the fuller story of the criminal's background and opinions.

The advert for Guthrie's pamphlet about John Davis appeared in the *London Evening Post*, just below an appeal by one Fletcher Gyles, bookseller, for the return of a twenty-pound banknote he had dropped ('of no Use to any but the Owner, Payment being stopt at the Bank') – considerably more money than Davis netted in the crimes for which he was hanged:

> To-Morrow at Noon (and not sooner) will be publish'd THE ORDINARY of NEWGATE'S ACCOUNT of the Behaviour and last dying Words of the several following Malefactors (viz. Thomas Granger for robbing his

Master, Col. Huffam, of 38 Guineas; John Davis for the Highway and for Murther; John Drinkwater, Bernard Fink, William Yates, John Armstrong, Nathaniel Lamprey, and Thomas Clarkson, for several Street and Highway Robberies) executed yesterday at Tyburn.

Anyone who paid three pence for this publication would have learned that Davis had been twenty-nine years old, was born in Portsmouth, and came to London with his parents as a child. His father having died, Davis showed early signs of trouble; 'a cross, perverse Boy, disobedient to his Mother, would not keep the School, and knew but little of Religion'. Apprenticed to a mason, he was said to have been too lazy to become a master craftsman, although he still made enough money sawing up stones for his employer in order to survive, and also to marry. Davis and his wife had three children, but soon, growing bored with masonry, he took up brewing instead, and acquired the skills necessary to make the beverage known as small beer.

At this point, his life story could easily have become the unremarkable tale of one who learns a trade and makes a tolerable living, and yet, according to the Ordinary's account, Davis threw his chance away:

> In this Way of Business he succeeded better, and made 50 l. a Year, and maintain'd his Family very well, but he lov'd not close Application to any Business, but getting into idle Company, he one Night (in a drunken Fit) listed himself, in the second Regiment of Guards, but repenting of this Action, when he came to himself, he absented from the Regiment, would not wear the Livery, and never learn'd the Exercise, and being liable to be taken up for a Deserter, he was obliged to hide, and when he went abroad to go in a constant Disguise.

An income of fifty pounds a year at that time would have been more than enough to live decently and support a family, so perhaps Davis had the idea of joining the army in order to escape a marriage he regretted, or was merely so drunk he had no idea what he was doing. Despite being listed as a deserter, he nevertheless made an attempt to resume his brewing activities. During this time he was fatally tempted into the business of robbery by a neighbour, identified as R——d J——s, who advised him to come along and buy some guns 'for raising of Contribution on the Highway':

> Accordingly they went into Holbourn, and purchas'd 2 Pistols and a half Blunderbuss, which was all the Arms he ever used on the High way.

John Davis's neighbour is portrayed as a bloodthirsty type, who also carried 'a sharp Knife, and sometimes a Dagger', and, perhaps predictably, Davis claimed it was actually his partner who had murdered Thomas Tickford. Whether this was the truth is impossible to say, but since they had long been engaged in this kind of business, the pair had indeed been lucky to have avoided trouble thus far. Nothing more is said of the mysterious R——d J——s, and so it can only be concluded that he successfully made himself scarce and so had escaped justice, at least on this occasion. As for Davis, he admitted to Guthrie that his crimes were 'very numerous, far above his Memory, he having had no Way of Living for some Years past, but by Thieving or Robbing in the Streets and Highway'.

All in all, the impression given in the pamphlet is of a chastened criminal who has seen the error of his ways – which is generally how the Ordinary's accounts liked to present these potted histories, but just how closely they match the realities of the situation is impossible to say. The John Davis that appears in this publication is very far from the hardened criminal his crimes might suggest; here, he is depicted as a remorseful man led astray by bad company, who has found comfort in religion during his imprisonment:

> He wept and groan'd much and seem'd very penitent. He behav'd well and acknowledg'd his Sentence most just. He declar'd his Faith in Christ, that he sincerely repented of all his Sins, and died in Peace with all Men.

John Davis had gone the way he probably always knew he would – 'kicking the clouds before heaven's door', as contemporary criminal slang termed it. His punishment, and the story of penitence and a life wasted recounted in the Ordinary's pamphlet, were intended to serve as a warning and a deterrent to those who might follow in his footsteps, yet on the very next day after the execution of John Davis a robber attempted to hold up a victim on a lonely stretch of road outside London. As the *Grub Street Journal* reported later that week, this time the victim fought back:

On tuesday Miss Worsley, Niece to the Lady Scawen, being out on Banstead Downs in an open Chaise, having a footman on horseback following, was attacked by one Highwayman, who shew'd his pistol after the usual greeting: the footman was disabled by the fright, but the young Lady struck at him with her whip several times, and company coming up, he thought fit to march off without any booty.

Clearly the spectacle of Tyburn and moral lessons such as those set out in James Guthrie's pamphlet had little effect upon this would-be thief. Despite the heavy penalties, throughout the eighteenth century there would always be a stream of candidates for the gallows making the journey along Oxford Street to the triple tree. Some had hopes of escape, even at the very last moment. Two years after the events described in this chapter, a prisoner managed to break free at the execution place itself, while the hangman was engaged in placing a rope around the neck of another of the condemned men. As the *Newgate Calendar* records, he 'jumped out of the cart, made his way through the astonished spectators, and ran over two fields; but, being knocked down by a countryman, he was brought back, tied up and hanged'. He, too, had apparently been involved in 'various daring robberies'.

His name? John Davis.

The green fields of Tyburn in 1750, showing one of the wooden grandstands from which spectators could view the hangings

NINE

MURDER AT TYBURN
1751

For centuries, England resisted the very idea of a police force. In the popular imagination, this was the sort of thing used by foreign despots to prop up their dubious regimes; against the spirit and letter of Magna Carta and the real or imagined ancient rights of the common people. There had long been constables and sheriffs, attempting to keep the peace on a local level, but when, in 1749, the magistrate Henry Fielding established the group later known as the Bow Street Runners, this was London's first organised police force. Admittedly, they did not wear uniforms, were part-time, could hire themselves out privately and there were only eight of them, but at least it was a start.

Since the beginning of that year, Fielding had been the principal magistrate for London, yet he was also one of the most famous novelists in the country. He lived at 4 Bow Street, in a house that was his private residence and also functioned as Bow Street Magistrates' Court. The irony of his being appointed by the government to such a position would not have been lost on him, since in his earlier career as a writer of satirical plays he had so angered their principal target, prime minister Robert Walpole, that in 1737 a censorship law was passed, effectively ending Fielding's days as a dramatist. Seeing the way the wind was blowing, he began studying to become a lawyer, but experienced the criminal justice system from the other side when imprisoned for debt in 1740.

By 1751, however, Fielding was the successful and well-rewarded author of some of the greatest novels of the age, such as *Joseph Andrews* (1742) and *Tom Jones* (1749) – the latter proving so popular that it sold out its entire print run before publication day. Once established in Bow Street, Fielding was at the heart of London's coffee house culture, just around the corner from Davies's in Russell Street, where Boswell would first meet Dr Johnson. That meeting was twelve years in the future and Johnson himself still hard at work compiling his masterpiece, the *Dictionary*, for which in 1746 he had received the very substantial advance of £1,500. Fielding's initial payment for *Tom Jones* had been £600, but his recent celebrity had also brought his controversial early plays back into print, and his salary as magistrate gave him a further £550 annually, in an era when the average domestic servant was earning roughly £5 a year. He had lately combined his legal and literary interests by writing a non-fiction work examining the problem of crime in the capital, the second edition of which was announced as follows in the *General Advertiser* in 1751: 'This Day is Published . . . *An Enquiry into the Cause of the late Increase of Robbers, &c., With some Proposals for remedying this growing Evil.* Price bound 3s. Or sew'd in blue Paper 2s. 6d.'

To judge from comments in the press at that time, the city was thought by both journalists and politicians to be teeming with criminals, and Justice Fielding was not the only one advancing suggestions for dealing with the problem. The December 1750 edition of the *Gentlemen's Magazine* carried a lengthy essay from one F.L., entitled *Castration Proposed for Capital Offenders*. The writer argued that far from inspiring awe and preventing crime, the present system of hangings at Tyburn had little effect; 'Their frequency renders them familiar; and the mob seems no more affected with this solemn scene, than with a puppet shew.' Instead of serving as an awful warning, scenes at the gallows frequently had something of a holiday atmosphere, 'whilst the mob secretly rejoices at the intrepid conduct of their hero, with wishes, that they may imitate a conduct so glorious, if their villainies should qualify them to act the same part, in this kind of publick entertainment.' In short, hanging was too good for them and should therefore be replaced by something that might prove more terrifying than death:

> What yet remains to be try'd? I am serious in proposing castration for the men, whenever they commit a crime that by the present laws would entitle them to the gallows. Intemperate lust is the most frequent cause of such crimes, and what more adequate punishment?

Such ideas might indeed have appeared to some criminals like a fate worse than death, but the grim carnival at Tyburn continued very much as it always had. Each batch of malefactors fresh from Newgate was met by a cross-section of rich and poor alike jostling for position to see them on the triple tree, 'riding a horse foaled by an acorn', as the saying went.

The most famous pictorial evocation of the scenes in London on execution day comes to us from Fielding's friend, William Hogarth, entitled *The Idle 'Prentice Executed at Tyburn*, from his series *Industry and Idleness* (1747), in which the prisoner is almost swamped among the shifting mass of people.

Not everyone journeyed to the gallows ground in order to spectate. Some were relatives of those being hanged, come to claim the bodies. Others were vendors of food and drink, hawkers of printed broadsides purporting to contain the last dying speeches of prisoners, or pickpockets, preying on the crowd. It was crowded, noisy, and could also be dangerous. Some of the deaths at London's execution sites were not part of the scheduled entertainment: when the eighty-year-old Jacobite leader Lord Lovat was brought out in front of huge crowds to be beheaded on Tower Hill in 1747, a specially built grandstand collapsed, killing a fair number of spectators. Lovat, much amused, commented, 'The more mischief, the better the sport.'

London's population in 1751 is estimated at around 650,000; small by the standards of today, but rather a handful for a mere eight Bow Street Runners to supervise. There were still the evening watch patrols, mostly consisting of older men armed with stout wooden staffs, but for every malefactor apprehended and brought up in front of Justice Fielding, there were probably countless others who simply melted away into the night. With many of the population armed, violence could break out at a moment's notice, on the least excuse. They were also frequently drunk. This was the year that Fielding's friend Hogarth published his famous pair of etchings, *Beer Street* and *Gin Lane*, deploring the effects of the latter foreign-inspired beverage on the working classes, and favouring instead what was seen as the wholesome English beer that had sustained the nation for centuries.

In November 1751, a day or so after Guy Fawkes Night, the *London Daily Advertiser and Literary Gazette* carried the following news item:

> On Tuesday Evening a Tradesman by Golden-Square, seeing a Youth standing by his wooden Rails, and suspecting that he was going to

take them away, as it is thought for the Bonfire, he came behind him with his Gun, and shot him in the Back, and it is thought he cannot recover. The Youth is the Son of a reputable tradesman in that neighbourhood.

Mid-eighteenth century newspapers were full of reports of commonplace, unprovoked violence; of gentlemen and ladies held up by highwaymen in their carriages when crossing the fashionable squares of the newly built West End; and of tavern landlords and shopkeepers robbed or assaulted at sword point for small change or the clothes on their backs. The depressing list below of just one day's proceedings at Bow Street Magistrates' Court – from the 16 November issue of the *Whitehall Evening Post or London Intelligencer* – gives something of the flavour of the time, the offences ranging all the way from trivial to despicable:

> On Friday John Hare was committed to the Gatehouse by Henry Fielding, Esq; for assaulting Rebecca Matthews, a Child about eight Years of Age, and Daughter-in-Law, to the said John Hare, with an intent to commit a Rape.
>
> And Saturday John Bickerton was committed to the same Place by the same Gentleman, for stealing a Quantity of Hair-Cloth, the property of Sarah Kennill of the Parish of St. George the Martyr.
>
> The same Day Thomas Ingham was committed to the same Place by the same Gentleman, for violently assaulting one Mary Coleton, a Child about seven Years old, with an Intent to ravish her.
>
> Last Friday three Persons were committed to Bridewell, for selling undersized Flounders, contrary to Law.

This would have been a typical day for Henry Fielding, yet in the same week other papers heralded the imminent publication of his new novel:

> *Next Month will be published, price 12s.*
> In F O U R V O L U M E S
> **A M E L I A.**
> *By* H E N R Y F I E L D I N G, *Esq;*
> Printed for A. Millar, in the Strand

As it happened, between this notice and the publication day, Fielding became involved in a crime that occurred some distance away from the teeming heart of the city, out on the extreme western edge, just where the metropolis ended and the countryside began. This was a murder in a place much accustomed to death; at Tyburn, practically in the shadow of the fatal tree.

In November 1751 Richard Shears made the journey west to Tyburn not as a prisoner or spectator, but merely to make some money. A carman by trade, which is to say, the driver of a cart, he had thought to take his vehicle out to the execution site and charge a few coins from spectators who might wish to view the proceedings from a higher vantage point. His wife Hannah later testified:

> 'He went between five and six o'clock in the morning, on the 11th of November, with his cart to Tyburn; it was the last execution but one: he went to let his cart for people to get up upon to see the prisoners die.'

As Jean Rocque's 1746 map of London shows, Tyburn lay in a rural setting at that time; the gradual urban development of the West End having only reached a little past Grosvenor Square, after which came the grassland of 'Hide Park' and the circular reservoir of the Chelsea Water Works, bordered by Tyburn Lane (the present Park Lane). The gallows at Tyburn stood at a crossroads at the end of Oxford Street, roughly where Marble Arch is now situated. On Rocque's map the execution site is shown just to the west of a milestone and a turnpike gate, with Tyburn Lane coming up from the south, and the insignificant path that will later become the Edgware Road joining from the northwest. On the corner is a building called Tyburn House, while a few yards to the south of the gallows is a spot which is chillingly marked 'Where Soldiers are Shot'; which must have given members of the military pause for thought when taking part in the frequent parades and reviews held in the park.

Execution days were something like public holidays, and as the nineteenth-century historian Macaulay later wrote, 'of all sights, that in which the English most delighted was a hanging'. Yet some in the crowd were not there to cheer; their chief concern after sentence had been carried out was to secure the bodies for burial, and guard against their being taken off for dissection. In many cases, relatives would not have access to any means of transport and would therefore pay others to carry away the deceased. Hence there was another group of people present on hanging day: those willing to engage in the gruesome casual labour of loading up fresh corpses onto carts.

On 11 November 1751, Richard Shears fell victim to a simple circumstance: he had come to Tyburn with a cart, hoping to rent it to spectators, while a certain Michael Magennis and his friends were there to carry off bodies for money but had failed to arrive with their own transport. The combination proved fatal.

A brief report in the *London Daily Advertiser* recorded the fact that a death had occurred, which was now a matter for Justice Fielding, who also, as usual, had more trivial matters to consider:

> On Saturday last Michael Magennis was carried before Henry Fielding, Esq; for the Murder of Richard Sheers on Monday the 11th ult. Between Tyburn and Bayswatering, by giving him two mortal Wonds [sic] on the Head with a Hanger, and breaking his Breast.
>
> The same Day two Boys were committed to Clerkenwell Bridewell, by Henry Fielding, Esq; for stealing two Jack-Asses from Mr. Thomas Emby, of Deptford.

The 'hanger' mentioned here was a short sword, so named because it was designed to be hung from a belt. Bayswatering – today's Bayswater – lay a short distance further west. It was a natural spring, originally known as Bayard's Watering, which for centuries had served as a wayside stop for refreshing horses and was also the source of one of the conduits providing water for the city of London.

Where the above report gave only scant information, more details were available to readers of the *Whitehall Evening Post*, although the names of both the accused and the victim had suffered from the customary mistranscriptions:

> Last Saturday Michael Mackenzie was committed to the Gatehouse by Justice Fielding, being charged with the Murder of one James, Master of a Sand-Cart, on the last Execution-Day. The said James was at Tyburn, with a View of getting something from Persons standing in his Cart to see the Execution; but the Prisoner, with five or six more,

came up to the cart with two dead Bodies, and insisted upon his going with them, which he refusing, the Prisoner pulled out a Hanger, and gave the Deceased a violent Wound in his Head, and then made his Escape. The Deceased was carried to St. George's Hospital, but died a few Days after.

St George's Hospital, founded two decades earlier, lay directly to the south, by the turnpike at Hyde Park Corner. Its countryside location was felt to be much healthier for patients than many of the older establishments inside the city, but given that surgery was still in its early stages of development in this era, and little was known of basic hygiene procedures, Richard Shears probably had small chance of recovering from his wounds.

Justice Fielding, as the preliminary magistrate involved, ruled that there was a case to answer, and Magennis was sent to the Gatehouse prison, in the shadow of Westminster Abbey. This building dated back to 1370, and at various times had held Sir Walter Raleigh, Samuel Pepys and the poet Richard Lovelace, who wrote *To Althea, From Prison* here in 1642 ('Stone walls doe not a prison make / Nor iron bars a cage').

Christmas came and went, shortly before which Fielding's *Amelia* was published, on a day when the author and magistrate was otherwise occupied sending a tradesman to the Bridewell prison for 'swearing 390 blasphemous Oaths'. Michael Magennis remained in the Gatehouse, waiting for the next Old Bailey sessions, due in late January. He had not yet been convicted but was certainly on dangerous ground. Ten years later, Dr Johnson would call the Gatehouse 'a building so offensive, that, without any occasional reason, it ought to be pulled down, for it disgraces the present magnificence of the capital', although Magennis might also have sympathised with a more famous quote of the good Doctor, published later by Boswell: 'Depend upon it, Sir, when a man knows he is to be hanged in a fortnight, it concentrates his mind wonderfully.'

On 16 January 1752, the judge and jury assembled at the Old Bailey Sessions House: the Lord Mayor of London, Thomas Winterbottom, was presiding, assisted by Lord Chief Baron Parker, Sir Michael Foster, Sir Thomas Birch and Richard Adams, the Recorder. There were two juries – one for London and one for Middlesex – each consisting of twelve men, as women were not allowed. The Lord Mayor was in charge, but the case of the murder of Richard Shears was heard by Sir Michael Foster and considered by the Middlesex jury, because the crime had taken place just to the west of London itself. Foster was a well-respected sixty-three-year-old judge of the King's Bench, with a reputation for fair dealing and justice, who went on to serve under the key legal figure of the age, Lord Chief Justice Mansfield. As usual, the majority of the cases brought before the court during these sessions concerned relatively minor crimes, and the punishments reflected this: Anthony Tamplin and David Wright transported for stealing lead from a roof; Joseph Taylor given the same punishment for the theft of five iron hoops from a brewer; Sarah Booth, indicted for the theft of a pair of stays, but acquitted; Robert Green and Thomas Humphys, transported for the theft of ten gallons of rum; or Richard Titten, who had his eyes on a wider variety of items, transported for making off with a haul that included 'one copper chocolate pot, one copper tea kettle, one brass candlestick, one brass knocker, one brass tinderbox, one bible and one common prayer book'.

Although the justice system of eighteenth-century London has a reputation for hanging malefactors for the theft of the most trivial of items, the overwhelming majority – twenty-five prisoners – of those before the court at this particular session were transported. One man was sentenced to be jailed for a year, then pilloried, and afterwards transported, but his crime was perjury, not theft. Two people were whipped for minor offences, four others branded, and several who had been indicted for the more serious crime of highway robbery were acquitted. A murder case, therefore, was still something a little out of the common run.

At the trial of Michael Magennis, the first person called was the deceased's wife, Hannah. She testified that on execution day, 11 November, sometime between twelve and one, she received information that her husband had been injured:

> I heard he was wounded, and gone to Hyde-Park Infirmary: I went there, and found him all in blood: I saw him everyday: I did not see his wounds till after he was dead. On his dying bed, he said, it was a short thick Irish Milkman, that gave him his death wound, that he was wilfully murdered,

and that they ran away with his cart and horses, and that murder will never
be hid.'

His wife said little more, except that Shears had offered her no reason
why he had been attacked. Next, however, came a witness who had a great
deal to say, none of which was helpful to the accused. Michael Munday
stated that he had been a spectator at the hangings – 'I went to Tyburn that
day, to see the prisoners die' – and witnessed the conflict between Shears
and Magennis. The former, standing by his cart, had been approached by
a group of men including Magennis, who had then taken it from him and
attempted to drive it away. Shears struggled with two or three of them
briefly, attempting to regain control of the reins, whereupon one of the men
'threatened to knock his brains out, if he did not go about his business'.

At this, Shears seemed to have either given up or merely lost his grip
on the horses, and the men were able to drive away due west for a quarter
of a mile to Bayswater, where they stopped for a drink, presumably
intending to wait for the hanging crowds to disperse before returning to
collect the bodies which they had agreed to transport. All the while,
Richard Shears remained in the general area of Tyburn, having not given
up hope of reclaiming his cart. Exactly what part the witness Munday
might have played in all this is unclear. Having stated that his only purpose
in attending that day was to watch the hangings, in his testimony he then
gave an elaborate account of the movements of Magennis and his accomplices which suggests that he might have been part of their group. Munday
claimed to have seen the initial struggle at the execution site, then told
of the cart-thieves' actions at Bayswater and their return to Tyburn, where
they argued once more with Shears and dealt him what proved to be a
fatal blow, then collected two bodies, driving them all the way across to
Tower Hill and leaving them there. Presumably, this was a drop-off point
that had been agreed with the families of the deceased. Crucially, Munday
said that he witnessed the moment at which Magennis struck Shears:

> '[the cart thieves] took his horses by the head, and drove them where they
> pleased: they drove them down to Bay's-Water, a place beyond Tyburn, about
> a quarter of a mile, where they staid and drank, and from thence back by
> Tyburn quite to Tower Hill, with two of the dead bodies in the cart, which
> they left on the Hill; I saw them use the horses very bad; the prisoner had
> a hanger under his coat; I saw him pull it out when the deceased came to

him, and cut him over the head. It was after they returned from Bay's Water, about ten yards on this side Tyburn; he went bare headed after his cart, with the blood running down his ears; I saw him following his cart almost by Nibs's Pound, that is on this side the Turnpike; he went to a surgeon to be dressed, and I saw him no more.'

For a supposed casual bystander, Munday was extremely lucky to have been a witness to all that transpired, not least because the crowds on hanging days could be as large as those at modern football matches (some 200,000 are said to have been at Tyburn for the execution of Jack Sheppard in 1714). In fact, Munday finally acknowledged under cross-examination that he knew the accused and 'had seen him many times before'. His surname suggests that he might have been Irish, like Magennis. As for Munday's vantage point – from which he had allegedly observed the accused producing a weapon and attacking Shears – he must have had good eyes, as he was standing some considerable distance away across the crowd:

Q: 'Who put the bodies into that cart?'
Munday: 'The prisoner and two or three more did, against Shears's consent.'
Q: 'How near was you when you saw the blow?'
Munday: 'I was standing about a hundred yards off under the wall.'
Q: 'Were there many people between you and them?'
Munday: 'There were not many; and I was upon a bank, I had a full
command of the mob, there was a scuffle with other people with sticks,
before the hanger was drawn.'

The prosecutor himself seemed not to have been certain of this witness and his connection to the accused, questioning him as to why he had later visited the Gatehouse prison, and about reports that he had spoken to Magennis – Did not you tell him there, that he was not concerned in this murder, but it was two other people?' – but Munday denied having said this. All things considered, he may well have been a hostile witness, attempting to direct the blame onto Magennis in order to shield someone else of his acquaintance. Certainly, London's courts had long seen groups of people touting for business outside, willing to swear to almost anything in return for money. There was also the question of why, if this crime was committed in such a public way, those nearby had not, in the custom of the time, banded together and apprehended Magennis. When this point was put to him, Munday replied that 'there was such a mob, no body would trouble themselves with him; there were near a quarter of a hundred chairmen and milkmen, seemed to be all concerned in taking away the cart horses, with the bodies'.

In the confused scramble to load up the corpses of the freshly executed – during which the friends and relatives of the hanged were trying to see that none of the bodies was taken away by unscrupulous persons and sold to doctors for dissection – it might be that few had time to worry about a fight apparently breaking out over the ownership of a cart. Of course, if you were looking to commit a murder, this was a very public place in which to do it, but the newspaper reports of the time were full of stories of people being assaulted and sometimes killed in crowded city thoroughfares.

Following on from the damning testimony of Michael Munday, the court then heard from an eyewitness who claimed to have seen many of the same events, but who was perhaps even more closely involved. William Latimore, who had gone to watch the hangings at Tyburn, later chanced upon Magennis at Tower Hill, prior to the local constables being summoned. Like Munday, Latimore seemed to have been present in different parts of London on that day, able to witness key parts of the story unfolding. His testimony, which appears to have been condensed or summarised by the court reporter, reads almost like confused jottings from a policeman's notebook:

'I saw the prisoner along with the deceased's cart and horses that day, driving them as far as Tower-hill; but I did not see the first beginning of it, I was at the execution and saw the first body put into the cart; there were several concerned in it; I did not follow the cart to Bay's-water; I saw the prisoner with the rest coming back from thence; I saw the cart come back thro' the Turnpike and the deceased came after it with blood running down half inch thick; I saw the prisoner with the rest of the mob, at Tower-hill; I followed them, they put the bodies down on Tower-hill, and the constables came and took hold of the prisoner, also another, named Kit. Williams, they were let to go away again, the prisoner was taken up, which was a fortnight ago, and had before justice Fielding, he denied that he was at Tyburn that day; but when Kitt Williams came there, the prisoner owned he was at Tyburn, but said he had nothing but a stick in his hand.'

Although Latimore firmly placed Magennis among the group that took away the cart from Richard Shears and later left the bodies of several executed prisoners on Tower Hill, there was nothing here to connect the accused with the striking of the fatal blow. What most counted against Magennis was his initial denial that he was ever at Tyburn that day – although he later admitted it – but this was perhaps understandable in a man arrested for a capital crime, whether guilty or innocent. After Latimore's original testimony, an interesting point was brought out in cross-examination, when he admitted that he had been the one who captured the accused at Tower Hill: 'He was in the street,' said Latimore, 'I met him by accident.'

So this witness was not merely an observer; he was actually the person who first seized hold of Magennis until constables could be summoned, making the kind of citizen's arrest that was rather common in those days. This suggests that he perhaps saw more of the crime than his earlier testimony implied, since he clearly felt that Magennis had been involved in the murder. However, as Latimore's cross-examination ended there, the exact motivations behind his own actions that day are much harder to determine.

The next witness, Edward Hilton, had no doubts whatever. He claimed to have been just near the cart when the violence began, and identified Magennis as the killer. To hear Hilton tell it, Shears responded with patience and calm words when the group initially attempted to steal his cart, having apparently said to them, 'Gentlemen I hope you will be so good, as not to throw these dead bodies up into my cart; for I am obliged to go home about some business.'

When the accused and his companions returned from drinking in Bayswater and proceeded to load up the bodies, Hilton was still on the scene, and described how the argument spiralled from a quarrel into murder, with Magennis apparently right at the centre of things:

'. . . the prisoner was riding on the top of the copses [sic]; he had a hanger under his cloaths, he drew it out, he swore by G——d, and other bitter oaths, if the deceased did not get away, and let go his horses, he would jump off, and cut him down; then he jump'd off and struck him on the right side of the head, close to his ear; after which the cart went forwards.'

In cross-examination, it then became clear that this witness too had known Magennis before the day in question – 'I have seen him carrying milk about the streets several times' – and had followed the cart across town to Tower Hill, in time to see the prisoner arrested by constables.

At this point it seems as if Michael Magennis was the best-known milkman in town, but one witness who had apparently never met him before was the man who actually drove the stolen cart to Tower Hill, Christopher Williams, known as Kit. He described himself as a passer-by, critical of the attempts of the gang to handle the horses, who found himself caught up in events and then fell foul of the law for depositing bodies on Tower Hill. Williams explained to the court that he had grabbed hold of the reins at Tyburn from these strangers, saying 'I can drive those horses better than you can.' By his account, the group of which Magennis was a part was even larger than others had said – 'forty or fifty men' – who then forced him to drive across town under their directions: 'They made me drive up one street and down another, just where they pleased; I was charged upon Tower-hill for bringing the dead bodies.'

Williams might have been driving the cart, yet provided no evidence that ought to have convicted Magennis. By his own account, he did not see the blow being struck, although he did speak sympathetically to Shears after it had happened, shortly before taking over the reins: 'I saw the man all bloody; I said go and get your head dressed, I'll drive your horses as well as I can.'

George Hale, the surgeon at St George's Hospital who treated Shears at around 2 pm that day, gave evidence as to the extent of the victim's head wounds and expressed the opinion that they had been caused by sticks. This tied in with the testimony of a defence witness, John Dawling, that the violence inflicted upon Shears was delivered 'either by a stick or a whip, I am sure it was no hanger, I saw several blows given'. Dawling went further, and stated that the one man among the group who was wearing a hanger had not used it: 'his name is Burk, I know him.'

As for the testimony of the prisoner himself, when charged with the crime, Michael Magennis uttered just a single sentence to the court: 'I know no more of it than the child in its mother's womb.'

There followed an impressive parade of character witnesses swearing to the previous good behaviour of the accused: his servant, Mary

Callowham ('I never saw a hanger or cutlass, or any such weapon in his house in my life'); his landlord, Thomas Reed ('I have known the prisoner between five and six years, I never saw any thing amiss of him in my life'); his fellow trader Mary Palace ('I never heard he was quarrelsome in all my life, or to have such arms as he is accused with'); and four or five others all attesting to his honesty and good nature.

It was to no avail. The testimony of the earlier witnesses prevailed, and Magennis once again became a news item in the *London Evening Post*:

> On Saturday 20 Prisoners were tried, at the Old-Bailey, two whereof were capitally convicted, viz. Michael Magginnis for the Murder of Richard Shears, And Joseph Saunders for the Murder of a Man on Smallbury Green, about two Years ago. Nine were cast for Transportation, and nine acquitted.

Having served out his time before the trial in the Gatehouse, Michael Magennis was taken from the Old Bailey around the corner to Newgate, to await the next hanging day, which fell in March. As he sat cooped up in one of the capital's most disease-ridden buildings, life outside went on much as it ever had. The *Daily Advertiser* for 23 January kindly informed its readers that at Horse Shoe Alley in Moorfields, there would be cockfighting; a special match at which 'The Mutton-Lane Shakebag fights the Winner of the last Welch Main For Four Guineas.' Alternatively, anyone reading this newspaper at one of the coffee houses or taverns in Covent Garden might have decided instead to walk westwards along the Strand, in order to witness creatures that defied the imagination:

> *To be Seen at the Red Lion, Charing-Cross,*
>
> The grandest Collection of WILD BEASTS, viz,
>
> The noble female Rhinoceros, or real Unicorn, a beast of upwards of eighty Hundred Weight, in a natural Coat of Mail or Armour, taken by the noted Kouli Kan from the Great Mogul, having a large Horn on her Nose, three Hoofs on each Foot, and a Hyde stuck thick with Scales,

Pistol Proof . . . allow'd to be the only complete Animal of its Kind ever shewn in Europe.

A surprising Crocodile alive, taken on the Banks of the River Nile in Egypt. Such a Creature was never shewn alive in the King's Dominions before. With others too tedious to mention.

Yet in among the classified adverts that day was one of a more sober nature, paid for by friends of Michael Magennis, appealing for witnesses in the case of the murder of Richard Shears, stating that:

> . . . Michael Maginnis, a poor Milkman, has been taken up and swore to by two Carmen, that he was the Person that struck the deceas'd with a Hanger . . . And after he was found guilty, several Persons who were in the Old Bailey Yard, that had been at the aforesaid Execution, declared that the said Michael Maginnis suffer'd wrongfully, for that he was inno- cent of the said Murder: These are therefore to desire all well-meaning People who were at the said Execution, and know any Thing of the Death of the said Richard Shears, or saw the said Richard Shears cut with a Hanger, that they would please to attend at Two o'Clock Tomorrow, at Mr George Long's, the Elephant and Castle in Fleet-Lane, near the Old Baily, in order to give any just Account thereof, and the Favour will greatly oblige the unfortunate Prisoner now under Sentence of Death in Newgate, and in so doing may prevent innocent Blood being shed.

Despite these efforts, no reprieve was granted, and on 23 March Michael Magennis was taken from Newgate back to Tyburn, along with fifteen others also due to be executed that day. They made the journey at nine o'clock in the morning in six carts. Around these, in the crowd, would have been tradesmen who had brought their carts along in order to hire them out to any spectators wanting to watch from a more elevated vantage point.

Two of those to die – James Hayes and Richard Broughton – arrived heavily shackled, having attempted to break out of Newgate armed with knives, viciously assaulting the warders. Their behaviour on the day, at least, matched the swaggering attitudes criticised by Henry Fielding in his *Enquiry into the Cause of the late Increase of Robbers*: 'The day appointed by law for the thief's shame is the day of glory in his own opinion. His procession to Tyburn and his last moments there are all triumphant.'

This was true for some, but does not match what is known of Michael Magennis. John Taylor, the Ordinary of Newgate, recorded the last words of the prisoner, and provided some background about the man himself:

> Michael Mac Gennis, aged 32, was born in the Kingdom of Ireland, of Parents whose Circumstances would not admit of giving him any Education; but they brought him up in a sober Way, in the Fear of God, and he was esteemed a quiet, harmless Youth by those who knew him in his early Days.

Here was a man who had come to England and found a living driving a milk cart. Married for the last nine years to a woman who was also in the milk trade, he 'had several Children, some of which are still alive, which he has left with a disconsolate Widow'. The overwhelming impression given by the Ordinary's account is of a man who believed himself to have been falsely convicted, and he certainly denied to the last having struck the blow. It may be that he was the victim of perjured testimony, designed to shield another man who committed the murder. At this distance in time, it is impossible to say. In his pamphlet, the Ordinary confined himself to simply relating the crime and stating that the verdict must have been just, since Magennis was found guilty. Having spoken to him on various occasions in the weeks leading up to his execution, Taylor seems to have grown to like Magennis despite believing him guilty, and concluded with this grim tribute:

> He has been very ill most Part of the Time since his Conviction, but for some Days before Execution he became more hearty, and was in good Health when he suffered, being as tight a little Man as might swing on Tyburn Tree: The Lord have Mercy on him. He died a Roman Catholick.

Reverend James Hackman as he appeared at his trial

Martha Ray

TEN

A MOMENTARY PHRENSY
OVERCAME ME
1779

Most killers, having committed a murder, generally make themselves scarce. If caught, they then spend the trial attempting to prove their innocence. However, in one of the most celebrated cases of the reign of George III, not only did the crime take place in a crowded part of central London before dozens of witnesses, but the murderer immediately passed a death sentence upon himself. He fired a loaded pistol at his own head, then tried to beat in his brains with the butt of the weapon. As the public and newspapers rightly concluded, this was no ordinary homicide.

The Covent Garden of 1779 was still a bustling centre of drinking dens, brothels, coffee houses and theatres. The Bow Street Runners carried on as before, and although Justice Henry Fielding had died back in 1754, his half-brother Sir John Fielding, 'The Blind Beak', remained the sitting Bow Street magistrate. The caseload was much the same as it had been in Henry's day, but prisoners lucky enough to escape the death penalty could no longer be transported to North America to work in plantations alongside the slaves because of the Revolutionary War. As a result, parliament had to look around for new options. Eventually, it was decided that the new lands in the southern hemisphere recently explored by Captain Cook might suit the purpose, and within a decade the first penal colony at Botany Bay had been established.

Transportation, however, was for the lesser criminals. As the century progressed, the number of offences carrying the death penalty had steadily increased, and Tyburn was always kept busy. Unsurprisingly, the kinds of people who passed before Sir John Fielding at Bow Street Magistrates' Court that year mainly came from humble backgrounds: Susannah Watson, seamstress, charged with picking pockets; Thomas Barnfield, apprentice carpenter (theft); Jane Jonas, market trader (assault and highway robbery); Peter Dubois, day-labourer (burglary). Yet in April, the prisoner brought before him was someone out of the common run – a man of the cloth, the Reverend James Hackman, whose love for a well-known opera singer had eventually driven him to murder.

On the evening of 7 April 1779, there were several entertainments on offer to tempt the Londoner. Anyone new in town might have seen adverts in the newspapers for a production called *Midas* ('With all the Scenery and Machenery incident to the Piece'), plus a masque entitled *The Apotheosis of Punch*, at the curiously named Patagonian Theatre, on the Strand, which had opened three years earlier, and was in fact devoted entirely to puppet shows. For live drama, there were only two options that evening: at Drury Lane His Majesty's Company were presenting a production of *Macbeth*, 'for the Benefit of Mr Brereton', while the Covent Garden Theatre – on the site of what is now the Royal Opera House – advertised an evening programme in three parts 'by particular Desire, for the Benefit of Mrs. Kennedy'. They began with *Rose and Colin* ('a Musical Piece'), followed by the main event, a revival of Thomas Arne and Isaac Bickerstaffe's comic opera *Love in a Village*, before concluding with an added attraction, *The Touchstone* ('a new speaking Pantomime').

The Covent Garden Theatre was built in 1731. Theatregoing was a volatile business in those days; crowds could be intensely hostile, and by 1779 the front of the stage was guarded by a row of spikes in order to afford the actors some protection. This was hardly surprising, given that a full-scale riot had taken place inside the building in 1763 after a change in the pricing policy, resulting in the destruction of most of the fixtures and fittings.

The London stage, and especially its female performers, held a great fascination for many gentlemen of the town, up to and including the sons of the king. In 1779 the Prince of Wales (later George IV) saw a production featuring the actress Mary Robinson, and was so taken by her that he offered her the colossal sum of £20,000 to become his mistress. The Prince's brother (later William IV), began a twenty-one-year relationship in 1790 with the comic actress Mrs Jordan, whom he had first noticed playing at Drury Lane.

The writer James Boswell, who kept a private journal upon moving to London in 1762, was also not immune to such temptations. He records numerous theatre visits, and also his affair with an actress of the Covent Garden Theatre, Mrs Lewis, which began rapturously but then fell victim to one of the hazards of the age, as he records:

> I this day began to feel an unaccountable alarm of unexpected evil: a little heat in the members of my body sacred to Cupid, very like the symptom of that distemper with which Venus, when cross, takes it into her head to plague her votaries.

Seventeen years later, the Reverend James Hackman developed a far more unhealthy obsession with the singer Martha Ray (or Reay) which led him ultimately to the gallows. Boswell attended his trial, mentioned it in his *Life of Johnson*, and even had to write to the press to deny reports that he had ridden in the carriage alongside Hackman on the way to Tyburn. The case understandably became a cause célèbre; not only was this a shockingly public murder – committed a few steps away from Bow Street Magistrates' Court – but the victim was a respected soprano singer of Handel's works, and long-term mistress of the fourth earl of Sandwich.

The first newspaper report (carried in the *St James's Chronicle or the British Evening Post*) pulled no punches:

> Last Night as Miss Ray (a Lady well known for her Connexion with a noble Lord in Administration) was coming out of Covent-Garden Theatre, at about a Quarter before Twelve, attended by another Lady, in order to take her Coach, near the Shakespeare Tavern, a Person came up to her, and discharging a loaded Pistol close to her Head, blew out her Brains, of which she expired immediately . . .

This would have been drama enough, but the subsequent actions of the assailant only added to the singularity of the event. Having killed his victim, Reverend Hackman made strenuous attempts in front of a horrified crowd of onlookers to end his own life:

. . . the Murtherer then instantly drew another Pistol, and applyed it to his own Forehead, in order to have done the same to himself, but the Priming, as supposed, having fallen out, the Pistol missed Fire, on which he struck himself so severe a Blow with it on the Head, that it fractured his Skull, but not Mortally.

According to another account, Hackman 'lay on the ground beating himself about the head, endeavouring to kill himself, and crying "Oh! kill me! kill me! for God's sake, kill me!"' Prevented from any further actions by the people around him, he was taken into custody. On the way to prison that night, he apparently said, 'What a change has a few hours made in me – had her friends done as I wished them to do, this would never have happened.'

Martha Ray was born in the Covent Garden area, probably in 1742. In the days before she was taken up by the earl of Sandwich, she lived just a few steps south of the Piazza at number 4, Tavistock Court. Her father was a stay-maker, and around the age of fourteen Martha was apprenticed to a woman who was also in the clothing trade, one Sarah Silver of St George's Court, Clerkenwell, who made mantuas (cloaks). Four or five years later, she was abruptly lifted out of these humble surroundings when she came to the attention of John Montagu, the fourth earl of Sandwich, who paid her father the considerable sum of £400 'for her honour'. Sandwich had been married since 1741 but was separated from his wife, who over the years had gradually become insane.

Unlike some attachments in those days, the relationship between Sandwich and Martha Ray seems to have been based upon genuine affection and was to all intents and purposes a marriage; they had five children together, and she acted as the hostess at his country seat Hinchingbrooke House in Huntingdon, Cambridgeshire. These days, the earl is often chiefly remembered for having given his name to the time-honoured habit of eating food between two slices of bread, but he also had an active political career – during which he did much to reorganise and strengthen the Royal Navy – and he was a patron of the arts who helped restore and foster Handel's reputation. He co-founded the Consort of Ancient Music in 1776, and Ray would frequently sing at the professionally staged musical events that he held at Hinchingbrooke. Although it was common for ladies to provide entertainment by singing or playing musical instruments at home gatherings, Miss Ray's talent far exceeded the usual standard, and had she not formed her attachment to a member of the aristocracy she would certainly have been able to earn a living singing professionally on the London stage.

Sandwich set Ray up with her own home in Westminster, near the Admiralty, and she often accompanied him to public functions. That they were an acknowledged couple in the eyes of their contemporaries is borne out by the satirical joint etching of the pair, produced in 1769, in which she is labelled 'Miss R——' and he is identified simply as 'Jemmy Twitcher', after the treacherous character from *The Beggar's Opera*. This was a reference to Sandwich having supposedly betrayed his friend, the MP John Wilkes.

On the evening of the murder, Martha Ray went to the Covent Garden Theatre accompanied by an Italian singer, Signora Galli, in order to see *Love in a Village*. They arrived at 6.15 pm, and were joined inside the theatre by a Mr McNamara of Lincoln's Inn. According to one newspaper account, Ray 'looked more than usually agreeable' that night, and 'it was also remarked that she was in an unusual show of spirits and good humour'. The *Newgate Calendar* said that the two women had been seen boarding their coach outside Ray's home in Whitehall by her admirer the Reverend Hackman, who had taken rooms, probably by design, a short distance away. His lodgings were in Duke's Court, off the eastern side of St Martin's Lane, roughly where the National Portrait Gallery now stands. He very likely knew where the coach was heading, but even if he did not, it would have been an easy matter to follow it on foot the short distance to Covent Garden. Although he is said to have spent that morning reading a book of sermons, something of Hackman's state of mind can be deduced from the *Calendar's* description of his actions in the early evening:

> Mr Hackman went into the theatre at the same time; but, not being able to contain the violence of his passion, returned, and again went to his lodgings, and, having loaded two pistols, went to the playhouse, where he waited till the play was over.

The 'violence of his passion' was raised to even higher levels by jealousy. Inside the theatre he had observed Miss Ray in conversation with Lord Coleraine, and suspected some romantic connection between the two. Having armed himself, Hackman waited in the nearby Bedford Coffee House, on the north-east side of the Piazza, until the performance ended.

So, one April evening in Covent Garden, as the rakes and the whores did business a few steps away at Haddock's Bagnio or in private rooms at the Shakespeare's Head Tavern, a clergyman dressed in black sat in a coffee house around whose walls hung playbills and etchings of actors and actresses, with two loaded pistols and murder on his mind.

James Hackman was twenty-six years old – nearly a decade younger than Martha Ray. Born by the sea in Gosport, just across the harbour from Portsmouth, he was the son of a Royal Navy officer. Although initially apprenticed to a mercer, James then decided to follow a military career, rising to become a Lieutenant in the 68th Regiment of Foot. It was army life that brought him into contact with Martha Ray, when he was part of a recruiting party of soldiers who visited the earl of Sandwich at Hinchingbrooke in the summer of 1775. He was smitten with Martha Ray from this point forward, but the exact nature of their relationship is not certain, although in the aftermath of her death pamphlet-writers claimed that they had become lovers. Whatever hopes James Hackman might have entertained, it seems unlikely that Ray would have left a long-term relationship with a man of some means and position – which had produced five children – in order to start afresh with him.

By 1779, Hackman had abandoned his army career in favour of the religious life, and in February of that year – less than two months before the night he brought his pistols to Covent Garden – he was ordained a priest.

In the immediate aftermath of the sensational killing, much was written both in the newspapers and in rush-released pamphlets seeking to explain the development of the relationship between the murderer and his victim. Among this outpouring of prose was a publication entitled *The Case and*

Memoirs of the Late Rev. Mr. James Hackman, And of his Acquaintance with the late Miss Martha Reay, which claimed to be based upon interviews with Hackman himself whilst in prison. Although very likely riddled with distortions and outright fabrications, it remains one of the most import-ant sources of information about the relationship between the Reverend and Miss Ray. Their first meeting at Hinchingbrooke, it alleged, led swiftly to a full-blown affair:

> It was here where the late Mr. Hackman first saw and became acquainted with the departed Miss Reay, a lady of an elegant person, great sweetness of manners, and of a remarkable judgment and execution in vocal and instrumental music. Frequently being in her company at his Lordship's house, where she lived under his protection, she impressed Mr. Hackman with the most tender and fond regard for her, which soon after ended in a mutual passion for each other. They indulged themselves in their love as privately as possible for a considerable time, unknown to his Lordship, and convinced each other (particularly on his part) that all-powerful love was involuntary and unrestrained, whatever prudence might dictate for the sake of appearances. But after revelling in all its rites by stealth, the suspicions of Lord Sandwich were set in motion.

There was also a publication with virtually the same title, purporting to tell the story from Martha Ray's point of view, yet although the victim was killed at point-blank range with a shot to the head, there were many who seemed to reserve their sympathy not for Miss Ray but for Reverend Hackman.

When the 7 April performance of *Love in a Village* drew to a close, some members of the audience stayed in their seats to watch the customary finale to the evening, a short farce or pantomime. Martha Ray and Signora Galli, having no interest in remaining, made their way outside in the company of Mr McNamara, to where Miss Ray's carriage was waiting. McNamara later testified that he had offered the lady assistance a few moments before:

'Seeing Miss Ray in some difficulties at the playhouse, and, being a little acquainted with her, I was induced to offer my assistance to hand her to her carriage; she took me by the arm . . . As we came out of the passage that leads into Covent-Garden playhouse, when we were in the piazzas, very near the carriage, I heard the report of a pistol.'

Signora Galli had already entered the coach, and McNamara was still holding Martha Ray's arm at the time of the shot. The street at that point in the evening was full of bystanders, and one of them – a fruit seller named Mary Anderson who was standing just near the carriage – later described the shock of the occasion:

'Just as the play broke up I saw two ladies and a gentleman coming out of the playhouse; a gentleman in black followed them. Lady Sandwich's coach was called. When the carriage came up, the gentleman handed the other lady into the carriage; the lady that was shot stood behind. Before the gentleman could come back to hand her into the carriage the gentleman in black came up, laid hold of her by the gown, and pulled out of his pocket two pistols; he shot the right hand pistol at her, and the other at himself. She fell with her hand so [on her forehead] and died before she could be got to the first lamp; I believe she died immediately, for her head hung directly. At first I was frightened at the report of the pistol, and ran away. He fired another pistol, and dropped immediately. They fell feet to feet. He beat himself violently over the head with his pistols, and desired somebody would kill him.'

James Mahon, an apothecary from nearby Bow Street, happened to be passing. Hearing the shots, he went forward to where Hackman was writhing around on the floor and clubbing himself on the head with the butt of his gun. 'I wrenched the pistol immediately out of his hand,' said Mahon. 'He bled very much.' The weapon was given over to the care of another eyewitness, a constable named Richard Blandy, who carried the wounded prisoner to the Shakespeare's Head Tavern, just near the theatre. In searching Hackman's pockets, Blandy found two letters, which the gunman had prepared beforehand.

By all accounts, Miss Ray died almost instantly. Her body was also taken to the Shakespeare's Head, where it was examined by a surgeon named Dennis O'Bryan, who could do little but confirm the obvious:

'I examined the wound, and found it to be a mortal one. I felt the vessels of sensation, and tried every other way to see if I could perceive any life, and pronounced the woman dead. The wound was received in the front of the head, in the Centra coronalis, and the ball was discharged under the left ear.'

In another part of the same tavern, James Hackman was under guard and bleeding profusely from his head wounds. These were cleaned and bandaged, and the two letters found on his person examined. One was addressed to Martha Ray, the other to his brother-in-law, Frederick Booth, who lived nearby at Craven Street, off the Strand. The first of these was said by the *Lloyd's Evening Post* to have been 'replete with warm expressions of affection to the unfortunate object of his love', while the other consisted of a 'pathetic relation of the melancholy resolution he had taken, and a confession of the cause that produced it'. Claiming that he could not live without Miss Ray, and being 'shut out from every hope of possessing her', he had decided upon this desperate course of action.

In fact, the letter to Booth, when read out in court, was not so clear-cut as this report suggested. That Hackman intended to die was not in doubt, since it began 'When this reaches you I shall be no more', but the conclusion of the letter suggested that killing Miss Ray was not necessarily a part of his original plan:

> May heaven protect my beloved woman, and forgive this act, which alone could relieve me from a world of misery I have long endured. Oh! if it should ever be in your power to do her any act of friendship, remember your faithful friend,
>
>   J. HACKMAN.

The last sentence could be taken to mean that he set out intending to kill himself in front of her, and that she would live on after his death. It certainly reads more like a suicide note than a warning of murder.

Mr McNamara, who was himself covered in blood from having helped bring the body of Miss Ray into the tavern, took the opportunity to talk briefly to Hackman, as he later testified:

> 'Upon the prisoner being secured, I was induced to ask him what could possess him to be guilty of such a deed? or some question of that sort; and he answered me by saying, that it was not a proper place to ask that question . . .

He desired to see the lady. I did not tell him she was dead; somebody else did. I objected to his seeing her at that time. I had her removed into another room. From the great quantity of blood I had about me I got sick, and was obliged to go home.'

The Shakespeare's Head Tavern – where the body lay in one room and Hackman in great pain in another – was a key Covent Garden location, its reputation anything but spotless. Indeed, it was here in the 1750s that Shakespeare's Head waiter, John Harrison, had reinvented himself as Jack Harris, Pimp General of All England, who lent his name to the long-running guide to the area's whores, *Harris's List of Covent Garden Ladies*. The tavern's upstairs rooms had seen much in the way of illicit gambling and paid-for assignations, although sometimes no money changed hands.

Into this seedy bastion of London nightlife at around 3.30 am on the night of the shooting strode a man who was himself something of a local landmark, Sir John Fielding, magistrate of Bow Street. Learning that Hackman was not in immediate danger of dying from his wounds, Fielding ordered the prisoner to be taken to Tothill Fields Bridewell, a prison in Westminster, near the Abbey, where he was placed under careful guard, as the *General Evening Post* reported:

[Hackman] is attended by two surgeons, and watched by two of Sir John Fielding's men, to prevent him destroying himself; he converses very little, and has a single fetter on. What induced the desperate man to this horrid act, we are yet to learn . . . Mr Hackman has appeared very calm and sane ever since the perpetration of the bloody deed; and what is very remarkable, fell into a sound sleep soon after he arrived at Tothill-fields bridewell, in which he continued several hours.

Back at the Shakespeare's Head, a coroner's inquest sat in the middle of the night, interviewing witnesses as the body was given a postmortem by two surgeons, who afterwards stated that 'they never saw so dismal and ghastly a fracture'. By 9 am the inquest had reached its verdict – wilful murder.

From the very beginning, newspaper coverage of these events was generally sympathetic to Reverend Hackman, perhaps because of his obvious
despair. One of the great literary successes of that decade was Henry
Mackenzie's novel *The Man Of Feeling* (1771), whose emotional protagon-
ist Harley regularly bursts into tears. This kind of sensitive behaviour was
seen as a sign of refinement and good breeding, and so the story of the
apparently love-crazed Hackman and his immediate regret for his own
actions would have struck a chord in the society of that time. In addition,
the pronounced unpopularity of the earl of Sandwich might have somehow
diminished public sorrow at the fate of his mistress. Certainly, whatever
the reason, concerns about the brutal death of the victim seem to have
taken second place to solicitude for the current wellbeing of the man who
had pulled the trigger. This seems also to have been the attitude taken
by Sir John Fielding himself when the prisoner was brought before him
at Bow Street for questioning on Friday, 9 April. The object was to enquire
into the events, preparatory to the case going forward for trial at the Old
Bailey. In order to give Hackman some measure of privacy, Fielding
invited him into his own room, where he was given a seat. This was
apparently done to prevent 'the unhappy prisoner from being exposed to
the view of wanton, idle curiosity, and to shield him from the impertinent
reflections of the illiberal and inhuman'. Heavily bandaged, Hackman was
in great pain throughout from his injuries, but the report of the questioning in the *General Evening Post* reads almost as if he had been the
victim of a crime, rather than the perpetrator:

> Sir John very pathetically and tenderly addressed him, desiring him to
> compose himself and behave as much like a man as such a situation
> would permit him, as he had still a great deal to go through . . .
> [Hackman's] sighs and tears, added to his polite and genteel appearance,
> made most people present give way to the finest feelings of human
> nature.

In what seems to have been a very civilised exchange of comments,
Fielding explained that he must now have Hackman transferred to Newgate,
to which the latter replied with a request for a room to himself in that
prison, so that he 'might not be confined in the same place with other
unfortunate wretches like himself'. This was granted, on account of the
prisoner's social standing – indeed the whole treatment of Hackman after

the killing was modified by the fact that he was seen as a gentleman rather than a common criminal, despite the savagery of his actions. There was a certain amount of sympathy expressed in the newspapers for Lord Sandwich, and although his long relationship with Martha Ray was common knowledge in polite circles, many reports declined to name him, referring to him simply as 'the noble gentleman' or something similar. Miss Ray herself, however, seems almost to fade into the background after the initial reports. A week after her murder, on Wednesday, 14 April, she was interred next to her mother at a country church in Elstree, Hertfordshire, two days before Hackman's trial at the Old Bailey. On the instructions of the earl of Sandwich, she was buried in the same dress and jewellery that she had been wearing on the night of the murder, worth the very considerable sum of £2,000, more money than the average workman might earn in several lifetimes, and surely a severe temptation for any grave robbers in the neighbourhood.

Reports from the gaol said that Hackman would be pleading guilty – 'he talks of dying with pleasure, and declares he will make no defence whatever', said one, while another claimed that the prisoner was being urged by his sister and others to enter a plea of temporary madness, 'which however he rejects with the utmost disdain'. In the event, Hackman seems to have changed his mind at some point during this week, and when his trial came up at the Old Bailey, he did indeed offer a defence. Perhaps, mindful of the overwhelmingly sympathetic press coverage, it occurred to him that he might yet escape the noose, or else he had been persuaded by his relatives to make the attempt. Meanwhile, there was news in the *London Evening Post* of Signora Galli: 'She says she fainted, but knows not what happened afterwards.' The lady was now at home in Chelsea, 'dangerously ill'. The earl of Sandwich had clearly been busy, for the same news item also contained the following: 'An attorney in the city is employed by a noble Lord to carry on the prosecution against Mr Hackman with the utmost vigour.'

Sandwich had in fact received a letter of apology and explanation from Hackman, to which the earl apparently replied sending both his forgiveness and pity, but also saying that Hackman had 'disturbed his peace of mind forever'. Robert Boyle-Walsingham, a friend of the earl, had questioned Hackman in prison, and concluded that the prisoner desired only to die. As for Sandwich's political enemies – those who regarded him as a man who had betrayed John Wilkes – they used the occasion of the murder to launch bitter attacks upon him in the press. Even on the day of Martha Ray's funeral, a repugnant anonymous letter appeared in the *London Evening Post* implying that if a lady was foolish enough to be the mistress of someone like the earl, then being shot in the head was only to be expected: 'Poor Miss——! I pity her untimely fate. But, lying in the monster's bosom, who can wonder that she was so early ripened for the reward of so intimate a connection?'

Reverend Hackman, while in gaol, was telling visitors that he had gone to Covent Garden not with the intention of killing Martha Ray, but only himself. He wanted 'to fall the heroic lover in the sight of his mistress', but changed his mind at the very last moment when, according to him, she had given him 'a look of anger at his presumption'.

Trials only lasted a short time in those days; however, because of the visiting arrangements at Newgate and the ability of newspapers to report the words of the accused, it was almost as if the week leading up to the proceedings constituted the preliminary arguments in the case. One way and another, Hackman's moment in court was shaping up to be one of the talking points of the year. The young reverend cut such a different figure from that of the average murderer: his remorse was there for all to see, while his guilt was hardly in question.

Right from the outset, the cause of the public's great fascination with this case was obviously not whodunnit, but why?

When the Reverend Hackman's trial took place at the Old Bailey on Friday, 16 April, one man present was the writer James Boswell. That morning, he had first visited his friend Thomas Davenport – one of the two men defending the prisoner – and was then led into the Old Bailey Sessions House personally by Davenport, who helped him secure a good seat at the counsel's table. From here, he had a fine view of the accused, and also the two judges in the case, Sir William Blackstone, Justice of the Common Pleas, and Baron Massieres, Deputy Recorder of London. In addition to his links to the defence counsel, Boswell was also friends with Hackman's brother-in-law, Frederick Booth, and had called on him several times in the week since the murder. Later, Boswell noted in his journal that it was 'affecting to see Hackman', and when dining that evening with Dr Johnson, Sir Joshua Reynolds and others, he gave them an account of the proceedings: 'Wine had no impression on me, I was so gloomy. Johnson, when I repeated Hackman's speech, . . . said with low-voiced piety, "I hope he shall find mercy."'

On the day of the trial, Hackman defended himself, but only very half-heartedly. Indeed, after the witnesses for the prosecution had been heard, he opened his own statement by saying that 'the justice of my country ought to be satisfied by suffering my offence to be proved, and the fact established by evidence.' Boswell's eyewitness account describes him as 'giving a decent and pathetic speech' to the court, which had been prepared beforehand: 'He was in great agitation, and I was afraid he would have been incapable of utterance; but he collected himself, and read it with much pathos and energy from a paper which he held in his hand.'

Hackman's main plea for understanding lay in his assertion that he had not gone to Covent Garden intending to kill Martha Ray, and that the letter in his pocket addressed to Frederick Booth supported this. 'I stand here this day the most wretched of human beings, and confess myself criminal in a high degree,' he began, but went on to claim that 'the will to destroy her who was ever dearer to me than life, was never mine till a momentary phrensy overcame me, and induced me to commit the deed I now deplore.'

Hackman's letter to Booth was then read out in full. Although the wording certainly suggests that Hackman intended to kill himself and that Martha Ray would survive, there were other factors counting heavily against him. Firstly, when considering a plea of insanity, there was Sir John Fielding's statement that when he had interviewed the prisoner at 4 am, Hackman had behaved in an entirely rational manner. A further point of contention was the fact that Hackman had brought two pistols with him on the fateful evening – a circumstance that, according to Justice Blackstone, suggested that the accused intended to shoot someone else as well as himself.

In the main, despite the attempts to portray the murder as a crime of passion committed while the mind was unbalanced, the element of cold-blooded premeditation was hard to banish. Martha Ray had done little except cross a short stretch of pavement, yet was met with a bullet in the forehead which killed her instantly. The *General Evening Post* reported the summing up as follows:

The prisoner had rested his defence upon a sudden phrenzy of the mind, but the Judge said, that it was not every fit or start of tumultuous passion that could justify the killing of another, but it must be the total loss of reason, and incapability of reason in every part of life.

In other words, Hackman seems to have been sane beforehand, and sane quite soon afterwards, therefore must be held responsible for his actions. The jury consulted amongst themselves for just a few minutes before returning a verdict of guilty. Accordingly, Baron Massieres then pronounced sentence, that the prisoner would be 'hung on Monday next till he was dead, and his body delivered to the surgeons to be anatomized'. At this, a composed Hackman bowed to the court and jury, and left the room.

Sentenced to death on the Friday morning, James Hackman had just the weekend to contemplate his fate before being brought to Tyburn on Monday. Twenty other people had been tried alongside him on that same day, and one of them, a burglar named William Walker, also received the death penalty. One who did not was John Vincent, who appeared in court that Friday charged with killing his lover, Mary Dollard, having shot her in the back with some kind of blunderbuss 'of which she languished and died'. Cleared of murder but convicted of manslaughter, he was merely burnt in the hand and then imprisoned for a year.

On the day of his execution, Hackman rose at 5 am, and spent the next two hours in 'private meditation'. Three close friends then joined him, and they went in a group to the chapel to hear prayers read by the Ordinary of Newgate. Until this moment, Hackman seems to have remained calm and composed, but soon, according to the account in the *Gentlemen's and London Magazine*, the horror of the occasion became too much for him:

> . . . between eight and nine he came down from chapel, and was haltered; when the Sheriff's officer took the cord from the bag to perform his duty, Mr. Hackman said, 'Oh! the sight of this shocks me more than the thought of its intended operation;' he then shed a few tears, and took leave of two gentlemen in a very affecting manner.

CAPITAL CRIMES

The prisoner then set out on the journey to Tyburn in a mourning coach, followed by a cart 'hung with black, out of which he was to make his exit'. Once at the gallows, the familiar grim procedure was enacted, and the Reverend James Hackman became yet another of the many to end their days on the triple tree: 'After some time spent in prayer, he was tied up, and about 10 minutes past eleven, he was launched into eternity. After hanging the usual time, his body was carried to Surgeon's-hall to be dissected.'

James Boswell had made several attempts to visit Hackman in Newgate over the weekend between the trial and the execution date. Indeed, he was rumoured in some quarters to have been the author of the latter's courtroom defence speech, and perhaps because he had so publicly concerned himself with the outcome of this case, it was widely reported that he then rode in the carriage that Monday with Hackman on his way to execution. Boswell wrote to the papers in order to set the record straight, and a correction published in the *London Magazine* for May 1779 quoted him as saying:

It was not Mr Boswell, but the Rev Dr Porter of Clapham, who so humanely attended the late unfortunate Mr Hackman. Mr Boswell had for a day that praise, which is so justly allowed to generous tenderness, but he has taken care that it shall be enjoyed by the worthy person to whom it is due.

The story had been so generally accepted that Dr Johnson told Boswell a week after the execution that he thought his friend had not only ridden in the carriage, but had also inserted a news story to that effect in the papers himself. It was just one small symptom of the strange fascination this case would continue to exert upon the public mind.

In the short term, that interest resulted in the publication of two similarly titled but opposing pamphlets – *The Case and Memoirs of the Late Rev. Mr. James Hackman, And of his Acquaintance with the late Miss Martha Reay*, which took the part of Hackman, and *The Case and Memoirs of Miss Martha Reay, to which are added Remarks on the Case and Memoirs of Hackman*, which replied from the victim's standpoint. Quite what the earl of Sandwich made of all this might easily be imagined, particularly as the former publication damned him with the faintest praise available:

Lord S—— , whatever may be his follies as a man, his conduct as a minister, or insincerity as a friend, according to the libellous fame of newspapers, and those who do not know him, is a character superior to malevolence . . .

To the modern observer, perhaps the strangest aspect of the publicity surrounding the case is that the fact that Hackman was a man of the cloth seems to have played no part in the public discussion. Admittedly, he had only recently been ordained, and in an age when all things were for sale, taking holy orders was perhaps more of a simple career choice, like working in a bank or joining the army. It was certainly not unknown for vicars to trouble the law courts: it was only two years since another clergyman, Dr Dodd – a friend of Dr Johnson, as it happens – had been hanged at Tyburn for forgery ('I am now a spectacle to men and soon shall be a spectacle to angels'); or, indeed, seven years since the death of the Reverend Luke Imber of Christchurch, Hampshire, who at the age of eighty-three had, in the words of the *Gentlemen's Magazine*, 'married a country girl of thirteen'. In the main, however, it was Hackman the distraught lover who caught the public attention, not Hackman the vicar.

James Hackman's posthumous fame probably reached its fullest flowering with the publication the following year of a volume entitled *Love and Madness. A Story too True, in a Series of Letters Between Parties whose Names would perhaps be mentioned were they less known, or less lamented.* Published by G Kearsley – who had been responsible for the *Case and Memoirs* soon after the trial – this purported to be a passionate exchange of letters between Ray and Hackman, but was in fact the fictional work of Sir Herbert Croft (a writer somewhat obsessed with the idea of revising Dr Johnson's *Dictionary*, who also happened to be the vicar of Prittlewell in Essex). The appetite of the public for this fanciful reimagining of the story proved considerable, and *Love and Madness* went through seven editions.

All things considered, although Martha Ray was to a certain extent already a public figure in her role as a singer and as mistress to a controversial peer of the realm, her tragedy seems in the public mind to have been obscured by the plight of Hackman. His death on the gallows overshadows that of hers in most accounts, not least that which was published in the *Newgate Calendar*.

Such was the end of a young gentleman who might have been an ornament to his country, the delight of his friends, and a comfort to his relations, had he not been led away by the influence of an unhappy passion.

The burning of Newgate prison during the Gordon Riots of 1780,
which prompted a major rethink of the application of the Riot Act

ELEVEN

DOWN BY THE JETTY
1798

In the late eighteenth century, the port of London was the busiest in the world, and the number of ships using it had almost trebled since 1700. For centuries, the sea and shipping had been of vital importance to the nation. London now stood at the heart of the British Empire's trade routes, and during the 1790s the country was also engaged in a maritime war with both Revolutionary France and Spain.

As the volume of trade rapidly increased, loading and unloading space was ever harder to come by, cargo theft from moored vessels and quaysides was reaching epidemic proportions, and virtually all of the port's traffic still had to tie up at wharves along the riverbank. A parliamentary committee was established in 1796 to consider proposals for the building of docks which would not only allow greater space for ships but also provide secure warehouses for storing valuable cargoes. When the first of these opened – West India Docks, in 1802 – it was guarded by a private police force consisting of one hundred heavily armed men.

These were the beginnings of the river police, but steps had already been taken to clamp down on theft with the establishment in 1798 of a Marine Police Office in Wapping High Street. Sitting as magistrates were two men who had campaigned for several years for just such a court: Patrick Colquhoun, who published his *Treatise on the Police of the Metropolis* in 1796, and John Harriott, who in 1797 sent his own plan for the formation of a river police to the Home Secretary and the Lord Mayor of London. As Harriott recalled a decade later in his autobiography, he did this because the river was plagued by 'numerous strong hordes of desperately-wicked water-pirates, that had long existed, without an attempt being made to impede their progress'.

To say that the riverfront at Wapping at this time was a rough and ready district would be something of an understatement. In October that year, a sailor 'being withal in liquor' in a pub in King Street jokingly aimed a pistol at one of the serving girls and shot her in the leg. That same month, two members of a press gang were arrested on charges of demanding money with menaces from a man in the street, and when he refused 'beat him unmercifully', then robbed him. Press gangs, forcibly recruiting men with seafaring experience for the navy, were a regular hazard for the unwary. They were sometimes just an excuse for demanding money with menaces: an enterprising robber named Charles Brown was charged with threatening a man in Wapping while armed with a cutlass, claiming to be a press master, and asking the considerable sum of three guineas to let him go free.

One evening in October 1798, when the Marine Police Office had only been in operation for a matter of months, it was attacked by a riotous mob who tore up paving slabs weighing twenty pounds and flung them at the windows, crying that they would tear the whole place to the ground before the night was through. Those inside feared for their lives. Pistols were fired, the Riot Act was read to the crowd, and before it was over, two men lay dead or dying.

The street names of Wapping emphasise the district's close links with the sea, such as Byng Street, after the powerful family of Admiral George Byng who owned land there, one of whose sons was the unfortunate Admiral Byng executed for alleged cowardice on the deck of *HMS Monarque* in Portsmouth Harbour in 1757. The more usual brand of seagoing malefactors, such as the pirate William Kidd, ended their days on the Wapping riverfront at Execution Dock, left hanging at the low-water mark until three tides had passed over them.

Today there is a pub named the Captain Kidd at 108 Wapping High Street, a little to the west of the former site of Execution Dock. Across the road is an open green space called Wapping Rose Garden, which in 1798 was the site of the Pichard & Company Brewery. This building and Execution Dock are clearly marked on Richard Horwood's superb map of the time, *A Plan of the Cities of London and Westminster*, published between 1792 and 1799. The map also shows five houses west of Execution Dock, a loading area called Phoenix Wharf, which still exists, and five houses further west another wharf whose name is not marked. The latter location would unquestionably have been one of the least fragrant in later eighteenth-century London, for this was Dung Wharf, where the contents of the city's thousands of cesspits were brought before being loaded onto ships so that they could be dumped out at sea.

Into this short stretch of riverside, in the late summer of 1798, came the specialist magistrates and their officers whose task was to clamp down on dockside violence and stem the rising tide of cargo theft. Their base of operations, the newly established Marine Police Office, stood on the river side of the street at 259 Wapping High Street, opposite the western end of Pichard's Brewery. It was a three-storey building, directly on the Thames bank, with a jetty and slipway for the River Police boats to tie up. The Office was twenty yards from Dung Wharf, thirty yards from a pub called the Rose & Crown, where the staff of the Office used to drink, and not far from Execution Dock. Much of the riverside has changed in the intervening two centuries, but the site of the original building is very easy to locate, because although it has been rebuilt several times, it has always been and remains a River Police station, with a sign saying 'Marine Policing Unit' on its land-facing wall to this day – reckoned to be the longest continually occupied police building in the world.

Businessmen whose trade was centred on the river had long been calling for such an establishment, and in the beginning it was their money that funded it, although the government became involved within a matter of years. The success of the new Office was noted by a newspaper which had itself only been in existence for little more than a decade – *The Times*:

> The Merchants have found themselves considerably relieved from depredations on the River, since the establishment of the MARINE POLICE OFFICE in Wapping. No person is better acquainted with the nature of these depredations than the worthy Magistrate who presides there, to whom the Public are very much indebted.

Importers, exporters and some sections of the public at large might have approved, but many locals felt quite the opposite about this new development. Judging by the routine cases that came before magistrates – such as that of Pierce Gogan, a coal-heaver, convicted of having a suspiciously large amount of coal at his own home for which he could give no explanation, or Joshua Jones, apprehended in Wapping with fifty pounds of sugar stolen from a ship lately returned from the West Indies – many thefts were carried out by those who worked on the docks surrounded by all kinds of valuable goods. The temptations must have been considerable, and when the new secure dock warehouses opened at the start of the nineteenth century, their contents were memorably described as 'the world's greatest concentration of portable wealth'.

As the magistrate John Harriott recalled, some who worked on the river unloading this cargo felt that a percentage of it was theirs by right, and 'had long considered plunder as a privilege'. Anyone standing up against this custom was treading a risky path, yet he knew that something must be done:

> The impunity with which these river-pirates were allowed to plunder induced others to do the same; until, with their numbers, their courage increased to so great a height as to threaten to overthrow the commerce of the Port of London.

Those elements who objected to the activities of the Marine Police Office eventually found a focus for their disapproval in protests over the seemingly routine theft conviction of another coal-heaver, Charles Eyres. Whether he was guilty or not seems hardly to have been the issue, but upon hearing the sentence, one spectator in the court was reported to have shouted out that 'it shall not rest here', and that the building itself would be torn down.

Clearly, the whole notion of policing the river was anathema to some.

Inside the Marine Police Office on 16 October 1798, it probably started out as an evening like any other. The magistrates in session were Mr Colquhoun and Mr Harriott, and at about half-past eight they heard the case of three defendants – two coal-heavers and a watchman's boy – accused of stealing coal. Charles Eyres was one of the accused. All three were found guilty and ordered to pay a fine of forty shillings. Some of this money was duly paid to Henry Lang, the clerk of the Office, but not all of it, as he later testified:

> 'Part of the money was brought to me, and there was some objection to the payment of the money: about five minutes after that, I heard a great noise in the street, which kept increasing till it grew quite outrageous; Mr. Colquhoun then ordered the constable in waiting, Richard Perry, to go out with the other constables, to see what was the matter, and if it could not be otherwise quelled, to bring the rioters in.'

Perry duly reported back after venturing outside, and at first, it seemed that the situation could be contained and that the authorities had the necessary power to keep the crowd under control. However, it soon became clear that their position was becoming dangerous; trapped inside the court with a mob of unknown size outside, determined to attack. The entrance to the Office was not directly on the street itself, but up a dark, narrow alley on the western side of the building, so to venture out would have been an act of some bravery in the circumstances.

That a riot quickly developed would have been no surprise to the average Londoner, since mob violence had been a regular feature of eighteenth-century life in the capital. Riots broke out protesting against the Hanoverian succession in 1715, cheap Irish labour in 1736, the employment of French actors at the Haymarket Theatre in 1738, and in support of the MP John Wilkes in 1768 and 1769. Sailors had several times rioted in Covent Garden at being regularly swindled in the brothels of the district. In all these cases, window-smashing was the usual precursor to the interior destruction of whatever building symbolised the displeasure of the crowd, so when the first heavy paving stones began shattering the glass of the Marine Police Office, those inside would have had little doubt of what might follow.

The law stated that troops were forbidden to fire upon a crowd until a magistrate had read the Riot Act of 1715 to them. Once this had been done, if the people failed to disperse, the force of the State could be unleashed against them (and soldiers, in the absence of any proper police force, were generally the only option open to the authorities). The most famous example was probably the week of the London-wide Gordon Riots of June 1780, in which 275 rioters died. During these disturbances magistrates were extremely reluctant to read the Riot Act, on the quite understandable grounds that their own houses might be destroyed if they stood up to the mob. After a bizarre week in which the troops stood by and watched the wholesale sacking of London, George III himself offered to read the Act to the crowd, which shamed a magistrate into doing his duty, and guns were then swiftly used against the mob, restoring order.

Lessons learned from the Gordon Riots were probably in the back of the minds of the magistrates now trapped inside the Marine Police Office, whose situation was clearly very serious. The wooden shutters and the glass in the windows facing the street had already been destroyed, and the danger inside from flying debris was evident. Magistrate John Harriott, who had seen action in the Royal Navy during the Seven Years War, and also been wounded while working for the East India Company, seems to have taken the decision to fire upon the crowd:

> 'They first attempted the door; when, finding that too strongly secured for them to force, they tore up the pavement in the street, and soon demolished the shutters of four windows of the room we were in . . . I believe I was the only person in the office, at the time, that had ever smelt gunpowder burnt in anger before, and many years had elapsed since I had been so engaged. I immediately saw the necessity of prompt resolute measures, for the infuriate madness of the assailants grew stronger every instant: ordering the fire arms, seeing to their loading, and giving necessary directions, seemed to electrify and make me young again.'

Shots were duly fired down at the rioters from a high vantage point, and it was then that one of the men attempting to break into the building, James Hanks, was killed, and his body dragged away by other members of the crowd. Several city gentlemen, apparently present at the Office in order to observe the proceedings, escaped by boat from the jetty at the rear of the building, while another climbed up to the top storey and hid near the roof. For the magistrates and their few men, trapped inside by a shouting mob and completely outnumbered, it must have been a very frightening moment.

Richard Perry, one of those who worked in the building, later gave his impression of the scene within the walls at that time:

'A large stone came in, which took me over the shoulder, and passed Mr. Colquhoun, the Magistrate . . . I expected every man there would be murdered; I directly went and fired a pistol off out of the place where that large stone came in . . . The moment it was done, I heard Mitchell, one of the officers, cry out, Oh Lord! Oh Lord! I saw him put his hand up.'

Despite the flying rocks, and the fact that guns had been brought into the equation, Colquhoun, Harriott and some of their officers then went out into that dimly lit alley to face the mob. Colquhoun stood up on a stone step at the roadside, placed there in order to assist people when entering carriages, and read the Riot Act to the crowd amid a hail of missiles. The rioters were mostly grouped a few yards down the road to the west, by Dung Wharf. There was a sound of 'shouting and huzzaing' coming from the crowd, and according to Perry, also 'several horrid expressions, that they would kill all the people belonging to the office'.

In the dark, stench-filled street alongside the river, jostling, shadowy figures confronted each other amid scenes of shouting, gunfire, threats and the hurling of any loose object that might come to hand. Gabriel Franks, a member of the casual staff attached to the office who had been drinking nearby when the trouble started, had asked Richard Perry to give him a cutlass before they confronted the mob. The latter did not do so, but apparently Franks was able to lay his hands on one before they made their way out in a body towards the rioters in the confusion down at Dung Wharf.

Exactly how many men of the police office faced down the rioters is hard to say, but it seems they were considerably outnumbered. Gabriel Franks had his cutlass, and may have attempted to use it. Certainly, he seems to have been very aware of the danger, as Perry later testified: 'Franks and I walked ten yards, I suppose, looking at the mob, and then Franks said, for God's sake, Perry, take care; he turned round, and, at that distance, I saw the flash of a pistol . . .'

Readers of the issue of the *General Evening Post* dated 16–18th October 1798 enjoyed a variety of news. The Lord Mayor of London, his aldermen and councilmen were responding to Admiral Lord Nelson's gift of a sword captured from the French Admiral Blanquet at the Battle of the Nile by presenting him with one of their own 'to the value of 200 guineas'. Moves were also underway to expand Britain, and the paper stated that 'the Projected Union between the two kingdoms of England and Ireland, we are well informed, will be submitted to the respective Parliaments early in the ensuing Sessions'. Political union and the war against Revolutionary France were, of course, a mere sideshow to really vital developments of the day:

> On Saturday night a man, known by the name of *Horseflesh Dick*, for a trifling wager, ate at the King's Head Public House, in Redcross-street, a shoulder of mutton of seven-pounds weight, a bunch of turnips, half a quartern loaf, drank two pots of beer, and eight half-quarterns of bitters. He finished this brutish repast in less than an hour.

Anyone glancing at this trivial anecdote of London pub life could also hardly fail to have noticed the news item directly above it, head-lined 'ALARMING RIOT', which gave a brief summary of the attack on the Marine Police Office, and reported the death of one of the staff, Gabriel Franks. The conviction for theft of Charles Eyres was said to have triggered this 'atrocious act of violence', but as yet the killer of Franks had not been identified. Nevertheless, there was the usual confident assertion that 'hopes are entertained of bringing them to justice'.

In reality, this was a crime that had taken place in a murky street at a time of much confusion. Gabriel Franks and one of the rioters had lost their lives, but establishing who was to blame would not be an easy task. Although newspaper reports were quick to accuse the rioters for the death of Franks, none of the eyewitnesses subsequently interviewed claimed to have seen anyone other than the men from the Marine Police Office using pistols. The rioters, it seemed, were solely armed with stones.

One interesting sidelight of this affair was the part played by a local voluntary peacekeeping organisation. Although the word 'police' was regularly employed at the time, London was still three decades away from having any properly constituted regular force, but increasing attempts were being made to keep order on the streets. A body called the Wapping United Volunteers mobilised themselves on the evening of the riot, helping to quell the disturbances, and in the days that followed, marched through the streets around the Marine Police Office alongside a guard of soldiers from the nearby Tower of London in a show of strength.

During the first inquiry into the events of that night, which took place the following afternoon, the man whose conviction had sparked the riot, Charles Eyres, was brought back to the Marine Police Office and examined by magistrates. Giving evidence alongside him were two fellow coal-heavers, Newman and Buff, who had come forward at the initial trial and paid the fine on behalf of Eyres.

The way Eyres told it, the events that followed his conviction were completely out of his hands; something frightening, from which he had soon made himself scarce. This is an understandable line to have taken, given that the charge of inciting a riot carried the death penalty. He explained that once his friends had paid the fine, he then left the Office and found a crowd of something 'between one and two hundred' persons outside. Hands were laid upon him, and some of the men criticised him for having submitted to the fine, saying that 'if he had refused the demand, they would have pulled the house down in ten minutes'. Portraying himself to the court as a man completely at odds with such behaviour, Charles Eyres said he had gone home straight away to his wife and family, 'terrified by the threats of the mob, purporting that he ought to be torn to pieces'.

Newman and Buff then gave evidence. The latter stated that he had not heard any in the crowd making threats against Eyres, but that one of those he took to be a ringleader of the mob was a man he recognised named Attey, whose sanity was somewhat in question owing to the results of a trepanning operation. Newman corroborated this, saying that he too had run into Attey, and had even gone so far as to warn him and his companions against starting any disturbances 'having been a witness to the fatal effects of them in the year 1780, while performing his duty as a soldier'.

More information emerged at this hearing concerning the previously unidentified rioter who had died that night. He was named in court as

James Hanks, said to have been shot whilst attempting to climb in through one of the windows of the Office. Hanks would very likely have died immediately, since he caught a bullet full in the face at close range. As for Gabriel Franks, he had been shot through the body, and although still alive the following day, was expected to die shortly from his wounds, which in the event he did.

At the close of this hearing, Charles Eyres – who in addition to being a coal-heaver was also a soldier in the Guards regiment – was remanded in custody pending further examination.

On Thursday, 18 October, two days after the riot, a coroner's inquest was held into the death of the rioter James Hanks. Sitting at the Workhouse of the Parish of St George in the East, the coroner Edward Walker interviewed a variety of witnesses and recorded a verdict of justifiable homicide – unsurprisingly concluding that anyone climbing through a window under such circumstances had only themselves to blame if those inside fought back.

The inquest also managed to throw a little more light upon the events of that evening. In particular, the mortally wounded Gabriel Franks had been questioned on his deathbed by officers of the court and said that he had heard one of the coal-heavers out in the street say to his companion 'Give me the ammunition'. Hearing this, Franks had turned away, and was almost immediately shot through the back.

One of the principal witnesses was a local resident, Josiah Culmer, a mathematical instrument-maker. The Marine Police Office was directly outside his windows, and upon seeing the mob attacking it, he had endeavoured to put up his own shutters for protection, out of fear that they would do the same to his house. Culmer testified that he had spoken to James Hanks at this point, who seemed to be one of the leaders of the mob. According to the account of the proceedings in the following day's newspapers, the latter had assured him that they had no quarrel with him and that his windows would be safe:

> The witness told the deceased [James Hanks], they had all better get away, as they could not but perceive the officers had fire-arms. He had scarce spoken the words, before the deceased received a shot and fell on his back.

Mr Lane, a solicitor attached to the Office, told the court that he had seen Gabriel Franks running back towards the building, crying out that he had been wounded. Lane was however certain that this particular shot had not come from inside the building. He also asserted that it was only after this that the rioter James Hanks was killed, and that 'the firing on the part of the Officers was necessary, in order to prevent the mob from pulling the house down, and murdering the Magistrate'. In addition, John Gibbons, a local mast-maker who had observed much of what occurred, gave his considered opinion that the officers should have opened fire even sooner.

In his summing-up, the coroner concluded that the objective of the mob was 'to have destroyed the Marine Police Office, and perhaps take the lives of the Magistrates and Officers, consequently they were justified in defending themselves'.

Gabriel Franks lingered in hospital for almost a week, dying on 21 October. By trade, he was a lumper, one of those who worked on the river unloading ships. He had also been assisting the work of the new Marine Police Office – although he was not a sworn constable – and this was to cost him his life. On 18 October, as Franks lay mortally wounded in hospital, *The Times* reported his comments when asked who had attacked him; he said that on the evening in question, he had been 'wounded by a very tall man, a coal-heaver, who was very active in the outrage that was committed'. Since virtually the entire crowd outside the Office that night was composed of coal-heavers, this was of limited help to those seeking the person responsible, particularly as Franks had been shot from behind.

Although a number of men had been rounded up on the evening of the riot and held for questioning, James Eyres, the man who was eventually tried for the murder of Gabriel Franks, voluntarily handed himself in at the Marine Police Office a few days after the shooting, probably because he knew he had been identified as a rioter. Since he was also the brother of Charles Eyres, whose initial fine at the Marine Police Office had been the original excuse for the riot, he would have almost certainly come under official scrutiny during the inquiries into the events of that night. In a close-knit community, the names of a fair few of those involved would have been common knowledge in the aftermath of such a disturbance. In giving himself up to the authorities, Eyres almost certainly had no intention of admitting responsibility for the killing, but was rather acknowledging that he had played a part in the disturbances.

The business of establishing exactly who had shot Gabriel Franks would not be easy – a fact admitted by the authorities later that month, when they took out advertisements in the newspapers offering a large reward in return for information. The notice began by stating that Anthony Kidman, 'alias Ante', William Bartel, John McGhee, James Harwood, George Batt, 'nicknamed Serjeant', Samuel Sawyer and Peter Fostley, 'nicknamed the Jumper' were among those who had been charged with 'a desperate and outrageous Tumult and Riot', but its main purpose was to seek information regarding the killer, and the king himself was involved in the appeal:

> His Majesty, for the better discovering and bringing to Justice the Persons concerned in the said atrocious Murder and Riot, is hereby pleased to offer his most gracious Pardon to any one of them (except the Person who actually shot the said Gabriel Franks), who shall discover his or her Accomplices therein, so that he, she, or they, may be appre-hended and convicted thereof. *And, as a further encouragement*, a REWARD of ONE HUNDRED POUNDS is hereby offered to any Person making Discovery of the Person or Persons who shot the said Gabriel Franks.

This was no mean offer, and anyone working as a coal-heaver in those days could have lived for a long time indeed on the sum of £100. Perhaps it was even enough to turn a few heads.

As the last months of 1798 played themselves out, still no one was brought to the Old Bailey to be charged with the murder of Franks. In November, after days of torrential rain, the river Thames rose up and flooded many cellars and basements in Wapping, requiring the use of pumps. Richard Neave, chairman of a group of subscribers to the fund for forming a Wet Docks at Wapping, advertised a general meeting of his group to be held at the Merchant Seamen's Office on 23 November.

Meanwhile Edward Ogle took out a similar notice calling for 'proprietors and lessees of the legal quays and warehouses, situated within the City of London' to attend a meeting at Batson's Coffee House in Cornhill on 3 December, with the aim of opposing the upcoming proposals currently before parliament to build these same Wapping Docks.

As the new year began, the authorities came to the conclusion that of all the people held in custody after the October riot, the man who should be charged with the murder of Gabriel Franks was James Eyres, the brother of the man whose fine had originally sparked the protests. His trial date was duly fixed to be held at the Old Bailey on Friday, 11 January 1799.

Clearly, after such a violent uprising against the whole principle of policing London's river and its goods, there must have been considerable pressure from various quarters that someone must be held responsible. Yet of all the many witnesses called, there was none who could specifically state that James Eyres had fired the fatal shot. That he had been involved in the riot itself was attested to by a fair few of those called, such as Gabriel Butterworth, a soldier and part-time coal-heaver – by his own account an 'intimate acquaintance' of the accused. Butterworth had been drinking at a local pub that evening and went along to the Marine Police Office with Newman and Mason, the two who had paid the fine on behalf of Charles Eyres. According to Butterworth, he witnessed the moment when James Eyres stirred up the beginnings of the riot, outraged that his brother had consented to be fined by the magistrates:

'I had not been there long before Newman and Mason, and then Charles Eyres came out; the prisoner said to his brother, Charles, d——n your long eyes, have you paid the money? to which Charles said, yes, I have; he took his brother by the collar, and dragged him towards the door, and said, come along, and we will have the money back, or else we will have the house down; shortly after that, in a very short space of time, there was a man in a blue coat began breaking the windows over the Police-office door with a stick; then the people began huzzaing and making a great noise, and took up stones . . .'

Butterworth and others testified that it was James Eyres who helped pick up and cart away the body of the dead rioter James Hanks, that he was armed with large paving slabs, and also that he had threatened to knock out the brains of anyone who ran away. Yet where the shot came from that killed Gabriel Franks, no one could say.

At this point, up to the witness stand came a woman named Elizabeth Forrester, who lived a short walk east of the Marine Police Office, past Execution Dock, in Gravel Lane. She certainly had a lot to say, and her evidence placed her in the thick of the events of that night. Indeed, it may well be that it was her initial testimony given shortly after the riot that persuaded the authorities that James Eyres had a case to answer.

Elizabeth and her husband George had been drinking at John Webb's pub, the Rose & Crown, and heard news of the events taking place a few steps along the road, as had one of the other customers, Gabriel Franks. Forrester told the court:

> 'We had something to drink, and then we heard of the riot; Mr. Webb, and Franks the deceased, and another man, wanted to go out, and I said, no, I will go, they will not hurt a woman; I went out, and they were knocking against the shutters of the Police-office, and beating them to pieces, then there was a pistol fired; I was so frightened that I kept my bed for three weeks.'

To hear Elizabeth Forrester tell it, James Eyres had been the ringleader and chief instigator of all that occurred; swearing such oaths as 'let us have some more fun, we have not had our revenge yet' and 'I will have the b——y Justices' heads off'. Crucially, she also claimed to have heard him say 'fire, you b——r, fire' just before the pistol shot which killed Gabriel Franks. Admittedly, she stopped short of asserting that she knew the name of the man who pulled the trigger, at whom Eyres had directed these shouts of encouragement, but insisted, 'I tell the truth, I do not tell a lye.'

Unfortunately for her, there were many others called as witnesses that day who stood up and essentially said that Elizabeth Forrester would not be capable of telling the truth if her life depended on it. George Hall, a butcher from Wapping Wall, when asked about her character, said 'a very bad one; I believe two-thirds of the parish would give evidence to the same effect', while George Fox, a coal-undertaker of Shadwell, testified that 'she bears as infamous a character, I believe, as any woman in the world; I am convinced she would as soon swear against any Gentlemen of the Jury, as against the man at the bar'. There followed James Nash, Paul Johnson and Robert Wood, all of whom swore that they would not believe her word about anything, and even the churchwarden, William Homan, when asked in court if he would trust anything she said on oath, replied 'No, I would not, if she was to swear for an hour.'

The accused himself said virtually nothing, except to assert his innocence, and although various people came forward to give evidence of his good character – including members of the regiment to which he belonged – the role he had played in the riot counted heavily against him, and he was found guilty of murder.

Pronouncing sentence, Mr Justice Heath informed Eyres that 'all persons who take an active part in a riot are answerable, by the sound policy of our law, for all the dreadful consequences which are most likely' – in other words, he might not have pulled the trigger, but he directly contributed to the circumstances in which the murder was committed, and therefore must pay the penalty:

'I do award, and this Court doth adjudge, that you, James Eyres, the prisoner at the bar, be taken from hence to the place from whence you came, and from thence, on Monday next, to a place of execution; that there you be hanged by the neck until you are dead, and your body is afterwards to be dissected and anatomized, according to the statute in that case made and provided. The Lord have mercy upon your soul.'

James Eyres's answer to this was simply, 'Amen. I hope he will.' In the event, against all the odds, mercy came from another quarter somewhat nearer at hand, as the *Whitehall Evening Post* mentioned briefly, after a note about the Prince of Wales being given the Freedom of Grantham:

James Eyres, who was convicted of the murder of Gabriel Franks, an officer belonging to the Marine Office, Wapping, and who was to have been executed yesterday, was reprised during his Majesty's pleasure.

No reason was given for this decision, although the authorities might have felt that, despite the verdict, the evidence directly connecting Eyres to the murder was vague in the extreme, and that an execution in this case might stir up further unwanted disturbances in Wapping.

James Eyres was fortunate indeed. With only a weekend separating his trial and his date with the gallows, the reprieve had come swiftly, and at the very end of a century in which there were over two hundred hanging offences on the statute books, one more man at least had cheated the hangman's noose.

The assassination of Spencer Perceval in the lobby of the House of Commons. His attacker, John Bellingham, stands calmly behind with a pistol.

TWELVE

'AN ACT OF BLOOD, HORRID ALMOST BEYOND EXAMPLE'
1812

These days, people visiting the Houses of Parliament on any kind of business have to pass through very strict security procedures. On production of the correct authorisation, they are then photographed and shortly afterwards given an ID tag featuring that picture, which has been stamped with the day's date and a barcode, on the rear of which is the following warning: 'This is a protected site under Section 128 of the Serious Organised Crime and Police Act 2005.'

Entry is only possible through full-body airport scanners, and the police on guard are armed with sub-machine guns.

It was not always this way.

In 1812, public access to the Houses of Parliament was much less controlled. There were guards at the entrance to the main lobby of the Commons, keeping a watchful eye on things, but members of the public wishing to view the proceedings in the chamber were generally at liberty to enter without prior arrangement and watch debates. Parliament at that time did not sit in the familiar buildings designed by Charles Barry and Augustus Pugin, and there was no iconic clock tower housing Big Ben. All this was to come midway through the nineteenth century, after the disastrous fire of October 1834 had swept away almost all of the old Palace of Westminster.

The palace had originally been a royal residence, although it had not been used for that purpose for two centuries, and now served to house the members of the Commons and the Lords. For years, the peers had occupied a medieval hall known as the Queen's Chamber, but the Act of Union with Ireland in 1801 increased their number and they subsequently relocated to the larger White Chamber, while the Commons had been meeting in the former St Stephen's Chapel since 1550. As for the business under discussion there in May 1812, MPs were debating whether to reform the electoral system, which still allowed so-called Rotten Boroughs with virtually no electors to return members to the House of Commons. This was presumably a matter of some interest to future Chancellor of the Exchequer Nicholas Vansittart – one of two MPs for Old Sarum, an unoccupied Neolithic hill fort in Wiltshire – whose seat had only five electors in 1802, the year he was nominated unopposed.

The metropolis in which parliament sat was vast by the standards of the day; ten times the size of any other in the nation, numbering 1,304,000 people at the census of 1811. Compared with the London of modern times, however, the city as shown on the map produced by R. Wilkinson in that census year looks decidedly compact. Immediately to the south and west of Parliament itself was the grassland of Tothill Fields – now covered by Millbank and the Vauxhall Bridge Road – which was still being used for bull-baiting. Green Park and Hyde Park marked the western edge of the metropolis; in the north, the city petered out just above Tavistock Square and Hoxton Square, while the eastern edge of the city gave way to fields around Cable Street and the Mile End Road. Directly across Westminster Bridge from the seat of parliament lay a thinly populated district which was also mostly agricultural. Lambeth Palace stood there, as it had in one form or another since the twelfth century, but otherwise the area housed the types of building that were typically located outside the main city: an asylum, the Magdalen Hospital and the Westminster Lying-in Hospital. This, then, was the scope of Regency London in the final years of the Napoleonic War.

The poet Shelley, aged twenty that year, once wrote that 'poets are the unacknowledged legislators of the World', yet for now, the person who had the job of running the British Empire on behalf of the Prince Regent was Spencer Perceval, the prime minister. Born in the capital fifty years earlier, he might have made decisions which reached out across the globe, but, according to the *Dictionary of National Biography*, 'he knew little at first hand of the world outside London and is said to have travelled no further than Knutsford [in Cheshire] and then only once'. Having variously been Solicitor-General, Attorney-General, Chancellor of the Exchequer and Leader of the Commons, he became prime minister in 1809, after the death of the then incumbent, the third duke of Portland. A staunch opponent of parliamentary reform and Catholic emancipation, he had nevertheless been strongly in favour of the abolition of the transatlantic slave trade in 1807, and above all had proved a firm pair of hands during the continuing war against Napoleon, whom he memorably compared to the beast with seven heads and ten horns from the *Book of Revelations*, 'drunken with the blood of the saints'. This choice of religious imagery was no accident, since Perceval was himself a very committed Evangelical Christian.

The prime minister was a steady leader in time of war, and, by all accounts, a modest, hard-working, generous man, untainted by scandal in an age ridden with stories of corruption and venery in high places. Perceval certainly cut an uncontroversial figure when placed next to his contemporary Viscount Castlereagh – who was singled out by Shelley in a verse ('I met murder on the way / He had a mask like Castlereagh'), and also by Byron, who later wrote an epitaph urging passers-by to urinate on Castlereagh's grave.

Spencer Perceval in all his public life seems not to have prompted such enmity, and yet, on 11 May 1812, a man walked up to him with a pair of pistols and shot him dead.

It was a relatively normal afternoon at the House of Commons. Shortly after five o'clock, the lobby of the House contained around twenty people. There were MPs, peers of the realm, a variety of officers employed by parliament, and also a mixture of 'strangers'. A guard was stationed at the entrance, and another inside the lobby, but even so, the general public was used to being able to gain access to Westminster Hall and to the public gallery of the Commons, and people were not searched on their way in or out. Some who came were regular visitors, their faces known to those who worked at the Palace of Westminster.

Parliament had been in recess since the beginning of the month, but there was always work to do. So far that year the Commons had debated matters such as the Sea Water Baths Bill – which proposed the building of a baths near London 'as being highly beneficial to the health of the inhabitants in the cure of cutaneous and eruptive disorders' – and the London Theatres Bill, concerning the licensing of a new theatre for the capital, which, according to *Hansard*, was supported by Lord Ossulston 'in a speech of considerable length, but in a tone of voice altogether inaudible'.

There was nothing to suggest that 11 May would prove to be anything other than a quiet day in which such members of both Houses who happened to be present would apply themselves diligently to paperwork, routine discussions or the contents of the building's well-stocked cellars, as the inclination took them. However, just inside the first doorway to the lobby of the Commons – the one through which anyone would have to pass in order to gain entrance to the building – stood someone later described by an eyewitness as 'a tall, large-boned man, about forty years of age, with a long thin visage, and aquiline nose'. His eyes were said to be sunken, and his complexion 'of a ghastly, pallid hue'.

The stranger's name was John Bellingham. He was born in London, around the year 1771. His father was a land surveyor and miniature painter, his mother 'the daughter of a respectable country gentleman'. It was later said that Bellingham's father had spent a year in St Luke's Hospital suffering from 'mental derangement', and died in that state when the boy was just nine. When Bellingham was fourteen, his mother apprenticed him to a jeweller in Whitechapel called Mr Love, but he soon absconded and signed up in 1787 as a sailor aboard one of the largest merchant ships of the East India Company, the *Hartwell*, which set sail with a cargo of silver on its ill-fated maiden voyage to China. It sank off Cape Verde after a mutiny in which the captain and a small number of officers and men held off most of the crew at gunpoint for several days. Exactly what part Bellingham might have played in this event – and on which side – is an interesting question. He eventually made his way back to England and, after an itinerant existence of several years, set up as a tradesman in Oxford Street in 1793, aided by financial backing from his mother. This latest venture ended in bankruptcy the following year, and it was also rumoured that he had set fire to his own house.

John Bellingham, still in his early twenties, but having hardly made a glowing success of his life to date, eventually opted to leave the country once again and wound up in the Russian city of Archangel, on the White Sea. Since the days of Ivan the Terrible nearly two hundred years earlier there had been trade between England and Russia, and Bellingham later said that in 1804 he went there 'on some mercantile business of importance to myself'. He worked there for a while as a clerk to a Russian merchant, but shortly before returning home, became caught up in a dispute between the owners of a local ship called the *Soleure*, which had sunk in the White Sea, and its insurers, Lloyd's of London, who refused to pay out on the loss. In some way blamed for this, Bellingham was then imprisoned for debt in 1804 by the Russian authorities – unjustly, so he claimed – and this was the beginning of the tortuous road that led him to the House of Commons in 1812.

From his prison cell, Bellingham appealed for help to the local British consul at Archangel, who forwarded his concerns to the British ambassador, Lord Granville Leveson Gower at the Russian court. Gower wrote to the governor of Archangel, but received the reply that Bellingham was being held legally, and had conducted himself 'in a very indecorous manner'. At this, the ambassador concluded that there was nothing to be done, and let the matter rest. Despite numerous requests written from a series of gaols in which he was held, Bellingham remained in prison until freed by the Russians in 1809, after which he returned to London.

The experience left John Bellingham with an overpowering sense of grievance against the British government, whom he felt had abandoned him to his fate. In their defence, they held to the opinion that the matter fell entirely under Russian jurisdiction and there was therefore nothing they could have done. Over the next three years, Bellingham relentlessly sought compensation from the government by letter and in person for all that he had suffered in Archangel, beginning with an approach to the Secretary of State for Foreign Affairs, the marquess of Wellesley (brother of the duke of Wellington). Eventually, he wrote to the prime minister himself, but when this failed, he began haunting the House of Commons, and was an everyday sight to some who worked there. The building was familiar territory to Bellingham, and he might well have known that the prime minister had a habit of arriving sometime around five o'clock each afternoon.

On 11 May 1812, some three years after his return from captivity in Russia, John Bellingham set off once more for the Houses of Parliament. Earlier in the day, he had attended mass at the chapel of the Foundling Hospital, and had then passed the time until four o'clock at the European Museum – an art gallery in St James's Square – in the company of a woman who lived in the house where he lodged. When he finally caught sight of Spencer Perceval, he did not hesitate.

It was all over in a matter of seconds. Henry Burgess, a solicitor, chanced to be in the lobby of the House of Commons. At around 5.15 that afternoon, he heard a pistol shot and then saw a man staggering in his direction with his hands against his chest, then falling forwards onto the ground. At this point, Burgess might not even have realised the identity of the injured person, but he soon noticed that the gunman had not run away, as he later testified at the Old Bailey:

> 'I heard some people say, that is the man, and I saw a man pointing towards a bench by the side of the fire place, at the side of the lobby. I immediately at the same instant went to the bench, I saw the prisoner sitting on the bench in great agitation, I looked at both hands, and saw his left hand on the bench, and in his hand, or under his hand I saw the pistol, I immediately took the pistol in my hand and asked him what could have induced him to do such a thing, or act; he replied, want of redress of grievance, and refusal by government.'

The man was also disarmed of a matching loaded pistol, similar to the one he had fired, which was found in his coat pocket together with a penknife, a pencil, a bunch of keys, and some money. Meanwhile, across the lobby, a small group had gathered around the body of the wounded prime minister. He was still breathing, but only just.

William Smith, MP for Norwich and a leading anti-slavery campaigner, had been near to Spencer Perceval when the attack happened. He heard the sound of the pistol, saw a group of perhaps ten people near the entrance, and heard some of them crying out that the doors should be secured and no one let out. Just at this moment, a figure came towards him, looking, as he recalled 'rather like one seeking for shelter, than as the person who had received the wound'. As the man moved closer, it became clear that he was injured: ' . . . taking two or three steps towards me, as he approached he rather reeled by me, and almost instantly fell upon the floor, with his face downwards.'

As the victim fell, Smith thought he heard him say the word 'murder, or something very much like that'. Not yet suspecting that the man was seriously hurt, the MP waited for him to pick himself up, but there was no further movement:

> 'I therefore immediately stooped down to raise him from the ground, requesting the assistance of a gentleman who stood close by me for that purpose. As soon as we had turned his face towards us, and not till then, I perceived it was Mr. Perceval. We then took him in our arms, the other gentleman on his left side, and I on his right. We carried him into the office of the speaker's secretary, and seated ourselves on a table there with Mr. Perceval between us also sitting on the table.'

A doctor was sent for; William Lynn, who lived nearby in Great George Street. By the time he arrived a few minutes later, Perceval was still being held up in the same sitting position on the table, with his feet placed on a couple of chairs, but there was no sign of a pulse. The prime minister had evidently died shortly after being brought into the room, although there was little blood to be seen on his white waistcoat or his shirt. Among those gathered around him during his last moments was his brother, Lord Arden.

Perceval had been killed, the doctor concluded, by a large-bore pistol ball through the chest, just above the heart. The bullet had travelled in a downward direction, since Perceval was a man of short stature, and Bellingham – who was tall – had apparently reached his arm over another gentleman in order to fire at the prime minister.

With the doors secured, and the victim dead, Bellingham was taken upstairs to the Commons chamber itself for questioning, along with various witnesses. He did not deny that he had pulled the trigger, yet seemed curiously unmoved by the horror-struck faces of those around him. Lieutenant General Gascoyne, MP for Liverpool, said 'I think I know the villain', walked up to him, and asked him to his face, 'Is not your name Bellingham?' The killer made no reply.

A constable from Bow Street was despatched immediately to search Bellingham's lodgings at 9 New Millman Street, south of the Foundling Hospital, near Russell Square. His name was John Vickery, and he later testified as to what he discovered there:

> 'I found in a drawer up stairs in a bed-room, a pair of pistol bags, in the same drawer I found a small powder-flask, this pistol key, it fits the pistol exactly, and a quantity of letters and papers; and I found a mould and some balls. This ball fits the pistol exactly, and it was made in this mould I have no doubt.'

Here was clear evidence of premeditation, and of the assassin calmly melting down lead to manufacture ammunition for his guns. It also became clear that Bellingham had recently approached a local tailor from Gray's Inn Lane and asked him to modify a coat so that it would have a nine-inch deep inside pocket on the left-hand side, large enough to hold a pistol.

If in doubt, as they say, go right to the top. John Bellingham felt badly treated by the British government, and so he took his complaint directly to the man in charge. No matter that the events of which he complained had happened, not on Perceval's watch, but under three previous prime ministers, two of whom were already dead. Indeed, by the time that his victim assumed office in October 1809, the Russians were flinging open the doors of Bellingham's cell and sending him home, but this would probably have cut no ice with the assassin. On the day after the killing, and later at his trial and when interviewed in his cell, John Bellingham remained calm, coldly polite and implacably convinced that his actions were logical and justified.

The newspapers published the following day reflected the national mood of astonishment mingled with revulsion at the killing. *The Times* called it 'a crime at which humanity shudders', and went on to voice the general opinion that it defied all expectations: 'We have said before that such occurrences do not often occur in England. God forbid they should! The Duke of Buckingham was, we believe, the last Minister that was murdered . . .'

Buckingham had indeed functioned as a kind of unofficial prime minister in the time of James I, long before such a post existed, and had been assassinated in Portsmouth almost two hundred years earlier. His killer was hanged, drawn and quartered, and there were probably those in Perceval's time who would have been happy to see Bellingham meet a similar end.

However, the idea that murderous assaults upon figures of authority was something unusual in London is not strictly true. George III, for instance, had been attacked with a knife outside St James's Palace in 1786 by a woman named Margaret Nicholson, and then shot at in the Drury Lane Theatre by a man named James Hadfield in 1800. Nevertheless, Spencer Perceval remains the only prime minister of Britain ever to have been assassinated.

The *Morning Chronicle* called it 'a most atrocious and afflicting event . . . under circumstances that find no parallel in history':

> The dreadful intelligence spread with amazing rapidity, and before six o'clock, the crowd collected on the outside was so great, that it was deemed prudent to close the doors of Westminster Hall, as well as to plant constables at all the entrances . . . The multitude kept augmenting every minute, and at length it was resolved, that in order to ensure tranquillity, and to produce a dispersion of the mob, that the Horse Guards should be called out . . . The environs of Parliament-street and Palace-yard were rendered almost impassable, notwithstanding the vigilance of the police officers.

As the evening progressed, the authorities also mobilised the Foot Guards, the City Militia and various volunteer bodies to keep order, as it was feared that this event might be the start of a general uprising against the Establishment. The French Revolution, and in particular the Terror of 1793–4, was fresh in the collective memory. One of parliament's actions on the evening of the killing was to prepare instructions which were sent out to the civic and military authorities in all parts of the country to help keep the peace, 'particularly in these districts where an inflamed and infatuated multitude have committed the most savage barbarities'.

Bellingham was sent off to Newgate, under strong and constant guard in case he might try to commit suicide, but this seems to have been the last thing on his mind. Arriving at 1 am on the Tuesday morning, he immediately went to bed and slept soundly until 7 am. After a breakfast of tea and buttered rolls, he told his keepers, 'They can do me no harm, but Government have cause to fear.'

Around the same hour that Bellingham was arriving at Newgate, the body of Spencer Perceval was taken out of the Palace of Westminster and brought to his home in Downing Street. The following morning, at 11 am on Tuesday, 12 May, the coroner's inquest into this major crime against the state took place a few yards away from the dead prime minister's house at the pub on the corner, the Cat & Bagpipes.

The stage was now set for a trial at the Old Bailey. Today, the gap between the crime and a murder trial of such importance might be months or even years. In 1812, the path of justice was frighteningly swift: Perceval was shot on Monday 11, and the Old Bailey trial was arranged for Friday 15.

The great and the good assembled at the Central Criminal Court at the Old Bailey around 10 am on the morning of 15 May. In addition to the presiding judge, Lord Chief Justice Sir James Mansfield, also present were the Lord Mayor of London, George III's son the duke of Clarence, the marquess of Wellesley, numerous MPs and virtually every one of the aldermen of London. According to the account in *The Times* the following day, 'the crowd was so immense that no distinction of rank was attended to'. Their reporter also noted the presence of 'a great number of Ladies, all led by the most intense curiosity to behold the assassin'. As an anonymous one-sheet pamphlet published soon afterwards put it, 'in the memory of the oldest person the Court was never so crowded'.

Soon after 10 am, John Bellingham appeared in a light-brown coat and a yellow striped waistcoat, and bowed to the court. He looked calm and self-possessed, just as he had done all week, 'with a firm step, quite undismayed'. This was in marked contrast to many others in the room, including the Lord Chief Justice himself. Indeed, Sir James Mansfield, on two occasions when addressing the court, found it hard even to say the name of Spencer Perceval without breaking down, as the trial transcript records: 'here the learned judge was so hurt by his feelings, that he could not proceed for several seconds'; and a few moments later, 'here again his lordship was sincerely affected, and burst into tears, in which he was joined by the greatest portion of the persons in court'.

Initially, Mr Alley, the counsel for Bellingham, moved to have the trial postponed, arguing that his client was insane and that time was required in order to establish this – although the assassin himself had maintained all week that he did not wish to plead insanity. The judge refused the application, and then a succession of witnesses was called who had been present in the Commons at the time of the killing. William Smith MP told how he had assisted Spencer Perceval in the moments after the shooting. William Lynn the surgeon gave evidence concerning the nature of the wound, and confirmed that the victim had certainly died as a result of the pistol shot. Henry Burgess, the solicitor who had disarmed Bellingham, expressed the opinion that at the time of the shooting the killer had seemed 'very much agitated' – an impression reinforced by other witnesses. Within a few minutes of the shooting, however, it seemed that Bellingham had regained his icy calm, and then remained that way.

The MP for Liverpool, Lieutenant General Gascoyne – who had helped search the pockets of the assassin as he sat in the lobby after Perceval had fallen – explained that he recognised Bellingham, because the man had come to his house in order to ask for help in his quest for redress against the government. Other witnesses included John Norris, who was in the habit of sitting in the Strangers' Gallery to watch debates in the House of Commons, and who chanced to be there at the time of the shooting. He testified that he had frequently seen Bellingham up in the gallery, as did Vincent Dowling, who had helped disarm Bellingham, and had on one occasion sat next to him while watching debates and conversed with him for half an hour or so.

The picture emerged of a man who had spent a great deal of time in recent months roaming the corridors of the House of Commons, watching the comings and goings, and preparing his ground. As a familiar face, he would have excited little notice when loitering near the entrance to the lobby on Monday, 11 May, least of all from the guards. He became part of the background, so that when he suddenly emerged into the foreground with a pistol in his hand, it was too late to stop him.

After a variety of such witnesses, there came the moment that most of those present had come to see – the testimony of Bellingham himself, in which he had his chance to explain his actions. This he proceeded to do, evidently to his own satisfaction, if not to that of anyone else:

> 'Gentlemen, As to the lamentable catastrophe for which I am now on my trial before this court, if I am the man that I am supposed to be, to go and deliberately shoot Mr. Perceval without malice, I should consider myself a monster, and not fit to live in this world or the next.'

Of course, this was precisely what many of his listeners thought him to be, and the truth is that nothing that followed was likely to have changed their minds. Bellingham detailed at length his Russian adventures, and gave extracts from his correspondence with various government bodies in the aftermath of his imprisonment and return to England. He said that in the past year, he had attempted to contact the prime minister himself, but had simply received an answer via a secretary that 'Mr. Perceval could not encourage my hopes'. In addition, Bellingham said that he had written to the Prince Regent 'with a statement of my sufferings'.

In arguing that until his Russian imprisonment 'there was not a spot on my character', he was somewhat glossing over his previous bankruptcy in England, and, of course, he might also have participated in the mutiny on board the *Hartwell* in 1787. Yet the picture Bellingham painted of himself to the court was that of a blameless man, cruelly abandoned in a foreign land by the representatives of his country. Having been told, during his recent correspondence with the Treasury, that he could expect nothing from them and that he was at liberty to take such steps as he thought fit, Bellingham was convinced that the blame for anything that followed was therefore a matter for the government, not him. Having made this dubious point, he then began issuing threats to the court:

> 'I trust this fatal catastrophe will be warning to other ministers. If they had listened to my case this court would not have been engaged in this case, but Mr. Perceval obstinately refusing to sanction my claim in Parliament I was driven to despair, and under these agonizing feelings I was impelled to that desperate alternative which I unfortunately adopted. My arm was the instrument that shot Mr. Perceval, but, gentlemen, ought I not to be redressed.'

As for his choice of victim, it seems that several other men would have done just as well, but the prime minister happened to arrive in the lobby first:

> 'If I had met Lord Gower he would have received the ball, and not Mr. Perceval. As to death, if it were to be suffered five hundred times, I should prefer it to the injuries and indignities which I have experienced in Russia.'

Small wonder that after a performance such as this, the only witnesses then called by the defence were several old friends of Bellingham, who dutifully lined up to declare that in their opinion he had not been sane for some years now, and that whenever the subject of his claim against the government had come up in conversation, he behaved as if deranged.

In summing up, Sir James Mansfield had difficulty in controlling his emotions but took care to discourage any thought in the minds of the jury that Bellingham might be insane. A lunatic, he suggested, would have needed care and attention, and therefore have been incapable of living on his own and planning such an action methodically over the course of some time. As for the case itself, Mansfield held it to be an essentially simple matter:

> 'The only question you have to try, is, whether the prisoner did wilfully and maliciously murder Mr. Spencer Perceval or not. It is not necessary to go very minutely into the evidence which has been produced to the fact, as there is little doubt as to the main object of your enquiry.'

Perhaps unsurprisingly, the jury sat for just two-and-a-half minutes in the box, and then asked to retire to consider their verdict. As they filed out of the court, according to the trial transcript, 'the prisoner regarded them separately with a look of mingled confidence and complacency'. It served no purpose. They returned after only fourteen minutes and delivered a unanimous guilty verdict.

The trial that Friday had lasted from 10 am until 6.15 pm – a marathon session by the standards of the day, when even murder hearings could still be wrapped up in an hour or two. John Bellingham was then given just the weekend in which to mull over his fate, for he was sentenced to be hanged on Monday morning, 18 May.

The following day, Saturday 16, the funeral of Spencer Perceval took place. He was taken from Downing Street at 8 am, and the cortege set off on the long journey to his family's ancestral manor house at Charlton, in Kent. He left behind his wife Jane, six sons and six daughters. Parliament debated the question of their upkeep on the day of the trial, and had voted in favour of a considerable sum of money to be provided for the purpose, as well as plans for a monument in Westminster Abbey. The results of their deliberations were then formally presented to the Prince Regent at Carlton House by a procession of 140 carriages from the Commons, led by the Speaker, and 56 carriages from the Lords led by the Lord Chancellor.

This was not the only activity to be seen on London roads. Five thousand troops had been brought in and quartered at Lambeth, and several country regiments were also ordered to the capital, in case this assassination proved to be the beginning of wider unrest. Huge crowds were expected outside Newgate for the execution on Monday, and the leader article in the Saturday edition of *The Times* specifically warned people to stay away. This may have been for fear of disturbances, but the main reason was to avoid a repetition of the horrific scenes that had accompanied the hangings of John Holloway, Owen Haggerty and Elizabeth Godfrey outside Newgate in 1807, when the crush was so great that scores of people died and many more were injured: 'If any should in the present instance become the victims of their own curiosity, either through the pressure of crowd, or any other accident, they will hardly deserve compassion.'

On Sunday, the day before the execution, readers of the *Observer*, curious to see the face of the assassin but not wishing to risk their lives in the mob, were presented with the following offer:

To morrow will be Published at MR DIGHTON'S, Spring Gardens, Charing Cross, a CORRECT LIKENESS of JOHN BELLINGHAM, taken during his Trial at the Old Bailey, May 15th, 1812.

Bellingham's final day, when it came, was cold and it was raining heavily, so the crowds were not as large as had been feared. Over the weekend, the prisoner, 'composed, but dejected', wrote a last letter to his estranged wife in Liverpool, and had also asked for jelly. He spoke at length on the Sunday evening to a clergyman called Daniel Wilson, vicar of St John's, Bedford Row, who later published a summary of their talk as a pamphlet entitled *The Substance of a Conversation with John Bellingham*, padded out with a vast amount of religious exhortation and windy moralising. Yet despite all this, Wilson concluded that Bellingham was still convinced that he had acted correctly in shooting Perceval.

The condemned man reportedly slept soundly each night over the weekend, and was then woken at 6 am on the morning of the execution. He was taken out by the Ordinary of Newgate, Dr Ford, and declared himself 'perfectly ready'. Bellingham's iron fetters were then removed and he was formally asked by Mr Sheriff Birch whether anyone else had been involved in a conspiracy with him to kill the prime minister, to which he replied, 'Certainly not.' He then expressed regret for the sorrow he had caused to Spencer Perceval's family and friends. Bellingham's hands were bound, and then, according to the *Observer*, the prisoner 'ascended the scaffold with rather a light step, a cheerful countenance, and a confident and calm, but not at all exulting air'.

At 8 am, as the clock struck, he was launched into oblivion, with some in the crowd apparently chanting, 'God bless you! God bless you!' He hung there for an hour, after which his body was taken by cart, covered with a sack, to St Bartholomew's Hospital for dissection.

Spencer Perceval died on a Monday afternoon. His killer, John Bellingham, was executed the following Monday morning. Five years later, they were reunited in the Strand, as part of *Ewing's Grand Exhibition of Royal Wax Figures*, which later toured the country.

Alongside life-size waxworks of 'celebrated Personages, highly gratifying to the Curious', depicting the likes of 'Bonaparte in Disguise, as he made his Escape from Moscow', and 'The Unfortunate Miss Vane, who was Burnt to Death at Bilby Hall', a sixpenny ticket would also allow the public to see:

A most correct Likeness of the assassin John Bellingham, as he appeared after condemnation, heavily ironed.

The Right Hon. Spencer Perceval, late Prime Minister – the only Wax Figure of him in the Kingdom.

Newgate prison in the early nineteenth century, designed by the architect
George Dance the Younger

THIRTEEN

EAST SIDE, WEST SIDE, ALL AROUND THE TOWN
1836

The London of 1836 was a city whose population had almost doubled since the turn of the century, and now stood at around two million. On its northern boundaries, the buildings now extended up as far as Camden and St John's Wood, with the new Regent's Park between them. South London was more sparsely developed, yet in among the fields and farms there were a fair few houses strung out along roads in places such as the Oval, Camberwell and Kennington, while areas like Walworth were quite densely developed. Bethnal Green, Stepney and the Mile End Road still marked the eastern edge of the city, and the main difference to be seen in that district was the rash of new dock basins which had been constructed since the beginning of the century.

As the West End pushed ever further outwards in the area of Hyde Park, a semi-rural turnpike called the Edgware Road currently formed the north-western extremity of the city, although houses had begun springing up along it in recent years. The green fields beyond, above what is now the Bayswater Road, were also being marked out for building. For the moment, however, the main distinguishing features of this nondescript area were the pair of large water reservoirs on either side of Praed Street, and above them the basin of the Regent's Canal.

The passing of the Metropolitan Police Act on 19 June 1829 had finally given London an organised body responsible for law enforcement in the capital. By the end of the century, their work would involve forensics, photography, telephones and telegrams, but for now these three thousand men – nicknamed Peelers or Bobbies after their founder, Sir Robert Peel – employed far simpler methods. Their principal job was keeping order, rather than detection, and they backed up their actions with stout wooden truncheons. Yet there were some crime cases at that time that called for intelligence rather than muscle, and one in particular which occurred in 1836 proved a fitting test of the investigative powers of the new force.

It was the Christmas holiday season towards the end of December, 1836, and London readers of the *Morning Post* had much to tempt them: amongst many attractions, they were cordially invited to view 'La belle giraffe' at the Cosmorama Rooms, Regent Street ('this noble Animal . . . the largest ever seen in this country'); buy shares in one of the many new railway companies springing up and touting for business; or subscribe money towards a proposed statue of the duke of Wellington to be sited near London Bridge. Anyone searching for the perfect Christmas gift might have considered Rowland's Macassar Oil ('for creating and sustaining luxuriant silken tresses'), some Indestructible Terrious Teeth made by Albert & Co., Haymarket, or, for those really pushing the boat out, Transparent Sperm Candles at one shilling-and-eleven pence a pound from Messrs. T Cane of Oxford Street. There was also a new book entitled *Sketches By Boz* – advertised by its publisher John Macrone as 'Appropriate Christmas Reading' – which marked the beginning of the success of a certain Charles Dickens. This collection of literary snapshots of London included one on Scotland Yard, in which he noted that the Police Commissioners had 'established their office in Whitehall Place'.

All of these tempting suggestions appeared in the same issue of the *Morning Post*, but a few pages later, news items highlighted the other side of the festive season:

SNOW BALLS – DARING OUTRAGE

On Wednesday afternoon last a gang of ruffians assembled in the neighbourhood of Grays Inn-road, and commenced pelting the passengers with snow balls, and their chief object of attack was upon old women, some of whom were pelted and rolled in the snow.

Unpleasant, certainly, but the city could offer far worse treatment to some, as another headline starkly proclaimed:

'A MUTILATED HUMAN BODY FOUND'

The press, and the public, have long been attracted to the kind of murder story where the corpse winds up in pieces – the classic example in recent times being the strip club homicide which gave rise to the 15 April 1983 *New York Post* front page, 'HEADLESS BODY IN TOPLESS BAR'. In the Edgware Road murder of Christmas 1836, all the elements for a sensational story were there from the beginning. On 28 December a torso had been found, lacking both head and legs. It was left in a spot right on the very edge of London, 150 yards south of the turnpike toll-gate known as the Pineapple Gate.

The remains were hidden in a new cluster of half-finished houses at the northernmost developed section of the Edgware Road, very close to where it petered out into open fields. On the eastern side of the street stood a run of occupied houses known as Clarendon Place, just above the point where the St John's Wood Road joined the Edgware Road. Opposite, not far from where the Regent's Canal crossed the road, nine new houses were under construction, known as Canterbury Villas. Four were already inhabited; the others would soon be ready. It was here – roughly opposite the place where today the St John's Wood Road joins the road now called Maida Vale – that a building worker named Bond discovered the torso of a woman hidden behind a large flagstone which leant against the front garden wall of one of the unfinished buildings:

> As he was passing the stone he observed something dark behind it, which, on nearer inspection, he found to be a wrapper of coarse canvas, sewed together, and resembling a bag used for bran. On removing the stone and lifting it up, he perceived a pool of blood, of about nine inches in diameter, which had apparently oozed through the canvas wrapper. Alarmed by the discovery, he instantly called to two men who had the care of the unfinished buildings, who, on their arrival, advised him to open the package, which he then did. In addition to the human trunk, it contained a child's frock, made of the commonest printed cotton, and in a very tattered condition from frequent wearing.

The sack also contained a very dirty old towel, cryptically marked 'C.J., 2B. (J.C.B.)', and a square piece of an old cotton shawl with a blue border. It was almost as if the killer was deliberately trying to leave a varied selection of clues to satisfy even the most jaded of detectives.

In the first instance, the torso was taken to the local poorhouse, and a Dr Girdwood was sent for, who lived a little further south down the Edgware Road. He concluded that the remains were of a middle-aged woman who seemed to have been married, to judge from the marks of a wedding ring still visible on her finger. Girdwood felt that death had probably occurred sometime in the last twenty-four hours, although because of the weather conditions, 'it might have lain in the situation in which it was found for three or four days, the severity of the frost and the snow preserving the fresh appearance which it exhibits'.

Here can be seen the beginnings of a much more thorough forensic approach to crime solving, and in contrast to the kind of news reports that would have appeared in the papers of ten or twenty years before, a new note was sounded of the Metropolitan Police in action: 'Inspector Feltham and Sergeant Hampton, of the S division, and constable Pegler, 104S, have been actively engaged all day in prosecuting their inquiries.'

At this stage, all the investigators had was the unidentified trunk of a body. There were initial theories that this might not be murder, but just some kind of a macabre prank played by medical students.

An inquest had been held at the White Lion Inn, Edgware Road, at which witnesses spoke of having observed a horse and cart near the spot where the body was found; they had suspected that the driver was loitering in the area intending to steal building materials from the unfinished houses. This was said to be before it had begun snowing: a significant point, since the sack containing the body did not have snow underneath it, suggesting that it had lain there since round about the same time. Dr Girdwood, who had examined the body, expressed the opinion that the throat of the victim had been cut, and the mutilations had happened after death. In the absence of the complete body, he estimated the height of the woman at between five feet seven and five feet eight. Having listened to extensive evidence over a six-hour period, the coroner's jury were then taken to the nearby Paddington poorhouse on the corner of Harrow Road, to view what there was of the deceased; a grim business: 'On entering they were conducted to a dark passage, where, on the lid of a shell, the mutilated remains of the unfortunate woman had been previously laid.'

Their verdict, unsurprisingly, was 'Wilful murder against some person or persons unknown'.

A week after the inquest, on 6 January 1837, the *Morning Post* excitedly claimed that the severed head 'of a woman about thirty-four' had been dragged out of a pond in leafy Watford by a dog. Jumping to the obvious conclusion, they stated that 'from the fresh appearance of the head in question there can be little doubt of its relation to the subject of the recent horrible and revolting murder'. This prompted a terse letter from a certain Mr Pugh, clerk of the magistrates at Watford, saying that no head of a female had been found in their area, and that they had no missing persons. However, on Monday, 9 January, the papers once again reported the discovery of a head – much closer to home – and this time it was true.

An East London lock-keeper named Mathias Ralph had an unpleasant start to his day's work on Saturday 7 at the Ben Johnson Lock on the Regent's Canal, in a part of Stepney known as the World's End. Around 8.30 am, having just let a coal barge through, he found that the lock gates would not shut properly because something was caught in the gap between them, so he called out to his colleagues, 'It is a dead dog, ease the gate.' As Ralph later testified, he certainly had something dead on his hands, but not what he expected: 'I pulled it up, and, to my surprise, I found the head of a human being . . . I saw the ear first – that made me know it was the head of a human being.'

From long experience of hauling bodies out of the canal, he judged that the head might have been in the water for four or five days ('I cannot exactly say,' he explained, 'because sometimes bodies will change in a short time, and sometimes not for a long time'). Whatever the explanation, it was hardly a pretty sight:

'I examined it, and found the right eye to be knocked out by a stick, or some other weapon. I found the flesh in a perfect state, not sodden, the left jaw-bone was broken, and penetrated through the skin, the bone itself was through the skin. I observed that the left ear had been pierced, and had had an earring torn through in youth.'

Having made his initial inspection, the keeper went into his house to fetch a cloth, wrapped up the head, with its plentiful quantity of long, greying brown hair, 'took it to the bone-house, and locked the door'. Mr Baker, the local coroner, was summoned, and then it fell to a surgeon from Mile End called Mr Birtwhistle to give his considered opinion. He agreed that the head had probably been in the water for something like five days, and 'had been very dexterously cut off with some sharp instrument, and the fifth cervical vertebrae sawn through, and not disarticulated as a surgeon might have done it'.

Yet again, the partial remains had shown up at a lonely spot on the very edge of London, where the city turned to countryside. In this case, the lock where the discovery was made was in the final stretch of the Regent's Canal as it heads down to meet the Thames at the Limehouse Basin. Ben Johnson Lock was below the Mile End Road, not far from the church of St Dunstan's in Stepney where the bone-house was located, but an isolated place set away from houses, with the grassland of Bow Common stretching away on the eastern side. It was possible that the killer had journeyed here to this out-of-the-way place in order to dispose of the remains, but also, since the Regent's Canal ran all the way across London from Paddington to Stepney, that the head had been thrown in the water somewhere near the place where the trunk had been found, and had spent the intervening time drifting down the channel.

Hearing of this new discovery, Inspector Feltham of Hermitage Street Police Station at Paddington Green, and Constable Pegler, who had been first on the scene when the trunk was discovered, travelled across to Stepney to view the head. In a further development, a couple had come forward from the outlying village of Willesden, saying that the published description of the victim closely resembled their former lodger, one Sarah Ricketts, who had not been seen since setting off to visit Buckinghamshire some time previously. Meanwhile, the trunk whose discovery had started off the investigation had been interred, it was reported, 'which was necessary, as the smell arising from it became very offensive'. However, it was exhumed shortly afterwards, so that the authorities could see if it fitted the head found at the Ben Johnson Lock.

A group of surgeons, together with the various police officers involved in the case, gathered on Sunday, 8 January, at the Paddington poorhouse in order to compare the head, which had arrived in a sealed parcel, with the mutilated torso that had been found a few streets away. The face of the deceased woman had fair skin, grey eyes 'with a shade of hazel' – although one was missing – and hair nearly two feet in length. The assembled doctors voiced the opinion that 'the profile struck all of us as being very much of the lower order of Irish'. Crucially, when they placed the head directly against the severed neck of the Edgware Road trunk, it corresponded exactly.

So now Inspector Feltham and his team had a trunk and a head that matched, but the identity of the victim remained a mystery, and no lower limbs had yet come to light. Nevertheless, as the saying goes, this case would prove to have legs.

<hr />

The discovery of the head was progress of a kind, yet until it became clear who the woman was, and where she had lived, the police were still a very long way from apprehending the criminal. One thing that could be ruled out immediately was the suggestion that this was the missing Sarah Ricketts from Willesden, since the couple who had come forward failed to identify the head when it was shown to them. However, this investigation was far more detailed and painstaking than would have been likely forty years earlier. In the eighteenth century, many of the murderers who were brought to trial at the Old Bailey had been caught literally red-handed at the scene of their crime, or had left such an obvious array of clues behind them that there was little hope of escape. The Edgware Road murder had something of an altogether more modern aspect, both in the efforts of the killer to dispose carefully of the body, and the scope and detail of the police investigation into the crime.

The case had already stirred up a great interest among the general public – indeed, so many people had gathered outside the bone-house in Stepney over the weekend when the head was there that Superintendent Young of K Division had to make special arrangements to prevent sightseers going in to view it. As a further measure, the man in charge of the Regent's Canal, a Mr Golding, had been in consultation with the police, and had drained and dragged a mile-and-a-half of it around the Stepney area, looking for the legs of the corpse, which it was felt might also have been thrown into the water. Golding gave the police his opinion that the head could very easily have travelled from a spot near the Edgware Road over to Stepney, particularly if it had been caught up against the side of a barge. He even made a 'neat model' of a canal barge and sent it to the officers in order to help them visualise his possibility. Perhaps understandably, the police were also pursuing a theory that the murderer might be someone who worked on the Canal, and were stopping and searching barges and questioning those on board. The government announced a £100 reward, and the parochial authorities a further £50, for anyone who could identify the murderer, while His Majesty's free pardon was offered to any accomplice who might bring the actual killer to justice.

All this, of course, was so much wasted effort, according to a newspaper called the *London Dispatch & People's Political & Social Reformer*, who reckoned the police were being hoodwinked:

THE SUPPOSED MURDER IN THE EDGWARE ROAD

This will, we suspect, be ascertained to be, after all, the result of the careless proceedings of some medical students. The head appears to have been kept, and the body brutally thrown away, till a suspicion being excited, the head was pitched into a canal. This appears a likely solution.

They had clearly convinced themselves, but it is unlikely that Inspector Feltham would have agreed with them. Yet until the following month, there was little in the way of further evidence to help him in his search. Thus far, the investigation had focussed on the western and eastern edges of London, but the breakthrough, when it came, was in the south.

South London was still only sparsely populated in 1837, when compared to the North. In the part nearest the docks, there were a fair few industrial developments – ropemakers, tanning yards, lead manufacturers – but a little further south, it was mostly a patchwork of open spaces. Here were found tenter grounds, market gardens and windmills, interspersed with the occasional brickworks, glue factory, workhouse or madhouse. The Grand Surrey Canal cut across the fields from west to east, past a few outlying houses which marked the southernmost extent of the city. Indeed, anything south of Kennington Oval, Walworth Fields and the

The north-west corner of the Tower of London, inside which
Sir Thomas Overbury lies buried

Lady Frances Howard   Robert Carr, Earl of Somerset

The executioner's axe which has been in the Tower since 1687, and the block upon which Lord Lovat was executed on Tower Hill in 1747

John Wyclif, Lollard leader, who translated the Bible into English in the fourteenth century

Portsoken Street, which follows the path of seventeenth-century Swan Alley

Milton Street, formerly called Grub Street

The popular romantic conception of highwaymen,
as seen on an early-twentieth-century cigarette card

The three-sided Old Bailey Sessions House, open to the
elements to guard against the spread of gaol fever

The Houses of Parliament at the time of
Spencer Perceval's assassination

Regent's Canal, from which a part of the victim of the
1836 Edgware Road murder was recovered

The Marine Policing Unit building, Wapping High
Street, home of the River Police since 1898

The grim corridor known as 'The Graveyard' connecting
Newgate and the Old Bailey, below whose stones
executed convicts were buried

A cell and gallery at Newgate, photographed shortly
before the prison's demolition in 1902

The site of 8 Baches Street, Hoxton

Claymore House, Hertford Road,
East Finchley

East Finchley in 1905

34 Deptford High Street today, which in 1905 was Chapman's Oil & Colour Shop

11 South Hill Park, Hampstead, former home of Styllou Christofi

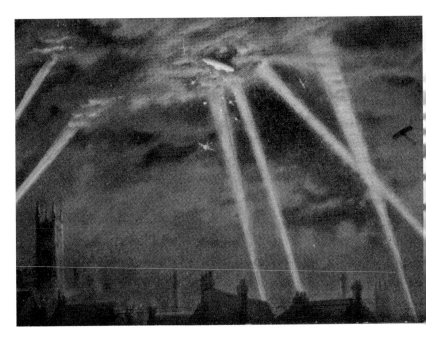

A 1915 postcard showing a Zeppelin raid over London

hamlet of Peckham was not even included on Christopher and John Greenwood's detailed 1827 *Map of London*.

Just off the lower edge of this map to the south lay Coleharbour Lane (now spelt Coldharbour), in the tiny countryside settlement of Brixton, one of whose windmills survives to the present day. Coleharbour Lane was a prime spot at that time for the planting of osier beds, the wet surroundings being ideal for growing willows, whose flexible branches were used for basket weaving. It was a quiet spot, away from town. Just the place for disposing of unwanted items, as the *Champion & Weekly Herald* reported on 5 February:

> On Thursday morning, as two labourers were employed in cutting osiers in a marshy piece of ground, situate close to Coleharbour-lane, Camberwell, they observed something tied up in a piece of coarse sacking and concealed amidst a heap of weeds and rushes. One of them lifted the bundle, and called his companion to witness the discovery. He then cut the cord which was tied around the bundle, and, to the horror and consternation of himself and his companion, the legs and thighs of a human body dropped from the sacking.

The osier bed was about forty yards square, in the corner of a meadow, about fifty yards from Coleharbour Lane. As luck would have it, Brixton Police Station had very recently been built only three hundred yards away, and so one of the labourers, James Page, went to fetch Constable William Woodward, P157, who came out to the osier bed to examine the discovery, where it lay partly shielded by blackthorn bushes and brambles. He took possession of the legs, and carried them up to Paddington Police Station. As he probably suspected, they proved to be an exact match with the Edgware Road torso. The battered corpse, which had been dispersed to three of the four corners of London, was now reassembled. However, the question still remained: whose body was it?

Inspector Feltham and Constable Pegler had spent the past month going through details of all missing females in London, to no avail, and the discovery of the legs represented a major advance in an investigation which up till then had been looking increasingly hopeless. The sack in which the limbs had been wrapped was identified by a local coal merchant, Mr Mosley of Camberwell, who had read in the papers that there had been parts of some words printed in red on it, of which 'sley', and 'erwell' were visible. If the sack had been obtained nearby, then perhaps the murder also had connections with South London. Upon examining the new find, Inspector Feltham decided that the rope with which the sack had been tied up seemed to be some kind of window sash-cord, and was identical as far as he could see to that used by the killer when binding up the torso.

An inquest upon the legs was duly held in the convivial surroundings of the Royal Veteran beer-shop in Coleharbour Lane, at which it was determined from the yellowness of the grass underneath the sack that it had lain there for some weeks. An interesting further detail was that the sack was found to contain wood shavings of deal, a type of yew commonly used for floors. The Edgware Road sack had also shown traces of wood shavings, but of mahogany. From this, Dr Girdwood, the surgeon who had first viewed the torso, told the inquest jury that it suggested 'the individual who perpetrated the horrid deed was connected with the trade. The bag found in the Edgware Road was formed of two carpenter's aprons sewn together.'

All this would be extremely useful once the police had a suspect, but as yet there was still no hint as to who might have committed the crime, or who the victim might be. As the *Examiner* reported on 19 February, 'Numerous letters have been received by the parochial authorities and police, giving accounts of persons missing, but none of them afford satisfactory information.'

What Inspector Feltham needed was a real breakthrough. A month later, as the disembodied head remained preserved in spirits in a jar at the Paddington poorhouse, this had still not come. There had been great excitement during the second week of March, following rumours of the arrest of two men, one of them a canal barge worker, but this proved to be a hoax. Similarly, a man who had written a letter from the Camberwell area, claiming to know more about the disposal of the legs, failed to turn up to his secret meeting with the police, despite the many assurances that had been given for his safety.

Thus far, the conduct of the case had been painstakingly thorough, and had much in common with police investigations of more recent times. Similarly, the turning point, when it came, would be familiar to any reader of contemporary crime stories, because this was an instance in which Inspector Feltham could justifiably be said to have been led to the killer by 'acting upon information received'.

In short, someone contacted the authorities, giving them the vital missing piece of the jigsaw puzzle.

On Monday, 20 March, the churchwarden of Paddington was approached by a man who wanted to view the head of the victim, which was in an ever increasing state of decay. The man's name was William Gay, and in recent weeks he had come to believe that the body that had been distributed to three different parts of London was that of his sister Hannah Brown. The two of them were the children of a farmer from just outside Norwich, where she had been born in 1790. Her life had been spent in service to various families, most recently that of a Mr Perring, a hatter from the Strand, but prior to this she had worked for two ladies in the Old Kent Road. Hannah was the widow of a shoemaker named Thomas Brown and was said to have saved a fair amount of money while in service. She lived in what is now Fitzrovia, just behind the Middlesex Hospital, in lodgings at 45 Union Street (which today is called Riding House Street). Her brother William lived nearby in Goodge Street, but they had quarrelled and were not on good terms.

Having gone through the grim and distressing business of examining the much-battered head, Gay concluded that it was indeed that of his sister, particularly on account of the fact that one ear had a scar where an earring had once been torn some years previously:

> 'I looked at the left ear, and found a similar appearance, there as that I had noticed in my sister. I noticed the eye in that head, and it resembled hers. I also noticed the hair, I took a lock of it from the workhouse—it was light hair mixed with grey—her hair corresponded with that I saw at the workhouse. I believe it was my sister's head, and no one else's. I told the overseer at the poorhouse he need not go any farther, for that was my sister's head.'

Despite all the public appeals that had been made during the previous three months to anyone who had knowledge of missing women in the capital, it had taken William Gay a while to suspect that anything untoward had happened to Hannah. He had not seen his sister since 24

December, the day before she had been due to marry a man named James Greenacre – a wedding which had then apparently been cancelled at very short notice. She had met her fiancé some time during the autumn of 1836; he lived on the Old Kent Road in a place called Carpenter's Buildings, opposite an institution on the corner of Mason Street called the Asylum for the Deaf and Dumb.

Since the couple had intended to emigrate to America, Hannah's brother William at first thought there must have been a reconciliation between her and Greenacre and that they had somehow gone ahead with the marriage and then left the country. However, as with much of the rest of London's population, William had been following the accounts in the newspapers of the discovery of various body parts, and eventually began to feel that the printed descriptions were worryingly close to that of his sister.

Growing increasingly suspicious, William Gay had questioned his sister's landlady at Union Street, and had also discussed the matter at length with his own employer in Goodge Street, Mrs Blanchard, who had known Hannah for several years. The mysterious James Greenacre had called in to see Mrs Blanchard on 27 December, telling her not to attend the proposed wedding dinner, saying that the marriage had been called off because he had discovered that Hannah Brown had lied about her financial situation. He claimed that she had now taken lodgings in the Old Kent Road rather than return to Union Street, 'it being too far to take her boxes back again'. Eventually, Gay's enquiries led him to speak with a couple called Mr and Mrs Davis, who told him that Hannah had said that her future husband lived at Carpenter's Buildings on the Old Kent Road.

By now, Gay was convinced that he was on the trail of the killer. On Sunday, 12 March, he travelled down to the furthest reaches of South London and knocked on the door at the address he had been given, only to be told that Greenacre had moved. Yet when he spoke to a Mrs Dillon, who also lived in that group of houses, she told Gay that she rented her home from Greenacre. She mentioned that he had called the previous week to collect his money and had promised to send a representative the following week to collect the next payment. Gay persuaded Mrs Dillon that when this messenger appeared, she should insist that she would only hand over the rent to Greenacre in person. Thus, when a woman in her early thirties knocked at her door demanding the rent, Mrs Dillon told her that Greenacre himself should call if he wanted his money. Having scored this small victory,

William Gay, who had been functioning these past weeks as a sort of unofficial one-man detective agency, told his wife on Sunday, 19 March, 'Oh heavens! I'm sure my poor sister has been murdered, and if the Lord spares my life until tomorrow I'll go and see her features.'

This was the state of Gay's investigations on the day he called in at the Paddington poorhouse and asked the churchwarden Mr Thornton if he could view the severed head of the Edgware Road murder victim. Gay made a positive identification, as did her former landlady and several others that week who had been part of Hannah Brown's circle. Inspector Feltham was notified, and in short order he secured a warrant for Greenacre's arrest, signed by the magistrates at Marylebone Police Office. Constables were mobilised all over the capital, and on the night of Sunday, 26 March, the word came through that a man answering Greenacre's description had for some months been living at 1 St Albans Street, Lambeth, a few yards away from the parallel street called Lambeth Walk, and adjoining Walnut Tree Walk. (Both of the latter are still there, but St Albans Street is now covered by a development of twentieth-century flats.) At 10 pm that evening, Feltham paid the house a call, accompanied only by a police constable from L Division. In a back room, they found James Greenacre in bed with the woman who had attempted to collect rent on his behalf. Her small daughter was in the other room. Greenacre, the *Standard* reported, 'nearly 50 years of age, of forbidding aspect, with an overhanging brow, is a widower, and has previously been in America, where he carried on the business of a washing-machine maker, but failed just before he left for England.'

His possessions were already packed up in several boxes and secured with strong cord, and he had been intending once more to emigrate, as he told the inspector: 'You are just in time – to-morrow I should have started to America.' Greenacre and the woman, who refused to give her name, were taken in a hackney cab to Paddington Police Station and locked up in separate cells, where, at some point during the night, he attempted to strangle himself with a noose made from his own pocket handkerchief. When discovered and saved by a police constable, Greenacre said upon regaining consciousness, 'I don't thank you for what you have done, I would sooner have gone off.'

Huge public interest accompanied these arrests, stirred up by headlines such as this from the *Standard*:

THE LATE MYSTERIOUS MURDER
IN THE EDGWARE-ROAD –
APPREHENSION AND ATTEMPTED SUICIDE
OF THE MURDERER

Around four thousand onlookers crowded all available roads in Paddington Green the following day when the prisoners were first brought from the police station to the court at Marylebone; people were jostled, tempers were short, and one man had his leg badly crushed by a cartwheel as it passed. It required, according to the *Morning Post*, 'a vast number of officers to keep back the mob' in order that the prisoners could be brought in. The woman was identified as Sarah Gale, and neither she nor Greenacre 'appeared to be in the least degree agitated'.

Witnesses were called, identifying Greenacre as the man who had planned to marry Hannah Brown, and swearing that shortly before her disappearance she had been seen in possession of several hundred pounds in cash, presumably having liquidated any assets she might have had in preparation for her proposed emigration to America. Here, it seemed, was a very powerful motive for murder. When it finally came the turn of James Greenacre himself to offer an explanation, he stated that the whole thing had been a terrible accident. While in discussion on Christmas Eve with Hannah Brown – who had allegedly spent the day drinking with some coachmen, and was becoming further intoxicated drinking tea spiked with rum – they had come to a disagreement, and he had kicked her chair. At this point, he claimed, Hannah had overbalanced backwards, 'her head coming with great violence against a great chump of wood'. Attempts to revive her failed; she was clearly dead. Convinced that no one would believe the truth and that he would be charged with murder, he decided upon the desperate course of attempting to dispose of the body. Greenacre was at pains to stress that Sarah Gale had no knowledge of his actions.

Both prisoners were further questioned at some length during preliminary hearings over the next few days, and finally remanded in custody at Newgate, awaiting trial at the Old Bailey. Their journey from the New Prison, Clerkenwell, to Newgate was accompanied by a large and angry mob, 'groaning and hooting all the way'.

The papers covered every detail and reported each rumour, some of which were instantly shouted abroad and then disproved the following day. One story that appeared frequently concerned allegations that Greenacre had some time earlier murdered his own illegitimate son. Nothing had come to court – indeed, he himself had sued several neighbours for making these accusations against him – but it all served to confirm the image of a monster in the public mind.

A few days after the arrests came the news that a certain penny showman in Ogle Street, Marylebone, 'who has for some years exhibited on a diminutive scale the atrocities which have occurred in domestic life' was presenting a new tableau representing 'the atrocious and horrible murder of Hannah Brown by James Greenacre, with the manner in which he divided the body of the unfortunate woman truly depicted'. The case had not yet come to the Old Bailey, but certainly the words 'innocent until proven guilty' were not of much concern in the London of the 1830s. Through it all, Greenacre had taken the same line: 'The occurrence was purely accidental . . . and I shall ever regret that I omitted to disclose the real facts of the case.' So great was the amount of unfavourable coverage published in the run-up to his trial, that Greenacre took the step of writing an account of his life and his actions to the press, which appeared on 9 April. In it he stressed his sober lifestyle and abhorrence of drink, and dealt specifically with the rumours that he had been responsible for the sudden deaths of his three previous wives. It is a very strange document, and probably did little for his prospects at the upcoming court case.

On Monday, 10 April, amidst intense public scrutiny, the trial began at the Central Criminal Court of the Old Bailey. In truth, although it ran for a reasonably long time compared to the murder trials of the eighteenth century – when ten or so sentences of life or death could be handed down in a morning – this was something of a foregone conclusion, despite the number of witnesses called and the painstaking presentation of the case by the police. The clamour for tickets to the court was phenomenal, and the admission price for spectators had been specially raised from its usual rate of one shilling up to a new level of ten shillings and sixpence. Needless to say, they sold out right away, and every inch of the court was packed.

Greenacre appeared in a dark coat with a velvet collar and brass buttons, a black waistcoat and black trousers; Gale wore a cap, a dark-coloured gown, and a shawl. The former was charged with murder, the latter with having knowledge of the crime, and that she 'did feloniously receive, harbour, maintain and assist him'. A bewildering range of witnesses was assembled, drawn from the friends and acquaintances of Hannah Brown, from the police and those who had played a part in the discovery of various body parts, and from many members of the medical profession giving detailed and often gruesome evidence of the state of the corpse. The trial went on into the early evening, and then adjourned until the following day. On 11 April the defence case was presented, which was largely based upon Greenacre's assertion that the death had been accidental. He argued that, although the manner of the body's disposal had been unpleasant, with each sensationalist article that appeared in the press, he had grown more nervous of coming forward, for fear of prejudice against him.

In this, he seems to have been correct. The jury retired for only fifteen minutes, returned and delivered a guilty verdict against both prisoners. James Greenacre was sentenced to death, and Sarah Gale to be transported for life.

Back in his cell at Newgate, being given pen and paper, Greenacre finally set down what he claimed to be the truth of the evening of 24 December. It had been a quarrel that had escalated out of hand, each accusing the other of having wildly exaggerated their own wealth in order to lure the other into marriage. He struck Hannah Brown in the right eye with a piece of wood, and having done so, held her up and cut her throat with a table knife. Greenacre described the process of dismembering the body, and how he himself had carried the head in a bag on the omnibus all the way up to the Ben Johnson Lock in Stepney and flung it in the water. The trunk he had taken in a sack on a cart, without the hired boy driver knowing what the package contained. He said he had found it very easy to hide the remains on the building site, but declined to give further details about the disposal of the legs, prompting suspicion that Sarah Gale had indeed assisted him with this part of the business.

Over the next few days, the blizzard of news reports continued, and Greenacre was even forced from his condemned cell to deny a wild rumour that he was a surviving member of the Cato Street Conspirators, who had plotted in 1820 to assassinate the prime minister and all of his cabinet. He also said to the authorities, 'If I am to be hanged, I wish they'd hang me at once.' Meanwhile, the residents of his old house at Carpenter's Place, where the murder had occurred, were reported to have made a considerable amount of money showing the curious around the death site.

Despite Greenacre's desire for a speedy resolution, it was not until 10 May, almost a month after his trial, that he was brought out in front of a vast crowd outside Newgate and led to the scaffold. 'So great was the anxiety to procure a commanding site,' said one report, 'that several persons remained all night actually clinging to the lamp-posts.' Barricades were erected by the police on all roads leading to the area in order to prevent stampedes and injuries, and every roof was filled with people perched up on the tiles. When 8 am approached, Greenacre appeared, almost unable to walk, and supported by his warders, to be 'greeted with a storm of terrific yells and hisses, mingled with groans, cheers, and other expressions of reproach, revenge, hatred and contumely'. He apparently gave the crowd a last look of contempt, said 'Don't leave me long in the concourse', and then died without a struggle.

His only dying wish was that his spectacles be given to Sarah Gale. As for the washing-machine that he had lately designed, hoping to make his fortune, Greenacre's sister applied to the magistrates for its return. She was refused.

The Railway Works at Blackfriars and Opening Towards Ludgate Hill, from the *Illustrated London News* 23 April, 1864

FOURTEEN

YOU CAN'T OUTRUN DEATH
1864

The Metropolitan Police of 1864 were a well-established feature of life in the capital, with almost forty years of experience in chasing criminals. This kind of uniformed force, unknown in the England of previous centuries, was enough a part of the social scene that Gilbert & Sullivan would include a chorus of policemen in their comic opera *The Pirates of Penzance* (1879), famously lamenting that their lot was not a happy one. Certainly, the constables of the Met would have had little time for singing; they worked seven days a week, walking an average of twenty miles a day, and if they were ill for more than a few days, their time away from the job was unpaid. Wages were around one pound a week, with an extra allowance for boots. Coppers did not yet wear the characteristic police-man's helmet, which only appeared in 1870, inspired by the German spiked helmet, the *Pickelhaube*. Instead, they were to be seen in top hats, and a long coat with buttons down the front, with their police number displayed at the collar.

Following the advent of photography, the Met had established in the 1860s the first systematic Criminal Records File, showing the likenesses of known miscreants, and listing underneath them some basic details, such as the following:

> *Mary Ann Travers*
> *Clever street thief*
> *26 old*
> *5ft 2½ high*
> *Brown eyes*
> *Brown hair*
> *Fresh comp*

Murder victims were also photographed, by the simple means of carrying the body in an open coffin out into the mortuary yard and propping them up against a wall for the camera.

If these attempts at modernisation suggest that a new era was dawning, some things remained unchanged. Hangings were still very much a public event, conducted outside the doors of Newgate prison in front of many thousands of people. (Indeed, the Royal Albert Hall, which was to open its doors at the start of the following decade, would have needed to be roughly fifteen times the size in order to accommodate the crowd that turned out for the most popular executions.) For those condemned to the gallows, death in London came courtesy of William Calcraft, who had been public hangman since 1829. Apparently an amiable man, in appearance not unlike Karl Marx, he had a fondness for breeding rabbits, and was paid a guinea a week, plus a further payment for every execution. Calcraft gained his start in this most exclusive of trades whilst selling meat pies in the streets around Newgate, befriending the then hangman and securing an initial job flogging younger prisoners for ten shillings a week. He served as public executioner for forty-five years, and when not sending people to their doom, worked as a cobbler.

Times were changing: it was Calcraft who would perform the last ever public hanging in London, on 26 May 1868, but for now, the grim business of justice was still one of the capital's most popular spectacles.

Travel can be a dangerous thing. Down through the centuries, numerous people had died in accidents when horse-drawn carriages turned over on England's less-than-perfect roads and lanes, and a smaller minority been murdered aboard them, by robbers, highwaymen or assassins. In 1825, the opening of the Stockton and Darlington Railway as a passenger service heralded the coming of the railway age, and it was feared in some circles that the early speeds of ten miles an hour were somewhat risky. The very public death of the politician William Huskisson, who mistakenly stepped into the path of George Stephenson's *Rocket* in 1830 at the opening of the Liverpool and Manchester Railway, alerted the general public to the fact that these new contraptions could indeed be dangerous, but it was not until almost a quarter of a century later that the shadow of murder fell across the train tracks.

Since the mid-1830s, the coming of the railways had also changed the face of London. Whole communities were swept away as houses were pulled down to make way for the ever-growing network of tracks, goods yards and stations. Across the Channel during the 1860s, Baron Haussmann was demolishing countless streets in order to create the wide new boulevards of Paris, but in London, it was the railway that drove a path through the houses of the poor. At the start of 1864, there were twenty-three separate proposed London railway schemes under consideration by parliament, and the *Illustrated London News* was moved to comment that 'there probably never was a city threatened at once by so many projects as the city of London is at the present time'. Dickens had described the visible effects of such schemes upon one metropolitan district in his 1848 novel, *Dombey & Son*:

> There were railway patterns in its drapers' shops, and railway journals in the windows of its newsmen. There were railway hotels, coffee-houses, lodging-houses, boarding-houses; railway plans, maps, views, wrappers, bottles, sandwich-boxes, and timetables; railway hackney-coach and cabstands; railway omnibuses, railway streets and buildings, railway hangers-on and parasites, and flatterers out of all calculation. There was even railway time observed in clocks, as if the sun itself had given in.

In May 1864, Dickens himself was involved in one of the great railway disasters of the age, when the train in which he was travelling crashed whilst crossing a bridge over a river at Staplehurst in Kent. Ten people died, many were injured, and Dickens, himself unharmed, spent much time giving brandy to the survivors.

The public was accustomed by now to the idea that the railway could be dangerous. Indeed, a book published in 1863 which gave a history of the early efforts to develop steam locomotion noted with scorn the fate of Brunton's Mechanical Traveller, whose boiler exploded in County Durham with fatal results in 1813:

> Next among the abortions of railway ingenuity came Mr. Brunton's 'Mechanical Traveller', with legs like those of a horse. This steam horse turned out to be 'broken-winded and vicious,' for it blew up and killed some of the bystanders.

Once passenger trains had become common in the 1840s, there was a string of fatal train crashes in places such as Yorkshire, Berkshire and Cheshire, while within and around London itself there had been fatalities at Farringdon (1846), Southall (1847), Ealing (1853), East Croydon (1854), London Bridge (1857), Lewisham (1857), Tottenham (1860), Primrose Hill (1861), Kentish Town (1861) and Streatham (1863).

Death on the railways was therefore hardly an unknown phenomenon to the Londoners of 1864 – indeed, in June that year seven people lost their lives in a collision between two trains at Egham, to the south of the city.

Murder on the railway, however, was quite another matter.

<hr />

Thomas Briggs arrived at Fenchurch Street station midway through the evening of Saturday, 9 July 1864. He was sixty-nine years old, with a full white beard, powerfully built, and reasonably tall for those days at around five feet ten. Originally from the village of Cartmel in Cumbria, Briggs was chief clerk at the bank of Roberts, Curtis & Company in Lombard Street. He lived at number 5 Clapton Square, just a short walk from Hackney station on the North London Line, where the city faded away into the fields and market gardens near the London Orphan Asylum and the Hackney Union Workhouse. Fenchurch Street station, which opened in 1841, was the terminus of the NLR, and by taking a train from there at the end of his working day, Briggs would journey in a semicircle through the East End, bypassing the city before arriving at Hackney station itself (today known as Hackney Central). This was a journey he took almost daily, between his workplace and home, and he was well known to the railway staff along the line.

Earlier that evening, Briggs had been dining with relatives – a Mr & Mrs Buchan in Peckham – and had then caught the bus up to Fenchurch Street from the Old Kent Road. He carried a black bag, and wore a watch and chain on his waistcoat, from which hung a small seal. At 9.45 pm, he presented his ticket to Thomas Fishbourne, the ticket collector at Fenchurch Street, who recognised him as a regular passenger, and took his place in a first-class compartment, number 69. Five minutes later, the train pulled out with Briggs on board, heading east at the then-impressive speed of twenty-five miles per hour. At 10.01, the train left Bow station (which is now Bow Church, on the Docklands Light Railway), and by 10.05 it had crossed Duckett's Canal, curved around Victoria Park, and arrived at the station called Hackney Wick. By now the train was travelling due west, through Homerton, and at 10.15 it reached Hackney station, the nearest stop to where Thomas Briggs lived. On this evening, however, he did not step out onto the platform.

Among the passengers waiting for the train at Hackney were two bank clerks, Harry Vernez and Sidney Jones, who intended to travel to Highbury station. By an odd coincidence, they worked for the same company as Thomas Briggs. They and two other people entered the same first-class carriage into which Thomas Briggs had stepped at Fenchurch Street some twenty minutes earlier. It was unoccupied.

As the train stood in the station, Jones noticed some blood on his hand and showed it to Vernez. They summoned the guard, Benjamin Ames, who brought along his lamp so that the scene could be examined properly. As Vernez later recalled, 'when the guard brought his lamp, I saw a hat, a stick, and a black bag in the carriage'. There was blood on the dark-blue cloth seats, blood on the walls, and blood trickling down the window pane. Some ladies who had been travelling in the next carriage then came forward. They had heard nothing during the journey, but upon arrival at Hackney, where the lights of the station better illuminated their surroundings, they had noticed that their dresses were stained with blood, which had apparently spurted through their carriage window as the train turned a corner. Clearly, something was terribly wrong, but as yet, there was no trace of a victim.

This train had been travelling west. Around the same time that evening, a locomotive pulling a group of empty carriages left Hackney Wick station, travelling in the opposite direction, heading for the Bow Locomotive Works, but soon had to halt its journey. The guard, William Timms, later explained what happened:

'I left about twenty minutes past 10. We have to go over the canal-bridge. When we arrived at about that point, the driver called my attention to an object in the six-foot way. We put on the brakes, and stopped the train as soon as we possibly could. On returning to the spot I found it was the body of a man lying there.'

When their train had rounded the corner of Victoria Park, on Old Ford Bridge which crossed the stretch of water called Duckett's Canal, they saw Thomas Briggs lying in the space between the two sets of railway lines, covered in blood, but alive. Attached to his waistcoat were a couple of links from a watch chain that had evidently been broken off. The guard and stoker from the train ran to the nearby Mitford Arms Tavern for assistance, and with the aid of James Hudson the landlord, carried the injured man to the tavern and then sent out for medical assistance. When examined, Briggs was found to have been savagely beaten about the head with a blunt instrument, so that part of his skull was caved in. The doctor expressed surprise that he was still living, although the injured man resisted all attempts to bring him round. In his pockets, they found a silver snuff-box, and four pound ten shillings in gold and silver coins, yet although Briggs had still had these about his person, the nature of his injuries led them to think that he had been set upon by a robber. There was also a bundle of letters in his pocket, addressed to *T Briggs, Esq., Messrs. Roberts, Curtis & Co's, Lombard Street*.

A local police constable, Edward Dougar, was patrolling Wick Lane, just by the railway line. Seeing a man being carried towards the pub by several others, he intervened, and then summoned his superiors. Inspector Kerressey, from Bow Police Station, then took charge. He sent a messenger to the Lombard Street address, who was able to track down the victim's employers, and then returned with a description of Mr Briggs which matched that of the person found on the railway line. Having obtained the home address of the victim from the bank officials, Kerressey despatched someone to Hackney in order to break the news. Soon, Thomas Briggs, Jr., several other family members, and the man's regular doctor arrived at the Mitford Arms.

Thomas Briggs had been found at a sparsely populated spot, where a body could perhaps be thrown from a carriage without being observed. At the start of the previous decade, the *Illustrated London News* sent a reporter to make a journey along this stretch of line, heading north through Bow as Briggs had done, to describe for their readers the experience of being a passenger on one of these new railway lines. The reporter tells of passing market gardens to right and left, going down the deep railway cutting running under Bow Road before the train arrives at Bow station itself, and, once clear of the latter, of leaving the built-up areas behind. The Hackney of those days was an agricultural region known for its watercress beds, a sleepy collection of rural hamlets only lately finding itself on the borders of the encroaching city:

> Soon after starting [from Bow] we found ourselves in open country: on the right, the newly-formed Victoria Park; on the left we had an extensive view over the Hackney marshes, terminating with a considerable portion of the well-wooded scenery of Essex. Passing onward, through the verdant fields, we came to the retired village of Homerton . . .

At night, as the train made its way through the darkened fields and marshy ground, the sound of a man falling from a carriage might easily have escaped notice.

Doctors sat up with the insensible Briggs all through that Saturday night, as the police conducted a meticulous search of carriage number 69, and of the ground near Duckett's Canal. The victim had been covered with his own blood, which was also to be found in goodly quantities both inside the railway carriage and on the exterior and handle of the door from which he had been ejected, prompting medical speculation that an artery in his severely wounded head had burst just as he was forced from the train.

Soon, as news of the assault spread, the pub was surrounded by such a mob that it was felt necessary to move the victim to his home, despite his poor condition. Thomas Briggs had survived repeated blows to the head and a fall from a moving train, but although he hung on long enough during the following day to be taken on a litter to his home in Hackney, there was little that could be done, and he died later that day, having not regained consciousness. When questioned by police, his son, Thomas Briggs Jr., identified the bag and cane that had been found in the carriage as items that had belonged to his father, but strongly denied that the somewhat battered hat left alongside these items was the one worn by the banker. The immediate supposition was that the murderer had picked up Briggs's hat by mistake in the confusion, and left his own behind.

The victim died on a Sunday, and when the news became public on Monday morning, it prompted an immediate outcry. Although violent death in the London of that time was a common enough occurrence, the circumstances of this killing tapped into pre-existing fears about the safety of rail travel in general, and especially the fact that when travelling between stations, passengers had no way of communicating with the guard in the event of danger, and were effectively at the mercy of anyone with malign intentions who might occupy the same carriage. An article in the *Globe* painted a picture of respectable citizens trapped on a journey in a confined space with evil-minded thugs:

> Railway carriages are now the scene of very shocking crimes and offences
> . . . It is not long since two men passed the greater part of the distance
> from Rugby to Watford sitting on a madman, who, with a knife, had furi-
> ously assaulted one for speaking to the other.

A week before the murder of Thomas Briggs, a woman had tried to fling herself from a moving railway carriage on a suburban train in order to escape being assaulted by a man, and survived by clinging to an open door for some miles. Both of these cases were widely reported, and questions raised about personal safety on this relatively new form of transport. The *Saturday Review* spoke in lurid tones of the prospect of being shut up in a confined space 'with a stranger of sinister aspect and dubious mien, with the consciousness on both sides that nothing but your physical power of resistance can repel any ruffianism that malignity, lust, or frenzy may prompt,' while the *Illustrated London News* summarised public concerns as follows:

> The railway managers set themselves against any change which shall enable
> a traveller to stop a train, and, so far, we heartily agree with them. No person
> can have travelled much without perceiving that nine people out of ten are
> utterly unfit to have the least control over anything, and least of all over a
> train containing several hundred people . . . What we want and ought to
> have is a means of summoning the guard.

One of the most frightening aspects of this murder was that Briggs had been set upon and killed during the very short space of time available between two East London stations – a matter of perhaps five minutes at most. This was no remote journey out into the wilds, where help might take hours to appear. This city worker died just a short distance away from his home station, and appeared to have been bludgeoned to death merely for the sake of his watch. It was a senseless opportunistic murder, committed by a killer or killers too stupid to realise that they had left their own hat behind at the scene of the crime. This was a basic mistake, which was quickly followed by another.

By all accounts, it was just an ordinary day for Mr Death. He appraised the man who came before him with a measured air born of long experience. Each new person was carefully judged, their appearance and behaviour taken into consideration, and their assets weighed in the balance. His decision, when arrived at, was final.

Every man has his price. On this occasion, Mr Death offered three pounds and fifteen shillings. For a man's soul, this would be cheap; for his gold watch chain, it was about the going rate.

John Death was a respectable man – a jeweller by trade – who bought and sold items on a regular basis from the premises he ran with his brother Robert in Cheapside. On Monday, 11 July, the day after Thomas Briggs died from his injuries, a man came into their place of business around 10 o'clock in the morning asking for a quote on a chain he wanted to exchange. Death's brother was minding the shop at the time, but he called John in to give his expert opinion. When the jeweller came upon the scene, the customer was already examining a range of watch chains that were spread out on the counter, as he later recalled: 'I examined the chain closely with a magnifying glass . . . I then went behind him to weigh it in some scales that were fixed there.'

Having heard Death's opinion on its value, after some haggling, the customer chose to exchange the chain he had brought in for one from Death's stock which was almost the same value, and accepted a five-shilling ring containing a white cornelian stone, carved with the head of a man, to make up the difference. Neither brother had ever seen this customer, who appeared to be a foreigner, before. They packed up his goods in a box marked with the name of Death, and he took it and departed.

Meanwhile, bills were being posted in public places across London offering various rewards for information concerning the murder of Thomas Briggs. The government put up £100, as did the bank that had employed the victim, and a similar amount was offered by the North London Railway. Briggs's distinctive watch and chain, stolen during the attack, were described as follows:

> A large, old-fashioned gold chronometer watch, white dial, second hands, with gold Albert chain, large gold key, with the figure of an animal on the top, gold swivel seal with two stones, one dark, one white, attached.

In addition, the public was asked for any information concerning the hat, bearing the maker's name *T.H. Walker, Crawford Street, Marylebone*, which had been found in the carriage.

When the news broke fully that Monday, it was clear that commentators regarded the crime as something quite out of the ordinary. The initial report in *The Times* called it 'one of the most atrocious crimes that probably ever disgraced this country.' By Tuesday, based on evidence provided by Briggs's son, it was stated categorically that the hat bearing the maker's name *Walker* had not belonged to the victim, and was therefore a vital clue to the identity of the attacker. A more detailed description of the stolen watch was also circulated: a gold lever chronometer made by S.W. Archer of Hackney, numbered 1,487.

Under examination at Bow, the rolling stock in which the attack had taken place showed ample evidence of the crime:

> The compartment in which the outrage took place is covered with blood in all directions, and shows that the struggle between the murdered man and his assailant must have been fearful. The handle of the door, the door itself, and the outside steps are also covered with blood. The stick found in the carriage is a thick cane with a heavy ivory knob. It is also covered with blood, and it looks as if it had been used in the struggle.

What was perhaps most remarkable, given the frenzied nature of the attack, was that the killer had been able to escape from the scene, presumably drenched in the blood of his victim, without being apprehended. Some argued that there had been several attackers, since although Thomas Briggs was getting on in years, he was by all accounts still a strong and powerful man. An initial inquest had been held at the Prince of Wales

Tavern in Hackney on the evening on Monday 11, but it had reserved judgement until an autopsy could be conducted. Pubs and inns had long been used for such inquests, since they generally had a large enough room available for the coroner's jury and witnesses to gather, as well as a sturdy table upon which the body could be displayed if necessary.

By the middle of that week, events were moving fast. The Death brothers had approached the authorities, having recognised the description of the victim's watch chain as matching that which had been brought to their jewellery shop on Monday morning by a man 'having the appearance of a foreigner'. This seemed to tie in with the fact that the brim of the hat left behind in the railway carriage had been turned up in an unusual style more common abroad, leading police to suspect that the killer was from another country. By Friday, 15 July, this suspicion had gained ground, to the extent that the *Manchester Guardian* felt confident enough to report the following account of the man who had exchanged the watch chain:

> On Monday morning a gentlemanly foreigner, apparently a German or Swiss, entered the shop of Mr Death, silversmith and jeweller, of 55, Cheapside. He appeared to be about 30 years old, 5 ft. 6in. or 7in. high, with a sallow complexion and thin features. He wore a black frock coat and waistcoat, dark trousers and a black hat.

Although the man in question had apparently tried not to show his face too clearly, in attempting to exchange a watch chain stolen from a murder victim he was either astonishingly confident or incredibly stupid. Having already left behind his own hat at the crime scene and made off with that of Briggs, the sensible thing would have been to throw away anything that might link him to the killing. Instead, despite having had the good fortune to escape unobserved from the train whilst covered in blood, the attacker seems to have behaved as if his luck would see him through all manner of risk-taking.

In the event, just over a week after the death of Thomas Briggs, the police were able to circulate a detailed description of the person they sought. The wanted man was said to be a German tailor named Francis or Franz Muller, who had been living for the past two months at a cottage in Bow, near the south-western corner of Victoria Park, at 16 Park Terrace, Old Ford Road. Muller rented a room from a couple named Blyth. They had noticed that their lodger was wearing a new watch chain on the

Monday after the killing, and on the Thursday they found a hat box in his room marked *Walker, 49 Crawford Street, Marylebone* – the same make as the hat left behind in the murder carriage. When they contacted the police, their description of the lodger matched that of the man who had exchanged the watch chain with Mr Death.

Another witness had come forward by the end of that week – a cab driver named Jonathan Matthews who had been friends with Franz Muller for two years. He told police that his young daughter had been given an empty jewellery box to play with, which, when she showed it to her parents, turned out to be inscribed with the maker's name *Death*. This rang a bell from newspaper accounts, so he went to Paddington Police Station and reported the matter. He told them that it was he who had given Muller the hat which he normally wore; in fact, he had it specially made by Walker's in Crawford Street after Muller had admired Matthews' own hat. This appeared to match the description of the one left in the railway carriage during the assault.

It almost seemed as if the killer had deliberately gone around leaving clues to his identity behind him, whether at the scene of the crime, at his lodgings or when disposing of jewellery. Less than a week after the murder, the police could now put a face and a name to their chief suspect. The only difficulty was that Franz Muller was no longer in Bow. In fact, by the time the Blyths came forward to identify him, he was already on his way across the Atlantic.

⸻

Heading for New York on board the sailing ship *Victoria*, Franz Muller took the time to write a short note to his former landlords at Park Terrace:

> Dear Friends, I am glad to confess that I cannot have a better time, as I have; if the sun shines nice and the wind blows fair, as it is at the present moment, everything will go well. I cannot write anymore, only I have no postage. You will be so kind to take that letter in.

Muller had told them earlier of the exciting trip he planned, and Mrs Blyth had washed six shirts for him in readiness. His destination was New York, already a great metropolis, but at around 850,000 people still less than a third of the size of mid-Victorian London. Having fled a city in which his actions had prompted a rash of stories about the safety of rail travel, Muller was sailing to a country entering the final year of its Civil War, in which control of the railways was of crucial strategic importance. Indeed, General William Sherman, commander of the Union forces in the West, was busy tearing up many miles of railroad tracks down in Georgia as part of the scorched-earth strategy he called 'hard war'. Trains had come a long way in the few short decades since Huskisson stepped in the path of Stephenson's *Rocket*.

A sailing ship passage across the Atlantic took several weeks, and so the discovery of the killer's identity was followed by a strange interlude in the summer of 1864 during which a slow-motion flight from justice took place, with Scotland Yard engaged in as hot a pursuit as was possible under the circumstances. The *Victoria* had set sail on Thursday, 14 July. Early the following week, after the discovery of evidence linking Muller to the crime, the police gave chase in a faster ship, the *Manchester*, which relied on steam, not sail, as was breathlessly reported in the *Sun*:

> The Home Secretary has granted passports, and Inspector Tanner, with Sergeant Clark, Mr Death, and the cabman [Matthews], have gone to the United States in pursuit of Muller, who left three days ago in a sailing ship for New York. The officers left in a Government steamer.

Even today, this would be a major operation, but for the time, the idea that the police would go to the trouble of taking a couple of witnesses on a month-long journey across the Atlantic in order to confront a murder suspect shows how far criminal investigations had come since the eighteenth century. As the wanted man strolled around the deck of the *Victoria*, unaware that the Metropolitan's finest were also crossing the ocean, the case against him was slowly being assembled back in London. The coroner's inquest had met several times and heard evidence, and then the case was referred to Bow Street Magistrates' Court.

On the day after Muller's ship left London Docks, Thomas Briggs was buried close to his home in Hackney at the Unitarian Chapel. As for the man sought in connection with his killing, he was said to be around twenty-four years old, originally from Cologne, and had latterly been working as a tailor at a firm called Hodgkinson's. Some acquaintances and colleagues came forward to testify that he had always been a quiet, considerate man with no hint of any violence about his personality.

Yet it was also said that he had expressed a desire in recent weeks to emigrate to America and fight in the Civil War.

The usual wild rumours prevailed, including one report that appeared in *The Times* claiming that police had travelled to Scotland in pursuit of the murderer. A number of suspects were temporarily detained in the London area on the flimsy grounds of speaking with a German accent and wearing a watch chain, and a certain Charles New approached a policeman in the Edgware Road while defiantly under the influence of drink, claiming to have committed the North London Railway murder.

One week after Muller had set sail, a hearing was held at Bow Street Magistrates' Court in front of the chief magistrate, Justice Henry. Robert Death, whose brother was currently crossing the Atlantic, testified that 'a young man of about thirty, with a foreign accent, having neither beard, moustache, nor whiskers, of a pale, sallow complexion and rather fair', had called at their shop the day after the death of Thomas Briggs and exchanged a watch chain. Briggs's son then identified the chain and clasp that had been left at the jewellers as being that which had belonged to his father.

A friend of Muller's named Elizabeth Repsch gave evidence to the court. She was the wife of a tailor named Godfrey Repsch, the man who had helped Muller obtain employment with the firm of Hodgkinson. She said that she had seen Muller at around 7 pm on the evening of the murder, and had left him at her house in conversation with his friend, John Haffa. On the morning of Monday 11, Muller had shown her his new gold watch chain and signet ring, claiming to have bought them both from a man at the Docks when he was there seeking a ticket for America. She noticed that he was wearing a different hat to the one he customarily wore, and told the court that his old one had a distinctive striped lining. As for the previous hat, Muller explained to her that he had 'smashed his old one and thrown it into the dusthole'. What Elizabeth Repsch failed to mention at this stage is that she also pawned a coat of Muller's on his behalf on Wednesday 13, at a time when he seems to have been wary of appearing in public too often.

Muller's friend John Haffa, who had shared lodgings with him during the week before he left London, told the court that when Franz had left him on the Saturday evening of the murder, he had said that he was on his way to visit 'his girl'. On Wednesday 13, the day Elizabeth Repsch pawned Muller's coat, Haffa was also involved in a financial transaction with him. Muller had already pawned the watch chain that he had obtained from John Death, apparently in order to raise money for his ticket to America. Now he sold the pawn ticket to his friend Haffa because he was still short of money for the passage. The pawnbroker who handled the transaction, Mr Annis, came forward to state that the chain had been brought in at 2 pm on Tuesday 12, by a man giving the name 'Miller'.

All this information emerged into the public domain a week after Muller had begun his journey, and although he was still at large, everything painted a picture of a man who had mysteriously come by a new hat and watch chain in the immediate aftermath of the attack on Thomas Briggs, and then pawned various items in a seemingly secretive manner in order to raise money for a trip to another country. Franz Muller had not been arrested, yet it was as if his trial in many ways had already taken place. Meanwhile, the two ships continued their steady journey across the Atlantic.

Although Muller might have imagined that he was leaving the scene of the crime far behind, he had chosen a very slow method of escape. As the *Times* reported on 9 August, 'the *Victoria* was freighted with a cargo of iron, and her sailing qualities are so far below mediocrity that it is not probable she will reach New York before the 20th inst.' Owing to information received from the pilot of the ship, who had been on board until it reached Gravesend, the police were now convinced that the hat which Muller was still wearing was the same one that had belonged to Thomas Briggs. To that end, the authorities had now sent by means of a second ship Inspector Kerressey and the son of the deceased, Briggs Jr., in order to help with identification in the US. News of the murder had in fact reached the *Victoria* during the early days of the voyage – but not of the identity of any likely suspect – and Muller's reaction is not recorded.

Back home more deaths occurred on the railways, but such news items were a depressingly regular occurrence: a collision at Margate caused a group of carriages to be 'heaped upon the roof' of the station, killing one woman and injuring many other passengers; four days later a railway track worker was decapitated by a train at Sudbury, and the same day an eleven-year-old boy was cut in two by an engine at New Cross station; the following week a locomotive exploded at Camden Road station, killing the stoker. These were just the train fatalities during a fortnight in early August, but they raised little of the commotion that surrounded the death of Thomas Briggs on the North London Railway.

While all this accidental carnage was taking place on the new railway system, the inquest was resumed into the death of the late Mr Briggs at the Vestry Hall in Hackney, at which another novelty presented itself that would not have been possible in earlier years – a *carte de visite* photograph of the suspect shown to the jury, of 'a well dressed, short, thick-set young man, with a firm, compressed mouth, and small, narrow, half-shut eyes'. He might be many hundreds of miles away, but in a sense, Franz Muller was already in the dock. At sea, however, as one of forty-eight passengers on the *Victoria*, he behaved himself at times as if he were on holiday. Having apparently no spare money, he wagered that he could eat five pounds of German sausages (he lost). He shared a cabin with an older Englishman, and on one occasion Muller got into a fight with another man, after having apparently called him 'a liar and a thief' (this he also lost).

The ship made very slow progress, owing to strong headwinds, which the passengers jokingly attributed to a suggestion that the murderer of Thomas Briggs was on board, since this well-publicised case was one of the conversational topics of the day. While Muller's vessel was at the mercy of the wind, the two faster steamships carrying police officers and various witnesses were steadily overtaking the slower ship – indeed, it is tempting to imagine Franz Muller standing on deck, watching one of these two passing him on the horizon, unaware of what passengers were on board, and that they would be there to meet him when he docked.

Finally, on 24 August, the *Victoria* landed in New York, where it was met by a selection of US and British authorities. Captain Champion lined his passengers up along the deck, and almost immediately Muller was picked out by Mr Death and Matthews the cabman, at which point he was formally arrested for murder by Officer John Tiemann of the New York police, accompanied by two London policemen who had brought the witnesses over, Inspector Tanner and Detective Sergeant Clark.

When informed that he was being arrested for the murder on the North London Railway, Muller replied, 'I did not do it. I was not there, and I can prove it.'

Now a prisoner, Muller began his long journey back to England, as his former fellow passengers were swooped upon by waiting newsmen. Some said he had behaved exactly like a 'gentleman', while the man who had shared a cabin with him told a different tale, claiming that he 'often, in punishment of Muller's profanity, had to administer a blow with the back of his arm'. Whatever the case, when the police searched Muller's trunk, the watch and hat that had allegedly belonged to Thomas Briggs were found inside.

When the case finally came to court at the Old Bailey on 27 October 1864, most newspaper readers had probably heard the key testimony several times over, so thoroughly had it been reported during the various sittings of the coroner's inquest and at the Bow Street Magistrates' Court. The insatiable public interest in this case meant that every detail had been picked over and examined in numerous feature and leader articles; indeed, it had become something of a matter of international tension, with sections of the German press convinced that Franz Muller had no hope of a fair trial purely on account of his nationality. Mr Beard, the solicitor acting for Muller, had requested that the jury be composed of 'half Englishmen and half foreigners,' but eventually twelve Englishmen were selected.

So great was the clamour for access to the court that chaotic scenes took place both inside and outside the Old Bailey, as large numbers of police struggled to process the demands of all manner of dignitaries desperately waving pieces of paper and claiming a right to entrance. The case was presided over by a selection of judges including the Lord Chief Baron, Baron Martin, the Lord Mayor, six aldermen and several sheriffs. The prisoner himself was said to have 'advanced with a steady step, although his face wore a pale and careworn appearance'.

Opening the case for the Crown, the Solicitor-General, R.P. Collier, commented that this was 'a case which had excited unusual interest, having been canvassed in every newspaper and every house in the kingdom.'

He then asked the jury to 'dismiss from their minds everything they had heard on the case, and to try the prisoner simply on the evidence which would be adduced.' In the event, however, the chances of finding any juror who had not been exposed to the story over the previous few months would have been slim indeed. One by one, witnesses were called to attest to the last railway journey undertaken by Mr Briggs, the state of the carriage when the murder was discovered, the provenance and disposal of the various hats, watches and chains of the victim and the accused – none of which would have come as any surprise to those who had followed the earlier preliminary hearings and coroner's inquest. After a full day of evidence, the court then adjourned.

The proceedings resumed the next morning, and continued in much the same fashion. While the defence admitted that the circumstantial evidence against their client seemed very strong, they argued nevertheless that nothing positive had been established to link Muller to the crime, and that it had not even been proved that the disputed hat that he was wearing when arrested was indeed the same one that had belonged to Mr Briggs. By the end of that day's hearing, the prisoner was described as looking completely exhausted, and when he took his place in court on the third and final day of the trial, his spirits seemed to have sunk even further. This was understandable; the sheer weight of evidence painted a picture of a man who had wilfully bludgeoned a defenceless fellow passenger to death for the sake of a few trivial possessions which he had then openly displayed to friends before pawning or exchanging them to buy a ticket on a sailing ship in order to flee the country. The Lord Chief Baron summed up the case as it had been presented, and when he sat down after addressing the court, it is reported that he wept. Nevertheless, when the jury retired to consider their verdict, they took only fifteen minutes to reach a unanimous verdict of guilty.

Franz Muller, looking pale and speaking very quietly, said after the judge had condemned him to death: 'I was prepared for the sentence. I have been convicted, not by a true, but by a false statement; and if I die according to the sentence, I shall die an innocent death.'

Returned to the same Newgate cell in which he had previously awaited trial, Muller was visited frequently during the next weeks by representatives of the German Legal Protection Society, and by Reverend Walbaum of a German chapel in London, who attempted to co-ordinate movement for an appeal against the sentence. The Society visited the Home Office and made their own attempts to solve the mystery of who might have committed the murder. Having examined the evidence and spoken at length to the trial judges, the Home Secretary Sir George Grey concluded on 13 November that 'there is no ground which could justify him in advising Her Majesty to interfere with the due course of the law.' Large crowds gathered each day outside Newgate, watching the temporary barriers being constructed in preparation for execution day, while Muller himself remained inside, praying a great deal, and also writing. His friend Haffa had been allowed to visit him twice, and reported afterwards that Muller denied ever having travelled on the North London Line, but expressed the hope that it would all be over soon. Meanwhile three people wrote to the authorities claiming to have committed the murder, but none of them signed the letters with their real names.

On 14 November 1864, at 4 am in the early morning darkness, the crowd which had already begun gathering outside Newgate despite heavy rainfall let out 'an unearthly yell, such as is only heard at the foot of the gibbet'. This was prompted by the doors having opened, and workmen beginning to assemble the scaffold. Streets were barricaded and shops were boarded shut, but the pubs were soon open, and the rain drove many spectators inside for an early-morning drink. Although there were only an estimated three or four thousand present during the night, by the time the rain ceased at 6 am, the number had swollen to over 100,000. This might be the age of the railway and the telegraph, but it was also, still, an age of public execution in London, and when they were discontinued four years later, it was hardly due to lack of interest.

Shortly before eight o'clock, Franz Muller was brought out of his cell and pinioned by William Calcraft, the executioner. The prisoner appeared calm and was accompanied by Reverend Mr Davis, the Ordinary of Newgate, and also by Reverend Dr. Louis Cappel, of the German Lutheran Church in Goodman's Fields. As Franz Muller stood on the scaffold, Cappel asked him several times in German whether he was guilty or innocent. Initially, he replied that he was innocent. When questioned again, he said, 'God knows what I have done.' Finally, when questioned a third time by Cappel, Muller replied in German, *'Ich habe es gethan'* – 'I did it.' They were his final words before the trapdoor was opened.

Out in the seething crowd, a young woman named Hester Collings was trampled so badly by the crowd that her life was despaired of, as was that of a young man named Benson. William Calcraft was paid his customary ten pounds for conducting the execution, and could expect more money from the sale of sections of the rope that he had used.

As for the international aspect of the case, Queen Victoria herself had received messages before the execution from the duke of Saxe-Coburg and also from the King of Prussia, asking her to intervene, but despite her own strong family ties to Germany, had declined. For the Berlin newspaper *Reform*, it was apparently a clear case of vindictive international politics:

> An execution we may call murder was the day before yesterday committed on the person of the unlucky journeyman tailor at London . . . But it was worse than murder – it was murder on the ground of national prejudice and hatred. The Schleswig-Holstein war, and the impotent rage of the English aristocratic mob, tied the noose by which was hung the man Muller.

The same issue of the *Observer* that reported these sentiments also carried an article about a proposal from a Mr Tattersall for the installing of a communication cord in railway carriages, enabling passengers to raise the alarm with the guard in the event of difficulty. A comfort for the traveller, no doubt, although a short item three pages later would tend to reinforce the impression that the age of railway travel was fraught with danger – a fifty-pound reward offered for information in connection with the death of a child found murdered in the first-class waiting room at Paddington Station. Franz Muller may have been the most famous early killer to operate on London's rail network, but he would hardly be the last.

A London bobby, from an illustration published in *The Graphic*, 30 August, 1884

FIFTEEN

SHOREDITCH IN SCARLET
1887

The year 1887 was a high-water mark of the Victorian era, with the queen celebrating fifty years on the throne. The population of the capital had just passed five million.

In London on 2 April, a crowd of 15,500 turned out at Kennington Oval to see Aston Villa beat West Bromwich Albion, 2–0, in the sixteenth FA Cup Final. On the south coast that same day, the *Hampshire Telegraph* reported on a football match played by Portsmouth, whose goalkeeper, a local medical man, was listed as 'Dr. Doyle'. In addition to his normal activities as a family GP in the city, he appeared reasonably often in their news pages as captain of the Portsmouth Cricket Club, Honorary Secretary of the Portsmouth Literary and Scientific Society, and lately as an aspiring local author. Indeed, although he had published various short stories, 1887 would see the appearance of Dr Doyle's first novel, introducing a character who, perhaps more than any other, would shape the image of late Victorian London which persists in the popular imagination to this day. In early December, the *Hampshire Telegraph* proudly reported:

> The publishers of *Beeton's Christmas Annual* (Messrs. Ward, Lock & Co.) have been fortunate to secure the services of our townsman Dr. A. Conan Doyle, who is now well-known in literary circles as a rising writer of fiction. Dr. Conan Doyle has prepared for Beeton's Christmas fare *A Study in Scarlet*, which for exciting incidents, clever construction, and artistic development of plot, will compare with any of the Christmas annuals with which the bookstalls are now deluged. This student in scarlet is one Sherlock Holmes, a consulting detective of most amusing eccentricities and strangely balanced powers.

The manuscript of *A Study in Scarlet* had previously been rejected by several publishers, so Conan Doyle had accepted a deal in which Ward, Lock & Co. acquired the copyright outright for twenty-five pounds. Despite the eventual worldwide success of the novel, as he later recalled, 'I never at any time received another penny for it.'

For the moment, though, in the early spring of 1887, Holmes was still just a completed manuscript awaiting publication in time for the lucrative Christmas market. Dr Doyle went about his normal round of hectic activities, and made a typical appearance in the local newspaper on 23 April as one of the brethren of a Portsmouth Freemasons' Lodge attending a '*recherché* banquet . . . interspersed with vocal and instrumental music'. The paper also noted the execution of a killer in London, which had taken place on the same day that Doyle attended his Lodge meeting. The press called the case the Hoxton Murder. The identity of the assassin was never seriously in doubt, but the motive for the killing, as Holmes once remarked in another context, was 'quite a three pipe problem'.

In 1887, the part of Shoreditch known as Hoxton was a crowded, poverty-stricken district of narrow streets, music halls, chapels, tabernacles, alms-houses, asylums and hospitals. At the beginning of February, one of the largest of the local music halls, the Britannia Theatre on Hoxton Street, was still drawing capacity crowds for its Christmas pantomime, *The Goblin Bat*, starring Mr Victor Vernon as the superbly named King Funky the First. However, life on the streets nearby was generally tough, as the local vicar, Septimuss Buss, discovered that month when he was assaulted near his vicarage in Hoxton Square by a labourer named Thomas Robson. Here could be found the itinerant dog-sellers, bone-grubbers, street herb-alists, long-song sellers, baked-potato men and Lucifer match girls, faith-fully documented by Henry Mayhew in his monumental study, *London Labour & the London Poor* (1851), as well as the 'crocks' who bartered household items for china plates and cups, crying 'Here we are – now, ladies, bring out your old hats, old clothes, old umbrellers, old anythink; old shoes, metal, old anythink; *here* we are!'

There were all kinds of ways of getting by in such a district. Lydia

Green, a thirty-one-year-old woman who lived at 8 Baches Street, Hoxton – next to the Haberdasher's Alms House and Aske's Hospital – worked as a 'surgical instrument-case coverer'. This area would be largely flattened during the Blitz, and although today the buildings along Baches Street are new, the thoroughfare itself is one of the very few from the old densely packed Victorian street plan that have not been obliterated during post-war map alterations. A short stretch of road a little to the north of Old Street, it runs between Brunswick Place and Chart Street (both of which are also survivals from the 1887 street layout). The pub on the northern corner of today's Baches Street, although also modern, is named in honour of one of the greatest figures from the area's music hall past, the bawdy singer Marie Lloyd, who would bring the house down with double-entendre songs such as 'I Sits Among The Cabbages And Peas'. (Perhaps not the kind of 'Victorian values' former prime minister Margaret Thatcher had in mind when choosing 'Two Little Boys' by Rolf Harris as her favourite song during her appearance on *Desert Island Discs*).

On the evening of Friday, 4 February 1887, Lydia Green retired to bed in her room at the rear of number 8. It was a four-storey building, divided up into various dwellings, which had been presided over for many years by Lydia's mother Ann, who was a tenant herself but also acted as landlady for the house, subletting the top three floors to a variety of families. Ann Green and her three daughters occupied the lower floors and basement. These daughters were: Alice Gauntlett, who had moved back in with her mother after becoming a widow; Amy Green, who was single; and Lydia Green, who was unmarried, but had been in a regular relationship for over a decade with Thomas Currell, who lived three minutes' walk away in Fanshawe Street. Although they were not formally engaged, the length of time Lydia and Thomas had spent together would have amounted to much the same thing in the eyes of their friends and family, as a report in the *Standard* explained:

> Lydia Green, a working woman, aged thirty-one, had for ten or eleven years been 'keeping company' with Thomas Currell, of nearly the same age, and in a similar rank in life. Among the humbler classes of London long engagements are rare, and early marriages the rule. Hence, a courtship of ten years must be regarded as out of the common.

A familiar couple, then, like many in their working-class neighbour-hood. Not married, but an established fixture in the local social scene. Lydia travelled every day to Walthamstow, where for fourteen years she had been one of a team working for a Mr Andrews. This was a journey away from the crowds and grime of the city to a much quieter location, since, at that time, Walthamstow was some distance outside London itself, a small hamlet of around a hundred houses, surrounded by fields. It was a steady job, for which she was paid eighteen shillings a week. Tom Currell, then unemployed, had last worked about a month earlier, in a similarly hands-on role trimming sponges at a warehouse in Red Lion Square. Currell was a frequent visitor to the house at 8 Baches Street, as, indeed, were a fair few other people. A few tenants had latch-keys, but the main door to the street was hardly ever locked.

Privacy would have been in short supply in such a household. A pair of elderly sisters, Mrs Fenn and Mrs Dodd, rented the front room on the first floor, and lived there together with Mrs Fenn's grand-daughter. Above them on the second floor were Mr and Mrs Attrell, and also Mr and Mrs Sinclair, while the third floor was occupied by Mr and Mrs Day and their three children. With Ann Green and her three daughters also in residence, there would have been plenty of arrivals and departures in the building throughout the daytime and evening. Thomas Attrell was a bricklayer; Mrs Fenn and Mrs Dodd worked as cleaners at the Sun Fire Office, as did Alice Gauntlett; William Sinclair sold muffins in the street for a living; John Day was a timber porter. All in all, it was a fairly representative selection of trades for this part of the East End. What money there was would go on the rent, a cheap supper of fish and chips – which had become popular during the last couple of decades – or a visit to the pub or the music hall. If there was an argument in the house, most of the fellow tenants would hear it.

On the Friday night in question, Lydia Green came home later than usual. Her working day at Walthamstow generally lasted until 7 pm, but on this occasion she did not reach Baches Street until shortly before 11 pm. At this point, her mother Ann, working in the kitchen, heard Lydia and Tom Currell in conversation at the street door. He was a regular visitor, but there had apparently been some kind of a dispute two weeks previously, since Lydia had told her mother that she had asked Tom not to come around any more. However, from what Ann Green could hear, their conversation on this particular evening sounded perfectly amicable, although she could not make out the words that were spoken. Shortly afterwards Lydia came into the kitchen and apologised to her mother for her late arrival, saying that she had gone with Tom to visit his parents in Stoke Newington, but making no mention of any quarrel.

Tom Currell was not necessarily the kind of man a mother would be delighted to have courting their daughter. Not only did he have a some-what casual attitude to the whole business of earning his keep, he had ceased living with his parents the previous year because, it was said, 'he was going on badly, and they could not sanction his doings'. Most damning of all, he had recently served eighteen months' hard labour for theft. As to her daughter's long engagement, Ann Green's explanation was simple: 'They were not married because he would never keep a place [job] to get enough money, and she would not marry him till he got a home.' Still, the relationship had muddled along for all those years, and there was no particular reason to suppose that it would not continue to do so.

Lydia ate some supper in the kitchen and then went to bed. Her mother recalled that she looked 'pale and ill', as if she was worried about something, but, for all that, 'was in her usual spirits'.

———— ◆ ◆ ————

The following day may have been a Saturday, yet for most of the residents of 8 Baches Street it was a working day much like any other. Mrs Fenn and Mrs Dodd, being office cleaners, rose early. Mrs Fenn went down and unbolted the street door, taking in the milk from the doorstep at 6.10 am, and leaving the door closed but not bolted when she went back upstairs. Fenn and Dodd left the house by 6.30, and Thomas Attrell set off to walk to his workplace at around 6.45. Alice Gauntlett, who shared a bedroom and parlour with Lydia Green, left at her usual time of 7 am.

One of the young children of the Day family on the top floor ventured downstairs at this time to fetch water and make some tea. Anyone moving around or opening the front door would very likely have been heard by various of the other residents of the house, but such sounds were part of everyday life in shared lodgings, and would not have excited any comment or curiosity. However, a very sudden noise at 7.15 made people on each floor take notice; some were even roused from their sleep as a result.

Everyone remembered the disturbance in their own way: for Amy Green, woken by the sound, it appeared to be the front door banging; Caroline Sinclair, up on the second floor, said, 'I cannot tell what it was, but the reverberation shook the house, and I heard the landlady screaming out in an excited manner for her daughter'; John Day, on the top floor, 'heard a kind of noise as if the children on the first floor were jumping down stairs – there were two or three noises'; his wife, Matilda, recalled 'a noise like a bang'; Mrs Attrell, in the front room on the second floor, thought 'it was like something exploding; it shook the whole house. I only heard it once, but it lasted longer than one explosion would have lasted'.

Ann Green, still in bed in the room above Lydia, had been waiting to hear the usual morning sound of her daughter knocking on the ceiling with a curtain pole that she kept for the purpose, as a sign that she was dressing and would soon be wanting breakfast. Instead, Ann heard a sudden strange commotion – 'a very great noise, three times . . . like something very heavy falling down', she recalled – and shortly afterwards, the sound of the street door banging, as if someone had left the house. Worried, or perhaps just mystified, she went downstairs to investigate:

'I got up and put my things on hastily; Amy remained in bed. I then went downstairs to the back parlour bedroom: the door was pulled close to, but not catched. When I got inside I found my daughter lying on the floor just inside the door, with her head towards a chest of drawers and her feet towards the bed, which is on the right-hand side of the room as you enter. She was fully dressed with the exception of her dress-body and her boots, and her hair was partly plaited. I saw some blood on the floor under her head, and some upon her face, and some under her right hand, which was thrown out under a chair. Mrs. Gauntlett's baby was on the bed crying dreadfully; it is eight months old.'

Something was terribly wrong, but at this point, Mrs Green assumed that there had been an accident and that her daughter had fallen, probably knocking her head on some solid object. Raising the alarm, she summoned Amy, and within minutes all the other lodgers still at home were crowded into the small room where the body lay. Matilda Day ran off to summon a local GP, Dr John Davis, who lived a short distance away at New North Road. He arrived at about 7.40 and found Amy Green in the bedroom, supporting Lydia's lifeless body. Davis made a swift examination of the body but was short of time, as he was on the way to attend to a woman in labour at a nearby house. As far as he was concerned, it was a straightforward, natural occurrence: 'I had no idea of any foul play. A rupture of a blood-vessel was the message brought to me.'

A busy doctor with a pressing engagement, Davis noticed only some blood and a fracture of the skull, which he took to be the result of Lydia's fall. Having confirmed that the woman was dead, he then left to attend to his other business. The ladies of the household therefore behaved as they normally would in the event of a death, and so a Mrs Coleman was sent for to come and lay out the body. Despite the loud noises that had preceded the discovery of the body, no one seems to have suspected that this was anything other than a tragic accident. However, Mrs Coleman apparently looked a little more closely at the body than Dr Davis, and mentioned her discoveries to Mrs Green, as the latter recalled: 'She then pointed out to me an injury on the right hand and two injuries upon the right side of the throat, and the right eye was very black as though bruised.'

If Lydia had suffered some kind of seizure, then fractured her skull when falling, where had these other marks come from? A good question, and indeed, Mrs Green eventually called the doctor back to re-examine her daughter's body, but she did not do this until 3 pm that afternoon, some six hours after her attention was drawn to these marks. For the moment, there were no real suspicions, and the main task in hand was to prepare the body for burial and make an initial attempt to clean up the room.

Alice Gauntlett learned the news of her sister's death when she arrived home at 10 am from her early-morning cleaning job in the city. She inspected the rooms that the two of them had shared, as she later testi-fied: 'I went into the parlour and bedroom, but found nothing disturbed or taken away . . . I assisted in clearing up the room, but I found nothing.'

The image that has come down to us from numerous detective stories – in which the body and the crime scene are carefully examined to determine the cause of death and any relevant circumstances which may have been contributory factors – owes a lot to the methods employed by Conan Doyle's Sherlock Holmes. He takes a meticulous approach, where no detail is too small or inconsequential to be of importance, based upon a thorough examination of the victim and their surroundings. In reality, Holmes was some years ahead of actual police procedure. It was relatively common until the beginning of the twentieth century for the police to arrive at a murder scene that had already been thoroughly cleaned and tidied by the residents of the building, mopping up all that nasty blood and setting upright any furniture that had been overturned. The idea that nothing should be touched, and the body itself left in its original position, had not gained ground by this stage, and many members of the public would have had no concept of the idea of preserving the integrity of the crime scene. There was a mess in the room, therefore it should be cleaned up. Of course, no one at Baches Street thought that there had been a murder. The body was found a little after 7.15 am, and it was not until mid-afternoon that the residents of the house began to suspect foul play, by which time the corpse had been washed and laid out, and the room returned to something approaching its normal state.

It was the arrival home of another lodger, the bricklayer Thomas Attrell, that prompted further inquiries into the situation. On his way out to work that morning, at around 6.45, he had seen no other members of the household. However, shortly after leaving, he had encountered someone familiar to him. Having walked the short distance to the southern end of Baches Street, he turned left into Brunswick Place, across the northern edge of Charles Square, until he came to the junction of Pitfield Street. (Although the map of the East End has greatly changed in the intervening years, all these roads survive today). As he reached the corner of Pitfield Street, near a pub called the Crosby Head, some two minutes' walk from his home, he saw Tom Currell, who greeted him with the words 'Good morning, Mister Attrell'. The two men exchanged pleasantries, then went into the pub together for a drink – quite a common thing for workmen to do of a morning. (Some years later, the regulations contained in the Defence of the Realm Act, 1914, banning pubs from opening until midday, were partly inspired by the fear that war workers in munitions factories might show up already drunk in the morning and then attempt to handle high explosives.)

Attrell did not know Currell well – indeed, he only knew him by his first name, and had never been for a drink with him before – but they were accustomed to saying a polite 'Hello' to each other when their paths crossed at Baches Street. On this particular morning, however, Currell seemed friendlier than usual, and showed a marked interest in the movements of the occupants of the house that Attrell had just left. As they each drank a half-pint of mild ale with a shot of gin, Lydia's boyfriend asked the bricklayer if anyone was 'up and about', and if Alice Gauntlett had already left for work. Although Currell often called at the house, he had no key to the front door – which is hardly surprising, since several of the residents themselves had none and relied upon knocking in order to gain entry. However, rather than doing the same on this occasion, Tom Currell gave Attrell a story about having left some of his tools in the house and asked to borrow the latter's front-door key. After some indecision, Attrell gave in and lent him the key, and at a few minutes before 7 am, the two parted.

When Attrell returned to the house that afternoon to news of Lydia's death, he told Mrs Green of his morning encounter with Currell. She seems to have been worried about the various injuries that Mrs Coleman had noticed, and this new information from the bricklayer caused her not only to call back the doctor but also to send for the police.

———————

The residents of the house who were becoming concerned about exactly what might have happened in Lydia's room at 7.15 am would have been even more disturbed had they been able to follow Tom Currell around during the rest of the day. While he was propping up the bar of the Crosby Head at 7 am, he certainly wasn't the only person in the neighbourhood having an early-morning drink. Close by in the Haberdasher's Arms, a resident of Bevenden Street named George Williamson was fortifying himself for the day ahead with 'twopenny worth of rum and milk and half an ounce of tobacco'. Suitably refreshed, he left the pub and walked down Great Chart Street and into Baches Street, where, at about 7.18 am, he saw Tom Currell and called out a greeting to him:

> 'He was 20 or 30 yards from No. 8, which I knew well and all the family. He was between No. 8 and Great Chart Street, just as I turned the corner by the Globe public-house, and before I saw him, I heard a door slam. I cannot say it was No. 8, but it came from that direction. He was buttoning up his coat and he walked very sharply across the road towards Great Chart Street. He did not reply when I spoke to him, and I went on and did not look back to see whether he turned up or down.'

So, just a couple of minutes after the loud noises that heralded the death of Lydia Green, Tom Currell was seen in the street outside her house, possibly having just left that building, and failed to respond to a greeting from a friend. Later that day, however, he was in a far more talkative mood. Annie Manton and Beatrice Stevens – work colleagues of Lydia Green's who also lived in Hoxton – were returning home, having completed their Saturday shift at Walthamstow. Since there was no direct train link, they had to break the journey at Hackney Downs, then walk across to Dalston station and take another train to Shoreditch. This was the route that Lydia had been using for many years, and sometimes Tom Currell would be waiting for her at Hackney when she alighted from the first train.

On this particular day, Manton and Stevens, noticing that Lydia had not shown up for work, collected her wage packet from the boss, Mr Andrews, in order to bring it home to her – something they had occasionally done in the past. At about 3 pm, as they were walking down Dalston Lane, the two women encountered Tom Currell, standing on the street corner reading a billboard. When Annie Manton called out to him and asked if he had seen Lydia, Currell replied that he had: 'I promised to take Lydia to the Hall to-night,' said Tom, 'but I don't suppose she will go now as her mother is ill. I told Lyd I was coming this way, and she asked me to meet you for her money.' Manton duly handed over the envelope containing Lydia's wages, and the three of them walked down to Dalston Junction, where they had a drink at a pub near the station. As Manton recalled, 'he joked with both of us. He seemed in good spirits; I thought he had had a glass too much to drink.'

A quarter of an hour later, Currell accompanied them to the station and bought their tickets for them before saying goodbye, adding cheerily, 'Look out for Lyd Monday morning.' As Annie Manton discovered the following morning, Lydia Green had been dead for eight hours at this point.

Having been in Hoxton and Dalston already that day, Tom Currell next appeared up in Hampstead around 7 pm, knocking on the door of his aunt, Elizabeth Hearn, at 32 New End Square. This was something of a surprise to her as he did not often visit, but she exchanged the usual pleasantries, asking after his parents and also Lydia, to which he replied, 'All right, I saw her last evening, and she will come up to see you shortly.' As in his earlier conversation at Dalston with Lydia's work colleagues, Currell appeared somewhat under the influence; 'a little heavy-eyed,' recalled his aunt, 'as if he had had a little something to drink'. They chatted for a while and then he left, giving no indication that he would then walk just a short distance around the corner into Flask Walk, where at number 22, the house of Charles and Martha Smith, he saw a sign that read 'Lodgings for single men'. Giving the address of his aunt Elizabeth as a reference, but nevertheless telling the Smiths that his name was Tom Cole, he took space in a room he would share with a Mr Mortimer. Currell's first action after settling into his new lodgings was to send out for a copy of the evening paper, and during the next few days he seemed concerned with little else other than obsessively reading the news. His new landlords also noticed that he liked to drink a fair amount more alcohol than was good for him.

While Tom Currell was finding new lodgings in Hampstead, the police and the medical profession were taking an interest in the events at 8 Baches Street. In Conan Doyle's *A Study in Scarlet*, faced with a similar crime scene in Brixton, Holmes is shown to be utterly meticulous, as Watson records:

> As he spoke, he whipped a tape measure and a large round magnifying glass from his pocket. With these two implements he trotted

noiselessly about the room, sometimes stopping, occasionally kneeling, and once lying flat upon his face. So engrossed was he with his occupation that he appeared to have forgotten our presence, for he chattered away to himself under his breath the whole time, keeping up a running fire of exclamations, groans, whistles, and little cries suggestive of encouragement and of hope. As I watched him I was irresistibly reminded of a pure-blooded, well-trained foxhound as it dashes backwards and forwards through the covert, whining in its eagerness, until it comes across the lost scent. For twenty minutes or more he continued his researches, measuring with the most exact care the distance between marks which were entirely invisible to me, and occasionally applying his tape to the walls in an equally incomprehensible manner.

Such an approach was hardly possible in the tiny bedroom at Baches Street, since it had already been cleaned up by some of the women of the house during the Saturday morning, when no crime was suspected. By early evening, however, the matter was in the hands of police inspector Joseph Fearn. News of the death reached him at Hoxton Police Station at 5 pm, and he despatched several constables to the house to investigate. When they reported back, Fearn then sent an Inspector Peel to fetch Dr Davis, and all three of them went in a group to Baches Street to examine the scene, where the body still lay. Davis, upon viewing the corpse again, found several wounds which he had not noticed that morning, and concluded that the victim had died of gunshots, perhaps three in all. Inspector Fearn then went over the ground, looking primarily for a weapon, as he later testified:

'I examined the walls and flooring, and under the bed and the carpet, and turned out some boxes, and examined the fireplace and window curtains, and behind, under, and in the drawers, but found no bullet or mark. I did not search for a bullet, but for any weapon with which the wounds might have been inflicted, and found none. I searched again on the Sunday and again on the Monday after the post-mortem, but discovered nothing.'

In classic detective fiction, all the occupants of a house where a murder had taken place would be considered potential suspects, but this was not how Inspector Fearn saw things. He later outlined his reasoning as follows:

> 'When I went to the house in the evening I heard that Lydia had been killed by three revolver shots in her head. I knew that no revolver had been found. I made inquiries at Mrs. Green's house. I knew all the respectable people living there, and I did not think it necessary to search. I did not cause the house to be searched. I had no clue at all to lead me to fix on anybody from first to last.'

He was a local policeman, and as far as he was concerned, the occupants of the house were all 'respectable people', and could therefore be excluded from the inquiry. Fearn may have been a public official looking for the weapon in a murder investigation, but it would not do to go bothering fine upstanding citizens. Incredibly to modern sensibilities, the inspector not only held these opinions, but also gave them publicly at the Old Bailey when the case came to trial.

In the world of fiction, Holmes would have looked closely into the faces of everyone in the building for signs of their inner character, having also gone over every inch of the ground looking for clues, while Agatha Christie's Poirot would have interviewed the entire household, and then rounded them all up in the parlour and explained that they all had good reason to have committed the crime but only one of them – the least likely – had actually done it. In reality, despite the lack of a thorough search and the refusal to regard any of the tenants as anything more than honest witnesses, the police had little doubt who they were looking for. Then again, this was no great mystery designed to tax the mind of a master detective. Indeed, Holmes himself, whose methods prefigured the rise of the forensic sciences in crime detection, deplored the lack of ingenuity in current murders:

> 'There are no crimes or criminals in these days,' he said, querulously. 'What is the use of having brains in our profession . . . There is no crime to detect, or, at most, some bungling villainy with a motive so transparent that even a Scotland yard official can see through it.'

The case certainly appeared simple. By the time the news broke in the papers on Monday 7, two days after the body was discovered, the focus of the inquiry was entirely on Tom Currell, and readers were left in little doubt as to his presumed guilt:

SHOCKING MURDER OF A WOMAN IN HOXTON
ESCAPE OF THE MURDERER

Suspicion pointed towards the young man who had kept company with the deceased, owing to recent quarrels having taken place between them, and inquiries were at once instituted with regard to his doings. It was found that he, or a person answering to his description, was seen about the neighbourhood of the house some time before the crime was committed, and that he had not been at home all day. The police have issued the following description of him:- 'Thomas William Carroll [sic], age 30; height 5ft. 6in., complexion fresh, mole on right ear; hair dark; slight side whiskers, and tuft on chin, sandy. Dress: dark blue Chesterfield overcoat, dark or check trousers, black hard felt hat, with mourning band. Respectable appearance. Seen at Dalston Junction at 3 pm, 5th. ultimo.'

By the following day, the police had revealed extra information about Currell, including that of his previous imprisonment for theft. The findings of the autopsy performed by S.L. Birchall, Divisonal Surgeon of Police, showed conclusively that Lydia Green had died from gunshot wounds to the head, but there was still no sign of the weapon, or of Currell himself. However, a search of the room at 22 Fanshawe Street, Hoxton, where he had been living for the past few months, yielded results. A locked box belonging to Currell, which Inspector Fearn and his sergeant managed to open, contained a package of thirty-eight bullets, labelled '50 powder 5 ½ grains. 50 bullets, 63 grains. Cartridges for revolver. Eley Brothers, manufacturers, London'. The suspect had not only been spotted near the scene of the crime both shortly beforehand and afterwards, he also possessed ammunition for a revolver that matched the mangled bullets recovered at the autopsy.

As the week went by, Tom Currell did little except stay in his Flask Walk lodgings at Hampstead, reading every daily newspaper he could obtain. On Thursday, 10 February, his landlady, Mrs Smith, happened to pick up one of the papers he was reading and asked him, 'What is this Hoxton murder?' Currell made no reply but immediately went upstairs to his room and then left the house, saying he would be back in two hours. This was the last anyone there saw of him, and on the following day his room-mate Mr Mortimer discovered that his own overcoat was missing. A letter then arrived, addressed to 'Mr Cole', from a pawnbroker in Upper Street, Islington, containing a pawn ticket for the overcoat. Mrs Smith decided to inquire further about her missing lodger, and having called on Mrs Hearn, whose name had initially been given as a reference, she discovered that his real name was Currell, whereupon she concluded that she had 'unknowingly been harbouring him'.

By now, Currell must have been in a very uneasy state of mind, after almost a week of reading articles about the murder in which he was repeatedly named as the killer. Half the city was looking for him – the proprietors of cafés, barber's shops, grocers, pubs and similar establishments had been provided with descriptions and a woodcut likeness of him made from a daguerreotype – and yet he remained in London.

In the end, it all seems to have become too much for Tom Currell. He was not a well man, suffering from what was described at the time as 'a congestion on the lungs', and the police expressed fears while he was still at large that he would commit suicide. As it happened, their sole suspect had some difficulty attracting the attention of the constabulary at all: unconfirmed reports suggested that he had gone to Scotland Yard and failed in an attempt to give himself up. Certainly, despite the descriptions and photographs of him in circulation, Currell seems to have walked around quite openly in the Islington area during the latter part of the week following the murder. A painter called Alfred Oram, who had known him for twelve years, spotted him in Upper Street at midday on Friday 11, and immediately notified a nearby policeman, Constable Pottinger, who challenged Currell rather politely, saying, 'I beg your pardon, I thought you was the man that was wanted.' In reply, Currell merely said, 'What makes you think that?', and walked away, leaving Pottinger under the impression that he had made a mistake.

On the following Tuesday, 15 February, Inspector Peel received a letter addressed to him at St Luke's Police Station, which read, 'To save you trouble I beg to say I shall be at Upper Thames Street Police-station at half-past 9 to-morrow morning, not inside. T.W. CURRELL.' However, the letter was dated 'Monday 14th', and by the time Peel arrived at the appointed place it was already 9.30 am. Although he waited for over an hour, there was no sign of Currell. Probably frustrated at having missed his chance, Peel sent a plain-clothes constable, Charles Mather, along Upper Street, in the company of Albert Oram, who would hopefully recognise the suspect. At 11.15, they spotted him, a little south of where Islington Town Hall now stands, just as he turned into Florence Street. After a very short struggle, it was all over. Mather said, 'I am a police officer, Currell; I arrest you for killing Lydia Green on the 5th of this month at Hoxton,' to which Currell replied, 'All right, I meant to give myself up.'

Far from being the cunning criminal who evades justice while laughing at the authorities, Tom Currell apparently made little serious attempt to escape. Indeed, a Hoxton local named Henry Barker came forward and gave evidence that at about 1.15 in the afternoon of the day of the murder, he had seen Currell outside a shop on the corner of Baches Street, 'standing and smoking and looking towards the house No. 8'. Having already learned of Lydia's death by this stage, Barker said to him, 'It is a serious thing round the corner for you,' to which Currell replied, 'Yes, it is,' and then walked away. Six hours after Lydia had been shot, he was just yards away, staring at the house, well aware that she was dead, and yet two hours later he was drinking with her colleagues in Dalston and telling them that she would be back at work on Monday.

Whatever his state of mind at the time of his arrest, statements from Holloway gaol delivered via his solicitor were to the effect that while offering 'sincere regret' over the death of Lydia Green, he professed himself entirely innocent, and said that he had only given himself up in order to clear his name. Currell also said that, contrary to some of the wild press speculation as to what he had been up to since leaving Mrs Smith's lodgings on Thursday 10, he had, in fact, simply rented another room nearby in Hampstead, and passed the time quietly.

On Wednesday, 15 February, when Currell was brought to Worship Street Police Court for his initial hearing, crowds besieged the building and all the roads leading to it. The prisoner had let his beard grow during the intervening week, and seemed unusually relaxed. *The Times* reported that: 'He showed considerable interest in the proceedings and conversed freely, sometimes smiling at parts of the evidence given against him by the sister and relatives of the deceased.'

Regardless of its lack of effect upon him, the testimony presented was considered sufficient, and Currell was sent to be tried at the Old Bailey on 30 March. On this occasion, in front of a packed courtroom, the prisoner apparently 'looked more careworn than when he was at the police court, but he still maintained the nerve and self-possession which distinguished him there'. According to the *Daily News*:

> For a man of his class he was exceedingly well-dressed in a dark overcoat, a tweed suit, and a white shirt and stand-up collar. He pleaded 'Not Guilty' in a perfectly calm and clear voice; listened intently to the evidence; and scribbled frequent notes upon it to his solicitor, Mr A. Newton.

There was a great deal of evidence to consider. Every member of the household at 8 Baches Street was brought into the witness box, barring the children, and so were all those who had met the accused either on the day of the crime or during the days that had followed, not to mention the various police officers and medical men involved in the case. Currell himself was not questioned. He remained impassive, and Mrs Green mostly wept whilst giving evidence, but among the crowd, the anonymous reporter from the *Pall Mall Gazette* found the whole event strangely amusing:

> A day at the Old Bailey is an admirable tonic, and it is astonishing that no doctor has ever prescribed it as a medicine for melancholia . . . [Currell] is only interesting because of the audacious manner in which he baffled the police and then befooled them by giving himself up. This affair of Lydia Green was very ordinary in other respects, and one says with a sigh, 'They do these things better in France.'

Women weeping over the senseless death of their daughter or sister, or the sight of a man on trial for his life, were not about to disturb this particular journalist's carefully constructed *fin-de-siècle* pose, but for the rest of those present, the three-day trial was a solemn affair. There were no great surprises for the newspapers to report, since most of the witnesses had already given evidence previously at the preliminary hearings some weeks before.

When the jury eventually retired on the third day, taking into the room with them the bullets retrieved at the autopsy and a map of the area around Baches Street, they were gone for less than an hour. Upon their return, they delivered a unanimous verdict of guilty. As for the prisoner, he made no comment when sentenced to death, and according to one report, 'did not appear to evince the least concern, and preserved the same callous and indifferent demeanour which has been evinced by him throughout the trial'. Currell also showed no emotion in the condemned cell at Newgate the following day, when news was brought to him that the date of 18 April had been set for his execution.

Various reports filtered out during Currell's time in prison, concerning his state of mind and motivations. Some learned men wrote to the newspapers arguing that he was insane – a view to which Currell's family also subscribed. It was also asserted that he had told a clergyman while in gaol that 'he was in the habit of taking large doses of chloral and laudanum, and that on the morning of the murder he was so stupefied by these drugs that he has no recollection of what took place'. The latter explanation was certainly the most convincing account of his motives. However, the Home Secretary concluded that there were insufficient grounds for him to request Her Majesty to interfere, and that the execution would go ahead as planned.

On the morning of 18 April, Sheriff Kirby, accompanied by various Under-Sheriffs, and the executioner James Berry, arrived at Currell's cell just before 8 am. Berry pinioned the prisoner's arms, then Kirby asked Currell if he wanted to say anything. 'No, I thank you, sir,' he replied, and walked steadily to the scaffold. Hangings were no longer public affairs and were conducted within the prison walls, but outside in the street, the crowd that had gathered watched as a black flag was raised by the prison authorities to signal that the execution had taken place.

Later editions of the newspapers that day, in addition to reporting that the sentence had been carried out, also printed the text of a confession that Currell had written the evening before. He admitted responsibility for the crime, blamed his own jealousy, drunkenness and drug habit, and claimed to have bought the revolver while intoxicated. After the killing, he had thrown the murder weapon in the Regent's Canal:

> We seemed, however, to be on the best of terms, and she seemed to be as true as steel to me. I loved her with all my heart, and up to within a short time of the murder I had no idea of taking her life any more than I had that of the greatest stranger.

There had been no quarrel. He had walked up and shot her with barely a word. A senseless crime, seemingly incomprehensible even to the person who committed it; a murder mystery without a solution, which would have been the despair of any writer of crime fiction.

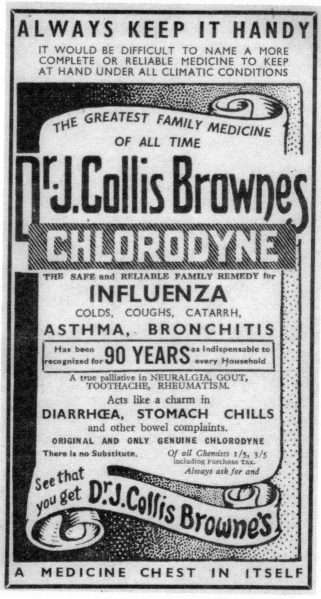

The patent medicine Chlorodyne, used to chilling effect by the
East Finchley baby farmers

SIXTEEN

THE EAST FINCHLEY
BABY FARMERS
1902

Newgate prison had long been part of the criminal landscape of London. There was a gaol on the site at least as far back as the twelfth century, and when the Great Fire swept it away in 1666, a new building rose to take its place. Demolished and then rebuilt in the 1770s, it was promptly burnt to the ground a couple of years later by the Gordon rioters, but emerged again in a new, robust design by the architect George Dance the Younger, which lasted all the way through the following century.

The worst malefactors were sent to Newgate. Situated next door to the Sessions House of the Old Bailey, it was a short step for a murderer from the gaol cell to the courtroom and condemnation. In addition, after the authorities abandoned Tyburn as an execution site in 1783, Newgate's gallows was also where their journey ended, and they were buried in quicklime beneath flagstones in the grim corridor that led from the cells to the Old Bailey next door.

To Londoners, it must have seemed as if the prison had always been there, and always would be, but in 1902, its six-hundred-year history came to an end. It was demolished to make way for the building of the current Old Bailey Sessions House, designed by E.W. Mountford, which would open in 1907. As they took Newgate down, stone by stone, there was great public interest in the ending of this city institution, and an auction of historic artefacts and fixtures from the old prison was held amid the rubble on the site of the old Press Yard on 4 February 1903. Auctioneer Herbert Hookey of Douglas Young & Co sold off all manner of items that day. The newly destroyed building was only a little over a hundred years old, but Hookey conjured up stories reaching further back into the past when delivering his sales patter. He claimed, for example, that the warder's key cupboard was the very one described by Dickens in his novel of the 1780 Gordon Riots, *Barnaby Rudge*, while the *Penny Illustrated Paper*'s drawing of a selection of items on sale included one labelled 'Staircase and iron grille by which Jack Sheppard made his last escape'. This was a remarkable survival, if true, given that Sheppard died in 1724, and the Newgate from which he twice escaped was pulled down fifty years later.

Still, there were genuine artefacts to be had: a Mr Meadows paid £13 for the door of condemned cell number one, while a Mr Booth acquired its twin from cell number two for £12. A set of leg irons made £4, some wall panels from the chapel went for £1, and one lucky buyer paid £2 for six stones from the prison wall. The wooden pole from which a black flag was flown to mark each execution went to a Mr Fox for 11½ guineas, and Madame Tussaud's paid over £100 for the iconic prison bell which tolled on these occasions, inscribed with the words, 'Ye people all, who hear me ring, be faithful to your God and King'.

These items were reminders of the long parade of felons who had come to Newgate under sentence of death. The drawing in the *Penny Illustrated Paper* mentioned above also showed bowler-hatted men rooting around in the ground at the auction with sticks on the site of the former corridor between the prison and the Sessions House, captioned, 'morbid seekers after human remains overturning the quicklime'. Clearly, if executions had still been conducted in public, there would have been plenty of people who would happily have shown up to watch.

As it happens, there had been a high-profile double hanging in London only the day before the Newgate auction. This was the first execution to take place at Holloway prison: the location may have changed, but the business of capital punishment went on much as usual. However, even at the time, it was recognised that there was something about this particular case that set it apart from the normal run of executions – the condemned pair were both women.

Nearly a century earlier, Charles Lamb wrote an essay about the treatment of women entitled *Modern Gallantry*, in which he said:

> I shall believe that this principle [gallantry] actuates our conduct, when I can forget, that in the nineteenth century of the era from which

we date our civility, we are but just beginning to leave off the very frequent practice of whipping females in public, in common with the coarsest male offenders. I shall believe it to be influential, when I can shut my eyes to the fact, that in England women are still occasionally – hanged.

In 1903, the execution of a woman was a rare enough occurrence that it merited a fair amount of attention in the press, and indeed it remained so until abolition came some six decades later. Yet there was something else about this particular murder case which prompted intense public scrutiny. Husband-kills-wife or wife-kills-husband stories were depressingly familiar to newspaper readers of this and every other era, but the executions carried out on 3 February at Holloway were not the result of any such domestic feud; this was a 'baby farming' homicide, the killing of a victim far too young to even fight back.

The London of 1902 displayed many of the elements that would transform the modern world of the twentieth century. Already, the horse-drawn traffic in the streets was having to compete with the first motor cars, with numerous reports of incidents in which animals were frightened by the new machines. For example, there was the case of a lady from Pall Mall, arrested for speeding in west London: 'Police constable 191B said that the defendant drove into Redcliffe-gardens, Kensington, from the Fulham-road at a speed exceeding 12 miles an hour.' This had frightened a horse, which overturned its cart and driver as a result. In her defence, the motorist, Miss Vera Butler, insisted that she had not been travelling faster than seven miles an hour. Meanwhile, a professor addressing the Royal Institution that year ventured the opinion that current attempts to develop a successful heavier-than-air flying machine might yet succeed, although the process 'involved dangers from the stoppage of the machinery which were frightful to contemplate'.

Telephones were an established part of the scene, although potential new subscribers were forever complaining about the many months it seemed to take the Post Office to run wires out to houses so that they might be connected to the system – indeed, one gentleman wrote an anonymous letter to *The Times* in September 1902 recommending bribing the engineers with a five-pound note in order to speed up the process. This was a significant amount of money; for just one fifth of that amount, the good people at the Phono Exchange in Berners Street in the West End would sell you one of the latest phonographs, gramophones or talking machines.

Despite all these signs of modernity, however, in other respects, London society had scarcely progressed since the eighteenth century. The Foundling Hospital was set up by Captain Thomas Coram in 1742 in an attempt to address the problem of the large number of unwanted babies in London, many of them simply abandoned in the streets, or, as he put it, 'left to die on dung hills'. Of course, there were the workhouses, or poorhouses, but they were hardly a safe haven for infants. As Lisa Picard notes, fifty-three children were admitted to the St Luke's parish poorhouse between 1750 and 1755, and at the end of that time, all of them had died.

In 1902, despite all the years that had passed since Coram's day, unmarried young London women of limited means still faced some very hard choices if they were about to have a baby. This was nearly half a century before the advent of the National Health Service, and workhouses were still very much in use. Any woman who could not afford to keep a child, had to make her own arrangements, with no help from the state.

For single women in Edwardian London, pregnancy could be a social and financial disaster. A considerable number of them would have been working as servants, usually with living accommodation included. There was simply no place in that arrangement for a small child, quite apart from the disgrace associated with unmarried motherhood. Anyone in that position, scanning newspaper adverts for a discreet nursing home in which to have their child, might view a coded hint about adoption in the text as a possible solution to their dilemma. Officially, adoption did not exist, since it was not until 1926 that an Act was passed making it legal. There had been pressure for some time before this, and as the First World War came to an end, groups such as the National Adoption Society, the National Child Adoption Agency, and the National Council for the Unmarried Mother and her Child all helped highlight the problem. Contraception was still a difficult subject to raise in polite society, and would remain so for decades, despite the work of people like Marie Stopes, who published her pioneering sex education book *Married Love* in 1918, and opened a first family planning clinic in Holloway in 1921. This, however, was all in the future, and the women of 1902 had to rely on the dubious services available in the shadowy world of 'baby farmers'.

Baby farming was a catch-all term that covered a number of activities. At its best, it was merely a kind of unlicensed fostering or adoption service; in return for an agreed amount of money, the baby farmer would agree to take a baby off the hands of its mother and find a home for it with a family seeking to adopt. However, owing to its clandestine nature, this business could be a cover for something much more risky. In the worst cases of baby farming, the danger was not to the mother, but to the child. The farmer would take a sum of money from the mother in question, promising to place the child with some suitable foster-parents, but instead of doing so, would simply kill it and dispose of the body.

As a result of various well-publicised cases in which this business of clandestine adoption was really a cover for murder, the term 'baby farming' achieved a fair amount of notoriety in late Victorian and Edwardian London. Despite its reputation, however, the underground trade inevitably continued, because most single women of limited means simply had nowhere else to turn.

East Finchley in 1902 was a quiet, leafy hamlet on the northern edges of London. Situated on one of the main routes out of the capital, it had long enjoyed good communications, which were further strengthened in 1867 with the building of the Great Northern Railway from Finsbury Park up to Edgware and High Barnet (these routes eventually became part of the Northern Line at the end of the 1930s), including a station at East Finchley. Here, as in so many other places, house building followed in the wake of the railway. Initially, many were substantial detached houses in their own grounds, but by the close of the nineteenth century, streets of typical Victorian terraced houses had been constructed. Amongst these was a grid built in the 1890s, fanning out east from the main High Road, whose streets were all named after the counties above London, such as Bedford, Lincoln and Huntingdon. The northernmost one, flanked by the trees of Coldfall Wood to the east, and open fields to the north, was called Hertford Road. It was a quiet spot, meeting the High Road at a place where three chapels gathered.

In the centre of East Finchley, at the crossroads where Church End Lane and Fortis Green Road join the High Road, a pub called the Bald Faced Stag – which survives to this day – had been serving the area since the 1730s. A little to the south, just past the station, the ribbon of houses petered out and East Finchley gave way to rural pasture on one side of the Great North Road, and the trees of Dirthouse Wood on the other (which also still exists, cosmetically renamed Cherry Tree Wood). The fields all around were fertilised by industrial quantities of horse manure collected from the streets of central London and brought up on carts to East Finchley. They would halt near the pub called the Old White Lion, formerly known simply as the Dirt House, in honour of this particular trade.

It was a semi-rural location, then, away from the crowded metropolis, but with its own character and amenities. Because of its transport connections, the area was home to a good many city workers, clerks and civil servants. They found it quiet and respectable, which was an improvement on the reputation enjoyed by the district a century earlier, when, under its former name East End, it was – according to one contemporary commentator – known for its 'drunkards, "godless persons", and general lack of moral restraint'. Those visiting the East Finchley of 1902 in search of wild living would probably have been disappointed – indeed, perhaps the principal local attractions were the two large graveyards, St Pancras Cemetery and Islington Cemetery, which lay a short walk north across the fields from Hertford Road. Serving the cemetery trade were several monumental masons scattered up and down the High Road, mixed in with a variety of commercial concerns. Although the area was only the size of a small village, it was served by more shops and pubs than it is today. Alongside the expected businesses – several butchers, chemists, a chip shop, plumbers, boot makers, grocers, cheesemongers – there were also some which spoke more of the surrounding countryside, such as a corn dealer, shoeing forge, a saddler, saw mill, timber merchant and a fair few dairies.

Some local amenities were hard to miss, for example the grandly named 'Convent of the Good Shepherd & Refuge for Catholic Female Prisoners & Home for Fallen Women' (close to the present-day site of Bishop Douglass School), or the towering gothic spire of the Congregational Chapel on the High Road (demolished in the 1960s; a supermarket now occupies the site). Others blended in more subtly to the local landscape. A small notice which regularly appeared in the newspaper *Dalton's Weekly* advertised the services of a nursing home for expectant mothers in Hertford Road, just a few steps away from the High Road, near an imposing coffee house called the Black Bess Temperance Hotel: 'Accouchement, before and during. Skilled nursing. Home comforts. Baby can remain. Claymore House, Hertford Road, East Finchley.'

Respectable enough, on the face of it. Yet, as several people who answered the advert later remarked, it was not so much the promise of professional care that attracted them, but those three loaded words, 'baby can remain'. The kind of baby farming implied by this modest advert would have hardly caused much of a stir in respectable society. The term had certainly been in general use for some decades. For instance, Little Buttercup, a character in Gilbert & Sullivan's 1878 comic opera *HMS Pinafore*, at one point admits in a song, 'When I was young and charming / as some of you may know / I practised baby farming', but in this case it was merely the mixing up of parentage, rather than anything more sinister.

Ada Galley was a young servant, single, living and working in a large East Finchley dwelling called Stanley House. In the summer of 1902, she found herself pregnant, and chanced to read the newspaper advert for the local nursing home at Claymore House. Plucking up courage, she wrote to the address concerned, and received a reply inviting her to visit the house in Hertford Road, where she met Amelia Sach, the person in charge.

Sach was a married woman, twenty-nine years old, with dark eyes and her hair tied back severely from her forehead. Her business cards looked reassuringly professional:

Mrs. A. Sach
Certificated midwife and nurse
Claymore House, Hertford Road, East Finchley
Private nursing home

She agreed to take Miss Galley into her house at a rate of one pound and one shilling per week, rising to three pounds and three shillings a week during confinement. Once installed in the nursing home on 24 September 1902, Ada saw that there were several other women also in residence awaiting delivery of their babies. By coincidence, one of these was Rosina Pardoe, a colleague of Ada's who worked as a servant for the same family at Stanley House.

Amelia Sach came to Miss Galley soon after she had arrived, asking if she had any plans for the baby once it was born, and would consider having the baby adopted for a fee. Galley later recalled:

> 'I said I should, and asked her how much it would cost. She said £25 or £30. I said I did not think I could afford that. Sach said she would write to the lady who was going to take it, and see if she could get it done for less. She did not tell me the lady's name or address. She said she was a lady of good position. One morning Sach came in and said that the lady would take the child for £25. I said I would try and get it.'

This was the regular approach that Amelia Sach seems to have taken with a number of the women who stayed at her house. In each case, the talk was of a wealthy lady in a good part of town – Kensington and Chelsea was often mentioned – willing to pay to adopt a baby. The picture she painted was of an ideal home in which the child would have money and affection lavished upon it in equal measure, but, of course, the adoptive parent was keen to preserve her anonymity, and once handed over, the child would have no further contact with its birth mother. It was a tempting solution. The baby would be safe and presumably happy, while the mother would escape from her present dilemma, and be able to retain her current employment and living quarters. Galley told Sach that 'whatever happened I must get rid of the baby'.

Ada duly wrote to the father of her child, who agreed to provide the money for the adoption. It was hardly cheap, but must have been an enormous weight off both of their minds, all the same. (To modern ears, £25 sounds like a small sum, but at that time a bicycle cost only £10, a sewing machine £2 and one of the new gramophones only £1.)

While waiting for her child to arrive, Ada passed the time making baby clothes. It was born on 15 November, delivered by a doctor who lived a short distance away in Fortis Green Road, Alexander Wylie, assisted by Amelia Sach. The baby was a boy, although Ada said later that she hardly had a chance to tell: 'I only saw the baby for a moment before it was washed. Sach said it was a boy. It was taken out of the room and in the afternoon I heard a child crying in the next room.'

This was the last she ever saw of her baby. The business side of the adoption arrangement was also attended to that day. With the help of Sach, Ada Galley sent a telegram to the father of her child, asking him to come to Claymore House in order to pay the bill. When he arrived at around 7.30 pm that evening, he handed over several banknotes to the value of twenty-five pounds, writing out a receipt for that amount, which Sach then signed in his presence and gave back to him. She asked if he would like to see the baby, and when he agreed, led him into the kitchen where it lay. Amelia Sach said that the child would be leaving for its new home the following morning. Having briefly viewed his baby, he went in to see Ada Galley for a while, and then left Claymore House. He, too, would never see the child again.

⁓⁓⁓

Rosina Pardoe, the other female servant from Stanley House who came to have a baby at the nursing home in Hertford Road, seems to have been slightly less accepting of the explanations offered by Amelia Sach concerning the details of adoption. She learnt of Claymore House through an advert in the *People* newspaper, paying the same fees as Galley. Shortly after her arrival, Sach asked if she had considered having the baby adopted, and suggested that it could be arranged in return for a further payment of thirty pounds. Pardoe questioned the reasoning behind this, as she recalled:

'[Sach] said she knew a lady who would adopt it for £30. I asked who the ladies were. She said they did not like the mothers to know their names or where they lived in case at any time the mothers wanted to take them from the ladies who had adopted them, and that I should have to sign a paper giving up all claim to the child. She said they were well-to-do ladies who had no families and wanted children to adopt. I asked her what the money was for; I thought if the ladies were wealthy ladies £30 would not be wanted and she said the ladies liked to buy presents for the babies.'

Despite her scepticism, Rosina Pardoe accepted the proposal, probably because she had few other ways out of her current dilemma. Yet her doubts were understandable. Amelia Sach, a twenty-nine-year-old living in no great style in a sleepy suburb of London, appeared to be on confidential terms with a string of wealthy ladies in some of the most expensive parts of the capital, who, when looking to adopt, placed all their faith in her to make the arrangements and choose a suitable child. Nevertheless, Pardoe, like Galley and several others, became a temporary resident of Claymore House, had her baby, and persuaded her gentleman friend to underwrite the cost of adoption.

In addition to the fees – thirty pounds from Pardoe, but twenty-five pounds from Galley – Sach also explained that the new babies would need clothes, and so the expectant mothers could either spend the time before the birth making them, or else they could buy them from her. Some of the women found this a little odd, because if the children were about to be placed in wealthy homes, it seemed natural that the new doting foster-mothers would surely want to outfit them to their own satisfaction. Sach, however, assured them that baby clothes were required, as Pardoe recalled:

'She said I should want a full set, and I made a full set. She said it was not the quantity which was wanted but that they must be very good. She said she kept sets in the house at £3 3s. a set. I said I preferred to make them.'

A stay at Claymore House could certainly prove expensive; for some, it was fatal.

Rosina Pardoe had her baby girl at 8.30 am on 12 November 1902, with Amelia Sach in attendance, but without the aid of a doctor. It would be three days later that Ada Galley gave birth to a boy in the same house. Each woman was permitted only a brief sight of her child before it was taken away to another part of the building. In each case, they were then reliant on Sach for what little information came their way.

Claymore House was not especially large – a normal late-Victorian four-bedroom semi-detached house – and so with at least two babies in residence, a certain amount of noise might be expected. In the event, it was strangely calm. On the afternoon that Ada Galley's baby was born, both she and Rosina Pardoe heard a child crying somewhere in the house, but this did not occur again. 'Baby can remain', said the adverts, but in fact, any baby born at Claymore House seems to have been removed from the building as swiftly as possible. Where they might have been taken was a more complex question. Pardoe had this to say:

'The baby was a girl. Sach took it straight away. She just lifted it up for me to see and then took it downstairs to wash it. She brought it back and told me to kiss it good-bye. I did so. It was taken downstairs and I never saw it again . . . I told her that I hoped, the baby would be good and that they would be kind to it. She assured me that they would be very kind. I did not ask if the child was in the house then because Sach had told me about five o'clock on the Wednesday that the lady had been down to fetch the child.'

Ada Galley's baby made a similarly swift departure just a few days later. The boy was born on Saturday, and on the following day, Dr Wylie returned to see Ada, and inquired after the child, as she recalled:

'Sach was present. The baby was not there. Dr. Wylie asked where it was. Sach said that my sister had it at Holloway. I did not say anything. After the doctor had gone I asked Sach if the child had gone. She said it had gone that morning.'

Before the doctor left the house, he looked in to see how Miss Pardoe was doing. Noticing that here, too, was a mother without her baby, he asked Amelia Sach where it might be and was told, 'Her mother has got it.'

The early-morning departure of Ada Galley's baby was noticed by Rosina Pardoe, who heard someone knocking at the front door that day. When Amelia Sach brought up breakfast to her room, she remarked, 'You have had an early visitor,' to which Sach replied, 'Yes, the lady has been to take away Miss Galley's baby.'

None of this was unexpected, given that both women had arranged for their children to be adopted. Sach's false statements to the doctor concerning the current whereabouts of both children – claiming that they had been taken by relatives – could easily be seen as the natural evasions of someone not wishing to admit to having taken money for co-ordinating the deal. For the mothers themselves, it was now just a question of a few more days of convalescence at Claymore House, accompanied perhaps by thoughts of the privileged life to be enjoyed by their offspring, doted on by wealthy foster parents.

Annie Walters, like Amelia Sach, was a married woman, but somewhat older, at fifty-four. She used a choice of two surnames, depending on circumstances. When she wasn't calling herself Walters, she was Mrs Laming. She told people that her husband was dead, that she had been a nurse St Thomas's Hospital, and now worked as a nurse for a Mrs Sach in East Finchley.

Walters lived in rented accommodation in Islington, at 11 Danbury Street, which should have been a law-abiding, respectable household, given that it belonged to a police constable, Henry Seal. He lived there with his wife and family, but also rented some of their rooms to lodgers. Annie Walters had only been resident since 29 October, and shortly after she arrived, told one of the other lodgers, Minnie Spencer, that she would soon be temporarily looking after the baby of her friend. The child would then go to 'a lady in Piccadilly, who was going to give £100 for it'. Sure enough, on the morning of 12 November, an enigmatic telegram arrived for her which simply said, 'To-night, at five o'clock'. It came from East Finchley, and where the sender's name should have been, was just marked 'Claymore House'. Walters duly returned that evening carrying a very small child, which she showed to Minnie Spencer, saying, 'I have got my baby, you see.' She claimed that it was about a week old, but Spencer, a mother herself, thought it looked even younger than that. In fact, this was Rosina Pardoe's baby, born at 8.30 am that morning.

Annie Walters regaled Spencer with stories of how the child would grow up to inherit a fortune, and then asked her if she would go out and fetch a few necessities, as Spencer later testified:

> [Walters] asked me if I would fetch it a bottle, a small tin of Nestle's, and a baby's teat, which I did. She gave me £1 to pay for them. She then asked me to fetch her a bottle of chlorodyne and a pennyworth of carbolic fluid. I fetched them, and paid for them out of the money she gave me.

Most of these provisions would not have surprised anyone accustomed to caring for young babies, but the request for chlorodyne might have raised an eyebrow. Marketed and sold as a cure-all for anything from consumption to gout or even cholera, it was the patent invention of Doctor John Collis Browne, under whose name this enormously successful medicine was sold, although he had been dead for nearly twenty years by the time Annie Walters was using it. Their adverts characterised it as 'a liquid medicine which assuages pain of every kind' – as well it might, since in those days it contained both opium and cannabis. Adults suffering from any of the vast range of diseases named in Collis Browne's publicity material, up to and including cancer, were probably able temporarily to numb the worst effects of their condition by drinking this mixture – although addiction was certainly a danger – but it was hardly suitable for newborn babies. Dr Collis Browne had originally devised chlorodyne in an effort to invent a patent cure for cholera, and had then widened his claims for his medicine in a way that was quite common in the nineteenth century, when it was hard to find a disease that couldn't apparently be cured by the various tonics sold at the local chemist.

On the day after Annie Walters brought Rosina Pardoe's baby to the house in Islington, Minnie Spencer came into Annie's room and noticed a shape on the bed, covered over with bedclothes. Walters told her this was indeed the child, but would not let her see it, because it was asleep. Persisting, Spencer asked if she could nurse the baby, but

Walters replied, 'It is asleep, and I want you to post a letter for me.' This document was addressed to Mrs Sach, Claymore House, Hertford Road, East Finchley. Despite her interest, Minnie did not succeed in catching sight of the baby that day. The following morning, Friday, 14 November, it was gone, and there was no longer any figure lying under the bedclothes.

Alice Seal, the landlady of the house and herself the mother of two children, had also seen the baby when it first arrived, and had later commented to her on how silent it had been during the night. Walters replied that the babies she looked after were always quiet. The chemical chlorodyne seemed to be at the heart of her methods, which disturbed Mrs Seal somewhat:

> 'I told her she would not keep one of mine quiet like that. She said she would if she had them, and that she was going to give the baby one or two drops of chlorodyne in its bottle. I said, "Oh, be careful, you cannot give a baby as young as that chlorodyne." She said she could drink a whole bottleful and it would not hurt her.'

At any rate, there was peace in the house thereafter, and on Friday morning, Mrs Seal saw Walters setting off from the house with something under her arm, closely wrapped up.

When, on Saturday, 15 November, another telegram arrived for Walters, Minnie Spencer asked her if it concerned the baby, but was told that it was about something else. Later that day Annie returned with a different baby, which also, she claimed, was destined for a fine life with a wealthy family – 'This one is going to a coastguard's at South Kensington,' she told Spencer, 'the mother gets £10 for the child, and I get 10s. for taking it to the lady.' Leaving aside the question of South Kensington's distance from the sea, it was also curious how Annie Walters had access to one baby after another, and rich families willing to take them. In this case, Minnie was able to see the baby itself lying on Walters's bed, since it was not covered over. As she later recalled, 'it seemed very healthy, and had not been born many hours'.

Only four days earlier, there had been a different newborn baby lying there, of which, however, there was now no sign. Annie Walters had an easy explanation for this – it had suffered from diarrhoea, because of a 'double rupture', and so she had taken it to a doctor.

Minnie Spencer saw the second child again on the Saturday, sleeping peacefully in Walters's room, but when she dropped in the following day, there was just a shape under the covers, apparently asleep. It was still there on the Monday, hidden from view, but emitting some rather disturbing sounds:

'While I was there I heard a kind of croaking like this coming from the direction of the heap on the bed. Walters said, "Do you hear it?" I said, "Yes." She said, "The mother must have been frightened by a dog, the way it coughs so." I went towards the bed to take the clothes off to look at the child. Walters got up and threw up her hands and said, "It is all right, I can see to it." She did not uncover the baby then, but made a motion for me to go out. I then left the room. I returned to the room several times during the day. The heap was still on the bed. I heard no sound coming from it.'

In a replay of the events of the previous week, on the morning of Tuesday 18, Mrs Seal caught sight of Annie Walters leaving the house with yet another bundle under her arm, in which Ada Galley's baby was wrapped. By now, she and her husband Henry had been suspicious for some days. When Walters had travelled to East Finchley on Saturday, 15 November – the day that Galley's baby was born at Claymore House – they had sent their son Albert to follow her secretly, in an effort to find out what she was doing. He shadowed her movements as she took a tram up to Archway, alighting just near the station, and going into the Archway Tavern, where, Albert reported, she met a 'stylishly dressed young person'. They then hailed a cab and set off in the direction of Finchley. Having seen this, Albert returned home, but later that evening Walters came back from this trip carrying the second baby. Mr and Mrs Seal also encouraged both their son and their daughter to try to gain access to Walters's room and see if they could catch sight of the mysteriously silent child under the bedclothes. However, Annie's response in these cases was very jumpy, and she would say sharply, 'Don't touch it, it is asleep.'

Having sent his fourteen-year-old son to follow Annie Walters on Saturday 15, PC Seal then took things further as a result of his suspicions, and notified his superiors, so that when Walters set off at 9 am on Tuesday 18 from Danbury Street with a bundle under her arm, she was tailed by Detective George Wright. His quarry seemed to be on edge and looked around several times, scanning the vicinity, before eventually boarding an omnibus, which Wright was also able to catch. It took them both across town to South Kensington tube station, where she alighted, closely followed by the policeman. Taking the bundle with her, Walters went in to the ladies' lavatory at the station. When she emerged, Wright approached her, as he testified in court, and said:

> '"I am a police officer; I want to see that baby." She said, "Why?" I said, "I have reason to believe it is not as it should be", I took her to the ladies' lavatory. She sat down in a chair, and before unwrapping the bundle she said, "I suppose you will take me to the station." I said, "I want to see the baby first." She unwrapped the bundle. There was the dead body of a male child in it. Its hands were tightly clenched, its lips were partly blue, the right side of the face was partly discoloured. I said, "It is dead." She said, "Yes." I said, "I shall now take you into custody on suspicion of murdering it." She said, "I never murdered the dear."'

Baby farming of this kind was something that filled the public with horror. The spectre was raised in the press of a shadowy industry which callously disposed of untold numbers of newborn children each year across the capital. When, soon afterwards, Amelia Sach was also taken into custody – accused of 'feloniously aiding and abetting' Walters – Claymore House was searched, and one detail which struck a chord was the discovery of over 300 baby garments in her room. If Ada Galley and Rosina Pardoe's children had both been killed in the space of less than a week, this prompted the question of just how many more might have suffered the same fate since Sach and Walters began their trade. The *Daily Express*, commenting on the case in December, gave some recent figures for the capital:

> Since the beginning of September over fifty babies have been found by the police in various parts of London, some dead, others merely deserted by their parents. In seven cases coroners' juries returned verdicts of 'Murder'.

When the police arrived on her doorstep at East Finchley, Amelia Sach denied any connection with the case: 'I do not know Mrs Walters, of 11

Danbury Street, Islington,' she said, 'and I have never given her any babies.' They said that it was a matter of murder, and she replied, 'Murdering? Never! Do you really mean to say that these babies are dead – that she has killed them?' Sach was taken to King's Cross Police Station and questioned, where she then admitted knowing Walters, but still maintained that she knew nothing of any plan to kill the children.

Walters and Sach were charged at Clerkenwell Police Court on Wednesday, 19 November, the day after the dramatic arrest at South Kensington. Walters said at this initial interview, 'I never killed the baby. I only gave it two little drops [of chlorodyne] in its bottle, the same as I take myself. I took the other baby back to her.' At this she pointed to Sach, and shortly afterwards, as she was being taken back to her cell, shouted that Sach would know the whereabouts of the other child. In the police station, she made a written statement, which thoroughly implicated Amelia Sach:

> If you go to East Finchley you will find telegrams addressed to Sach. She has sent me telegrams to meet her at Finchley Station, where I took the baby from her, and on occasions other babies, and took them back after three days.

She also stated that she was in a very distressed state of mind on the day of her arrest, and was in fact planning to commit suicide that evening: 'I intended to wander about till it was dark and end myself. I never intended to kill the baby.'

Initially, the investigation was centred on the murder of Ada Galley's baby boy, found in the bundle carried by Walters when arrested. However, there was also the question of the fate of the first child that she had brought to Danbury Street, that of Rosina Pardoe. As a result of the publicity, a woman named Ethel Jones came forward who was able to throw some light on this question. She worked as a waitress at Lockhart's Coffee Rooms in Whitechapel, and at around 3 pm on that particular Friday, had served Annie Walters. Noticing the bundle she carried, which had become partly uncovered, Jones inquired, 'What is that you have there, a doll?', to which she received the remarkable answer, 'No, it is a baby under chloroform.' Walters claimed that she had brought it straight from hospital where it had just had an operation for a double hernia, and she was on her way to take it to 'an accouchement home in Finsbury'.

From what Jones could see, the baby looked waxy and immobile, even dead: 'The child's face was pale,' she recalled, 'and it was not making any sound or movement whatsoever.' Nor did it, during the hour that Walters was there.

Newspaper reports of the case as it progressed through the various preliminary hearings in November and December unfolded a gruesome tale in which one of the defendants felt it perfectly normal to wander the streets of London carrying dead or dying infants, and this hardened public opinion against the accused. Women convicted of murder in England were very seldom executed, but in this case, if the trial judge were to hand down a capital sentence, it looked as if there would be few voices raised in protest.

On 15 January 1903, Annie Walters appeared at the Old Bailey, charged with the murder of the unnamed child of Ada Galley, while Amelia Sach appeared alongside her, charged as an accessory before the fact, and the two of them were indicted together for conspiring to commit the murder. On that first day, Walters admitted having given the child chlorodyne 'because it was cross', and claimed that she had later found it dead on the bed. She showed little emotion, in contrast to her fellow defendant, who seemed more troubled by the experience, but had made the effort to put on a show, 'conspicuous in a light blue coat trimmed with fur'.

Galley and Pardoe both gave evidence of their experiences at Claymore House, and of the financial arrangements into which they had entered with Sach. Supporting them were the fathers of their children, who were given leave to appear without their names being read out publicly in court – a courtesy denied to the women in the case. Galley's gentleman friend testified as follows:

'I swear that my correct name and address are on this card (Produced). I have known Miss Galley for some time and in consequence of our intimacy last year she became pregnant. It was with my knowledge that she went to Claymore House to be confined. On November 15th I received a telegram, and in consequence went to Claymore House about 7.30 p.m..

In consequence of something I had heard from Miss Galley I took with me £25 in bank notes, Nos. 09978 to 09982, dated September 3rd, 1902. I saw Sach there and handed her the notes. I got this receipt.'

Rosina Pardoe's gentleman said much the same, and, when cross-examined, admitted that he was married.

At the end of the first day's evidence, the case was adjourned till the morning and the jury taken away by an officer of court and locked in for the night. The trial resumed the following day, with various residents of the house at Danbury Street giving evidence about the behaviour of Walters during her time there. Following this, there was expert testimony from members of the medical profession, including Augustus Pepper, FRCS, who had this to say about Annie Walters's favourite medicine:

'I am familiar with chlorodyne. One of its constituents is chloroform, and it smells strongly of it; morphia is also one of its constituents. I should say that two drops of chlorodyne would be fatal to a child of this age.'

When the jury retired at 6 pm to consider their verdict, they took forty minutes before returning. During that time, according to one report, 'the face of Mrs Walters was as stolid and expressionless as ever. Only in the fixed expression of her younger companion, and the deep lines under her eyes, were any evidence of mortal strain'.

They were both found guilty, but with a recommendation of mercy. The judge, Mr Justice Darling, asked the reason for this stipulation, to which the jury foreman replied, 'Mainly that they are both women.' Walters and Sach were duly sentenced to death, then to await the final decision of the Home Secretary, who would often commute such sentences to life imprisonment in the case of female murderers.

In the week following the trial, the *Penny Illustrated Paper* printed photographs of Claymore House and 11 Danbury Street, together with a drawing showing the two women in the dock, captioned 'A Very Bad Case at the Old Bailey', which seems to have summed up the public mood. Walters and Sach were convicted on a sample charge of having killed the baby of Ada Galley, yet the question remained as to how many other children born at Claymore House, or Sach's previous East Finchley nursing home in Stanley Road, had met a similar fate. There seems to have been little popular call for mercy in this case, and indeed, on 31 January, it was announced that the Home Secretary had decided that the law must take its course.

Amelia Sach and Annie Walters were hanged together at 9 am on Tuesday, 3 February, at Holloway, which had recently become a women-only prison. The executioner himself was said to have little enthusiasm for this particular job, and the staff were especially uneasy, as the *Daily Express* reported:

> None of the prison staff at Holloway has ever assisted at an event of this kind, and today's grim duty is looked forward to with certain misgiving. One wardress said yesterday, 'We have been hoping these women would be reprieved, because we do not like to aid, even indirectly, in their execution.'

There was said to be 'intense bitterness' between the two women, who were no longer on speaking terms. Walters was quoted as saying, 'I have been betrayed,' but Sach apparently maintained a calm disposition to the end, visited several times by her husband, a builder's foreman.

Despite the public horror engendered by this case, those who hoped for an end to the practice of baby farming would not have been cheered by a report in the newspapers only two days after the executions:

MORE BABY FARMING

> At an inquest on the body of a child found in the gutter at St Pancras the coroner yesterday said that since the conviction of Sach and Walters he had noticed that there was a great reduction in the number of children found in the street dead. They were, however, again increasing, and it appeared as if there was another baby-farming business going on.

Over a century later, Amelia Sach's house still stands, at number 5 Hertford Road, East Finchley. Such was the notoriety of the case, however, that at some stage, the inscribed stone panel on the wall above the front window has been carefully filled in and painted over, so that passers-by can no longer read the original name, Claymore House.

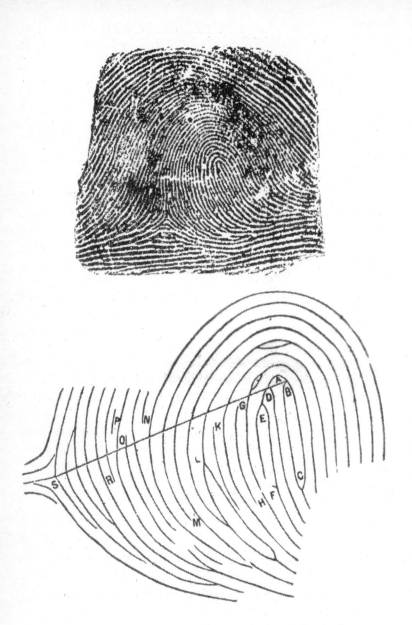

The thumb-print of a murderer, from *Harmsworth's Universal Encyclopedia*, 1921

SEVENTEEN

DEPTFORD – PRINTS OF THIEVES
1905

The East Finchley baby farm murders of 1902 took place in an era of modern inventions such as the cinematograph, the motor car and the gramophone, but the method of detection was straightforwardly traditional; the suspect was caught red-handed in charge of the body of one of her victims. Three years later, in the case of a homicide in Deptford High Street, the investigation and trial incorporated fingerprint evidence, a process developed in the nineteenth century, but only now coming to the fore in English legal cases. So novel was it considered that the *Daily Mirror* (itself only two years old) felt the need to explain the system to their readers, accompanying their article with large-scale examples of prints from the Deptford case. Learned letters were exchanged in the press, and newspaper leader writers discussed the reliability of such evidence.

As might be expected, Conan Doyle's Sherlock Holmes had already been down this path, in a 1903 story called *The Adventure of the Norwood Builder*. A bloody thumbprint found on a whitewashed wall at the murder scene is triumphantly pointed out to Holmes by Inspector Lestrade of Scotland Yard:

'Look at that with your magnifying glass, Mister Holmes.'

'Yes, I am doing so.'

'You are aware that no two thumb-marks are alike?'

'I have heard something of the kind.'

'Well then, will you please compare that print with this wax impression of young MacFarlane's right thumb, taken by my orders this morning?'

In the event, this particular piece of evidence was not as trustworthy as it first appeared. Outside the world of fiction, there were also those in the legal profession and the wider public who were sceptical about the reliability of fingerprint technology and its admissibility in court cases. That each person's fingerprints were unique had been observed centuries ago in the Far East, but in the western world, it was not until the late eighteenth century that this first became apparent. By 1858, William Herschel, a British administrator working in India, was regularly taking prints which he called 'hand marks' from locals as a way of recording their identity, to prevent anyone impersonating someone else. Then, in 1880, a Scottish doctor named Henry Faulds wrote to the magazine *Nature* to recommend taking fingerprints at crime scenes:

> When bloody finger-marks or impressions on clay, glass, etc., exist, they may lead to the scientific identification of criminals . . . There can be no doubt as to the advantage of having, besides their photographs, a nature-copy of the forever-unchangeable finger furrows of important criminals.

A little later, inspired by what he had read of Herschel's discoveries, a wealthy Birmingham man named Sir Francis Galton conducted his own research into the subject at the South Kensington Museum, culminating in his landmark book, *Finger Prints* (1892), which identified eight broad types into which all prints could be grouped. This work then directly inspired that of Edward Henry, born in London but at that time serving in the East as Inspector General of Police for Bengal. His fingerprint research produced the first proper classification system, identifying five distinct patterns: plain arches, tented arches, radial loops, ulnar loops, and whorls. Having put his theories into practice in Bengal, he published a book in 1897 on the subject, entitled *Classification and Uses of Fingerprints*. Back in London, the police were still using the Bertillon method of identifying suspects, which involved taking a variety of body measurements, but in 1900 the British government set up a committee to investigate the possibilities of a fingerprint system. Edward Henry gave evidence to the committee, and the following year, he became head of the Criminal Investigation Department (CID), just as Scotland Yard's Fingerprint Department was established, and was promoted to Metropolitan Police Commissioner in 1903.

Thus the London constabulary in 1905 was led by a man who firmly believed in the value of fingerprinting methods, and the department had for several years been building up an archive of many thousands of examples taken from known criminals. Yet the value of this kind of evidence in a court case was still far from being generally accepted, and the average jury member might well never have heard of the process. However, those on the other side of the law were fast learning their lessons. Thieves who made off with £1,000-worth of jewellery from a shop in Holborn in April, 1905, not only disabled the telephone, but also first stole pairs of gloves from a nearby dressing room in order, it was said, 'to obviate the dangers of finger-prints'. The process was certainly in the news; Inspector Collins of the Yard's Fingerprint Department, speaking to the press about a Liverpool case that year, claimed that 'the chances are a hundred thousand millions to one against the suggestion that the impression on a piece of glass was not made by the prisoner's right ring finger'. The implications of such a development in the fight against crime were much under discussion.

Even so, there were a few teething problems. Francis Gadd, a thief who was only four feet seven inches tall, managed to have his fingerprints labelled on the police files as those of a woman, owing to the smallness of his hands, and thus avoided detection – although this was hardly the most remarkable of his escapes that year, as the *Daily Express* noted in a report entitled 'How Man Was Mistaken for a Dustbin':

> With the skill of a trained contortionist he rolled himself up until, to use his own words, he appeared no bigger than an ash-bucket. He declared, in fact, that the police had more than a dozen times mistaken him for a small dustbin as he lay curled up after committing various burglaries.

It is tempting to conclude that any police department incapable of distinguishing between a diminutive thief and a household waste receptacle would probably also find the analytical comparisons necessary in any fingerprint system somewhat beyond their grasp.

Whereas some outlying parts of the London of 1905 had been little more than fields or farmyards a century earlier, Deptford was not in this category. A settlement just south of the Thames which grew up around the bridge over a waterway called the Ravensbourne, Deptford lay on the ancient route between London and Canterbury – indeed, Chaucer's Pilgrims passed this way ('Lo, heer is Depford', says the Reeve). Wat Tyler's men came calling in 1381 during the Peasants' Revolt, as did Jack Cade's rebels in 1450, but the district really started to make its mark a century later, when Henry VIII established his Royal Dockyard in Deptford, as a shipyard for building or servicing the huge warships of the time. A largely working-class district – although the wealthy diarist John Evelyn lived close by the dockyard in a house called Sayes Court, and once had the Russian Tsar Peter the Great as his house guest – its pubs could be rough, and there was much poverty here. In the mid-nineteenth century, Henry Mayhew recorded the sight of a well-known criminal named Captain Moody, a 'lurking patterer', in one of the area's watering holes:

> Old, and worn-out by excesses and imprisonment, he subsists now by 'sitting pad' about the suburban pavements; and when, on a recent evening, he was recognised in a low public-house in Deptford, he was heard to say, with a sigh: 'Ah! Once I could "screeve a fakement" (write a petition) or "cooper a monekur" (forge a signature) with any man alive, and my heart's game now; but I'm old and asthmatic, and got the rheumatis, so that I ain't worth a d—n'.

Gentlemen of the criminal persuasion could, of course, also be found in the Deptford pubs of 1905, alongside the law-abiding. By then, the Royal Docks were no more. In their place had come the Foreign Cattle Market, the landing-point for vast quantities of livestock, much of which met its end at the twenty-three-acre Deptford Slaughterhouse, a major employer in an area where jobs were often hard to come by.

Deptford High Street ran from north to south, down to where it met the Broadway, just to the west of the Ravensbourne and Deptford Bridge. At its halfway mark, it was crossed by the suburban railway line running out to Greenwich. At the southern corner of the High Street, just across the tramlines from the imposing dome of the Broadway Theatre, stood Brooks' Cash Drug Stores, which had been serving the area since 1820. Huge iron-and-glass lanterns jutted out from the fronts of such buildings, overhanging the pavements, as did a wide variety of canvas awnings. The traffic in the streets – trams and handcarts aside – was still almost exclusively horse drawn, and a motor car would have been an expensive luxury for this district (in 1905, a new horse-drawn landau carriage could be had for 50 guineas, whereas a Daimler motor car cost a whopping £750).

The High Street then, as now, was lined with shops, and at number 34, a short walk up from Brooks' on the right-hand side, could be found Chapman's Oil & Colour business, which for many years had supplied materials to painters and decorators. This shop, one of several owned by George Chapman, was managed and run by Thomas Farrow, aged seventy-one, who lived on the premises with his wife Ann. Both husband and wife worked in the shop, whose opening hours were from 8 am to 9.30 pm, together with their young assistant, William Jones, who described Mr Farrow as 'active' and 'bald headed'. Jones would normally arrive at around 8.30, by which time Mr Farrow would already have conducted a reasonable amount of business. Although the official opening time was 8 am, Farrow was in the habit of standing out on the pavement in front of the shop about an hour earlier than this, enjoying a pipe of tobacco before work began. People in the painting trade knew of this, and he would quite often serve customers before his official start time.

On the morning of 27 March 1905, Thomas Farrow was seen at the door of his shop by several passers-by. He was not smoking a relaxing pipe, however. A painter called Alfred Purfield, on his way up the road to catch the 7.35 am train at Deptford station, later recalled that he had noticed Mr Farrow on the way:

'The shop door was closed when I first saw it, but I saw it open and an old gentleman standing there. He had blood on his face, shirt and hands. He stayed at the door in a vacant kind of way for a short time, and then closed it. I lost sight of him. I looked for a policeman, but there was not one there and I went on to catch my train.'

A similar disturbing sight greeted Edith Worth, who was walking up Deptford High Street on her way to work at around 7.20 am:

'I know Chapman's shop; I saw an old man at the door. He appeared to have been very seriously injured. He had blood on his face and hands. He stayed at the shop door for a short time and then closed it.'

However strange this may have been, no one at this point raised the alarm. Several years later, when Sir Melville MacNaghten, Assistant Commissioner of the Metropolitan Police, recorded his memories of this case in his autobiography, he offered the explanation that such gory sights would have been common in the district:

> As a matter of fact there are a good many slaughterhouses in Deptford and its vicinity, and the sight of blood is not so abhorrent to those who dwell in the East, as to those who dwell in the West, End of London.

That may be, but the testimony of Edith Worth suggests that she knew that she was looking at a man who was wounded, not a worker from the local abattoir. Similarly, if this was an everyday sight, hardly to be remarked upon, there would surely have been no impulse on the part of the painter Alfred Purfield to seek out a policeman.

Something was clearly wrong, but at 7.20, Mr Farrow was still on his feet, and had gone back inside his place of business and closed the door. The early morning traffic in Deptford High Street of pedestrians, barrows and horse-drawn carts continued to pass in front of Chapman's Oil & Colour Shop, and it was not until a little over an hour later, when the assistant, William Jones, arrived for work, that the alarm was raised.

In the normal course of events, William Jones would have walked through an open door to find Mr Farrow, and perhaps Mrs Farrow also, filling orders for a selection of workmen from the decorating trade at the start of their day. It was a Monday morning, so Chapman's had been closed on the previous day, but on the Saturday it had been open for business as usual. Nothing was amiss when Jones was last at work, as he testified, describing his last sight of the Farrows:

'We all three served in the shop. On Saturday night, March 25th, I saw them alive. On Monday morning I arrived at the shop a little after 8.30 am. I went to the street door, but was unable to get in. After knocking I went to Mr. Chapman's Greenwich shop, and came back with Louis Kidman.'

Kidman worked at the Greenwich branch, and, as a more senior member of staff, accompanied Jones back to Deptford, determined to gain access to number 34 and find out why the door was locked and the shop not open to the public. Peering through the letterbox, they noticed over-turned furniture and the signs of a struggle. The two men eventually mananged to enter from the rear via a neighbouring house, and found the bloody corpse of Thomas Farrow lying in the parlour; he had evidently suffered extensive head injuries. Kidman sent Jones off in search of a policeman, and when a Sergeant Atkinson arrived, they explored the rest of the premises. Even at this stage, it seems that members of the public had been learning the lessons gained from reading murder reports in the popular press, and the two shop workers were reasonably careful not to interfere unduly with the crime scene. Kidman, who acted as his owner's representative in this matter, described the search:

'I sent Jones for the police and I waited there until Sergeant Atkinson came. I went upstairs with him, where we found Mrs. Farrow lying in bed severely injured and apparently dead. I remember seeing a cash box on the bed-room floor. I did not touch it nor anything else.'

Ann Farrow had been savagely beaten about the head where she lay. Though still alive, she was in no condition to speak about what had happened. Broken crockery was strewn around the place, a chair had been turned over, a bowl of bloody water had been left as if one of the attackers had attempted to clean themselves up, and, perhaps strangest of all, a parrot was missing from its cage.

As for the cashbox, although William Jones had worked for the Farrows for three years, he had never seen it before, and had not been aware that they had one. Yet the box had been rifled, and the motive for these two brutal attacks appeared to be theft. A shop such as this would hardly have enjoyed much of a cash turnover each week – this was no Hatton Garden jewellery store with a small fortune in precious stones on the premises – but Sir Melville MacNaghten had a theory about this:

> It was rumoured in the neighbourhood that these old people had saved money and were hoarding it up. It turned out in this case, as in most others, that Dame Rumour was a lying jade. I do not think that they had more than six or seven pounds in the house.

In fact, those responsible made off with the week's takings for the shop, the princely sum of just thirteen pounds. In addition to the looted cashbox, the police discovered several stockings which had been cut up and converted into masks. The number found led them to conclude at first that three intruders were involved, but the breakthrough clue was initially overlooked. On closer inspection, the empty cashbox – which had been moved a little way under the bed by a detective sergeant so that the stretcher-bearers would not trip over it when taking the injured Mrs Farrow out of the room – was found to have a distinctive mark upon it. The thieves might have covered their faces, but they appeared to have left behind a fingerprint.

'Brutal Murder in Deptford,' said the following day's headlines, 'Masked Burglars Suspected'. It was reported that Mr and Mrs Farrow were aged 'between 70 and 80', that the former was dead and the latter in 'a very precarious condition'.

Crucially, however, a pair of witnesses had already come forward upon hearing of the killing. In a community such as this, most locals would have known old Mr Farrow and his wife, and in this case Henry Jennings, a local milkman passing down the High Street on his morning round with his eleven-year-old assistant, Edward Russell, had briefly caught sight of something at 34 about the time of the murder, which with hindsight he felt worth mentioning to the police. It was just a minor moment in his day – on the face of it, nothing worth interrupting his routine for – as he explained:

'We were going down High Street, Deptford. I know Chapman's shop. As we came down High Street I saw the shop and noticed two men come out. As we came up the door was shut. When they came out it was left open. I called out, "You have left the door open." One of them turned round and said, "Oh! it is all right; it don't matter." They walked away towards New Cross Road. They crossed the road from Chapman's shop. I saw them for about 15 yards from the shop. I did not take any more notice. That was about 7.15 a.m.'

The milkman's young helper also remembered these two men. According to him, they slammed the shop door behind them, 'but it flew back'. He was able to describe them as follows:

'One was a little bit taller than the other and was dressed in a dark blue serge suit, a dark bowler hat, and a pair of black boots. I noticed that he walked very stiff and quickly. The other one, who was not so tall, was dressed in a dark brown suit, a cap and a pair of brown boots. I cannot say if the taller was thin or broad. When I went home to breakfast I told father something.'

A fuller description of both men appeared in the morning papers on the day after the break-in. They were both said to be about five foot six inches tall, and aged somewhere in their middle twenties. One had 'a round face, a rather dark moustache' and the other had light-brown hair.

Of course, in this neighbourhood, such descriptions could have applied to any one of dozens of young men out in the streets. Yet whoever the suspects were, they had taken little trouble to disguise themselves when leaving the place. If they were the ones who inflicted such terrible head-wounds on the elderly couple, then it was also possible that they had some of the blood of the victims on their clothes. However, there was also the question of the masks found at the scene. Despite their casual reply to the milkman, they had apparently been keen to disguise their identities while inside the shop. Three customised stockings were found, but only two men were seen emerging from the shop. One theory was that the third man had remained behind to close and lock the door, before perhaps escaping another way. Certainly, although the two who were seen by the milkman had left the door open, it was firmly secured when Jones the shop assistant arrived for work.

Mrs Farrow, suffering from similar appalling head-wounds to those which had killed her husband, was taken to the Seamen's Hospital in Greenwich. Here she developed pneumonia and died on 31 March. She had recovered consciousness only once during her time in hospital, but was unable to speak.

Around Deptford High Street, this savage murder, all for a few pounds, would have been the talk of the district. Just as the Farrows had been familiar figures in the community, any local villains would have been equally well known to the police of Deptford and New Cross. The descriptions provided by Henry Jennings and Edward Russell were frustratingly general, but when faced with a shocking crime such as this, the constabulary was under considerable pressure to trawl through the district's pubs and feel the collars of any criminal who might fit the bill. Something had to be done, it was clear. (As the police chief Captain Renault remarks at the end of *Casablanca*, 'Major Strasser has been shot. Round up the usual suspects.') Reasonable suspicions were enough to justify many people being pulled in off the streets. Indeed, three days after the murder, the House of Commons happened to be debating the national figures for arrests, and the Home Secretary, for one, seemed quite happy that the actions of the authorities were usually justified:

> Considering that the annual number of apprehensions in England and Wales exceeds 350,000, the number of complaints I receive alleging arrest on insufficient grounds is extraordinarily small, and affords a striking testimony to the care and discretion with which the police exercise the powers which the law confers on them.

In the case of the double murder at Chapman's Oil & Colour Shop, a couple of likely prospects were brought in for questioning within a week of the murder. They were two brothers, Alfred and Albert Stratton, both locals in their early twenties, said to be 'men of the labouring type'. It had not been necessary to look very far afield for either of them. Alfred was arrested in the bar of a pub called the King of Prussia in Albury Street – a road which joins Deptford High Street just north of the Station. When searched, his purse contained eighteen shillings, which was hardly a fortune, but might have seemed so to some in this poverty-stricken neighbourhood. They found Albert just a few yards further north, at the top end of the High Street, where it meets Evelyn Road. Neither of the brothers seems to have displayed any great distress at being detained by the constabulary, which is perhaps understandable, since they were not entirely unknown to the authorities. When told of the charges, Albert simply said, 'Alright'. His brother asked the police what evidence they had, and received the following reply:

> 'A milkman and his boy saw you together come out of a shop door at 34, High Street, Deptford, at a quarter past seven on Monday morning, and a young woman, who knows you, saw you and another man run across the top of Deptford High Street.'

Alfred disputed this at once, saying that he had been in bed until 9.15 am, at Brookmill Road, Deptford – just south of the High Street – with a woman named Hannah Cromarty. Nevertheless, both Strattons were taken to Blackheath Road Police Station, just across Deptford Bridge. Here they were lined up in the yard with fourteen other men for an identity parade, and were picked out by a woman called Ellen Stanton. On the morning of the murder, she had been walking up the High Street on her way to work, and had seen two men running from there into New Cross Road. She recognised one of them as Alfred Stratton, and came forward on 31 March to tell the police. Despite the fact that Alfred claimed to have been elsewhere at the time both of them were remanded into custody at Greenwich Police Court on 3 April on suspicion of having been concerned in the murder of Thomas and Ann Farrow, and also on a charge of having stolen 'between £12 and £14'.

On 6 April, the *Daily Mirror* informed its readers that one Robert Brown had been sentenced to five years' penal servitude and eighteen strokes of the lash for highway robbery, and that London's 76,000 beggars were earning an estimated total of £100,000 a year. They also printed a photograph of Alfred Stratton, in a white, open-collared shirt, looking barely out of his teens, alongside a report stating that a third man, John Milligan, had been arrested in connection with the killings. However, on a later page in the same issue, it was revealed that the latter suspect had been released without charge, so he might have been picked up on little or no evidence, or even implicated by an enemy who had given a deliberately false tip-off to the police. Before the case came to court, there were certainly examples of witness intimidation, so the arrest of Milligan might indeed have been an attempt on someone's part to muddy the waters.

Essentially, the chief factors that had kept the events at Chapman's shop in the news were the sheer brutality of the killings and the disguises used by the perpetrators. The press swiftly named the case 'The Deptford Mask Murders', which gave them an air of glamour that in reality, this pitiless, squalid homicide sorely lacked. Yet the chief aspect that was to distinguish this case from dozens of other murders in the capital that year would shortly become apparent to the public. Wearing a mask or clubbing someone over the head with an iron bar might land you in the papers, but it was hardly novel behaviour – people had been doing this sort of thing for centuries. What really attracted attention in this instance was the pivotal role played by fingerprint evidence. Suddenly, it seemed as if commentators and figures from all spheres of life were falling over themselves either to explain the nature of fingerprints themselves or to argue about their admissibility as evidence in trials. Three days after the arrest of the Stratton brothers, the *Daily Mirror* duly revealed that the key focus of the inquiry into the Deptford killings hinged upon this new crime detection technique: 'The finger-prints of the men have been taken, and compared by the police with those found upon the cashbox that was left behind by the men who committed the crime.'

On 11 April, the two prisoners were charged at Greenwich Police Court with murder, and remanded in custody for another week to give the police more time to complete their investigations. The case was ordered to be transferred to Tower Bridge Police Court, on account of the large number of witnesses to be called at the next hearing. That total might have been reduced, if the efforts of Ellen O'Leary had been successful; she was convicted on 12 April of assaulting Mary A. Compton of Hale Street, Deptford, a witness in the Farrow murder case. Aiding justice could be a dangerous business – indeed, on the same day that O'Leary was convicted, a prisoner in another London courtroom named John James succeeded in flinging a heavy glass bottle at the head of the judge who was sentencing him. The magistrate, who narrowly escaped injury, remarked that the accused should have been more thoroughly searched as he might have had a pistol, to which James replied, 'I wish I had. You would not be there to give any more sentences, you old villain.' To great applause, the judge then increased his sentence of eighteen months to five years' penal servitude.

While the Strattons remained in prison on remand, the police continued building their case. Acting on information received, they discovered two sovereigns and half-a-crown, thought to be part of the stolen money from number 34, buried in a narrow passage between Deptford and Lewisham. Much time was also spent interviewing witnesses, in particular various women friends of the accused.

On 18 April, the results of all this activity became clear when the Stratton brothers appeared at the Tower Bridge Police Court and were charged on remand. It was a measure of the seriousness of the case that Melville MacNaghten, Assistant Commissioner of the Metropolitan Police, appeared, in addition to Chief Inspector Fox of New Scotland Yard, the officer who had been leading the investigation.

At the time of the murders, Alfred Stratton was living with Hannah Cromarty at 23 Brookmill Road, while Albert and a woman named Kate Wade had been jointly renting a back room in the house of Sarah Tedman, at 67 Knott Street, Deptford. At the Tower Bridge hearing, Mrs Tedman testified that she had found stocking masks under Albert's bed. The court also heard that his clothes had smelled strongly of paraffin when he returned home on the morning of the crime, as if he had been trying to clean them, and that he had been asking women of his acquaintance in the days prior to this whether he could borrow some stockings. Alfred, meanwhile, had blackened his own brown boots that day, in order to change their appearance, and told Cromarty that he had given away his brown coat. It was noted that the description of the suspects printed in the newspapers stated that one of them wore brown boots and a brown jacket. Furthermore, it was revealed that Alfred had pointed out a place to Hannah Cromarty where he had buried some money, which was exactly where the police then found the sovereigns while he was in gaol. As if this were not enough, Hannah Cromarty told the court that after she had read the news of the murder in the paper, Alfred had told her that, if questioned, she should swear that he had been in bed with her all night and had not left the building.

At the close of this day of significant revelations, the Strattons were once again remanded in custody for a week. All things considered, although this was merely a preliminary hearing and not the murder trial itself, the circumstantial evidence against the brothers looked very incriminating. In addition, alongside the verbal testimony, there was also the physical evidence: 'The thumb-print upon the cash-box was submitted to Inspector Collings [sic], and he had identified it as that of Alfred.'

The Strattons might well claim that they had never set foot inside the door of number 34 Deptford High Street, and that at least one of them had been in bed at the time of the murders, but this relatively new type of evidence, if accepted by the courts, suggested that at least one of them was lying.

On 19 April, the Coroner for South East London opened his inquest into the deaths of Thomas and Ann Farrow, and the two Stratton brothers were brought into court. The testimony heard added weight to the case against them. Their mother, Maria Ann Stratton, gave evidence in a state of high emotion, and when leaving the witness stand, cried out to Alfred and Albert, 'You have killed me; you have killed me, if you have done it.' She was led weeping from the courtroom by another of her sons, while the two accused themselves broke down in tears. Meanwhile Kate Wade, who had lived with Albert for a while, testified that 'she had left him because he went out so frequently at night'. She also claimed that she had no idea what either brother did for a living. This they hotly disputed, saying that she knew very well, and had 'often changed "stuff" for them'. In other words, she implied very strongly that they went out thieving at night, and they responded by naming her as a receiver of stolen goods. Given the incriminating evidence already offered at the previous hearing by Alfred's lady friend, Hannah Cromarty, it was becoming obvious that whatever affection had existed between the brothers and these women was now in very short supply. In a district where poverty was common, it would hardly be surprising to discover that a certain number of the people propping up the bars at local hostelries were sometimes involved in crime. However, while burglary was one thing, battering a defenceless old couple to death was clearly another.

Once again, Alfred's thumbprint had a starring role in the proceedings:

Inspector Collins, chief of the finger-print department of Scotland Yard, stated that there were eleven distinct points of resemblance between finger marks on the cashbox and an impression obtained from Alfred Stratton's thumb. Whenever he found four points of resemblance he invariably found they agreed in other details. During ten years' experience he had examined no fewer than a million finger prints. The chances that the mark on the cashbox was made by Alfred Stratton's thumb were one hundred thousand millions to one.

On the following day, the inquest resumed, and now, far from bursting into tears, the two brothers went out of their way to show how little they cared about the proceedings; as they were brought into the court, they 'assumed an air of bravado', and 'whistled snatches of popular tunes, keeping time by stamping their feet on the floor'. Inspector Fox said that Alfred Stratton's hands were injured on the day before the robbery, but not to the extent that would have prevented him from carrying it out. Further, he stated that these injuries 'were caused by assaulting a woman' – who turned out to be his girlfriend, Hannah Cromarty, which perhaps explains her willingness to testify against him.

At the close of the inquest, both men were found guilty of wilful murder, paving the way for the trial proper. Their bravado continued, as the newspapers reported: 'On hearing the verdict, the accused laughed.'

The coroner's inquest had delivered a verdict against the Stratton brothers, and now, when the case resumed at Tower Bridge Police Court on 25 April, the counsel for the defence chose to cast doubt upon the reliability of fingerprint evidence, and the expertise of Scotland Yard. Inspector Collins took the stand – 'a short, slim, keen-eyed man, with a dark complexion and a heavy moustache' – and showed the court photographic enlargements of the thumbprint found on the cashbox, while explaining once again the business of identification and the probabilities involved. Appearing for the defence, a Mr Budden strove to cast doubt on the whole procedure, as the *Daily Express* reported: '"Do you call it a science?" demanded Mr Budden, with a scornful emphasis on the closing word.' Collins seemed unsure, although he eventually said that he would, and Budden sarcastically retorted, 'But you are an expert, you know.' When questioned about the literature upon which the fingerprint system might base its claims to accuracy, Collins cited the works of Francis Galton and that of Edward Henry. 'Can you give me the name of any medical or legal authority who takes any notice of this so-called science?' asked the defence counsel, to which Collins replied that he could not. Budden then attempted to cast a fundamental doubt upon the reliability of the work of the inspector's department:

> 'I might, if I had a favourable opportunity, bring as a witness a gentleman recognised as an authority in the finger-print science who would say that the system in vogue at Scotland Yard is based on error, and is a system that is a positive danger to the public.'

Budden requested that the case be adjourned, but the magistrate, Mr Baggallay, having asked the identity of this proposed expert witness, refused, saying, 'I cannot consent to an adjournment. Any faddist may write offering to give evidence.' The hearing was ended, and the accused were then committed for trial at the Old Bailey.

Although several women had given evidence against the Stratton brothers in the various hearings so far, doing so was not without its dangers, as could be seen from the assault case quoted earlier. On 1 May, there was another incident, when Jennie Cutler, a woman who worked at the Crosse & Blackwell factory in the Charing Cross Road, was shot in the leg. She could think of no reason why anyone might attack her, and the authorities suspected that the culprit might have shot the wrong person, since another woman who worked there was known to have recently given evidence at the Deptford murder hearings.

The Strattons' trial was set for 5 May at the Old Bailey. Three days prior to this, in his opening remarks at the May Sessions of the Central Criminal Court, the Recorder of London highlighted this particular upcoming case to the grand jury, because of the relative novelty of finger-print evidence:

> The Recorder pointed out that there was a most important piece of evidence against Alfred Stratton. A new method of identifying persons committing crime had been discovered, by noting finger-prints. It was suggested that this method was infallible. He was glad to hear this, because there were considerable differences of opinion with regard to identification, and some witnesses who swore positively to identifications were undoubtedly mistaken. He did not know that this system of identification had had sufficient trial in the courts of justice for the judges to be able to say whether the confidence which was placed in it by those who believed in finger-marks was well founded or not.

Although fingerprint evidence had already been used in a variety of trials in 1905 alone, the vicious nature of this particular double murder and the intense public interest which it therefore generated, turned the Stratton hearings at the Old Bailey into something of a test case.

When the proceedings began, much of the evidence for the prosecution had already been made public during the preliminary hearings and cor-oner's inquest the previous month. However, there was one dramatic piece of new testimony offered during the first day which caused something of a sensation in the court. Taking the stand was William Gittings, assistant gaoler at Tower Bridge Police Court, who had been one of the people looking after the Stratton brothers on 18 April, during their remand hearings. While Alfred and Albert had both been waiting in separate cells, Gittings had a conversation through the cell door with the younger of the two, which he recalled as follows:

> 'He [Albert] spoke first and said, "How do you think I shall get on?" I replied, "I do not know." He said, "Is he listening?" meaning his brother in the adjoining cell. I looked in and saw that Alfred was sitting down reading a newspaper. I said to Albert, "No, he is sitting down reading a newspaper." He said, "I reckon he will get strung up, and I shall get about ten years; he has led me into this; he is the cause of me living with a woman. Don't say anything to him, I shall not say anything until I can see there is no chance, and then— " He stopped speaking and started walking round the cell. He came back to the door, and said, "I do not

want to get strung up. He has never done any work in his life, only about a month, and then they tried to put that Brixton job on him, but they found out at the time he was at work. I have only been out of the Navy about seven months."'

The prosecuting counsel alleged that this provided overwhelming proof of Albert's guilt but was not evidence against Alfred. Having both pleaded 'not guilty', the brothers listened to the familiar testimony which then followed during that first day. According to one report, 'Alfred sat bolt upright, impassive as stone; Albert leaned back in the dock and occasionally shut his eyes, as though anticipating his fate and resigned to it'. When the court adjourned for the day, the case against them certainly looked strong.

⋅⋅⋅⋅⋅⋅⋅⋅⋅⋅⋅⋅⋅⋅⋅⋅⋅⋅⋅⋅⋅⋅⋅⋅⋅⋅⋅⋅⋅⋅⋅⋅⋅ ◆◆◆◆ ⋅⋅⋅⋅⋅⋅⋅⋅⋅⋅⋅⋅⋅⋅⋅⋅⋅⋅⋅⋅⋅⋅⋅⋅⋅⋅⋅⋅⋅⋅⋅⋅⋅

The trial resumed on 6 May, and the star witness was Inspector Collins of Scotland Yard's Finger Print Department, whose expert testimony the defence counsel, Mr Rooth, did his best to disparage. In particular, Rooth claimed that the print found on the cashbox did not match the one taken from Alfred Stratton in police custody. Collins, however, responded to this challenge by pointing out that the first was made by the perspiration from a thumb on the metal surface of a box, whilst the other was produced by running a roller of ink over the thumb and pressing it onto paper, and that any other variation noticeable would be due to differences in the pressure applied. Collins went into great detail about the characteristics visible in the photographic enlargements he showed to the court, and the conclusions he drew from them. Then he played his master-stroke by offering to take the fingerprints of a jury member. One of them submitted himself to the process there and then, and it was shown that slight variations were possible if the same thumb was printed several times with differing amounts of pressure being applied. Although Collins had given lengthy testimony in which he described the parts of a fingerprint by using terms like *ridges, spurs, pronged forks, islands, lakes* and *peninsulas* – even throwing in the word *bifurcation* for good measure – it is likely that the members of the jury, for whom this science was an obscure novelty, were most convinced by the down-to-earth reality of the practical demonstration he gave, when he told them:

'I have my apparatus here for taking prints. This is a copper plate. A thin film of ink is spread over it by a roller, the finger is placed upon the inked plate, the ridges take up the ink, the finger is then placed upon the paper and leaves an imprint. We have paper forms for the purpose. This is the print I took of Alfred's finger.'

Despite his determinedly technical explanations, the inspector succeeded in sufficiently demystifying the process to convince the jury that the print still visible on the cashbox – which had been brought into the courtroom as evidence – matched the photographic enlargement of the print taken from Alfred Stratton. In response to this display, Mr Rooth for the defence mounted a counter-attack, calling in his own fingerprint expert, Dr John Garson, who 'with a great flourish of papers' began by implying that he had a greater knowledge of such matters than the Scotland Yard officers who had so far given evidence:

'I have had experience of the finger print system since about 1890. I was engaged by the Home Office in 1894 to undertake the organisation of this, and also the Bertillon system, and I was engaged in training a staff of officers in prison and police service. I had Inspectors Collins and Steadman as pupils in one of my classes at Wandsworth Prison.'

His detailed testimony was also littered with descriptive terms like *interval, shoulder, upper fork, ridge* and *junction*, together with a blizzard of measurements designed to illustrate his position:

'As to point 10, it is distinctly a perennial end in the lower print but in the upper it appears to me to be placed on the cross of an arch, which is running onwards to join the one above it. I have not got the measurement from 9 and 10, but I have from 1 to 10, and from 11 to 10; from 1 to 10 in the upper print measures eighty-four millimetres; in the lower one seventy-eight, a difference of six millimetres or a quarter of an inch.'

Garson spoke in a similar vein for a long time, but his essential point, when he finally came to it, was that the impression taken from the cashbox and the one from the accused were not the same: 'I accept the statement that one of those prints is the finger of the right thumb of Alfred Stratton and I am prepared to swear before the jury that the one above is not.' He also ridiculed statements by Collins about the probabilities involved in fingerprint identification which had been reported in the press ('I, as a scientific man, came to the conclusion that it was nonsense').

Into this war of the experts then stepped the presiding judge, Mr Justice Channell. The court was shown a letter Garson had written, offering to testify for the defence, and then a similar one in which he had offered to testify for the prosecution. When asked, 'How do you justify writing two such letters?', Garson replied, 'I am an independent witness', at which the judge intervened, saying, 'I should say, after having written such letters, an absolutely untrustworthy one', and dismissed him shortly after. According to one observer, 'the face of the elderly Justice Channell on his hearing of the two letters, had gradually become crimson with rage'.

Once the case for the Crown had closed, Alfred Stratton took the stand, and although he denied that he had carried out either the murder or the burglary, admitted that he had for some time been living 'an utterly degraded life, and had been in trouble before'. In fact, unknown to the jury at this point, the Stratton brothers were responsible for a string of burglaries in the area. As for the defence counsel, in their closing speech, they were reduced to casting aspersions on Scotland Yard's fingerprint system by saying that such evidence 'savoured of the French courts', implying that it was somehow foreign, unsporting and generally below-the-belt.

In his summing up, the judge singled out the fingerprint evidence for attention, remarking on the very close similarity between the print on the cashbox and that later obtained from the accused, although he warned the jury not to rely too heavily upon it.

It had been a very long day in the courtroom. The entire room was filled with men – since, it was said, the case was too brutal to have attracted women spectators. Outside in the road, a crowd of around 2,000 people waited in expectation of the verdict, while inside the courtroom 'was crowded with men who, rather than risk losing their chance of seeing two men sentenced to be hanged, had gone without food since morning'. The jury retired to consider its verdict at 8 pm, and returned two hours later, watched stonily by the accused. As the *Daily Express* reporter commented: 'Alfred, the master mind of the two, stood in sulky anger, his hands in his trouser pockets, his small, wolf-like eyes partly closed in malicious gaze upon the foreman of the jury.'

To the surprise of no one, let alone the Stratton brothers, the accused were pronounced guilty.

Alfred and Albert Stratton were taken from the Old Bailey to Wandsworth gaol, where they spent three weeks waiting in the unlikely expectation of a reprieve from the Home Secretary. It was not to be, and on 22 May, the relatives of the Stratton brothers received an official communication saying that no reprieve would be forthcoming, and therefore the two prisoners would be executed the following morning.

Three sisters and two brothers of the condemned men visited them later that day at Wandsworth. Alfred, the elder of the two, was stoic, but Albert, who was twenty but 'looked sixteen', had been crying the whole day. Both of them told their siblings that they held no grudge against the other. At 9 am the following morning, they were hanged together, side by side.

As far as the press was concerned, despite all the verbal testimony, it was the fingerprint evidence that had tipped the balance. 'The Thumb Prints That Convicted The Masked Murderers' ran one *Daily Mirror* headline, above a photographic reproduction of the two fingerprint blow-ups which had been presented in court by Scotland Yard. Of course, the considerable publicity given to the fingerprint system in this and other cases helped alert even the most simple-minded criminal to the advisability of disguising such a distinctive feature, as the *Mirror* went on to stress:

> The up-to-date professional criminal now seeks to prevent the leaving of tell-tale prints by covering the finger-tips with thin india-rubber, gold-beater's skin, or silk finger-stalls. Some even go so far as to wear kid gloves.

Indeed, although the average member of the public at the time of the Deptford Mask Murders had little or no knowledge of the fingerprint system, so much was heard of it in the following years that by the time Agatha Christie wrote her classic novel *The Murder of Roger Ackroyd* in 1926, she was able to include the following fine piece of sarcasm from the narrator, Dr Sheppard, who has been warned by the police not to touch a murder weapon because it might have fingerprints on it:

'I do not see why I should be supposed to be totally devoid of intelligence. After all, I read detective stories, and the newspapers, and am a man of quite average ability. If there had been toe marks on the dagger handle, now, that would have been quite a different thing. I would then have registered my surprise and awe.'

Special. "ONE OF THE BOMBS FELL LESS THAN TWENTY YARDS FROM WHERE I WAS ON DUTY THE OTHER NIGHT."
She. "REALLY! HOW EXCITING! DID IT WAKE YOU?"

Punch magazine tackles the subject of the new air-raids, 9 June, 1915

EIGHTEEN

MEAT IS MURDER
1917

In July 1915, the bloody war which had been raging for much of the year across the battlefields of France and the Low Countries descended from the skies over London, wrecking buildings and killing members of the civilian population. The idea of dropping high explosives from flying machines onto urban areas was something that had been predicted by H.G. Wells in his novel *The War in the Air*, first published in 1908:

> He had seen airships flying low and swift over darkened and groaning streets; watched great buildings, suddenly red-lit amidst the shadows, crumple at the smashing impact of bombs.

The initial raids on London were carried out using Zeppelin airships, dropping an incendiary mixture made from manganese dioxide and magnesium. The military use of such dirigibles had begun almost as soon as the war broke out, when Zeppelin Z6 rained down high explosives over Liège in Belgium on 5 August 1914, but it was not until 1915 that the Kaiser gave permission for German aircrews to bomb London.

Zeppelins were slow, could not fly at especially high altitudes, and their huge size made them a very prominent target. Yet throughout 1915 and 1916 they were almost unopposed in the skies over England – a terrifying sight for those down below. In a London raid carried out on the night of 13 October 1915, four Zeppelins converged over the City and the Docks, killing 71 and wounding 128. In 1916, a new class of Zeppelins darkened the skies that were much larger, faster and could fly at higher altitudes, but the tide had begun to turn against them. On 2 September that year, a brand-new Zeppelin called the SL11 was shot down in flames over

London by Lieutenant William Leefe Robinson of the Royal Flying Corps, followed on 23 September by the destruction of Zeppelins L32 and L33.

The year 1917 would gradually see the end of the Zeppelin campaign, highlighted by the loss of five of them in a single raid, but in their place that year came a new aircraft, a twin-engine biplane called the Gotha bomber. Measuring forty feet from nose to tail, with a giant wingspan, for the time, of eighty feet, and machine guns mounted fore, aft and centre, the Gotha appeared over London on 13 June 1917. The intended target was Liverpool Street station. However, accuracy was hard to achieve, and the destruction inflicted that day by a squadron of twenty Gotha bombers not only resulted in great loss of life at the railway terminus itself, but also a direct hit on a school, in which forty-six children were killed or wounded. Not surprisingly, four days later the British Royal Family changed its surname by official proclamation from Saxe-Coburg-Gotha to Windsor. It has often been said that the First World War was basically an argument between the grandchildren of Queen Victoria, who between them sat on many of the thrones of Europe, including those of Russia and Germany. It would not do to remind the public too obviously that the chief enemy, Kaiser Wilhelm II, was himself a grandson of the late revered queen.

By the autumn of 1917, Londoners were well used to Gotha raids. Andrew Home-Morton, president of the British Association of Rotary Clubs, attempted to sum up the experience for the benefit of an American audience in these words:

As I lie in my bed on a quiet night – so very many nights – between midnight and three o'clock in the morning probably I can hear the pounding of the guns in Flanders . . . I hear a sudden sound . . . a slight bang and a soft boom. It is quite familiar to us. It is the fire from one of our neighbouring fire stations, and if you could see it you would see a coloured light in the sky. It is fired to tell us that the enemy machines have crossed the coast and are making for our town, and that now is the time for us to take cover and shelter against the shrapnel and the falling bomb . . . Then the sound comes nearer and nearer. The gun-fire concentrates over your house; the shrapnel falls, zips down and pounds on the pavement, misses your windows or perhaps gets one; zips down to the back of your garden into the soft ground with a little mushy thud. Then your windows rattle with the intensity of the gun-fire because they have concentrated the gun-fire from all parts into that part of town in which the enemy machines are heard. Your windows rattle, your doors rattle, the china rattles, the pictures rattle, and you brace yourselves together and try to think that you like it. You don't, but you are not going to show anybody that you don't.

War was as old as time, but air raids like this were something new. In the chaos and confusion of such a night, people sought whatever shelter they could, just like the men in the trenches, whose philosophy was summed up in Bruce Bairnsfather's famous cartoon of the time – 'Well, if you knows of a better 'ole, go to it'. Purpose-built air-raid shelters were largely a feature of the Second World War; in these earlier days, many people took cover down in the Underground stations, others in cellars or anywhere that offered some sense of security. While the planes or airships droned overhead, normal nightlife was suspended, till in the morning the official estimate of the damage would be released, carefully censored in the press with all geographical references deleted so as to give no help to the enemy, as in this report from 1 October:

The people had crowded into the cellar of a corner public-house, and a high explosive bomb fell through into the cellar, killing two women and injuring very many others, but few of them seriously. The first floor is heaped with debris and unbroken barrels. The upper floors, with windows shattered and furniture flung in all directions, are otherwise intact, though the force of the explosion knocked a big door right across the street and into a shop opposite.

On 19 October 1917 it was Zeppelins, not Gotha bombers, that attacked London, but then, on the last night of the month, the twin-engine biplanes came again to the skies over the capital. It was a large raid, which would have been a terrifying sight, though singularly ineffective, according to the *Manchester Guardian*:

Wednesday night's aeroplane attack was made in seven waves, and there were odd machines besides. All the attacks were driven off by the barrage and other arrangements. In the seventh attack two or at most three got through and dropped bombs.

No mass casualties, not even a great amount of damage to property. Yet if anyone went missing overnight during such a raid, it might easily pass unnoticed for a time, and even then, be accounted for as simply a by-product of the war.

However, not all the sudden death in London came from above.

Death was very much a fact of life for Londoners at that time. At the last census before war broke out, the population of London stood at 7,160,000, but by the autumn of 1917, because of recruitment, there were fewer men on the streets of the capital, and the conflict across the Channel was annihilating them at a shockingly high rate. All around the Belgian town of Ypres in West Flanders, a savage battle had been underway since 31 July and would come to a futile halt on 6 November, swamped in acres of mud and choking slime. An estimated 300,000 members of the British Expeditionary Force lost their lives in this engagement, fighting over a few thousand yards of ground and the wreckage of a town long since shelled into rubble. One survivor, Alfred Finnegan of the Royal Field Artillery, wrote in his diary during the battle:

> I lost my Sergeant, Corporal and two Bombardiers, several gunners killed and wounded and several sick as it was ammunition carrying day and night. Everything was mud and water and continuous shelling. Hell with the lid off.

One death more or less back in London might not have seemed so much, particularly during an air raid, but there were limits.

The overnight bombing raid which had taken place late on 31 October was covered in the newspapers in a matter-of-fact way. Certainly there had been casualties, but nothing that London had not witnessed many times in the previous two years. An exhibition had just opened that week in the East End at the People's Palace, in which the wreckage of various enemy aircraft and Zeppelins was displayed, including a Gotha bomber shot down off Southend back in August – 'There is little of it except twisted tubes, tangles of wire, and burnt woodwork which were fished out of the water.' The general mood was one of confidence; that the city could take whatever might be thrown at it – a feeling borne out by the 'Sayings Of The Week' in the *Observer* for 4 November: 'What every German ought to know is that, far from striking terror into the heart of London, air-raids merely stiffen British backbone.' On the other hand, this admirable sentiment was lined up next to another utterance deemed worthy of note, from a Mrs Pember Reeves: 'It tears at one's heart strings to have to abandon onion sauce.' Clearly, life for some on the Home Front was troublesome indeed.

There was, however, another story making the headlines that week, typified by this graphic front-page report in the *Daily Express* on 3 November:

THE MYSTERY OF REGENT SQUARE

The most sensational murder since that of Mrs Crippen was discovered yesterday morning, when the headless and dismembered body of a young woman was found in Regent-square, Bloomsbury. The head had been cut off close to the trunk – probably in two cuts, the first of which penetrated as far as the vertebræ. Both legs had been severed at the knee-joints and both arms at the wrists. A parcel containing the trunk was found just inside the railings of the square. Another, containing the legs lay a little distance away. The head and hands are missing.

Despite the numbing effects of three years of war, this was gruesome enough to stand out from the general run of events. Presumably, the object of any murderer in carving up a body and removing the head and hands would be to hinder identification, yet in this case, they had in fact managed to provide an embarrassment of other clues by way of compensation. Doctor John Gabe, the police surgeon called to the scene, saw evidence of enough methodical expertise in the way that the body had been partitioned to speculate that the perpetrator might well be a butcher by trade. In a short statement, he said:

The remains were those of a woman about 30 years of age, well-nourished, some 4ft. 11in. in height. She had been the mother of several children. There was no trace of disease. She had apparently been dead about 24 hours.

The authorities were said to be working on the theory that the victim was a Belgian, whose remains, discovered at 8.30 am on Friday,

2 November, had probably been brought to Regent Square in a van or a handcart.

The gardens at the centre of Regent Square, like many in London at that time, were enclosed by spiked railings and not intended for use by the general public. Residents of the surrounding buildings were issued with keys to the various gates leading to the gardens, although in this case, two of the four in Regent Square were not usually locked. Dumping a couple of parcels of human remains in such a location was not quite as public as leaving them on the pavement in Oxford Street, but could hardly have been expected to remain unnoticed for very long. In the event, a local man employed to clean the streets – and known in the district as Jack the Sweeper – passed by the railings early on the November morning on the south side of the square, near the spot where the large sack lay. However, he simply remarked to his companion, 'More rubbish to clear', and then went off for his break-fast.

A short while later at 8.30 am, one of the residents of the square, a male nurse named Thomas Henry, who lived at number 17, spotted the large sack lying in the grass. Rather than return home to fetch his key to the garden's gates, he climbed over the railing at a point where several spikes were missing and jumped down in order to investigate. Not only was he convinced immediately that something was wrong, he also happened to have with him a police whistle, which he then blew enthusiastically to summon help – the immediate consequence of which was that people living nearby 'flocked into the roadway thinking that it was an air-raid warning'. Mr Henry was clearly not the type to pass by on the other side:

'I was on my way to work, and, as I usually do, I crossed the road to the path opposite. When I was about half-way down towards Sidmouth-street my attention was arrested by a large parcel inside the railings, which I at first took to be a soldier's kit-bag. I put my hand through the railings and felt the parcel. It was soft to the touch, and I became curious to know what the contents were, fancying anything but what they proved to be. I thought at first that it contained half a sheep's carcass . . . The parcel was done up in sacking and tightly bound with a thin rope, very firmly knotted. It struck me at the time that the person who tied it up was used to fastening parcels. As I could not untie the knots, I cut the rope with my knife. I was shocked to see the top of the trunk of a body. The head had been cut away close to the shoulders as if with a very sharp instrument.'

Many people at this point would probably have run away in horror or simply moved to one side in order to be sick, but Mr Henry – who would no doubt have seen a variety of troublesome sights in his work as a nurse – proved to be made of sterner stuff, and delved further into the interior of the sack:

'I then opened the package fully, removing an inner white sheet, in which the trunk of a woman was tightly wrapped. The body was clothed in a beautifully-made undergarment, with lace and a blue ribbon round the upper part. On it lay a piece of torn brown wrapping paper, on which I read the words, "BLODIE BELGIM".'

It was at this point that he had blown his whistle; then, while waiting for the authorities to arrive, he looked around further and discovered the smaller parcel containing the legs, which he also opened. Together, the packages were found to contain various other items in addition to the cryptic message pinned to the body, any of which might prove of help to the police. These were listed in one report as follows:

Two fine white sheets, one bearing the laundry mark 'II.H.'.
A fine chemise with lace embroidery and bows of blue ribbon.
A piece of sacking bearing the name 'Rank'.
A piece of rope.

Any crime novelist scattering quite that many suggestive clues around a murder victim might reasonably be accused of overdoing things, but then, the urge to dismember one's fellow human beings and parcel them up for collection in a London square is hardly a rational impulse in the first place.

Owing to the activities of the public-spirited Mr Henry, by the time the police finally appeared on the scene from the local station two streets away, half the neighbourhood had turned out to watch, and news of the grisly discovery was spreading throughout the district. Today the immediate area would be cordoned off in an effort to secure the crime scene prior to the search for evidence, but it was still early days for forensic science – indeed, the specialist called in to help with this investigation was one of the pioneers of such methods, Bernard Spilsbury. Sometimes called the 'father of forensics', Spilsbury had first come to wider public notice when giving evidence at the trial of Dr Crippen in 1910. However, the gardens at Regent Square appeared to be simply a disposal point for the remains, following a murder which had taken place elsewhere. The killer might, of course, have left traces of his visit in the grass around the two sacks, but when the police discovered two deep footprints near the place where the torso had been left, they turned out to have been made by Mr Henry when he first jumped down from the railings.

It seemed that perhaps the best lead available to the police was the laundry mark visible on the sheet. In those days, many people would have regularly taken their household linen to a nearby laundry to be washed and collected later; to avoid confusion, each item was usually embroidered with a small mark identifying the place of business and the individual customer. A by-product of this was that the marks were commonly used to assist police investigations, and in this case, the relevant details were immediately made public in the hope of securing an identification:

> It is to be anticipated that sooner or later the laundry mark will be recog-
> nised. Any laundry that can throw light on the mystery should immediately
> communicate with the nearest police station. The mark is very faintly
> worked in the right-hand corner of the sheet in red cotton. There is a dot
> over the top of the 11, and a line underneath the H. The faintness of the
> marking leads to the belief that the sheet has not been sent to the laundry
> for some time.

This element of mystery, and the plethora of clues in the case, certainly caught the imagination of the newspaper copy-writers. The *Daily Mirror* seemed especially taken with the business:

> The 'Great Sack Mystery' is a kind of super-crime. It contains all the
> elements of a great drama. It reminds one of the sensational stories of
> Fergus Hume [prolific crime novelist of the day]; it rivals Edgar Allan Poe
> in its weird details.

Contradicting other sources, their report stated that the body was 'nude' (which it was not), and added that the trunk was 'still warm'. As for the motive – at a time when the papers were full of stories warning about 'aliens' and foreigners in general – the fact that the deceased might have come from another country seemed to suggest sinister practices not usually found in England:

> Among the theories given to the police are:-
> (1) That the woman was a foreigner
> (2) That she was the victim of 'the unwritten law'.

Stirring stuff indeed for a public used to the sensational best-selling novels of Sax Rohmer, whose characters such as the Oriental super-criminal Fu Manchu or the French detective Gaston Max, lent an air of exoticism to his tales. As opposed to the average domestic murder, in which one member of a happy couple simply beats the other over the head with a blunt instrument and then sits around waiting for the police to arrive, the initial details of this case suggested elements of mystery and cunning, perhaps even ritual execution. *The Times*, however, had an alternative theory, in which the killing was directly linked to the war being fought in Flanders:

> There is a strong belief locally that the crime may have been committed
> by a German, his victim being a Belgian woman, and his motive hatred
> of the people who stood in his country's way.

The man responsible for making sense of this tangled web of evidence and rumour was Detective Inspector Ashley of Bow Street. As things stood, he had perhaps eighty per cent of a body, a sample of what might be the murderer's handwriting, and the suggestion that the dismember-ment had been carried out by someone with surgical or butchery skills. Most promising of all, there was the telltale laundry mark.

The post-mortem was carried out upon the available remains on Saturday, 3 November by Dr Spilsbury and Dr Gabe. They concluded that death had been caused by 'some terrible injury to the head, which drained the blood from the body'. The head being absent, it was speculated that either it had been 'battered to pieces', or the victim's throat had been cut.

On 4 November, two days after the discovery of the torso, further details were made public by the police in the hope that someone would come forward to assist them in their inquiries. In particular, they were exploring the idea that the embroidered letters on the sheet might not be the mark of a commercial laundry, but rather that of a private hotel or lodging house. As for the garments worn by the victim, they were listed as a 'ribbed cotton undervest marked as follows: "Unshrinkable underwear, heron make, unsurpassed",' together with 'a white embroidered chemise and combinations'. The torso itself was further surrounded by 'a piece of butcher's sacking bearing the stamp, "Argentine La Plata Cold Storage",' which might suggest that the killer either had an extremely dry sense of humour, or was deranged, or perhaps both. On the other hand, there was always the simplest explanation – that the murderer was indeed a butcher by trade.

Those curious for more details about the sack used for transporting the torso – which had given the headline writers a name for this mystery – were duly informed that it had originally contained bran, and was marked 'Joseph Rank Limited, Premier Flour Mills, Victoria Dock, East'. The latter was a sizeable firm – whose former mill in Gateshead is now the Baltic Arts Centre – so there would probably be little chance of tracing this one sack among the many thousands they would have handled each year. Nevertheless, the impression remained of a murderer who showed little concern for the number of clues they left behind, except in so far as they had taken the precaution of removing the victim's head and hands.

Finally, the police announced that their unknown suspect was likely to be 'a man of considerable strength with exceptionally strong fingers, and that he was probably accustomed to cutting up carcasses'.

The latter statement was issued in time to be carried in the Sunday papers; by Monday morning, the headlines read:

REGENT SQUARE MURDER

~

BUTCHER DETAINED ON
SUSPICION OF THE CRIME

It all happened surprisingly quickly. The body was found on Friday morning, and before the weekend was over a man had been arrested. As it turned out, it was the laundry mark '11. H' that played the decisive role. Having seen it reproduced in Saturday's newspapers, the manageress of the Danish Laundry in Judd Street, just around the corner from Regent Square, contacted the police with the name and address of one of her customers whose items were identified by that particular code. Despite the fevered speculation of the previous days, it turned out that the woman who matched the laundry mark was in fact French, not Belgian, and the man pulled in on suspicion, instead of being an aggrieved German with 'hatred of the people who stood in his country's way', was also from France. He was, however, a trained butcher, as the investigators had suspected.

The Danish Laundry used the mark '11. H' when handling the washing of a woman called Emilienne Gerard or Girouard, who lived near Warren Street tube station in a rented room at 50 Munster Square, roughly ten minutes' walk from where her body was discovered. They told the police that she had failed to collect her last parcel of washing left with them. According to those at her lodging house, Emilienne Gerard had gone missing during the air raid on Wednesday night and had not been seen since. She seemed a likely match for the body found in Regent Square, but as yet there had been no positive identification. With the head and hands still unlocated, there were obvious difficulties in this respect, and if the victim was indeed Madame Gerard, the police could not immediately locate anyone who had known her well. Although Mrs Rouse, her landlady at 50 Munster Square, stated that Emilienne had lived there since 3 April 1916, no one at that address seemed to have been on particularly close terms with the lady, probably because her English was relatively poor.

One neighbour, Mrs Barker, thought that Madame Gerard would have been unlikely to leave London to escape the air raids, saying that she had not been frightened by them, and had said to her during a previous raid, 'Don't be scared. Your husband is going through much worse at the front than we are.' A nearby dairyman, who was accustomed to selling the missing lady milk every day, said that her hands had been very recognisable, being 'heavily scarred, apparently from burns, and the marks were so prominent as to amount to a disfigurement'. If she turned out to be the person found in Regent Square, this might be why the killer had felt the need to remove the hands. Yet other reports from those claiming to have known the woman stated that she had 'delicate hands and feet, of which she was proud'.

Emilienne Gerard was known to be married, but her husband Paul had volunteered for the French Army, and was away fighting on the western front. According to the landlady, they were a 'devoted couple', yet one of the lodgers, Mrs Adelaide Chester, formed a very different impression, as if something was very wrong in Madame Gerard's life:

'I do not think she was particularly happy. Sometimes she seemed to me as if she had been crying for hours. She had a most depressed, unhappy expression, and whenever she spoke to me I could not help being struck with the mournfulness of her conversation.'

This, of course, could well be a case of someone reading far too much into otherwise everyday occurrences, now that they suspected that an acquaintance of theirs might be a murder victim. However, Mrs Chester also mentioned Madame Gerard in connection with a third party:

'Once or twice I have seen her in the company of a middle-aged man, who, she said, was a relative of hers. Once, when they passed me at the corner of Munster-square they were quarrelling violently, speaking in French. I spoke to her, but she took no notice. I could hear her shrill voice a long way down the street, and she was gesticulating wildly.'

In the confusion of an air raid, some people chose to leave their houses, feeling safer elsewhere, and so for a woman to go missing during the bombing was not necessarily a sinister occurrence. However, the fact that Madame Gerard had been seen publicly quarrelling with someone shortly before her disappearance was certainly suggestive, and the middle-aged man in question found himself being visited by the constabulary on Sunday, 4 November, the day after the landlady from the Danish Laundry had come forward with her suspicions. His name was not immediately given to the newspapers, but readers were certainly invited to join the dots: 'The man detained is stated to be a relative of the dead woman. He is a butcher.'

The formula used by the police when arresting a suspect had by this time already been in place long enough for it to have become well known. In

E.C. Bentley's pioneering detective novel, *Trent's Last Case* (1912), the hero teases his Inspector friend that he has been eyeing up a likely suspect with the following: 'Your lips were mutely framing the syllables of those tremendous words: "It is my duty to tell you that anything you now say will be taken down and used in evidence against you."'

Fine words, but in this instance, it is possible that the suspect could not even understand them, since he barely spoke English at all. This was the man 'of foreign appearance' said to have often visited Emilienne Gerard at Munster Square, 'who drove up in a two-wheeled conveyance of French type, and was believed to be her brother-in-law'. The vehicle in question, pulled by a mule, would, of course, have been handy for transporting heavy items, such as a couple of sacks containing body parts, through the streets of Bloomsbury. Mrs Rouse, the Munster Square landlady, recalled that the gentleman had been a frequent visitor to the house and had called again on Friday afternoon – some hours after the sacks were discovered in Regent Square – to say that Madame Gerard had gone to the country for a fortnight, and that he was sending her a sack of potatoes.

Chief Detective Inspector Wensley, who was in charge of the investigation, found evidence at Munster Square of the missing woman's connection to this middle-aged man, which led him to an address a little to the south, at 101 Charlotte Street, in the basement of which lived Louis Marie Joseph Voisin, a Frenchman aged fifty. He currently worked as a stableman at Smithfield Market but had formerly been a butcher. When told of the reason for the police visit, Voisin protested his innocence, but his command of English was so shaky that it was felt necessary to call in an interpreter in order to question him.

With one suspect in custody, and a possible name to match up with the body, Inspector Wensley and his team then made a thorough search of Louis Voisin's home. Today, the building is no longer there, and this section on the west side of Charlotte Street is home to the halls of residence for University College, with the offices of Saatchi & Saatchi across the road. In 1917, number 101 was a run-down Georgian terraced house, with an alleyway on the left-hand side leading to stables at the rear. Inside, the impression of neglect was even more apparent. Voisin's kitchen was a dingy, rubbish-strewn affair, which gave the appearance of last having been cleaned sometime around the date when Queen

Victoria came to the throne. Hanging on hooks on the walls above the cooker were several large saws, of the kind that might be used for cutting down a tree, or dividing up a carcass. If this room was unlikely to win prizes in the *Daily Mail*'s newly created Ideal Home Exhibition, it was a model of cleanliness when compared to Louis Voisin's cellar – a grim, tunnel-like structure resembling a railway arch, oozing damp from bare bricks and littered with offcuts of wood, stone drinking jars and old barrels.

The police diligently picked through all this detritus as the evening of Sunday 4 wore on, and what they found corroborated their tentative theories. The kitchen turned up nothing conclusive, but the cellar was a different matter, as the *Daily Express* reported:

> Late last night, during their search of the premises in Charlotte-street of the butcher who has been detained, the police found a woman's head immersed in a brine tub containing some of the coarser parts of beef which are usually salted. They continued their search and found, not far away, the missing hands. This second discovery placed it beyond doubt that the head belonged to the mutilated body . . . In spite of its immersion in the brine, the head is said to be easily recognisable by any one who knew the original.

When examined, the severed right hand was seen to be scarred, as if from severe scalding, which further strengthened the impression that this was indeed the body of the missing Mrs Gerard.

They searched the cellar with torches and candles, and found a blood-stained towel, to which an earring was attached, matching another earring found in the victim's ear. In the adjoining stables, which Voisin leased, they discovered 'a piece of butcher's meat covering stamped "La Plata Cold Storage, Argentina".'

As a consequence of their thorough examination of the building, the police also took into custody a woman named Berthe Roche who shared the accommodation with Voisin, said to be his housekeeper. She was also French, aged thirty-one, and spoke equally few words of English. Jointly protesting their innocence as best they could, they were taken to Bow Street Police Station.

Now that the police had located both the head and the hands, Doctors Gabe and Spilsbury could make a further examination of the remains, after which they concluded that all the pieces found in Regent Square and in Charlotte Street matched up exactly with each other, and that the victim had died from repeated savage blows to the head. On Tuesday, 6 November, less than a week after the night of the air raid on which Madame Gerard was last seen alive, the inquest opened into the murder, and the *Daily Express* printed a photo of the presumed victim, captioned:

MISSING WOMAN OF MUNSTER SQUARE
Portrait of Mme. Emilienne Gerard who has not returned to her residence
since the discovery of the murdered woman in Regent Square.'

At the coroner's inquest, two days after Voisin was arrested, an initial identification of the body as being Madame Gerard was made by a man named Noel Bissi, the proprietor of a Belgian café in Whitfield Street called the Lanterne, just around the corner from 101 Charlotte Street. He said that she had often visited his café. However, the definitive identification was imminent, since Paul Gerard had been given leave from front-line service with the French Army, and had just arrived in London to face the grisly task of viewing the remains.

On 8 November, Voisin and Roche appeared before the magistrate at Marlborough Street Police Court and, via an interpreter, were formally charged with being concerned together in the murder of Emilienne Gerard. Berthe Roche wore a grey mackintosh, a black hat, and fur wrap. Her fellow accused, despite appearing on charges involving murder and dismemberment, did little to avoid giving the impression that here was a man who spent much of his day slicing up carcasses, as the *Daily Mirror* noted:

Voisin, a heavily-built man, of medium height, with swarthy complexion and dark, heavy moustache, came in hatless. He wore a drab butcher's overall such as is common in Smithfield Meat Market, and a pair of black leggings.

Inspector Wensley ran through the police case so far, and the two prisoners were remanded for seven days. Such was the public interest in the case that despite the abundance of war news as the Third Battle of Ypres drew to its bloody conclusion that week, it was photographs of Inspector Wensley, various witnesses, and the crowd outside the Police Court that made the front page of the *Daily Mirror*.

While onlookers waited to catch a glimpse of the accused at Marlborough Street, across town at the St Pancras Mortuary, Paul Gerard went through the sad and painful business of identifying his wife for officials of Scotland Yard. Unsurprisingly, 'he was much affected, and was led weeping from the mortuary'. On 12 November, Paul gave evidence at the inquest at St Pancras Coroner's Court, formally stating that the deceased was his wife. Unlike the accused, he spoke English extremely well, having lived in Britain and worked as a pastry cook before joining the French Army. Gerard shed some light upon the relationship between his wife and Voisin. He said that although she had originally been working in a café, she then wrote to him at the front line to say that she had now taken work as a servant to a Mr Voisin, whom Paul Gerard then met when he briefly returned to London, as he testified:

'My first leave was on December 28, 1916. My wife was at Munster Square, and Voisin. We had supper together, and Voisin said to me: "Your wife was off duty today and I thought it would be better for me to come here and have my supper."'

During the rest of his eleven days' leave, Voisin was a frequent visitor, and he and Paul Gerard often played cards together. Once he had returned to the trenches, however, Madame Gerard had not written to him nearly as often as before. On the occasions that she did write, she mentioned Voisin in her letters, and even claimed that he would be able to help Paul find a job when he returned.

On the face of it this seemed like a story which had been played out in thousands of homes across the country: the husband away at war, and the wife back in England forming an attachment to someone else. Various other witnesses called at the inquest only served to strengthen this impression. The landlady from the house at Munster Square gave evidence that Voisin had been introduced as the brother-in-law of Madame Gerard, was a frequent visitor to her rooms, and had stayed overnight at least once. Conversely, a Frenchman named Georges Everard stated via an interpreter that in the four weeks prior to her disappearance, Voisin had met with Madame Gerard roughly twenty times. If Emilienne had indeed become romantically involved with Louis Voisin whilst her husband was overseas, the relationship between the butcher and Berthe Roche had yet to be explained.

The inquest was adjourned once more, and on the following day, 13 November, some 800 people attended the funeral of Emilienne Gerard at St Pancras Cemetery, East Finchley, at which her husband 'broke down completely and sobbed loudly for some time', as, indeed, did Reverend Father Boyland, the priest officiating, who for a while was unable to continue reciting the burial service.

When the inquest resumed on 15 November, the public image of Louis Voisin took a further turn into the realms of the macabre. Giving evidence, Madame Luppens – the porter at 101 Charlotte Street who supervised the tenants on behalf of the landlord – stated that for the past month and a half, Berthe Roche had been living with Voisin and using the name Madame Martin. On the night of the air raid, she had warned them of the impending bombing, as was her custom. The following morning, she noticed that Roche was up and about much earlier than usual, and asked her why. According to Luppens, Roche replied:

> '"Voisin came in just a minute before, and he has just killed a calf, and he is full of blood and I washed his underclothes . . ." She said that he gave a very bad hit with his axe, and the calf was struggling very badly on account of the bad hit . . . She said that his shirt and jacket were full of blood.'

Further to this gruesome image, Detective Sergeant Stephens testified that in searching Madame Gerard's rooms at Munster Square, he had found 'a piece of butcher's longcloth and two corn sacks', and on the counterpane there had been a smear of blood. On the washstand, there was a pail which contained blood and water, and in a cupboard, six bed-sheets marked '11.H'. All this was certainly suggestive of foul play, but it was as nothing compared to the roll-call of lethal implements discovered in various parts of Louis Voisin's residence by Detective Sergeant Collins:

> On top of some furniture he found four butchers' overalls, bloodstained, one very much so inside. Three pieces of butchers' meat covering were also bloodstained, and also a wood block. On the door of the back kitchen

– produced in court – were observed bloodstains, and a glass panel was broken. The witness [Collins] produced eight butchers' choppers found in the back yard, and a number of butchers' implements, including a heavy axe and a wooden hammer. Among the ashes in the kitchen grate he found the head of a small hammer which had apparently been through the fire. In the kitchen table drawer were a number of large knives, sharpeners, and steels, among them being a large carving knife, recently sharpened, with blood spots on it. On the handle was a large finger impression in blood. In the same drawer was a stone knife sharpener with spots of blood on it.

Voisin had trained as a butcher and worked at Smithfield looking after horses for a sausage maker, so many of these things might well have been simply the tools of his trade. If, however, he had wanted to bludgeon someone to death and then divide up the victim into various pieces, he would not have had to look further than his own front room for the means with which to do it.

Not entirely surprisingly, the inquest jury returned a verdict of wilful murder against Voisin and Roche on 20 November, and in court a dramatic statement by the former was read out, in which he swore that his Berthe had nothing whatever to do with the murder. By his version of events, the whole thing was a conspiracy, designed by the real murderer – identity unknown – to frame him for the crime. He had gone innocently to Emilienne's rooms, he said, and discovered evidence of a brutal killing:

'I went to Mme. Gerard's place last Thursday at 11 am, and when I arrived the door was closed but not locked. The floor and the carpet were full of blood. The head and hands were wrapped up in a flannel jacket, which is at my place now. They were on the kitchen table. That's all I can say. The rest of the body was not there.'

Faced with such a scene of medieval gore, with the disembodied head of a very close friend lying on the table, he did what he felt anyone would have done in the circumstances – took it home and hid it in a barrel, whilst carefully avoiding notifying the police. 'I thought that a trap had been laid for me,' he said. 'I began to clean up the blood, and my clothes became stained with it.' (Some contemporaries might have been tempted to pre-empt the 1963 words of Mandy Rice-Davies and respond, 'Well, he would, wouldn't he?')

Although the coroner's inquest had ended, the hearings continued at Marlborough Street Police Court, where the accused sat – Voisin 'dressed in a black Melton overcoat . . . cool and collected', but Roche showing 'signs of sleeplessness, her eyes being swollen, and her face very pale' – as the evidence piled up against them. The butcher had been asked while in custody if he had any objection to writing the words 'Bloody Belgium' on a piece of paper for the police. He agreed and performed the task several times, in each instance misspelling it as 'Blodie Belgim'. Forensic specialist Dr Spilsbury gave evidence that Emilienne Gerard could not have been killed at her home in 50, Munster Square, but rather that Voisin's kitchen showed various distinct signs that it was the site of the murder. In addition, some items of jewellery belonging to Madame Gerard had been found in a concealed drawer at Voisin's home, for which he had no convincing explanation, and a search of the victim's bedroom had revealed an IOU for the considerable sum of fifty pounds lent by her to Voisin, and signed by him.

The contention of the prosecution was essentially that Louis Voisin and Berthe Roche were having an affair, and had conspired between them to murder the butcher's former lover, Emilienne Gerard.

The hearings ran all through December, with the suspects repeatedly remanded in custody. Air raids continued as Christmas approached, with the leader writer of the *Daily Express* impatiently calling for reprisal attacks on German cities, under the headline 'Bomb And Burn Them Now'.

As the new year, 1918, began, the *Daily Mirror* printed photographs of men who had just been awarded the Victoria Cross by King George V, alongside pictures of Louis Voisin and Berthe Roche. The butcher, who with his jaunty moustache and fashionable hat looked more like an easy-going, successful music hall comedian than an axe-wielding killer, had declared once again at the most recent hearing that Madame Roche was entirely innocent of the crime, and still stuck to his story of having been framed by a third party. Whether anyone in the country believed either of them by this stage is another matter entirely.

Finally, on 16 January, the case came to trial at the Old Bailey, with the prosecution advancing the theory that this was a lovers' triangle, with jealousy as the motive for the killing. It was stated that Gerard and Roche probably never met, but the implication was that once the latter appeared on the scene, Madame Gerard was surplus to requirements, and this senseless butchery had been Voisin's solution to the problem. Both suspects denied the charges.

Within a day, Berthe Roche was found not guilty of murder, but then held in custody to await trial as an accessory after the fact. Meanwhile, the jury was presented with an impressive amount of physical evidence designed to prove the case against Voisin:

> Among the seventy-five exhibits brought into court and shown to the jury were the blood-stained door leading to the yard at Charlotte-street, near which, it is suggested, the murder was committed; the cask in which the head and hands were found, and butchers' knives with finger prints of blood on the handles.

In addition to this display, the jury were taken on the second day of the trial to visit 101, Charlotte Street, in order to inspect the kitchen and cellar for themselves. It was certainly not a case for the faint-hearted. As with many trials of the day, by the time it reached the Old Bailey, there were few dramatic revelations, since the vast majority of evidence had already been previewed at the preliminary hearings during the intervening two months since the arrest of Voisin.

On 18 January, to little surprise, Louis Voisin was found guilty of murder. Asked if he had anything to say, he merely replied in French that he was innocent. Owing to the language difficulty, the judge, Mr Justice Darling, then pronounced sentence of death first in French out of courtesy, and then in English as required by the law. Voisin, 'who had only paled a little', then left the court without a backward glance.

Louis Voisin's counsel launched an appeal in early February, largely on the grounds that it was not proper that he had been asked to write out the words 'Bloody Belgium' while in police custody, but this was dismissed on 8 February. His execution date was set, and then delayed by several days, in case he would be needed to testify at the trial of Berthe Roche. In the event, he was not required, and was therefore promptly executed at 9 am on 2 March at Pentonville prison, the day after Berthe Roche had been sentenced to seven years' penal servitude for her part as an accessory.

Over in mainland Europe that week, Gotha bombers were attacking Venice, the Royal Flying Corps were carrying out raids over Germany, and the Germans were also conducting daytime raids over France.

The French, of course, had their own military aircraft: their principal bomber manufactured by a company named Voisin.

Broadcasting - Page 8

Daily Mirror

THE DAILY PICTURE ● NEWSPAPER WITH THE LARGEST NET SALE

No. 9,581 | Registered at the G.P.O. as a Newspaper. | SATURDAY, AUGUST 11, 1934 | One Penny

FAMOUS
BARONET
MARRIED
AT 74

CINEMA CRIME: YOUTH ARRESTED

Found at Yarmouth

RECOGNISED IN HOTEL

John Frederick Stockwell, a nineteen - year - old youth, whom Scotland Yard wished to interview in connection with the London cinema crime, was found last night at Great Yarmouth.

Stockwell was arrested at the Metropolitan Hotel, Great Yarmouth, at 6.30. Members of the hotel staff communicated with the police after recognising Stockwell from photographs in the newspapers.

Chief-Inspector Sharpe, who has been in charge of the inquiries, left London immediately for Yarmouth.

The discovery followed a number of dramatic developments during the day.

CLOTHES FOUND ON BEACH

First came the news that a neatly-folded bundle of clothing, had been found on the beach at Lowestoft.

Ten minutes after the clothes were found Stockwell was seen in Lowestoft.

Stockwell was employed at the Palace Cinema, Bow-road, E., where Mr. Dudley Hoard, the manager, was found dying, and his wife injured, after they had been attacked by an intruder. The thief got away with £100. After the clothing had been found, Scotland Yard issued this statement:—

"Stockwell was positively seen in Lowestoft at 8 a.m. to-day. He has abandoned the clothing and is now wearing a new blue suit, new black shoes or boots, and is carrying a new fawn mackintosh.

"It is possible he will make for Yarmouth or elsewhere on the coast.

"Members of the public, especially landladies, coach-drivers, railway servants, and caterers, are asked to keep a special look-out for this man, and to inform the nearest police station or constable immediately he is seen."

"Going to Yarmouth"

The police established the fact that a man answering Stockwell's description stayed on Thursday night at a house in Albany-terrace, Albany-road, Lowestoft. He left about nine o'clock yesterday, saying he was going to Yarmouth.

In the bedroom occupied by the man the police found a blue suitcase in which were a pair of flannel trousers and a camera.

Mrs. Tripp, the landlady, said yesterday that "a nice boy" called at her house on Wednesday afternoon and booked a room.

"When asked about terms," added Mrs. Tripp, "he said he could pay anything from 30s. to £2 a week, and we agreed on 35s. He said he had only 10s. with him, but would go for his suitcase in which he had his money.

Landlady Suspicious

"At 7.30 this morning he went out and returned to breakfast at 8.30. He took up a picture paper and opened it.

"Almost at once he threw it on the table and took up a book he had been reading. About two minutes later he got up from the table saying, 'I'm fed up. I think I'll go out. I'm going to Yarmouth and won't be back all day !'

"After he had gone I became suspicious and went into the bedroom. I shook his suitcase, which did not appear to have anything in it, and I asked my next door neighbour, Mr. Howell, to go for the police."

The late Mr. Hoard.

J. F. Stockwell, who was found at Yarmouth last night.

Mrs. Hoard.

Dr. Temple Gray (centre) following Dr. R. L. Guthrie, the coroner, after the inquest.

LONDON'S FIRST SKY POLICEMAN ?

Ex-Flying Officer S. J. Chamberlain, of the traffic department of Scotland Yard, who is mentioned as likely to be the first sky policeman in the auto-gyro from which observation of London traffic is to be made.

EAST LINKED WITH WEST.—Japanese women athletes at the International Telephone Exchange in London yesterday, when they spoke with friends in Tokio at the inauguration of the Britain-Japan telephone. They are in London for the world games.

J F Stockwell (with dog) shares space with Mr and Mrs Hoard on the cover of the *Daily Mirror* on 11 August, 1934

NINETEEN

DEATH AT THE PALACE
1934

For the majority of Londoners seeking evening entertainment in 1934, outside of time-honoured options such as the music hall and pubs, or newer attractions like radio, a visit to the cinema was the preferred option.

Television existed in a primitive form, yet could not rival the popularity of the picture palaces. The BBC had been broadcasting TV programmes since 1932, but these only reached a very limited audience of wealthy people. Those on a tighter budget had the option of picking up one of the build-it-yourself television kits being promoted by the *Daily Express* at five pounds each, complete with instructions to 'switch on the motor 10–15 minutes before the broadcast is due to commence, to allow the motor to warm up and settle to a steady speed'. Still, the fuzzy 'yellow orange'-toned pictures on the sixteen-inch by eight-inch screen could scarcely compete with the majestic expanse of the pin-sharp images projected in cinemas.

Silent films had been enormously popular, but ever since the night in 1926 when Warner Brothers showed a moving picture with synchronised sound in which the tenor Martinelli sang *'Vesti la Giubba'* from the opera *Pagliacci*, the irresistible rise of the Talkies had begun. Films were now a worldwide business generating colossal amounts of money, and London's cinema-goers alone were spending a formidable £300,000 a week (at a time when the average ticket cost one shilling, or five pence today). All of which was good news for the likes of Louis B. Mayer, head of MGM, barely struggling by on a salary of £156,000 a year, or canine star Rin Tin Tin, whose pay packet of £500 a week would have bought him a veritable mountain of dog biscuits.

H.W. Cruss, the manager of one of London's largest picture houses, the Empire Theatre, Leicester Square, stated in a 1933 article that his cinema alone welcomed between 50,000 and 100,000 customers a week. The money changing hands at that single venue was considerable – they took over £10,000 in one week showing the Greta Garbo blockbuster, *Mata Hari* (1931) – but then the Empire employed a far larger workforce than most, as Mr Cruss noted:

'In my own cinema I have a "service Staff" of forty. These, the uniformed men of the house, are under a chief of service, an assistant chief, and five captains, all being supervised by myself and my three assistant-managers. On the technical side there is the chief engineer, with his staff of six engineers and six electricians who are responsible for the lighting, ventilation, and general mechanics of the building. Then there is the chief projectionist, with his six assistants . . .'

The Empire also boasted an accounts department, a restaurant with six chefs and twelve waitresses, and even a tailor's shop in the basement 'where the uniformed staff's liveries are valeted and kept in trim'. This, of course, was the high end of the cinema trade – a showpiece building fit for celebrity-studded premieres and gala occasions. Spread out across London were literally hundreds of smaller picture houses, from the local Odeons owned by Oscar Deutsch which had been springing up since 1928 ('**O**scar **D**eutsch **E**ntertains **O**ur **N**ation', as his publicity had it), to the tiniest fleapit, struggling by on fewer staff than Mr Cruss had chefs.

This was the age of the classic stars such as Clark Gable and Claudette Colbert, whose romantic comedy *It Happened One Night* broke box office records that year. The Hollywood glamour machine was operating at full throttle, with the major studios able to spend the then colossal sum of £250,000 for a prestige production like *Grand Hotel* (1932), although this was a bargain compared to the £800,000 Howard Hughes had spent on the air warfare picture *Hell's Angels* (1930). The average American film at that time cost around £70,000 to produce, which was considerably more than the £20,000 spent making the equivalent British production.

Home-grown films were certainly popular, shot at eleven major studios in and around London, including Gainsborough in Islington; Gaumont-British at Shepherd's Bush; Associated Radio Pictures at Ealing; Warner Brothers/First National at Twickenham; or the giant Elstree with its ten sound stages, home of British & Dominion, British International and others. Here the major stars were people like Gracie Fields – the music hall singer from Rochdale – or the husband and wife team of Jack Hulbert and Cicely Courtneidge, who turned to film after a stage career in revues in order to pay their debts.

Pictures featuring well-known musicians were also popular. The bandleader Roy Fox, familiar to the public through his regular Wednesday night radio broadcasts for the BBC and his stage shows at the Palladium, showed up in films such as *A Night Like This* (1932), which was adapted from a Ben Travers play, or *Britannia of Billingsgate* (1933), a glamorous tale set in a London chip shop. In both of the latter, Roy appeared simply as an unidentified bandleader, but in 1934, his new film placed him centre stage under his own name in the radio-themed musical, *On The Air*.

On 6 August 1934, East End residents had the opportunity to see this picture, in a double bill with a 1933 US film called *The Girl From Georgia* (aka *Her Secret*), at the Palace Cinema, 156 Bow Road. This picture house opened for business in 1923, but the building in its former incarnations had also been home to a pub, then a Victorian music hall and later a theatre. As it turned out, the present cinema structure was not long for this world, and would be rebuilt in the Deco style the following year. (This in its turn was demolished in 1960, and today the site, just to the east of Bow Church DLR station, is occupied by modern flats.)

While certainly not as grand as West End flagship cinemas like the Empire, Leicester Square or the 5,500-seat Trocadero, Elephant & Castle (the largest in the country), it still held almost a thousand people. Jointly owned by David Weinberg and Neville White, the Palace was managed by thirty-year-old Dudley Hoard, who lived on-site in a second-floor flat at the rear of the balcony together with his wife Maisie.

Many families visited the pictures several times a week in this era, long queues at the box office were common, and the Palace would have taken a respectable amount of money on most days. For this reason, like all cash businesses, it presented a tempting target for local criminals.

The last evening show was over. On the night of 6 August, the audience at the Palace had gazed at the big screen showing Roy Fox conducting his big band jazz, comedian Max Wall as a character called 'Boots', and popular music hall 'sand dance' act Wilson, Keppel & Betty pretending to be Egyptians. Suitably entertained, they made their way home, leaving Dudley Hoard and his staff to count the takings and lock up, after which Mr Hoard and his wife went to bed. To all intents and purposes, it was just another ordinary night.

At 8 am the following morning, Mr C.J. Bannister happened to be walking past the cinema when he was stopped in his tracks by the sound of female screaming from inside the building: 'A woman cleaner ran out and told me that Mr and Mrs Hoard were terribly hurt. I ran down the road and fetched a policeman.'

Mrs Brinklow, who gave him the alarm, had herself been alerted by a fellow-cleaner, Mrs Earrey, who discovered something was terribly wrong when she went up as usual to tidy the balcony area and the manager's flat. As she told reporters:

'I found Mr Hoard lying bleeding on the balcony near the stairs to the flat. He had been battered about the head, and looked as if he was dead. I ran up to the flat, and in the bedroom found Mrs Hoard lying on the bed, covered with blood. She was in her nightdress and was moaning faintly. I gasped: "My God, mum, what's happened?" She looked at me, only moaned, and turned her head away. I dashed from the flat, and in my haste, tripped up and fell headlong down the stairs, injuring my left leg. I screamed, and told another cleaner about my discoveries, and she ran out, screaming "Murder! Fetch the police!"'

Plain-clothes and uniformed police swiftly arrived, some of them in patrol cars fitted with the very latest technology available – 'wireless receiving sets in constant touch with Scotland Yard'. They combed the interior, as well as the roof and neighbouring buildings. Scuff-marks on the balcony staircase walls were found to match with paint scrapings on the soles of Mr Hoard's leather slippers, apparently dislodged as he kicked out in the frantic struggle for his life. There was blood everywhere, and on the wall near the body, the gory print left by a man's hand.

Mr Bannister, who had run off to raise the alarm, returned in time to watch from outside on Bow Road as grim evidence of the night's events was revealed:

'I saw the couple carried out of the cinema. Both had been wrapped in blankets. Mrs Hoard had terrible cuts on the back of her head and Mr Hoard was covered in blood from a wound on the top of his head. They looked as though they had been attacked with a bludgeon.'

News quickly filtered through to the owners of the cinema. One of them, David Weinberg, arrived and was allowed inside to inspect the scene and offer any assistance the police might require, in particular concerning the likely motive for the assault. If the object was robbery, there would have been a fair amount of cash in the building, because the Monday had been a bank holiday, so the entire takings for the three-day weekend would still have been in the safe. As with many of those caught up in this affair, Mr Weinberg appeared happy to keep the waiting newspaper reporters informed:

'It seems that Mr Hoard and his wife were suddenly attacked in their bedroom. Mr Hoard must have put up a desperate struggle. There were bloodstains running all the way from his room along the vestibule outside the balcony to the roof. The detectives have explored every inch of the cinema, but so far they are puzzled as to how anybody could have got in. Until I arrived here with my duplicate keys, it was thought that the safe had not been touched. It was empty, however, when I opened it, and it seems that the thieves must have taken Mr Hoard's keys and ransacked it at leisure. Search has been made to try and find the instrument with which the couple were bludgeoned but so far no trace of it has been discovered.'

Over £100 in banknotes and coins was missing, a fair sum in a year when a double room including breakfast at the Regent Palace Hotel in Piccadilly was sixteen shillings (roughly eighty pence in today's money). Even so, this was hardly a fortune, yet it cost manager Dudley Hoard his life. He died shortly after 3 pm that afternoon, while his wife lay seriously ill at nearby St Andrew's Hospital.

Maisie Hoard, though suffering from terrible injuries, had been conscious at the time the cleaner raised the alarm and later that day was able to speak about the circumstances of the attack. Her words appear to have been paraphrased or tidied up before being released by the police to the press, since she was still in very poor health:

'In the early hours my husband and I were awakened by the ringing of a bell. Mr Hoard hurriedly put on some clothes, and I remember him remarking, "Who on earth is that at this time of the night?" Then he went into the sitting room, which adjoins the bedroom, and the next moment I heard sounds of a struggle and of men's voices raised in anger.'

Rising from her bed, she went to investigate, and saw her husband 'struggling desperately with a tall, fair-haired man, who had a mallet or hammer in his hand'. Mrs Hoard had just a moment to take in the scene, before she herself was struck down from behind: 'I did not see the man who attacked me, but I would recognise the man who was struggling with my husband.'

Maisie was in fact too ill at this point to be given the news that her husband had died. She was very lucky to have survived, and her evidence allowed the police immediately to issue a detailed description of the suspect. Their current theory was that the man had concealed himself somewhere in the building after the last show had finished, but their published statement – in which the suspect's hair had mysteriously changed from fair to dark – made no mention of a second attacker:

A man, who is described as being 22 years of age, 5ft 10in. or over, complexion pale, clean shaven, long, dark hair, dressed in a dark suit, and no hat, is believed to have left the cinema by an exit door at the rear at about 4.30 a.m. on August 7. It is possible that he hired a taxi cab near the scene of the crime. His clothing is probably considerably blood-stained.

The person responsible was clearly a very dangerous individual, who had turned a simple robbery into a lethal attack, leaving one person dead and very nearly killing another. He probably thought that he had left behind no witnesses, yet the front-page reports in the newspapers of Wednesday 8 will have told him that he had been seen, and his description was being circulated all over London.

All things considered, it was a good time to run.

At the Palace Cinema, there might have been a murder, but the film shows continued, and the stalls were packed as the building rang to the sounds of Roy Fox and His Orchestra while the police continued their investigations up in the sealed-off balcony area. There had been long queues down the street on Wednesday 8, the day the story first appeared in the newspapers, and the cinema was late in opening due to the police presence. The careful search conducted that day yielded results – the most important of which was the discovery of a hatchet (mistakenly described in some reports as a hammer) lying on waste ground behind the building. The section of wall with the bloody handprint was carefully removed and sent away for forensic examination, as were several hairs found nearby, thought to have been wrenched off from the attacker's head by Mr Hoard.

One result of the intense publicity surrounding the case was that a man had come forward that day to tell that police that he had been passing the cinema at around 3 am on the night of the murder and had seen someone answering the general description of the fugitive running out of the alleyway leading from the rear of the building. The suspect in question then boarded a taxi around the corner in Campbell Road.

On Thursday 9, two days after the murder was discovered, the front page of the *Daily Express* devoted a fair amount of space to the continuing relationship problems of a pair who had been Hollywood's most glamorous couple in the silent cinema days, Mary Pickford and Douglas Fairbanks, Sr. The page was dominated, however, by the murder at the Palace:

CINEMA CRIME
DETECTIVES' ALL-NIGHT WAIT FOR MAN

The great man hunt for the murderers of Dudley Hoard, the thirty-five-year-old manager of the Palace Cinema, Bow Road, E, took a dramatic turn last night. Three C.I.D. officers visited a house in the Poplar district, where they wished to interview a young man who has not been seen at his work since Monday night . . . The detectives made a thorough search of the rooms and dug in a small garden at the back of the house.

It was described as the 'biggest East End man-hunt since the Ripper', with over two hundred statements already taken from members of the public. Unsurprisingly, the police were said to be on the lookout for impecunious young men who might have been spending unusual amounts of money in the last two days. They also sent plain-clothes officers into picture houses during shows in order to eavesdrop on conversations, on the theory that the suspects were 'possibly unemployed and inveterate cinema-goers'. Meanwhile, at the hospital, Mrs Hoard remained unaware that Dudley was dead, although she must have been suspicious, since she kept asking, 'Where is my husband? Why doesn't he come to me? Are you sure he is quite safe?' The medical authorities, eventually judging that she was now able to withstand the shock of the news, duly informed her that he had died. It was Thursday, 9 August – their wedding anniversary.

Later that day came a breakthrough: Scotland Yard issued a photograph of their chief suspect, together with the following description: 'The police require to interview John Frederick Stockwell, aged nineteen; height 5ft. 7in. or 8in.; complexion pale; hair light brown, fairly long, parted at the side; eyes brown; long face.' Stockwell was said to be dressed in a brown suit, cream shirt and brown shoes, and was described as someone who 'seldom wears a hat or cap, and has a small camera'. Also, as if to confirm the theory that many victims of murder are killed by people they know, rather than by strangers, the police revealed that John Stockwell was one of the staff at the Palace: 'He left his employment at the cinema early on Wednesday, August 8, and he may be accompanied by another young man, slightly his senior, description not known.'

Despite the heroic efforts of inventive crime novelists through the decades, it seemed once again that a murder suspect would turn out to be exactly the person nearest at hand, and glaringly obvious. At the time of the Hoard murder, two of England's queens of crime fiction were at work on new novels: Agatha Christie was writing the next Poirot case, *Death In The Clouds*, in which virtually all the passengers on a cross-Channel flight are suspected of murder, while Margery Allingham had just started a new book, *Flowers For The Judge*, featuring her detective hero Albert Campion unravelling a case involving mysterious disappearances, carbon monoxide poisoning and a missing manuscript. Both authors would probably have been unimpressed by the idea of a plot in which Scotland Yard stake out the house of the sole likely suspect, owing to the fact that he has absconded from his workplace shortly after a theft and murder have been committed there.

There was also little mystery surrounding the identity of the murder weapon. The bloodstained hatchet found just behind the cinema had samples of human hair clinging to it, which, when analysed, proved to have come from the head of the victim. However, since it might provide a further link to the murderer, the police also issued a picture and detailed description of the item:

> The attention of the public residing or trading in the East End of London is drawn to the photograph of the hatchet or chopper. This implement was used by the murderer and left behind at the scene of the crime. Its dimensions are 15¼in. in length overall, the blade is 5¼in. wide, very rusty and blunt; the head of the blade is very much blurred from rough usage. Anyone in the east End missing such an implement, which may have been left lying about in some yard, mews, stable, coal yard, wood yard or work-shop, is requested to communicate immediately with the nearest police station or New Scotland Yard.

As if the murderer had not left enough incriminating evidence behind, the rubber flooring of the stalls also revealed bloody footprints and hand-prints, so the relevant section was removed and taken away for forensic examination. Having satisfied themselves that the building had yielded up whatever clues it contained, the police then lifted their restrictions and allowed the balcony to open once more during film shows.

It was by this time mid-August, and the traditional English seaside resorts were crowded with holidaymakers. One of the most popular, Brighton, had recently been in the news for crime-related reasons; there were two so-called 'Brighton Trunk Murders' that year. Sun-seekers not wishing to encounter dismembered bodies in packing cases could have opted instead to visit the East Anglian coast, but even that turned out to have links to homicide.

People pick up all sorts of things on the seashore; pebbles, drift-wood, shells. On the beach at Lowestoft in Suffolk on the morning of Friday, 10 August there was something more substantial, which had not been thrown up by the tide. It was a 'neatly folded bundle of clothing', and in one of the pockets, half a third-class return ticket from London to Lowestoft, and a Post Office savings book in the name of John Frederick Stockwell. In response to this, at the request of the police, BBC Radio began broadcasting a description of the man over the air, and the morning papers were full of his name and image. He had arrived in Lowestoft two days earlier, paying a week's rent on a room at the house of Mrs Tripp in Albany Terrace. He gave his name as Jack Barnard, and she thought him 'a nice boy', as she said that day:

'When asked about terms, he said he could pay anything from 30s to £2 a week, and we agreed on 35s.. . . At 7.30 this morning he went out and returned to breakfast at 8.30. He took up a picture paper and opened it. Almost at once he threw it on the table and took up a book he had been reading. About two minutes later he got up from the table saying, "I'm full up. I think I'll go out. I'm going to Yarmouth and won't be back all day!"'

A short while after he left her house, Mrs Tripp became suspicious and decided to check her lodger's room. Picking up his suitcase, she thought it seemed far too light, and indeed it appeared to have nothing inside. Convinced that something was amiss, she asked her neighbour to run and fetch the police. The suspect had temporarily escaped their grasp, but he had kindly given the constabulary notice of where he was heading. Duly forewarned, and also aided by Mrs Tripp's description of his current appearance, the police issued a further statement to the public:

Stockwell was positively seen in Lowestoft at 9 am today. He has abandoned the clothing and is now wearing a new blue suit, new black shoes or boots, and is carrying a new fawn mackintosh. It is possible he will make for Yarmouth or elsewhere on the coast.

The suspect turned out to be a man of his word: having told Mrs Tripp where he was going, he duly appeared just after 6 pm at the Metropolitan Hotel, Great Yarmouth, a short distance up the coast from Lowestoft. He checked in under the uninspired false name of J.F. Smith, but, in view of the considerable publicity surrounding the case over the previous few days, it was hardly surprising that he was identified by the staff, who called the police after recognising him from newspaper photographs. Stockwell was arrested at 6.30 pm and held in custody by the local constabulary to await the arrival from London of the officer in charge of the case, Chief Inspector Fred Sharp. He gave up without a struggle.

Having spent the days since the murder scanning the newspapers for clues to the police pursuit of him, John Stockwell might not have been shown all the articles about him that appeared on many front pages the morning after his arrest. Of course, there were other stories that day: Greta Garbo was rumoured to be coming to England to make her next film; baseball legend Babe Ruth – 'The Sultan of Swat' – announced his retirement; Scotland Yard's first police pilot was pictured next to his gyrocopter, ready to monitor London's traffic from above. There were also large adverts for an article by former prime minister Lloyd George to run in the following day's *Sunday Express* under the reassuring title 'War Impossible For Ten Years', so presumably he took his crystal ball back to the shop five years later and asked for a refund.

Despite all this competition, the lead story in the *Daily Mirror* was the apprehension of suspected hatchet-murderer John Stockwell. He stared out from the cover, wearing an open-neck shirt and holding up what appeared to be his pet dog for the camera. He was not smiling and looked very young – but then, at nineteen he was still two years away from being able to vote.

Back in London, the inquest into the death of Dudley Hoard opened at Poplar Coroner's Court, outside which stood crowds of onlookers. Dudley's wife was still confined to hospital, but his mother, Mrs Jane Hoard, appeared and gave evidence. The coroner, Dr R.L. Guthrie, asked her if her son had any enemies, to which she replied, 'Well, there were two men he had to dismiss when he was at Camden Town . . . on the instructions of the proprietor because of the expense. These two men had wives and children.' There followed medical evidence from pathologist Dr Temple Gray, who stated that death was due to multiple scalp wounds and fractures of the skull. Hoard 'must have been a powerful man, and the evidence showed there had been a tremendous struggle', said Gray, reconstructing the grim last moments of the manager as he fought for his life:

'It was obvious that he must have been struck from behind, and that the weapon had a cutting edge and also a serrated edge. After being hit it was obvious that Mr Hoard must have got up because that explained the blood on the mirror [in the sitting room]. He must have left the room and then have had his head dashed against an uncovered stone wall . . . I think he was seized by the throat when his head was dashed against the wall.'

On Saturday, 11 August, having spent the night in the cells at Yarmouth Police Station, John Stockwell was taken back to London by Chief Inspector Sharp and charged with murder soon after his arrival at Bow Road. The body of Dudley Hoard, meanwhile, was released from Poplar mortuary and conveyed to his mother's house in Croydon, awaiting burial. As for Dudley's wife, she remained in hospital, though showing signs of recovery.

It may have been the height of the summer holiday season, but violent storms battered London on the Sunday, with severe flooding and houses struck by lightning. Stockwell remained in custody throughout the weekend, and was then taken to Thames Police Court on Monday 13 and charged with wilful murder. This was also the day that Mr and Mrs W.H. Hoard, together with their three daughters, watched the interment of their son Dudley at Mitcham Road Cemetery, Croydon in a quiet ceremony, the details of which had not been announced, in an effort to avoid crowds arriving to watch. The hearse was preceded by a police car, and there were more police dotted around the cemetery. Despite these precautions, at least one press photographer learned of the event, and a photo of the mourners at the graveside duly appeared on the front page of the *Daily Mirror*.

Making his first appearance in court, John Stockwell, apparently still dressed to blend in with seaside holidaymakers, 'stepped into the dock briskly, wearing a blue suit, an open-neck tennis shirt and white canvas shoes'. Although pale, he seemed composed, but when Chief Inspector Sharp began to give evidence of Stockwell's arrest on a charge of the wilful murder of Dudley Hoard 'by striking him on the head with an axe at the Palace Cinema, and also for wounding Mrs Hoard by striking her with an axe', he put his head in his hands, and the magistrate allowed him to sit down. Sharp reported that upon arrest in Yarmouth, the prisoner had responded, 'The only thing I can say is that I did not intend to kill him', and had repeated virtually the same phrase the following day, during questioning at Bow Police Station.

The magistrate Mr Dixon granted the prisoner legal aid on the grounds that he had 'no means', and also gave permission for him to be visited by 'a woman . . . and some other friends', before remanding him in custody at Brixton prison for eight days. Four days later, it was announced that Stockwell was ill and had been moved to the prison infirmary. The condition of Maisie Hoard, still in hospital herself, was described as 'comfortable'.

John Stockwell had recovered sufficiently by the time proceedings resumed at Thames Police Court on Tuesday, 21 August. While the initial hearing had only served to outline the crime and give a description of the injuries suffered by the Hoards, considerably more was now revealed. The accused, an attendant at the Palace, had worked there for several months. He had been on duty on the night of 6 August, but had left the building as normal at the end of his shift, and was not the last member of staff there. He had then been seen in the High Street at around 11.20 pm. However, there remained the question of the possibility of a second man being involved, and the witness who had seen someone running from an alley down the side of the cinema late that night swore that it had not been Stockwell.

The court heard that on the day that Stockwell had left Lowestoft and fled to Yarmouth, the Lowestoft police had received a handwritten letter from him, which had been posted earlier that morning, probably around the time that he left the bundle of clothing on the beach. It read:

Dear Sir,
By the time you get this letter I shall be dead, as I am going to drown myself. I want to confess to attacking Mr and Mrs Hoard at 7.40 am on Tuesday. I am very sorry I killed him, as I did not intend to. I am writing you this as I cannot possibly go on any longer. I do not get any

sleep as a picture haunts my brain, and I cannot face the ordeal of a trial. I cannot go into details. I cannot bear to think of it. I am sorry for what I have done.

J.F. Stockwell

Sending a letter and leaving clothing and a Post Office book on the beach might simply have been aimed at throwing the police off the scent, but conversely, it is possible that he fully intended to drown himself and at the last moment could not bring himself to do it. The note of remorse in the letter seems genuine. (Despite the undoubted savagery of the hatchet attack on the unarmed cinema manager and his wife, the impression created by Stockwell both at the time of his arrest and during his various court appearances is hardly that of some flinty-eyed murderer like Clyde Barrow or Bonnie Parker, the psychopathic couple gunned down three months earlier in Texas, who once drove up to a policeman directing traffic purely for the 'enjoyment' of blowing his head off with a shotgun and then driving away laughing.) The sense of Stockwell as someone horrified by what he had done was further strengthened by the testimony of Chief Inspector Boulton of the Yarmouth police, who told the court that, when arrested, the suspect had said, 'Every bit of it is true. I am guilty of the crime.'

The account of his movements that Stockwell gave to the Yarmouth police, covering the days since the murder, had been thoroughly checked in the interim, and it appeared that he was telling the truth. The details concerning his living arrangements, and actions on the morning that the murder was discovered, were revealed to the court:

> Stockwell lodged with Mrs Roake and her family in Empson Street, and had done so for about three years. On August 7, Stockwell got up, and, as was his custom, left the house with Miss Violet Roake, with whom he was on affectionate terms. Miss Roake would say she did not notice anything unusual. They walked to the Seven Stars public house, where Miss Roake caught an omnibus. The last she saw of Stockwell he was walking along High Street, Bow, in the direction of the Palace Cinema.

The High Street in question is Bromley High Street, a few hundred yards south of where the cinema then stood. (The Seven Stars is no longer open for business, but the building still stands at 94 Bromley High Street, on the corner where the road joins St Leonard's Street. Empson Street is a little further south, not far from the current site of Devons Road DLR station.)

Although in her initial statement to the police, Mrs Hoard had spoken of being attacked 'in the early hours', it was suggested to the court that the crime was in fact committed by Stockwell that morning, between 7.40 am when he parted from Miss Roake and 8.35 am when he arrived back at Empson Street. That evening, Stockwell and his girlfriend went out for a date as normal – in fact, even after all that had happened, he still chose to go to the pictures, and took her to the Stoll Theatre in Kingsway. Having brutally attacked two people with an axe earlier in the day, for relaxation he chose a programme comprised of *The House of Connelley* (a Janet Gaynor romance set during the American Civil War), *Search For Beauty* (a comedy drama starring Buster Crabbe, shortly before he became Flash Gordon) and one of Walt Disney's Technicolor 'Silly Symphony' shorts, *The China Shop*. It would prove to be the couple's last date. The following morning, Stockwell saw Miss Roake to the bus stop as usual, but then made his escape to Lowestoft.

The most startling evidence of all came from Chief Inspector Sharp of Scotland Yard, who told the court that in the car on the way back from Yarmouth to London, Stockwell had allegedly made a detailed confession, which contained the following:

'I first thought of doing this last Saturday. On Sunday night I found the axe in the yard where I was living . . . When I went with my girl to the bus on Tuesday I carried the axe under my coat. I left her and went straight to the cinema. I got in by shaking the door at the front and twisting the handle. I went to the flat, rang the bell, and Mr Hoard came to the door. I said, "I have lost a ten shilling note in the hall," and asked him if I could look for it. He said, "Certainly." He went to close the door when I pulled it open and tried to hit him with the axe. He ran into the room and I followed him and hit him on the head with the axe from behind. He fell and I hit him several times again with the axe. His wife came out of the bedroom and I hit her on the head with the axe. I don't know if I hit her on the ground.'

If this testimony was to be believed, the accused had just convicted himself out of hand.

After a further few days on remand, John Stockwell appeared yet again in court, and Chief Inspector Sharp was questioned about the sensational statement that Stockwell had apparently made to him on the journey between East Anglia and London. He admitted that three hours had elapsed between the statement being made and the time when he, Sharp, had written it out from memory. He also said that he had not read it back to the prisoner afterwards. The remainder of the hearing consisted of the defence asking questions about the mysterious second man – seen by an informant who himself gave a false name – said to have run away from the cinema at 3 am after dropping a pair of pliers and some keys, then boarded a taxi. Clearly, in the face of apparent confessions from John Stockwell, this confusion surrounding another man was the only real possibility of avoiding a guilty verdict. The keys, however, turned out to have nothing whatever to do with the cinema, which helped put paid to the 'second man' theory. Things were looking decidedly grim for the accused, not least when Sergeant Archie Vickers of the Lowestoft police gave evidence that he had searched the room occupied by Stockwell at Mrs Tripp's boarding house, and found several items of bloodstained clothing which had been left behind.

The hearings continued intermittently through September. At one of these the celebrated forensic witness Sir Bernard Spilsbury, who had performed the post-mortem on Mr Hoard, testified that the victim had died from at least fourteen separate blows. Stockwell's London landlady, Mrs Roake, gave evidence of his home sleeping arrangements, and her daughter Violet – Stockwell's girlfriend – also took the stand, refusing to look in his direction as she testified about their meeting on the day that news of the murder first appeared in the papers:

> 'He had bought a newspaper, and I passed a few remarks about the murder in the cinema. I said it was a funny thing to kill a man for money. He replied that it was a ghastly trick to kill someone for money.'

The case concluded on 18 September, and John Stockwell was duly sent for trial at the Central Criminal Court, Old Bailey, on a charge of murder, to which he pleaded not guilty and reserved his defence.

The front page of the *Daily Express* on 23 October recorded a rare moment in the UK justice system – a judge twice putting on the traditional black cap used when condemning a prisoner to death, in other words handing down two capital sentences in one day:

> WOMEN JURORS SEE TWO DEATH SENTENCES
> They Would Not Look At The Black Cap

One of these sentences, after an extremely short trial which mostly reiterated the evidence already laid out in the preceding hearings at the Thames Police Court, was that of John Stockwell, found guilty of murdering Dudley Hoard at the Palace Cinema. The other man sentenced to death that day was a Cypriot, Georgius Georgiou, who killed a Bloomsbury boarding-house keeper. In Stockwell's case, however, there was a plea for mercy, apparently from two female members of the jury:

> The two women, both middle-aged, seemed deeply affected when they listened to the black-capped judge utter the words which doomed this boyish-looking, self-confessed murderer to the gallows. The jury added a humane rider to their verdict – they recommended the youth to mercy.

Normally, if a jury had returned a guilty verdict in a capital trial, they were excused, and a new jury was selected for the next one, but Stockwell had altered his plea to guilty shortly after the Crown outlined its case, thus ending the trial almost before it had begun. Therefore the jury delivered their verdict without retiring from the room, and were then retained for the next case, which also concluded that day.

The date for the execution was set for 14 November. In the weeks following the trial, it was thought that the plea for clemency might well

succeed. By this era, the beginnings of the anti-capital punishment movement were stirring, and Stockwell's youth provided a focus for calls from
various quarters that the Home Secretary should commute the sentence
to life imprisonment. A petition was organised, which garnered many
signatures. However, one person who was vehemently set against this –
understandably so – was Mrs Maisie Hoard, who told the press from her
bed at St Andrew's Hospital:

> 'How can I forgive the man who murdered my husband, the man who has
> robbed me of everything that counted in the world to me?. . . I cannot
> forgive. I cannot forget . . . he struck until he almost hacked him to pieces.
> Could any woman forgive a man who did that to her husband?'

The Home Secretary apparently agreed with her, and on 12 November
announced that the sentence would be carried out. This was greeted with
headlines that announced 'BOY MURDERER HEARS "NO REPRIEVE"
DECISION'. His reported words upon learning this were, 'Why should
I worry? I don't mind dying. There is nothing to live for.'

His appetite was said to be hearty, and each night in the cell he was
allowed one bottle of beer, which he drank 'with the invariable toast,
"Here's to the next world."'

After a last conversation in the condemned cell with his brother the
night before, in which Stockwell predicted that the England football team
would win the next day's international fixture because they had picked
so many Arsenal men, he went to the scaffold on the morning of
Wednesday 14, apparently with a firm tread.

On the day of the execution, Dudley Hoard's widow once again spoke
out from her sick-bed of the terrible cost of the crime:

> 'I am not sorry for him. He was a degenerate of the worst kind . . . I
> have a scar across my eye which I shall carry for the rest of my life.
> He hacked my forehead to the bone . . . When my husband died,
> another manager was appointed to the cinema. I have now no
> home – nothing. I have nowhere to go, for I have no mother, brother
> or sister. My husband was uninsured – so I have no money. I do not
> ask for charity. All I want is work. Will someone give me a job as a
> housekeeper?'

Styllou Christofi on the front page of the *Daily Mirror*, 29 October, 1954

TWENTY

STYLLOU CHRISTOFI, THE OTHER RUTH ELLIS

1954

Anyone visiting the part of Hampstead around South End Green today – a short stroll from Keats's House, where the edge of the Heath meets the back gardens of large mid-Victorian houses and a two-bedroom flat costs upwards of half a million pounds – might be forgiven for thinking that this amenable location had always been expensive. Yet the area was portrayed with no great affection by George Orwell in *Keep The Aspidistra Flying* (1936), a novel written the previous year while he was working at the bookshop on the corner of South End Green, and living a few steps away at 3 Warwick Mansions.

The story's narrator, Gordon Comstock, holding down a job in a thinly fictionalised version of the same bookshop, describes the area as 'not definitely slummy, only dingy and depressing'. Yet he goes on to say that there were 'real slums hardly five minutes walk away. Tenement houses where families slept five in a bed.' At one point, Comstock gazes out of the bookshop window and imagines, with something like enthusiasm, a vast aerial bombardment flattening the district: 'squadron after squadron, innumerable, darkening the sky like clouds of gnats'. Five years later, when real bombs fell on London, there were anti-aircraft batteries and barrage balloons on Hampstead Heath, local people slept underground on the Northern Line platforms at Hampstead Tube, and Orwell himself served in the Home Guard, digging trenches in Regent's Park.

The war brought other changes. A considerable number of once-grand dwellings in roads like South Hill Park were converted into cheap rooming houses. By 1954, a journalist named Eve Perrick, writing a feature article in the *Daily Express* about her recent house-hunting activities, was moved to comment that although Chelsea was on the up, and some of those 'one-time meaner streets off the further reaches of the King's Road' had been reclaimed by what she termed the 'smart set', the part of Hampstead near the overground station – in other words, South Hill Park and South End Green – was really not acceptable. The house that she had viewed was, she explained, 'on the wrong side of the tracks'.

By no means everyone at the time would have shared that view. Back in 1914, London Transport memorably promoted the attractions of the district with a poster captioned 'Take Your Son and Heir Where There Is Sun and Air'. Orwell died in 1950, and Booklover's Corner, the bookshop where he had worked had, by 1954, become a café called Prompt Corner, with tables set out for endless games of chess. Writers, artists and actors continued to be drawn to Hampstead, just as they had since the time of Keats, and like Chelsea, the area provided a haven for those of a bohemian persuasion. A local pub, the Magdala, at the bottom end of South Hill Park, was the haunt of many such characters, as writer and Hampstead resident Oswell Blakeston reported at the end of the 1950s:

> Here, sooner or later, one may sample the full delights of Hampstead drinking, comparing news notes with film producers and television men, actors and actresses, writers and artists, psychiatrists and philosophers who know all about life because they're in it too, and maybe an eccentric like the lady who is rewriting the history of the world and leaving out all the nasty wars and the nasty generals.

It was here, in one of the lavatories, that Blakeston spotted a piece of graffiti which spoke volumes about the clientele; other pub conveniences might harbour scrawled threats directed at rival football teams or teenage gangs, but this particular message read 'Down With The Hallé Orchestra'.

Few of the locals would have thought that Hampstead was about to become the site of not one, but two separate front-page murder cases within the space of a year, both of which happened within a hundred yards of each other on South Hill Park.

On 28 July 1954, prime minister Winston Churchill was busily reshuffling his cabinet; among the appointments was that of Mr Henry Brooke, Conservative MP for Hampstead, who became Financial Secretary to the Treasury, on the princely salary of £2,000 a year. The previous evening, MPs had voted through the bill that would pave the way for the country's first commercial television channel, while on this day they were deeply involved debating the rising tensions developing in one of Britain's colonies, the Mediterranean island of Cyprus. Television had come a long way since its early days in the 1930s, with the coronation of Elizabeth II in 1953 prompting many to invest in a TV set, but the cinema was still big business. Occasionally, film stars could also be seen on the London stage, like Richard Attenborough, who was currently treading the boards in Agatha Christie's whodunnit *The Mousetrap* (soon to chalk up an impressive two whole years at the same theatre, although the Windmill Theatre's motionless nude extravaganza, *Revuedeville*, was already in its twenty-third consecutive year).

That summer evening in South Hill Park, close to Hampstead Heath overground station, John Young noticed a fire in the back garden of a neighbouring house. It was nearly midnight. Moving closer, he came to the conclusion that one of the occupants was burning a life-size shop window dummy – a 'wax figure', as he later described it. A woman was bending over the flames, stirring up the fire in order to encourage it. Satisfied that everything was in order, he went back into his own house and put the matter out of his mind. A little later the same night, at around 1 am, a passing motor car was flagged down in the street near number 11 South Hill Park, by a middle-aged woman. According to the occupants of the car, a Mr Harry Burstoff and his wife, the woman was apparently in distress: 'Please come,' she said. 'Fire burning. Children sleeping.' When they followed the woman to her house to investigate, they could see no sign of a fire, but, as she led them through the building, the Burstoffs were confronted with the sight of what appeared to be a body on the floor, its head covered with blood. Horrified, they asked for a phone in order to call the police. Having done that, they tried to get some sense out of the woman about what precisely had happened, as Mr Burstoff later testified: 'My wife said, "Was that your son lying there?" The woman said "No, my son marry

Germany girl he like. Plenty clothes, plenty shoes. Babies going to Germany."'

It was not her son, but her daughter-in-law lying there. This was a strange tale, that was to become stranger as it unravelled.

--------------------◆--◆--◆--------------------

As Mr and Mrs Burstoff would have immediately noticed, the woman who had flagged down their car spoke very little English. Her name was Styllou Christofi. She was from Cyprus, aged fifty-three, and had come over from her home village in order to stay with her son, a wine waiter who worked in the West End at the Café de Paris. The *Manchester Guardian*, in an unrelated feature article about London's Cypriot community which appeared two weeks after the strange events in South Hill Park, estimated that there were 20,000 Cypriots living in the city:

> It is mostly the young peasants who come to London now from Cyprus; with care they can manage it for £20, often the life savings of the family. The parents watch the sons go from the melon farms and the hot vineyards, knowing often that they are going to the other heat of basement kitchens but believing they will come back with the big money. London wages, even scullions' wages, sound rich to the villagers or fishermen of Cyprus . . . The majority of the Cypriots here work in catering trades. Nobody knows exactly why.

The article went on to assert that integration was rare, and that they kept mostly to their own communities, but Stavros Christofis, the wine waiter who lived at 11 South Hill Park, had broken the mould in several ways. Not only had he settled for good in the UK, but he had also married a German woman, Hella Christofis, née Bleicher. She was thirty-six, came originally from a mining town in the Ruhr, and had been in England for fifteen years. The couple had three children: Nicholas, eleven, Peter, ten, and Stella, eight – young, but hardly the 'babies' Styllou had made them out to be. As a mother, Hella was entitled to claim free orange juice for her children from the government, the local distribution point for which was the Drill Hall, a short walk away on Pond Street, a road running north off South End Green.

Martin Hart, who grew up in South Hill Park, was six years old in 1954, and remembers being taken to the Drill Hall at that time by his mother:

'We were living in South Hill Park, and the Drill Hall in Pond Street, that is where as children we were taken to get our free orange juice. When my grandfather moved to South Hill Park in 1926, a lot of the houses were single occupant. It was due to the war that a lot of these houses were, I won't say requisitioned, but the owners of the houses didn't live there, so they rented them out as rooming houses.'

Martin's mother and Hella Christofis, two women with young children, got to know each other when visiting the Drill Hall, as Martin recalls:

'We children would have been of a similar age. Yes, so mothers would talk together, and my mother said this German girl had very good English. She spoke it with a slight accent. My mother used to say, you know, Mrs Christofis, who lives down the road, she's complaining about her mother-in-law.'

Hella clearly blended in well with the local community, assisted by her language skills. She worked as a waitress in the West End, while her husband's workplace was one of London's most star-studded nightspots. Only a few weeks' earlier, on 21 June, Hollywood legend Marlene Dietrich had opened there, introduced by Noel Coward. Stavros would have served champagne to the 500 diners who had paid three guineas a head for cabaret and dinner, packed into the exclusive club which normally held only 350. Among the first-night audience enjoying Marlene's sultry renditions of songs like 'Falling In Love Again' were David Niven, Laurence Olivier and Deborah Kerr, dining on smoked salmon, pâté de foie gras, consommé, sole, chicken and strawberries. London might still have been in the midst of post-war austerity, but inside the walls of the Café de Paris there was little sign of it.

Both Mr and Mrs Christofis had come to London and made a life in Hampstead. A neighbour spoke highly of Hella to reporters on the day after her death:

'She was beautiful. So were her clothes. She was a laughing, gay young woman, attractive in appearance as well as in dress. My boy used to play with their three children, who were all looking forward to a holiday with their mother in Germany this week.'

Stavros's mother, Styllou, who spelled her second name Christofi, without the final 's', came over to live in the same house in the middle of 1953 and seems not to have integrated so well. Although one contemporary report stated that she spoke Greek, Italian and French, her English was extremely limited, and she needed an interpreter in order to answer the initial questions put to her by the Hampstead police that night. By all accounts, relations between her and her daughter-in-law Hella were strained during her extended stay, perhaps because of differing expectations of their respective roles in the family, as Martin Hart suggests:

'From what I understand his mother came from a small village in Cyprus. Which would have been very traditional, because you would have had the man of the house running the house, and the mother of the house – if you like, the *matriarch* of the house – was very powerful.'

None of this would have been out of the ordinary, and families across London where several generations shared the same accommodation probably encountered similar tensions. A particular point of contention was the fact that Hella was due to take the children off to Germany later that week, which her mother-in-law objected to for some reason. Now, in the early hours of the morning of 29 July, Hella lay dead, and Styllou was using what little English she knew to paint a very confusing picture. The police arrived at 2 am, and Stavros returned sometime around 4 am, having worked his normal late shift at the Café de Paris. What exactly had happened at number 11 was far from clear, but the deployment of a senior team of CID led by Superintendent Leonard Crawford, together with Scotland Yard fingerprint specialists, showed that the matter was being taken very seriously indeed.

The newspaper headlines the following day were full of Sir Winston's cabinet reshuffle and speculation about the future of Cyprus. Detectives had been questioning Styllou, Stavros and assorted neighbours while the dawn came up. At 6.30 am, as the first editions were on the streets,

Stavros was taken to the local police station, and at 7.15 am Styllou was also put in a car and taken there. The couple's three children were sent away to stay with family friends. Although Stavros was later allowed home by the authorities, Mrs Christofi was still being questioned with the aid of interpreters. Meanwhile, towards the end of the day, the post-mortem conducted by Home Office pathologist F.E. Camps – who had worked the previous year on the infamous case of John Christie, the multiple murderer of 10 Rillington Place – revealed that Hella Christofis had been strangled, apparently with a nylon stocking, then hit on the head, before her body was covered in petrol and set on fire.

During the first full day of their investigation, the police initially had a theory that the murderer might have been someone whom Hella had met in her day job in the West End, so the front page headlines when the story broke to the wider public on 30 July were full of speculation about the identity of the possible killer. 'Yard Probes The Double Life Of A Mother' was the *Daily Mirror*'s cover story, in which they reported that detectives had 'scoured the West End, asking people who knew her "Was there anyone who wanted her out of the way?"' The paper backed this up with information from the police that a blind neighbour, Mrs Isabella Boult, reported hearing a conversation between two unidentified men in the back garden of the Christofis house sometime around midnight. There was a suggestive tone given to the information that 'attractive Hella, mother of three, used to leave the quiet of Hampstead each evening and spend her nights in the clubland area of Mayfair and the West End', yet this was her job, and would have been entirely natural behaviour for many thousands of women who, like her, were working as waitresses. Still, putting the two pieces of information together, it was thought that she might have gone out on the night of the murder, and that two men might have followed her back to her home.

London clubs, mysterious killers, a late-night rendezvous, the possibility of someone having led a double life, and a police dragnet through the West End – this was all prime tabloid fodder. However, by the following day, 31 July, the focus narrowed sharply, and it seemed that the answer to this case lay much closer to home: 'MOTHER IN LAW OF 53 ON MURDER CHARGE,' said the *Daily Express*;

'CHARGE OF MURDERING DAUGHTER-IN-LAW,' said *The Times*.

Taken into custody and formally accused of the crime, Styllou Christofi replied in Greek, through an interpreter, seeking to account for some of the forensic evidence against her:

> 'I did not make use of any petrol, but some few days previously some petrol spilled on the floor. I did not pay any attention to it. I stepped on it and probably the smell was the result of that petrol. From this story I know nothing more.'

Remanded in custody at Hampstead Magistrates' Court for the first of several occasions in the coming months, Styllou kept essentially to the policy she had adopted since first running out into the road to flag down the car driven by the Burstoffs. All along she had claimed to be a bystander to events, unable to account for them, and just as mystified as anyone else. As the weight of forensic evidence mounted up, she retreated ever more into this uncomprehending stance. Three pieces of the scarf that was thought to have been used for strangulation were discovered under wet ashes in her dustbin; the fourth part was in the back yard. Hella's wedding ring had been found wrapped up in paper, hidden behind an ornament in Styllou's bedroom. The latter testified at the preliminary hearing that she had found it on the floor and mistaken it for a curtain ring, yet the police stated in response that there were no curtain rings of any kind being used at number 11. The evidence of the pathologist, Dr Camps, painted a grim picture:

> 'Death was due to asphyxia by a scarf, such as the one which had apparently been cut off the body after it had been burned. There was a fracture of the skull at the back, injuries to the face, bruising above the right ear and lacerations on the top of the scalp.'

As the prosecutor J.F. Claxton explained, these injuries were consistent with the deceased having been beaten over the head with a blunt instrument 'such as the ash plate of the kitchen boiler', and with a subsequent fall. On inspection, the ash plate proved to be bloodstained. L.C. Nickolls, from the Metropolitan Police Laboratory at Scotland Yard, further testified that two of the legs from the kitchen table had bloodstains, and there were further bloodstains on the lino floor. Both the table legs and the floor covering showed signs of having been washed or wiped afterwards.

Appearing at this preliminary hearing in Hampstead, the accused's son Stavros stated openly that his mother and his wife had not been on good terms. He agreed that Styllou's English was not good, and said that some three weeks before the murder, he and his wife had suggested to her that she should return to Cyprus, to which she had apparently responded, 'If you feel that way I'll go back.' Stavros Christofis also said that he felt that the wedding ring worn by his wife was a very tight fit, and could not possibly have fallen off accidentally.

Taking all the evidence into account, including the short statements in Greek uttered by the accused, whose own counsel described her in court as 'absolutely bewildered by the proceedings', it was no surprise that the Hampstead magistrates formally committed her on 7 September for trial at the Old Bailey.

Styllou Christofi was tried for murder in the autumn of 1954 – still a hanging offence at a time when, after many centuries of capital punishment in the UK, serious debates had been taking place as to its effectiveness as a deterrent. Since 1948, the MP for Nelson and Colne, Sydney Silverman, had been campaigning in parliament and outside for the abolition of hanging. There had been a Royal Commission on Capital Punishment which sat from 1949 to 1953, and public debate had been stirred by cases such as the execution of Timothy Evans on the perjured evidence of John Christie. Then, in 1953, the hanging of Derek Bentley prompted petitions, demonstrations outside the Home Secretary's house and Wandsworth prison and much debate in the press, especially in the pages of *Picture Post*.

Hanging was therefore a controversial issue in a way that it had not been in the eighteenth or nineteenth centuries. Yet in being tried for a capital crime, Styllou Christofi was more unusual: men were hanged every year, but no woman had suffered the death penalty in London since 1923, when Mrs Edith Thompson and Frederick Bywaters were hanged for murdering Edith's husband Percy. The most recent case in

Britain had been the previous year, when Louisa Merrifield was hanged at Strangeways in Manchester for murdering the woman she worked for by means of rat poison. Indeed, until 1954, only nine women had been hanged in England and Wales since 1900, compared to over 600 men. However, as the case came to trial at the Old Bailey on 25 October, the evidence proved every bit as damning as that presented at the initial sessions in Hampstead.

On the opening day of the trial, Mr Christmas Humphreys, for the prosecution, described the affair as 'a stupid murder by a stupid woman of the illiterate peasant type'. Humphreys, a well-known Crown Prosecutor who had appeared in both the Timothy Evans and Derek Bentley cases, went on: 'She really believed that by washing the floor she could eliminate bloodstains, and that with a small tin of paraffin she could so burn a body that it could not be recognised.' Mrs Christofi was, he concluded, 'a murderess who is remarkably tidy in clearing away the evidence of the murder'.

The following evening, in order to help the jury picture the events of the night of the killing, they were taken in a police coach up to Hampstead in the pouring rain to see the house at number 11 South Hill Park – by then sporting a 'For Sale' sign – in particular its kitchen and back yard area. A photo of them peering over part of the garden wall appeared on the front page of the *Daily Mirror*. The ten men and two women of the jury were also pictured by a *Daily Express* photographer who was there, while the paper's reporter described the scene as follows:

> With coat collars turned up against the pouring rain, an Old Bailey jury last night inspected a weed-ridden garden where a murder is alleged to have been committed on July 28. They squelched through the mud, clambered over a broken-down fence, and pointed down to where the body of 36-year-old Mrs Hella Dorothea Christofis was found . . . Furniture was brought from the court and put in the lounge to set the same scene as on the night of the alleged murder.

Styllou's defence was that two unknown men had killed her daughter-in-law and then escaped. Through the interpreter, she testified that on the night in question, she woke up, having smelled smoke. Going downstairs from her room on the fourth floor, she saw 'a man with a suitcase', and another man, who both ran away. Then she discovered Hella lying in the back yard 'with fire all around her'. She stated that twice within the previous eight months she had left the house where she lived with her son and daughter-in-law, but denied that this was because they had argued. Christmas Humphreys for the prosecution picked up on the question of antagonism between the two women:

Humphreys: 'You were jealous of Hella, weren't you, with her youth and pretty clothes?'
Christofi: 'I was not jealous of her.'
Humphreys: 'You thought you were not wanted and were being sent home to Cyprus?'
Christofi: 'No.'

Styllou's defence counsel, David Weitzman, QC, having presented her story that two unknown men were responsible, finally sought to reinforce her case by asking for categorical statements of innocence:

Weitzman: 'Did you kill your daughter-in-law?'
Christofi: 'Never.'
Weitzman: 'Did you strangle your daughter-in-law?'
Christofi: 'Never.'
Weitzman: 'Did you try to burn her?'
Christofi: 'Never.'

Summing up on 28 October, the trial judge Mr Justice Devlin said that if it could be shown that there was a reasonable possibility, rather than a figment of imagination, that the murder could have been committed by anyone else, then Styllou Christofi should be acquitted.

Having retired to consider the evidence, the jury at Number 1 Court at the Old Bailey took just two hours to decide that she was guilty of murder. Her son Stavros, husband of the deceased, was not present that day, as Styllou heard the verdict translated for her, flanked by three female warders. Mrs Christofi requested that she might address the court from the witness box, but this was denied, and she was taken to the condemned cell at Holloway prison.

On the day that Styllou Christofi was sentenced to death, life went on as usual. The morning papers reported that crime writer Sydney Horler, known for ingenious ways of murdering his characters, had died in Bournemouth: 'poison arrows, daggers, death rays, supernatural influences – he killed with them all'; that a magistrate from Worcester had declared it a disgrace that Oscar Wilde's house had just been honoured with a plaque, saying that he was 'nothing more than a common criminal convicted of one of the foulest crimes'; and that Marilyn Monroe had been in court and in ten minutes had secured a divorce from Joe DiMaggio.

An appeal was lodged against Styllou Christofi's conviction, but when it was heard on 29 November, it was dismissed in just four minutes. This was not surprising, since her defence counsel, David Weitzman, said that, having studied the case, he could find no point to put to the court. He described the trial judge's summing up as 'faultless, and indeed, put the case favourably from Mrs Christofi's point of view'.

Although it was unusual for a woman to be under sentence of death in England in the mid-twentieth century, the sympathy that Styllou Christofi might otherwise have aroused in the public mind was probably tempered by the conviction that she seemed to be guilty, and had brutally murdered another woman on the strange grounds that she did not want her to take her grandchildren off to Germany for a holiday. Opinion would have hardened against her on the day after her sentence, when it was revealed that she had stood trial for murder once before, at the age of twenty-four, back in Cyprus. Incredibly, the victim in that case was said to have been Styllou's own mother-in-law, who had been gruesomely killed by having a burning piece of wood rammed down her throat. Mrs Christofi and two other women had been found not guilty, but this information, when taken together with her 1954 offence, probably convinced many that she was a deeply disturbed individual. This was certainly the conclusion that Martin Hart's mother came to, as he recalls: 'My mother said, "God, Mrs Christofi's been killed by her bonkers mother-in-law." No, sorry, her "*nutty*" mother-in-law.'

By contrast, the public perception of the next, and last, woman sentenced to death in England, Ruth Ellis, was very different. This killing happened only six months after Mrs Christofi's trial, and, strangely enough, it happened in the same road where Hella was murdered, outside the Magdala pub at the bottom of South Hill Park. Ellis gunned down her lover, David Blakely, as he emerged from the Magdala, and several of the bullet holes are still visible today on the pub's exterior. What is even more of a coincidence is that Martin Hart and his father witnessed the latter killing, from a vantage point roughly thirty yards away outside Hampstead Heath overground station:

'I was by the station. It sounded like a car back-firing. I was on the corner, she [Ruth Ellis] was right outside the pub. Blakely ducked behind his car. They'd been in Tanza Road – he'd been to a party, they'd run out of booze, and that's the reason he had come down. I was with my father, and we were walking up the road. Well my father went forward to see if he could help. I think he forgot I was with him. And Mr Blakely was just lying there, with the blood going glug, glug, glug . . . My father thought he was dead. My grandfather was coming down the road to have a drink in here [The Magdala], and my father said to him, "I wouldn't go down there, someone's been shot." So my grandfather walked past him, looked at the body, said "Oh yes, so he has", and then walked up the road with us.'

Ruth Ellis was still holding the gun when an off-duty policeman, PC Thompson, rushed out of the pub and took it off her. The early headlines and pictures used by the newspapers speak volumes about the different perception of this crime compared to the earlier Christofi case: 'BLONDE MODEL ACCUSED OF KILLING ACE CAR RACING DRIVER', 'ASH BLONDE MODEL NEVER LOOKS AT THE GUN', 'THE BRIGHT LIGHTS LED HER TO THE DEATH CELL'. Here was a case involving nightclubs, fast cars, and a twenty-eight-year-old killer repeatedly identified not by her own name but just as a 'model'. By contrast, the few photos of Mrs Christofi that had been used in the press showed her unsmiling and middle-aged. More often, articles about the killing at 11 South Hill Park were illustrated with smiling shots of Hella and her husband, or featured the jury inspecting the crime scene. The avalanche of press which accompanied the trial and execution of Ruth Ellis far outweighed the attention given in the same media to the Christofi case a few months before – Ruth even had her exclusive memoirs of her relationship with David Blakely serialised in one of the Sunday papers in the weeks leading up to her death. Yet there were numerous similarites between the two cases. Not only did the murders happen within a hundred yards or so of each other, but the prosecuting counsel was the same man in each case, Christmas Humphreys. He secured a conviction against Ruth Ellis by asking just one simple question:

> Humphreys: 'When you fired the revolver at close range into the body of David Blakely, what did you intend to do?'
>
> Ellis: 'It is obvious that when I shot him I intended to kill him.'

After this admission, as the law stood, there was only one verdict that could have been reached, and no room for a reprieve.

In the case of Mrs Christofi, the new Home Secretary Gwilym Lloyd-George was petitioned by a group of MPs led by Sydney Silverman, attempting to persuade him that she should be spared execution on account of insanity. The prospect of this kind of plea had been raised during the time of her trial by the prison doctor at Holloway where she was held, Dr Thomas Christie. In his report, submitted on 5 October 1954, he wrote:

> The clinical picture is that of a non-systematised, delusional mental disorder. This is a disease of the mind. In my opinion, the fear that her grandchildren would not be brought up properly induced a defect of reason due to the above disease of the mind whereby, however much she may have been capable of appreciating the nature and quality of the acts she was doing, at the time of the acts, the defect of reason was such that she was incapable of knowing that what she was doing was wrong.

Yet the Home Office stressed that the Home Secretary had taken all such matters into consideration before turning down a reprieve, and he himself issued a statement the following week saying he had consulted three other doctors after 5 October to examine these claims, who had concluded 'that the prisoner was not, in their view, insane'. Her son Stavros Christofis told the press that Mrs Christofi had absolutely refused to plead 'guilty but insane', commenting: 'All the time my mother kept saying "I am a poor woman of no education – but I am not a mad woman. Never, never, never."'

On the morning of 15 December, Styllou Christofi was taken from the condemned cell at Holloway by Albert Pierrepoint, the public executioner, who had hanged John George Haigh, the acid bath murderer, Derek Bentley, Lord Haw Haw, John Christie and hundreds of others, and would go on to hang Ruth Ellis. In his remarkable autobiography, *Executioner: Pierrepoint*, he called her 'a grey-haired and bewildered grandmother who spoke no English', although in photos of her taken at the time of her arrest she appears to have dark hair. The journalist John Thompson, in an opinion piece published that morning, noted the fact that the vast majority of murders were committed by men, and that they were much more likely to hang for it when caught: 'Roughly, about one murderer in two is reprieved; but about nine murderesses in ten are reprieved.'

Seven months later, on the morning after Ruth Ellis's execution, the discrepancy in public reaction to the two cases was noted in the *Daily Mirror*'s front-page article ('Should Hanging Be Stopped?'), in which they asked the following bluntly phrased question:

> Some murderers – like Ruth Ellis – attract much public sympathy. There has been more talk about the fate of PRETTY YOUNG Ruth Ellis than there was about the similar fate of UGLY Mrs Christofi, aged fifty-three, who strangled her daughter-in-law.

Styllou Christofi and Ruth Ellis became the last two women to be hanged in Britain, although men were sent to the gallows for almost another decade. On the Sunday before Mrs Christofi's execution, long-time habitués of Hampstead's South End Green, sitting playing chess at Prompt Corner, might have noted that a former bookshop employee and resident was suddenly receiving a great deal of posthumous publicity, not all of it good. The BBC had transmitted a live two-hour television play based on George Orwell's final novel, *Nineteen Eighty-Four*, starring one of the finest actors in the country, Peter Cushing, as Winston Smith. Nine million viewers tuned in for the broadcast, and to judge from the number of phone calls and telegrams it prompted, a fair few of them were moved to complain about the graphic scenes of rats and torture in Room 101.

In 1946, the year he began writing *Nineteen Eighty-Four*, Orwell published an essay in the *Tribune* called 'The Decline of the English Murder', which might have struck a chord in the week of Styllou's execution. Advancing the argument that the public would not remember the crimes of today in the same way as those of the classic era, 'between 1850 and 1925' – the days of Jack the Ripper and Dr Crippen – he suggests that this is to do with the poor quality of crime in recent years. Orwell cites the case of Elisabeth Jones and Karl Hulton, convicted of a series of squalid, senseless wartime murders. The man was executed, the woman reprieved, despite widespread public calls for her to suffer the same punishment. He notes how few women have been hanged in Britain during the twentieth century, and asserts that 'the practice has gone out largely because of popular feeling against it'.

Oddly enough, Orwell had addressed the question of capital punishment at the very start of his literary career; one of his first published pieces was 'A Hanging', which appeared in the *Adelphi* magazine in 1931. Drawing on his experiences in the Indian Imperial Police in Burma during the 1920s, it depicts the banality and the matter-of-fact horror of a condemned man's last moments, observed by a policeman. Although it is often taken for straightforward reportage, some argue that it is in fact imaginative fiction and that Orwell never actually witnessed an execution. In the end, it probably does not matter. At the time he was writing, people had been judicially hanged in England for something close to a thousand years, but almost within a decade of his death – too late for Mrs Christofi or Ruth Ellis – this was to change. Until then, however, the grim procedure which had been enacted so often at Tyburn, Newgate and elsewhere in London would play itself out much as it always had:

He and we were a party of men walking together, seeing, hearing, feeling, understanding the same world; and in two minutes, with a sudden snap, one of us would be gone – one mind less, one world less.

Books

Thomas Allen: *The History and Antiquities of London, Westminster, Southwark, and Parts Adjacent,* London: George Virtue, 1839

Anonymous: *A Warning for Faire Women, Containing the most tragicall and lamentable murther of Master George Sanders of London Marchant, nigh Shooters Hill, Consented unto by his owne wife, acted by M. Browne, Mistris Drewry and Trusty Roger agents therein: with their severall ends,* London: Valentine Sims for William Aspley, 1599

Anonymous: *The Case and Memoirs of the Late Rev. Mr. James Hackman, And of his Acquaintance with the late Miss Martha Reay,* London: G. Kearsly, 1779

Richard Arnolde: *The Customs of London, Otherwise Called Arnold's Chronicle,* London: F.C. & J. Rivington (et al), 1811

Max Arthur: *The Last Post – The Final Word From Our First World War Soldiers,* London: Phoenix Books, 2006 (first published 2005)

T.F.T Baker & C.R. Elrington (eds.), A.P. Baggs, Diane K. Bolton, M.A. Hicks, R.B. Pugh: *The Victoria History of the County of Middlesex, Volume 6: Friern Barnet, Finchley, Hornsey with Highgate,* Oxford: Oxford University Press, 1980

Andrew Barrow: *The Flesh is Weak – An Intimate History of the Church of England,* London: Hamish Hamilton Ltd., 1980

E.C. Bentley: *Trent's Last Case,* London: Penguin Books, 1950 (first published 1912)

James Boswell (Frederick A. Pottle, ed.): *Boswell's London Journal, 1762–1763,* Edinburgh: Edinburgh University Press, 1991 (first published 1950)

James Boswell (Joseph W. Reed & Frederick A. Pottle, eds.): *Boswell, Laird of Auchinleck, 1779–1782,* Edinburgh: Edinburgh University Press, 1993 (first published 1932)

James Boswell (George Birkbeck Hill, ed.): *Life of Johnson,* New York: Harper & Brothers, 1891 (first published 1791)

Geoff Brandwood, Andrew Davison & Michael Slaughter: *Licensed to*

Sell – The History and Heritage of the Public House, London: English Heritage, 2004

Tom Brown: *The Works of Mr Thomas Brown in Prose and Verse; Serious, Moral and Comical*, London: Sam Briscoe, 1707

R.W. Chambers & Marjorie Daunt, eds.: *A Book of London English, 1384 –1425*, Oxford: The Clarendon Press, 1967 (first published 1931)

Thomas Codrington: *The Roman Roads in Britain*, London: The Society for Promoting Christian Knowledge, 1903

G.G. Coulton: *The Medieval Village*, Cambridge: Cambridge University Press, 1925

Sir Herbert Croft: *Love and Madness. A Story too True, in a Series of Letters Between Parties whose Names would perhaps be mentioned were they less known, or less lamented*, London: G. Kearsly, 1780

R.B. Dobson, ed.: *The Peasants' Revolt of 1381*, London: The Macmillan Press, 1983 (first published 1970)

Arthur Conan Doyle: *Memories and Adventures*, Oxford: Oxford University Press, 1989 (first published 1924)

The Penguin Complete Sherlock Holmes, London: Penguin Books, 2009 (first published 1930)

Philip Edwards: *Pilgrimage and Literary Tradition*, Cambridge: Cambridge University Press, 2005

Markman Ellis: *The Coffee-House – A Cultural History*, London: Phoenix, 2005 (first published 2004)

James Elmes: *A Topographical Dictionary of London and its Environs*, London: Whittaker, Treacher & Arnot, 1831

John W. Forney: *Letters from Europe*, Philadelphia: T.B. Peterson & Brothers, 1867

Celina Fox: *Londoners*, London: The Museum of London, 1987

John Foxe: *Foxe's Book of Martyrs – The Acts and Monuments of the Church, Book II*, London: George Virtue, 1851 (first published 1563)

Rowland Freeman: *Kentish Poets, Volume 1*, Canterbury: G. Wood, 1821

Francis Galton: *Finger Prints*, London: Macmillan & Co., 1892

Chris Given-Wilson: *Chronicles – The Writing of History in Medieval England*, Hambledon and London: Hambledon Continuum, 2004

John B. Gleason: *John Colet*, Berkeley: University of California Press, 1989

Arthur Golding: *A briefe discourse of the late murther of Master George Saunders, a worshipfull Citizen of London: and of the apprehension,* *arreignment, and execution of the principall and accessories of the same,* London: Henry Bynneman, 1573

Dennid Griffiths: *Fleet Street – Five Hundred Years of the Press,* London: The British Library, 2006

Edward Hall: *Hall's Chronicle – The Union of the Two Noble and Illustre Famelies of Lancastre and York, beeyng long in continual discension for the Croune of this noble realme,* London: J. Johnson & others, 1809 (first published 1542)

Mark Hallett & Christine Riding: *Hogarth,* London: Tate Publishing, 2006

T.C. Hansard, ed.: *The Parliamentary Debates from the Year 1803 to the Present Time, Volume XXII,* London: T.C. Hansard, 1812

Francis Hargrave: *A Complete Collection of State Trials and Proceedings For High Treason – The Fifth Edition,* Dublin: Graisberry & Campbell, 1793

John Harriott: *Struggles Through Life,* London: C. & W. Galabin, 1807

J.F.C. Harrison: *The Common People – A History from the Norman Conquest to the Present,* Beckenham, Kent: Croom Helm, 1984

William Harrison: *An Historicall Description of the Iland of Britaine,* London: Henry Denham, 1587

Peter Haydon: *Beer and Brittania – An Inebriated History of Britain,* Stroud, Gloucestershire: Sutton Publishing, 2001 (first published 1994)

John E.N. Hearsey: *Bridge, Church and Palace in Old London,* London: John Murray, 1961

Mark Herber: *Criminal London – A Pictorial History from Medieval Times to 1939,* Chichester, West Sussex: Phillimore & Co., Ltd, 2002

Edmund Hickeringill: *The Vindication of the Character of Priest-craft,* London: B. Bragge, 1705

Raphael Holinshed: *Holinshed's Chronicles of England, Scotland and Ireland, Volume IV,* London: J. Johnson & others, 1808 (first published 1577)

Edward Horton: *The Age of the Airship,* London: Sidgwick & Jackson, 1973

Philip Howard: *London's River,* London: Hamish Hamilton, 1975

Gerald Howson: *It Takes a Thief – The Life and Times of Jonathan Wild,* London: The Cresset Library, 1987 (first published 1970)

David Jardine: *A Reading on the Use of Torture in the Criminal Law of England,* London: Baldwin & Cradock, 1837

John Heneage Jesse: *London and its Celebrities,* London: Richard Bentley, 1850

Samuel Johnson (Rev. Robert Lynam, ed.): *The Works of Samuel Johnson, L.L.D.,* London: George Cowie & Co., 1825

William Kemp: *Kemp's Nine Daies Wonder: Performed in a Daunce from Norwich to London,* London: Camden Society, 1840

Andrew Knapp & William Baldwin: *The Newgate Calendar – Comprising Interesting Memoirs of the Most Notorious Characters Who Have Been Convicted of Outrages on the Laws of England., Volume 1,* London: J. Robins & Co., 1824

The Newgate Calendar – Comprising Interesting Memoirs of the Most Notorious Characters Who Have Been Convicted of Outrages on the Laws of England., Volume III, London: J. Robins & Co., 1825

Charles Lamb: *The Essays of Elia,* London: J.M. Dent & Co., 1900 (first published 1823)

J. Baxter Langley: *The Illustrated Official Guide and Tourist's Handbook to the North Eastern Railway and its Branches,* London: W.H. Smith & Sons, 1863

Jacob Larwood & John Camden Hotten: *English Inn Signs – The History of Signboards,* New York: Arco Publishing, 1985 (first published in London, 1866)

John Lewis-Stempel: *England: The Autobiography – 2,000 Years of English History By Those Who Saw It Happen,* London: Penguin Books, 2006 (first published 2005)

Fergus Linnane: *Madams – Bawds & Brothel-Keepers of London,* Stroud, Gloucestershire: Sutton Publishing, 2005

Thomas Babington Macaulay: *The History of England from the Accession of James II,* London: Longman, Brown, Green & Longmans, 1849–1861

Tim William Machan: *English in the Middle Ages,* Oxford: Oxford University Press, 2003

Sir Melville MacNaghten: *Days of My Years,* London: Edward Arnold, 1914

H C G Matthew & Brian Harrison, eds.: *Oxford Dictionary of National Biography,* Oxford: Oxford University Press, 2004

Henry Mayhew: *London Labour & the London Poor,* London: Charles Griffin & Company, 1864 (first published 1851)

R.J. Mitchell & M.D.R. Leys: *A History of London Life,* London: Pelican Books, 1964 (first published 1958)

Robert Nares: *A Glossary; or, Collection of Words, Phrases, Names and Allusions to Customs, Proverbs, &c.,* London: Robert Triphook, 1822

David Nokes: *Samuel Johnson – A Life,* London: Faber & Faber, 2009

Mavis & Ian Norrie: *The Book of Hampstead, Revised Edition* Hampstead: High Hill Books, 1968 (first published 1960)

John Northbrooke: *A Treatise against Dicing, Dancing, Plays, and Interludes, with Other Idle Pastimes,* London: H. Bynneman for George Byshop, 1577

George Orwell: *Decline of the English Murder and Other Essays,* London: Penguin Books, 1979 (first published 1965)

Keep the Aspidistra Flying, London: Penguin Books, 1975 (first published 1936)

Sir Thomas Overbury (Edward F. Rimbault, ed.): *The Miscellaneous Works in Prose and Verse of Sir Thomas Overbury, Knt.,* London: John Russell Smith, 1856

Henry Peacham the Younger: *The Worth of a Peny,* London, 1641

Edward Pearce: *The Great Man – Sir Robert Walpole: Scoundrel, Genius and Britain's First Prime Minister,* London: Jonathan Cape, 2007

A.H. Phillips: *Georgian Scrapbook,* London: T. Werner Laurie Ltd, 1949

Liza Picard: *Dr. Johnson's London – Everyday Life in London, 1740–1770,* London: Phoenix, 2003 (first published 2000)

Albert Pierrepoint: *Executioner: Pierrepoint,* London: Coronet, 1977 (first published 1974)

Henry R. Plomer: *A Dictionary of the Booksellers and Printers Who Were at Work in England, Scotland and Ireland from 1641 to 1667,* London: The Bibliographical Society, 1907

Raymond Postgate: *Murder, Piracy & Treason,* London: Jonathan Cape, 1925

J.B. Priestley: *The Prince of Pleasure and His Regency 1811–20,* London: Sphere Books, 1971 (first published 1969)

Peter de Rosa: *Vicars of Christ – the Dark Side of the Papacy,* London: Corgi, 1993 (first published 1988)

Cathy Ross & John Clark: *London – The Illustrated History,* London: Allen Lane, 2008

Richard Savage: *The Tragedy of Sir Thomas Overbury: As it is Acted at the Theatre-Royal in Drury-Lane by His Majesty's Company of Comedians,* London: Samuel Chapman, 1724

John Stow: *The Survey of London,* London: J.M. Dent & Sons, 1965 (first published 1598)

Philip Stubbes: *The Anatomie of Abuses – A Discoverie or brief Summarie of Such Notable Vices and Corruptions, as now raigne in many Christian Countreyes of the Worlde,* London: Richard Jones, 1584 (first published 1583)

'A Student of the Inner Temple': *The Criminal Recorder; or, Biographical Sketches of Notorious Public Characters,* London: James Cundee, 1804

Keith Thomas: *Religion and the Decline of Magic,* London: Penguin Books, 1991 (first published 1971)

Jürgen Thorwald: *The Marks of Cain,* London: Pan Books, 1968 (first published in German, 1964)

Geoffrey Trease: *London – A Concise History,* London: Book Club Associates, 1975

G.M. Trevelyan: *Illustrated History of England,* London: Longmans, Green & Co., 1956 (first published 1926)

Edward Walford: *Old & New London, Volume VI,* London: Cassell & Company, 1880

Ned Ward (Paul Hyland, ed.): *The London Spy,* East Lansing, Michigan: Colleagues Inc. Press, 1993 (first published 1709)

W.L Warren: *The Governance of Norman and Angevin England, 1086–1272,* Stanford, California: Stanford University Press, 1987

Ben Weinreb & Christopher Hibbert, eds.: *The London Encyclopedia,* London: Book Club Associates, 1986 (first published 1983)

H.G. Wells: *The War in the Air,* London: George Bell & Sons, 1908

Peter Whitfield: *London – A Life in Maps,* London: The British Library, 2006

Richard Whitmore: *Victorian and Edwardian Crime and Punishment from Old Photographs,* London: B.T. Batsford, 1984 (first published 1978)

Sir Roger Wilbraham: *The Journal of Sir Roger Wilbraham, Solicitor-General in Ireland and Master of Requests, for the Years 1593–1616,* London: Camden Society, 1902

Daniel Wilson: *Sermons and Tracts, Volume II,* London: George Wilson, 1825

H. Raynar Wilson: *Railway Accidents – Legislation and Statistics, 1825–1925,* London: The Raynar Wilson Company, 1925

Clarence Winchester, ed.: *The World Film Encyclopedia,* London: The Amalgamated Press Ltd., 1933

Alexander Wood: *Ecclesiastical Antiquities of London & its Suburbs,* London: Burns Oates, 1874

Various authors: *A Collection of the Yearly Bills of Mortality From 1657 to 1758 inclusive,* London: A. Miller, 1759

Various authors: *Journal of the House of Commons, Volume 9, 1667–1687* London: House of Commons, 1802

Articles, pamphlets, etc.

'The Abominations of the Church of ROME', *London Gazette,* Issue 998, 14 June 1675

'About six o'clock on Wednesday evening', *General Evening Post,* Issue 7064, 8–10 April 1779

'Accidents, Offences &c.', *Examiner,* 19 February 1837

'Accused Woman "Bewildered"', *The Times,* 27 August 1954

'Air History', *Manchester Guardian,* 1 November 1917

'Air Raid Defences', *Manchester Guardian,* 2 November 1917

'Air Raid Night Murder', *Daily Express,* 16 November 1917

'Alarming Riot', *General Evening Post,* 16–18 October 1798

'Alarming Riot', *Lloyd's Evening Post,* 15–17 October 1798

'Apprehension and Attempted Suicide of the Murderer', *Standard,* 27 March 1837

'Arrests and Surveillance', *The Times,* 31 March 1905

'Assassination of Mr. Perceval', *Morning Chronicle,* 12 May 1812

'At Clerkenwell, yesterday', *The Times,* 2 November 1902

'At the Desire of several Ladies of Quality', *Daily Courant,* Issue 4740, Saturday, 29 December 1716

'At West London, Miss Vera Butler', *The Times,* 21 August 1900

'Baby Farm Case', *Daily Express,* 3 December 1902

'Baby Farm Trial', *Daily Express,* 16 January 1903

'Behaviour and Execution of Bellingham', *Observer,* 24 May 1812

'Berthe Roche Found "Guilty"', *The Times,* 2 March 1918

'Biggest East End Man Hunt Since The Ripper', *Daily Express,* 9 August 1934

'Blonde Model Shot Lover in the Back', *Daily Mirror,* 29 April 1955

'Bloomsbury Murder Mystery', *The Times,* 3 November 1917

'Bloomsbury Murder Mystery', *Observer,* 4 November 1917

'Bloomsbury Murder Mystery', *The Times,* 7 November 1917

'Boarders threaten "Teddy-boy" boats', *Daily Express,* 16 July 1954

'Bomb And Burn Them Now', *Daily Express,* 12 December 1917

'The Bow Cinema Murder', *Observer*, 12 August 1934

'Boy Murderer Hears "No Reprieve" Decision', *Daily Express*, 13 November 1934

'Brutal Murder in Deptford – Masked Burglars Suspected', *Manchester Guardian*, 28 March 1905

'The Burnt Child dreads the Fire', *London Gazette*, Issue 998, 14 June 1675

'But Winston Holds On!', *Daily Mirror*, 29 July 1954

'The Camden Town Railway', *Illustrated London News*, 15 November 1851

'Caruso at Covent Garden', *Daily Mirror*, 23 May 1905

'Castration Proposed for Capital Offenders', *Gentlemen's Magazine*, December 1750

'Catastrophes', *Observer*, 7 August 1864

'Central Criminal Court, Monday', *Morning Chronicle*, 11 April 1837

'Charge of Murder Against Baby Farmers', *Manchester Guardian*, 16 January 1903

'Charge of Murdering Daughter-in-Law', *The Times*, 31 July 1954

'Child at a Railway Station', *Observer*, 7 August 1864

'The Christian's Defence against the Fears of Death', *London Gazette*, Issue 1000, 21 June 1675

'Cinema Attack and Robbery', *Manchester Guardian*, 8 August 1934

'Cinema Crime – Detectives' All-Night Wait For Man', *Daily Express*, 9 August 1934

'Cinema Crime: Man Detained', *Daily Express*, 11 August 1934

'Cinema Crime: Police and Youth of 19', *Daily Mirror*, 10 August 1934

'Cinema Crime: Youth Arrested', *Daily Mirror*, 11 August 1934

'Cinema Manager and Wife Attacked', *The Times*, 8 August 1934

'Cinema Manager's Death', *The Times*, 9 August 1934

'Cinema Manager's Death', *The Times*, 10 August 1934

'Cinema Murder Charge', *Manchester Guardian*, 22 August 1934

'Cinema Murder Charge', *The Times*, 22 August 1934

'Cinema Murder Charge', *Manchester Guardian*, 29 August 1934

'Cinema Murder – Hatchet Found By Police', *Manchester Guardian*, 9 August 1934

'Cinema Tragedy – Foot and Hand Prints On Floor', *Manchester Guardian*, 10 August 1934

'The Cinema Tragedy', *Manchester Guardian*, 11 August 1934

'A Complete Narrative of the Trial of Elizabeth Lillyman', London: Phillip Brooksby, 1675

'The Confession and Execution of Currell', *Pall Mall Gazette*, 18 April 1887

'Confession of the Convict Greenacre', *Morning Chronicle*, 14 April 1837

'The Convict Currell', *Observer*, 17 April 1887

'The Convict Greenacre', *Morning Chronicle*, 18 April 1837

'The Convict Muller', *Manchester Guardian*, 4 November 1864

'The Convict Muller', *Manchester Guardian*, 14 November 1864

'Coroner's Inquest', *Star*, 20 October 1798

'Court of Criminal Appeal', *The Times*, 9 February 1918

'The Cypriots in London', *Manchester Guardian*, 14 August 1954

'Daily Express Television Kit', *Daily Express*, 23 March 1934

'A Day at the Old Bailey', *Pall Mall Gazette*, 31 March, 1887

'Day of Sorrow, Day of Shame', *Daily Express*, 28 July 28, 1954

'The Dead Warrant is come to Newgate', *Evening Post*, 29–31 January 1717

'Death Sentence in French', *Daily Express*, 19 January 1918

'The Deptford Murder', *The Times*, 6 April 1905

'The Deptford Murder', *Daily Express*, 14 April 1905

'The Deptford Murder', *Observer*, 7 May 1905

'The Deptford Murders', *The Times*, 4 April 1905

'The Deptford Murders', *Manchester Guardian*, 21 April 1905

'Detectives Hunt in Great Sack Mystery', *Daily Mirror*, 3 November 1917

'Diary of the War for October', *Manchester Guardian*, 1 November 1917

'Discovery of the head of a female', *Morning Post*, 9 January 1837

'Discovery of the legs of the woman', *Champion & Weekly Herald*, 5 February 1837

'Discovery of the legs', *Morning Post*, 6 February 1837

'Divers of the Conspirators against His Majesty's Life', *London Gazette*, Issue 3162, 27 February, 1696

'A Door Makes Me Ashamed', *Daily Express*, 10 February 1954

'The Edgware-road Murder', *Morning Post*, 6 January 1837

'The Edgware-road Murder', *Champion & Weekly Herald*, 12 March 1837

'The Edgware-road Murder', *The Times*, 3 April 1837

'The Edgware-road Murder', *The Times*, 10 April 1837

'Evidence of a Thumb', *Daily Mirror*, 8 May 1905

'Execution of Franz Muller', *Manchester Guardian*, 15 November 1864

'Execution of Greenacre', *Morning Post*, 2 May 1837

'The Execution of Muller', *Observer*, 20 November 1864

'Fatal Affray at the Marine Police Office, Wapping', *Oracle and Daily Advertiser*, 18 October 1798

'Finger Print Clues', *Daily Mirror*, 8 April 1905

'Finger-Prints Evidence', *Manchester Guardian*, 26 April 1905

'Finger-Prints Evidence', *Manchester Guardian*, 3 May 1905

'Freemasonry in Portsmouth', *Hampshire Telegraph*, 23 April 1887

'Friday's Post', *Ipswich Journal*, 16 May 1812

'Gagged the Telephone – Burglary As a Fine Art in a Holborn Shop', *Daily Express*, 14 April 1905

'Gay Wife Murdered', *Daily Express*, 30 July 1954

'The Gotha Biplane', *Manchester Guardian*, 28 August 1917

'The Home Secretary has intimated', *The Times*, 31 January 1903

'Horrible Murder in a Railway Carriage', *Manchester Guardian*, 12 July 1864

'Horrible Murder in a Railway Carriage', *Observer*, 17 July 1864

'Horror of "1984" Angers TV Viewers', *Daily Express*, 13 December 1954

'How Finger Marks Convict Criminals', *Daily Mirror*, 8 May 1905

'The Hoxton Murder', *Daily News*, 8 February 1887

'The Hoxton Murder', *Standard*, 14 February 1887

'The Hoxton Murder', *Pall Mall Gazette*, 16 February 1887

'The Hoxton Murder', *Penny Illustrated Paper*, 19 February 1887

'The Hoxton Murder', *The Times*, 24 February 1887

'The Hoxton Murder', *Daily News*, 31 March 1887

'The Hoxton Murder', *Manchester Guardian*, 4 April 1887

'The Hoxton Murder', *Manchester Guardian*, 14 April 1887

'The Hoxton Murder', *Hampshire Telegraph*, 23 April 1887

'I Did Not Mean To Kill Mr Hoard', *Daily Mirror*, 14 August 1934

'I Thought It Was a Wax Model Burning in the Garden', *Daily Mirror*, 25 August 1954

'I Was Not Jealous', *Daily Mirror*, 28 October 1954

'"IF" For Murder Jury', *Daily Express*, 28 October 1954

'Importance of Finger Prints', *Daily Mirror*, 13 April 1905

'Injuries of Dead Cinema Manager', *Daily Express*, 5 September 1934

'Inquest', *The Times*, 31 March 1905

'Inquest on Cinema Manager', *The Times*, 11 August 1934

'It appears on a further investigation', *The Times*, 18 October 1798

'It Is My Wife', *Daily Mirror*, 13 November 1917

'Judge bars five from Teddy boy clothes', *Daily Mirror*, 11 November 1954

'A Jury Goes By Night To House Of Echoes', *Daily Express*, 27 October 1954

'Last Monday Mr. Burdet and Mr. Webster . . . .', *Evening Post*, Issue 1156, 1 January 1717

'Last Night as Miss Ray', *St James's Chronicle or the British Evening Post*, Issue 2819, 6–8 April 1779

'Last Night Capt. Robert Faulkner', *Evening Post*, Issue 1158, 3–5 January 1717

'Last Night was buried in the Vault of St. Bride's', *Daily Courant*, Issue 4746, 5 January 1717

'Last Saturday fifty-five children', *Penny London Post*, 10 April 1751

'Last Saturday Michael Mackenzie', *Whitehall Evening Post or London Intelligencer*, Issue 915, 7–10 December 1751

'Last Saturday Night a great Quarrel', *Original Weekly Journal*, 12 September 1719

'Last Thursday Night his Royal Highness', *Weekly Journal or British Gazetteer*, 8 December 1716

'Last Wednesday a woman was try'd', *The Country Journal or The Craftsman*, Issue 263, 17 July 1731

'The Late Horrible and Mysterious Murder in the Edgware Road', *Standard*, 10 January 1837

'The Late Mysterious Murder in the Edgware Road', *Morning Chronicle*, 12 January 1837

'The Late Mysterious Murder in the Edgware Road', *Morning Post, 12* January 1837

'A Letter from Mr J. Burdett', London: J. Baker & T. Warner, 1717

Letter to *Spectator*, No. 28, 11 April 1711

Letter to *Spectator*, No. 324, 12 March 1712

'Life of Greenacre (Written by Himself)', *Champion & Weekly Herald*, 9 April 1737

'The Life Or Death Ordeals of Mrs Christofi', *Daily Mirror*, 29 October 1954

Log Book, 'Poor Miss ___ !', *London Evening Post*, Issue 8895, 13–15 April 1779

'London, February 2', *Post Man and the Historical Account*, Issue 11520, 31 January–2 February 1717

'London, Feb. 2', *Evening Post*, Issue 1170, 31 January–2 February 1717

'London, Feb. 2', *Post Boy*, Issue 4293, 31 January–2 February 1717

'London Houses Struck By Lightning', *Daily Mirror*, 13 August 1934

'London, May 4', London News-Letter with Foreign and Domestick Occurrences, Issue 3, 1–4 May 1696

'London Telephone Service', *The Times*, 30 September 1902

'The Man of Destiny's Hard Fortune, or, Squire Ketch's Declaration', London, 1679

'"Mask" Murder', *Daily Mirror*, 6 April 1905

'"Mask" Murder', *Daily Mirror*, 8 April 1905

'The Masked Murderers', *Manchester Guardian*, 20 April 1905

'"Mask" Murder Plea', *Daily Mirror*, 26 April 1905

'Mask Murder's Second Victim', *Daily Express*, 1 April 1905

'Masked Murders Confession', *Daily Mirror*, 6 May 1905

'Masterpiece at 77', *Daily Mirror*, 23 May 1905

'The Merchants have found themselves', *The Times*, 12 January 1799

'Middlesex Sessions Rolls', 1675

'Midnight Murder in London Cinema', *Daily Express*, 8 August 1934

'Missile From The Dock', *Daily Mirror*, 13 April 1905

'Model Tells Court – Yes, I Intended To Kill', *Daily Express*, 21 June 1955

'More Baby Farming', *Daily Express*, 5 February 1903

'Mother-in-Law of 53 On Murder Charge', *Daily Express*, 31 July 1954

'MP's' Attempt To Save Condemned Woman', *The Times*, 15 December 1954

'Mr Burdett and Mr Webster', *Weekly Packet*, Issue 235, 29 December 1716–5 January 1717

'Mr Hackman, the unfortunate murderer', *Lloyd's Evening Post*, Issue 3401, 9–12 April 1779

'Mrs Christofi's Appeal Fails in Four Minutes', *Daily Mirror*, 30 November 1954

'Mrs Christofi Sensation', *Daily Express*, 15 December 1954

'The Murder by Masked men', *Manchester Guardian*, 4 April 1905

'Murder in a First Class Carriage on the North London Railway', *The Times*, 11 July 1864

'The Murder in Edgware Road', *Morning Chronicle*, 2 January 1837

'The Murder in the Edgware-Road', *Morning Post*, 28 March 1837

'The Murder Mystery', *Manchester Guardian*, 6 November 1917

'The Murder Mystery', *The Times*, 9 November 1917

'The Murder Mystery', *The Times*, 16 November 1917

'The Murder of Mme. Gerard', *The Times*, 18 January 1918

'The Murder of Mr Briggs', *The Times*, 23 July 1864

'The Murder of Mr Briggs', *Guardian*, 9 September 1864

'The Murder on the North London Railway', *The Times*, 12 July 1864

'The Murder on the North London Railway', *Manchester Guardian*, 14 July 1864

'The Murder on the North London Railway', *Manchester Guardian*, 15 July 1864

'The Murder on the North London Railway', *Manchester Guardian*, 19 July 1864

'The Murder on the North London Railway', *Manchester Guardian*, 20 July 1864

'The Murder on the North London Railway', *Manchester Guardian*, 9 August 1864

'The Murder on the North London Railway', *The Times*, 9 August 1864

'A Murder Was Committed', *Illustrated London News*, 16 July 1864

'Murder Witness Threatened', *Daily Mirror*, 13 April 1905

'Murdered Woman Identified', *The Times*, 6 November 1917

'The Mutilated Body', *Morning Post*, 2 January 1837

'A Mutilated Human Body Found', *Morning Post*, 30 December 1836

'The Mystery of Regent Square', *Daily Express*, 3 November 1917

'The Mystery of Regent Square', *Daily Express*, 6 November 1917

'Newgate Sold Up', *Daily Express*, 5 February 1903

'The North London Railway Murder', *Manchester Guardian*, 28 October 1864

'The North London Railway Murder', *Manchester Guardian*, 31 October 1864

'Notable Invalids', *Observer*, 19 August 1934

'Oh, What a Turn-Up for the Café Society Book!', *Daily Express*, 22 June 1954

'Old Bailey, Friday, 15 May', *The Times*, 16 May 1812

'On Friday John Hare', *Whitehall Evening Post or London Intelligencer*, Issue 906, 16–19 November 1751

'On Monday Night last', *Weekly Journal or British Gazetteer*, 5 January 1717

'On Saturday Joshua Jones', *Oracle & Daily Advertiser*, 29 October 1798

'On Saturday last Michael Magennis', *London Daily Advertiser*, Issue 241, 9 December 1751

'On Saturday night a man, known by the name of Horseflesh Dick', *General Evening Post*, 16–18 October 1798

'On Saturday 20 Prisoners', *London Evening Post*, Issue 3784, 18–21 January 1752

'On The Threshold Of The Beyond', *Daily Mirror*, 23 May 1905

'On Thursday Night a Watchman', *Weekly Packet*, Issue 235, 29 December 1716–5 January 1717

'On Tuesday Evening a Tradesman', *London Daily Advertiser and Literary Gazette*, Issue 215, 8 November 1751

'On Tuesday night last John Davis', *Daily Courant*, Issue 9244, 24 June 1731

'One Mr. M—— d of Greys Inn', *British Mercury*, Issue 309, 12–14 March 1712

'The Ordinary of Newgate, His Account,' 1 February 1717

'Particular correction of an ERRATUM in our last', *London Magazine*, May 1779

'A Penny Showman', *Morning Post*, 31 March 1837

'The Perils of the Railway', *Manchester Guardian*, 13 July 1864

'Pierce Gogan, a coal heaver', *Courier and Evening Gazette*, 25 January 1799

'Pigmy Burglar's Ruse – How Man Was Mistaken for a Dustbin', *Daily Express*, 14 June 1905

'The Police Courts', *The Times*, 12 April 1905

'The Police Courts', *The Times*, 19 April 1905

'Police Radio Broadcast', *Daily Mirror*, 11 August 1934

'Portsmouth Literary and Scientific Society', *Hampshire Telegraph*, 22 January 1887

'Professor Hele-Shaw on Locomotion', *The Times,* 9 January 1903

'Railway Imprisonment', *Manchester Guardian*, 18 July 1864

'Railways in the City of London', *Illustrated London News*, 13 February 1864

'The Railway Murder – A Sham Confession', *Observer*, 31 July 1864

'Regal Cinema, 156 Bow Road', www.cinematreasures.org

'Regent Square Murder', *Daily Express*, 5 November 1917

'Regent Square Murder', *Daily Express*, 8 November 1917

'A Restricted Raid', *Manchester Guardian*, 1 October 1917

'The Sack Mystery', *Daily Mirror*, 16 November 1917

'Sack Mystery Told In Police Court', *Daily Mirror*, 8 November 1917

'Sack Victim's Funeral', *Daily Mirror*, 14 November 1917

'Sayings of the Week', *Observer*, 4 November 1917

'Sentenced to Death', *Daily Express*, 8 May 1905

'Sentenced to Die', *Daily Express*, 17 January 1903

'Shocking Murder of a Young Woman in Hoxton', *Daily News*, 7 February 1887

'Shooting Outrage', *Daily Mirror*, 2 May 1905

'Should Hanging Be Stopped?', *Daily Mirror*, 14 July 1955

'Sir H. Irving as Shylock', *Daily Mirror*, 23 May 1905

'Snow Balls – Daring Outrage', *Morning Post*, 30 December 1836

'So notorious is the Calumny', *Weekly Journal or British Gazetteer*, 2
February 1717

'Some Account of the Trial and Execution of John Bellingham',
Anonymous pamphlet, 1812

'Status of Cyprus: Self-Government by Steps', *The Times*, 29 July 1954

'Stockwell in Hospital', *Daily Express*, 17 August 1934

'Stockwell Sent For Trial', *Daily Express*, 19 September 1934

'Suspected Murder of a Sweetheart', *Reynolds Newspaper*, 13 February 1887

'Stop Smoking!', *Daily Mirror*, 21 November 1917

'The Supposed Murder in the Edgware Road', *London Dispatch & People's
Political & Social Reformer*, 15 January 1837

'Test of Finger Prints', *Daily Express*, 26 April 1905

'The Trial of Muller', *Manchester Guardian*, 25 October 1864

'There was some evidence given yesterday', *Standard*, 11 February 1887

'This Day is Published', *General Advertiser*, Issue 5328, 16 November 1751

'This Day is Published', *Daily Courant*, Issue 4757, Friday, 18 January 1717

'The unfortunate Mr Hackman', *London Evening Post*, Issue 8894, 10–13
April 1779

'To Be Hanged Today', *Daily Express*, 3 February 1903

'To Die Today', *Daily Mirror*, 2 March 1918

'To Morrow will be published', *Post Man and the Historical Account*, Issue
11520, 2–5 February 1717

'To Morrow will be Published', *Observer*, 17 May 1812

'Traffic in Babies', *Daily Express*, 12 December 1902

'Tragedy of babies', *Daily Express*, 28 November, 1902

'Two cases of railway outrage', *Illustrated London News*, July 16, 1864

'U S Public Enemy Number One Shot Dead', *Daily Express*, October 23, 1934

'We are requested to state', *Morning Chronicle*, 9 January 1837

'We have said before', *The Times*, 12 May 1812

'We hear that the unfortunate Mr Hackman', *General Evening Post*, Issue
7066, 13–15 April 1779

'What Makes a Woman Want To Kill?', *Daily Mirror*, 15 December 1954

'Who killed Mme. Gerard?', *Daily Express*, 17 January 1918

'Widow Refuses To Sign Reprieve Petition', *Daily Express*, 6 November 1934

'Women Jurors See Two Death Sentences', *Daily Express*, 23 October 1934

'The World War – A British View', *Rotarian*, August 1918

'Yard Probes The Double Life of a Mother', *Daily Mirror*, 30 July 1954

'Yesterday five Malefactors', *Weekly Journal or British Gazetteer*, 2 February 1717

'Yesterday morning, at half an hour past nine', *General Evening Post*, Issue 7067, 15–17 April 1779

'Yesterday Morning, at nine o'clock', *General Evening Post*, Issue 7064, 8–10 April 1779

'Yesterday the Sessions ended at the Old Baily', *Evening Post*, Issue 1162, 12–15 January 1717

'Yesterday the Son of the Right Hon. The Lord Townshend', *Daily Courant*, Issue 9263, 16 July 1731

INDEX

385